THE
TALENT
DEVELOPMENT
PLATFORM

THE TALENT DEVELOPMENT PLATFORM

PUTTING PEOPLE FIRST IN SOCIAL CHANGE ORGANIZATIONS

HEATHER L. CARPENTER

TERA WOZNIAK QUALLS

with **ALEXIS S. TERRY** and **RUSTY STAHL**

Foreword by Trish Tchume

WILEY

Published by Jossey-Bass
A Wiley Brand
One Montgomery Street, Suite 1200, San Francisco, CA 94104-4594—www.josseybass.com

Library of Congress Cataloging-in-Publication Data
Carpenter, Heather L.

  The talent development platform: putting people first in social change organizations / Heather L. Carpenter and Tera Wozniak Qualls; with Alexis S. Terry and Rusty Stahl; foreword by Trish Tchume. – First edition.
      pages cm. – (The Jossey-Bass guidebook series)
  Includes bibliographical references and index.
  ISBN 978-1-118-87388-5 (pbk.)
  ISBN 978-1-118-87384-7 (pdf) –ISBN 978-1-118-87395-3 (epub)
  1. Nonprofit organizations–Personnel management. 2. Manpower planning. I. Qualls, Tera Wozniak, date- II. Title.
  HD62.6.C2665 2015
  658.3'01—dc23
                                              2014036903

Printed in the United States of America
FIRST EDITION
PB Printing 10 9 8 7 6 5 4 3 2 1

The Jossey-Bass Nonprofit Guidebook Series

The Jossey-Bass Nonprofit Guidebook Series provides new to experienced nonprofit professionals and volunteers with the essential tools and practical knowledge they need to make a difference in the world. From hands-on workbooks to step-by-step guides on developing a critical skill or learning how to perform an important task or process, our accomplished expert authors provide readers with the information required to be effective in achieving goals, mission, and impact.

Other Titles in the Jossey-Bass Guidebook Series

Contents

For more information, please visit talent4socialchange.com/talentdevelopment platform

List of Tables, Figures, and Exhibits

Tables

Figures

Exhibits

Foreword

In 2011, my colleague Dan Dobin and I published a report based on a survey of 1,100 respondents within the Young Nonprofit Professionals Network (YNPN). That year we asked young professionals to take a look at five often-cited strategies for developing and retaining talent in the nonprofit sector:

- Nonprofits should offer more competitive compensation.

- Nonprofits should invest in building "bench strength."

- Nonprofits should engage in inclusive succession planning.

- Nonprofits should prioritize diversity.

- Nonprofits should move away from traditional organizational structures and chief executive roles.

We then asked the young professional to tell us

- whether they were excited about the strategy's potential for impact;

- whether the nonprofits they worked for currently were implementing these strategies; and

- if so, whether the strategies were having their intended impact.

We wanted to know which strategies were having the greatest impact on emerging nonprofit leaders and the organizations they represented, with the goal of helping organizations and funders channel their resources.

The survey results were truly startling. Young professionals revealed that while there was quite a bit of buzz throughout the nonprofit sector about strategies for developing talent, fewer than 60 percent of nonprofits were actually implementing these popular talent development strategies. And as the survey probed deeper, we learned that fewer nonprofits were implementing these talent development strategies effectively. Given these results, it came as little surprise that when we asked these same respondents about their plans for staying in the nonprofit sector, only 34 percent of respondents were committed for the long haul, citing limited professional development opportunities as a key factor for leaving the sector.

We named our report "Good in Theory, Problems in Practice" because the survey revealed that the nonprofit sector seemed to know how to develop talent but struggled with follow-through.

Lack of funding, strained capacity, and competing interests are many of the barriers that YNPN members hear about when discussing why the sector cannot invest in its talent. These barriers are what lead many young professionals to start chapters and volunteer their time to serve as chapter leaders of YNPN. They are young people who are passionate enough to believe in change and practical enough to know that change can't happen on passion alone. They are creative and committed, and they know that if something is critical and resources are scarce, you find a way to do it anyway.

In light of this, I was thrilled, but not at all surprised, to hear that Tera and Heather were writing this book. I've had the privilege of knowing each of them for many years—as colleagues, as YNPN chapter leaders, and as friends—and rising to a challenge such as this is what I have come to expect from each of them.

I first came to know Tera Qualls (Tera Wozniak at the time) in 2007 as a blogger. Her Nonprofit2020 and Social Citizen blogs were two of the only online spaces that consistently and poignantly focused on issues facing the next generation of nonprofit leaders. Years later when we finally met through YNPN, I was (perhaps ironically) surprised to discover that the insightful voice I had come to rely on as my go-to reference for emerging leadership trends was so young herself! Through our work together as fellow board members for YNPN National, I came to learn how driven Tera is by her belief in the power of the nonprofit sector as a force for social change.

Within my first few minutes of meeting Heather Carpenter at a conference in 2007, she confessed to me that she was a "total nonprofit geek." Serving alongside Heather on committees such as the Nonprofit Workforce Coalition, I've come to learn that her passion for the nonprofit sector goes beyond wanting to do her own work well. She is devoted to elevating the level of discourse and practice throughout the sector and is eager to bring data, solid research, and a deep level of academic rigor to the process.

As I read through *The Talent Development Platform*, I found myself thinking—and sometimes exclaiming out loud—"*Yes!*" and "*Finally!*" There are so many reasons that social change organizations should celebrate the publication of this book, but I'll focus on two reasons in particular.

First, Tera and Heather have lived many of the challenges as well as much of what works when it comes to leadership development. So, the frameworks offered in this book are grounded in both thorough research and experience. Second, the tools in this book are so incredibly practical. The book lays out a straightforward path for all organizations but will be especially transformative for those 60 percent of organizations we surveyed that understood the value of leadership development but simply struggle with implementation.

My hope is that this book can serve as one important step in closing the gap between theory and practice when it comes to leadership development. The talented 66 percent of emerging leaders fleeing the sector for greater professional development and the professionals at every level of their careers who are committed to building vibrant, stronger communities deserve more than talk. They deserve strategic investment in their development.

The sector is ready for *The Talent Development Platform*.

TRISH TCHUME

Preface

It is a cliché to say this book is our labor of love, but it really is. This idea has been percolating in us for years, and we can trace it back to when we served on our first national committee together. We were by far the youngest participants in the Nonprofit Workforce Coalition, which the Nonprofit Leadership Alliance (then American Humanics) formed in 2006 with the mission to connect talented, skilled, and diverse young people to nonprofit sector careers and "help nonprofit organizations recruit, retain, and cultivate the diverse leadership they will need in the decades ahead" (Nonprofit Workforce Coalition, 2009). We then both joined the Next Generation Leadership Forum and served on the advisory board for Independent Sector's NGen Program. We are both founders of Young Nonprofit Professionals Network chapters in two different cities (Heather in San Diego; Tera in Grand Rapids). We've both been discussing and blogging about nonprofit talent and leadership issues since 2006, and our blogs have gained national recognition. All of those experiences gave us the fuel for this book.

We decided it was time to stop discussing the challenges with nonprofit talent retention and start implementing a solution. This book is our contribution to a solution for addressing talent and turnover issues within nonprofit organizations, but it is also applicable in any type of social change enterprise. Some organizations will find this process too difficult to go through, some of you will find pieces of the book helpful, others will be too busy to even pick up the book to invest in talent, but so be it. We want the organizations interested in long-term sustainability and truly effective change for their mission to pick up this book and make it happen!

We both have a passion for talent development and helping people—managers, staff, volunteers, and leaders—to be better equipped for the roles they are meant to play within their organizations. Our formal training and experiences working in social change organizations paired with the extensive research we conducted for the book make our perspective unique. We built tools that social change workers and organizations need in order to stay and thrive in the sector. We've lived and worked in the social change sector for many years and believe in the power that a committed, nourished workforce can have on some of the most vulnerable populations in the world.

Come along on this journey with us. Invest in your people! It's worth it!

Acknowledgments

The journey to writing this book started early in our careers. Many individuals have both inspired us and challenged us over the years, leading us to what we have become today. We want to thank each one of them for all they have done for us to make this book and our vision possible.

We would like to thank those whom we call our mentors, who spent countless hours inspiring us and developing us along our journey. We are forever grateful for your support of our careers: Salvatore Alaimo, Anne Bunton, Janean Couch, Laura Deitrick, Robert Donmoyer, DeDe Esque, Emily Stoddard Furrow, Shannon Garrett, Mark Hoffman, Rich Jelier, Lucy Joswick, Paula Krist, Pat Libby, Wesley Lindahl, Roseanne Mirabella, Donijo Robbins, Jane Royer, Melvene Tardy, Caitlin Townsend Lamb, and Milinda Ysasi Castanon.

Thank you to those who are thought leaders and experts within the field of talent development. We appreciate that you took the time to provide us feedback on our book and support our efforts, specifically Mary Jo Baweja, Debra Beck, Teresa (Teri) Behrens, Jeanne Bell, Lisa Brown Morton, Marla Cornelius, Emily Davis, Matthew Downey, Terry Horton, Beth Kanter, Kim Klein, Kivi Miller, Debra Minton, Michael Moody, Kevin Rafter, Paul Schmitz, Maya Enista Smith, Steve Strang, Gene Takagi, James Weinberg, and Steve Zimmerman.

We would like to thank our graduate assistants, without whom this book would not be possible. They developed the third-party professional development guide, proficiency mapping tools, and numerous other items. Thank you to Inchan Choi, Gayane Selimyan, Lauren Spangler, and Olesya Tykhenko.

We want to thank all the managers who came before us, who challenged and inspired us, and who run amazing social change organizations: Kathy Agard, William Crawley, James Edwards, Ken Druck, Beverly Grant, Allen Gunn, Diana Spatz, Anita Rees, and Mike Woodruff.

Thank you to the executive directors of our four pilot organizations, Bridget Clark Whitney, Susan Kragt, Holly Johnson, and Chris Zahrt. Thank you to the organizations that sent out the national professional development survey: Public Allies, the Institute for Nonprofit Education and Research at the University of San Diego, CompassPoint Nonprofit Services, and the Council on Foundations.

Thank you to Rusty Stahl and Alexis S. Terry who wrote the guides. Thanks to Trish Tchume for writing the foreword and thanks to our reviewers for their helpful feedback in refining the book: Laura Gassner Otting, Nelson Lyang, and James Shepard.

Thank you to our employer, Grand Valley State University, for supporting this work: the School of Public, Nonprofit, and Health Administration, the Dorothy A. Johnson Center for Philanthropy, the College of Community and Public Service, and Dean George Grant. Thank you to our editor, Alison Hankey (and her editorial team), for believing in this project and supporting us from the proposal process through delivery.

And most of all, thank you to our parents, who believe in us, and our wonderful husbands, John Carpenter and Rob Qualls, who supported us through working full-time while writing the book and taking care of our toddlers, Kristin and Eli, during countless hours of us bent over our laptops.

About the Authors

Heather L. Carpenter, PhD, is assistant professor in the School of Public, Nonprofit, and Health Administration at Grand Valley State University. She is an experienced and highly networked nonprofit manager, researcher, trainer, and blogger.

She earned her bachelor's degree in business administration from San Diego State University with a certificate in nonprofit management from the Nonprofit Leadership Alliance, her master's in nonprofit administration from North Park University (Chicago, Illinois), and her PhD in leadership with a specialization in nonprofit leadership and management from the University of San Diego. She has been employed as a full-time tenure-track assistant professor since 2012. She teaches graduate and undergraduate courses in nonprofit management (using the competencies she and Tera developed), financial management, fund development, nonprofit technology, leadership, and human resources management. In 2012, she was awarded the prestigious Russell G. Mawby Faculty Fellowship in Philanthropic Studies, which is awarded to only one faculty member per year at Grand Valley State University.

Heather has conducted several national and local studies about professional development in the nonprofit sector. She was recruited by the Nonprofit Leadership Alliance to conduct research on nonprofit education, Idealist.org to conduct research on nonprofit careers, and HR Solutions to conduct research on nonprofit employment trends. Her most recent study, a statewide professional development needs assessment of nonprofits in Michigan, received national press coverage and is being used by many infrastructure organizations in Michigan, including the Dorothy A. Johnson Center for Philanthropy.

Heather authors the well-known Nonprofit Leadership 601 blog (www.nonprofitalternatives.org/page/blog), where she provides practical advice and information about nonprofit management, professional development, nonprofit education, and nonprofit leadership. Her posts have been featured on the Chronicle of Philanthropy, Brazen Careerist, Employee Evolution, PhilanTopic, and NP2020 websites. Nonprofit

Leadership 601 has been listed in the "Top 150 Social Capital Blogs," "Top Nonprofit News" on "Alltop.com," and "Top 50 Nonprofit Blogs" on Networked Blogs.

Heather previously served as nonprofit manager for ten years in California and Illinois, she cofounded the Young Nonprofit Professionals Network in San Diego (with Emily Davis), and she served as an advisory board member to Independent Sector's NGen Program, the Nonprofit Workforce Coalition and the Next Generation Leadership Forum.

Tera Wozniak Qualls, MPA, is founder of Momentum, a consulting shop that brings nonprofit organizations from strategy to impact by focusing on engaging people more deeply in mission work and equipping staff to work more effectively. Most recently Tera served as the director of communications and advancement for the College of Community and Public Service at Grand Valley State University and as communications manager for the Dorothy A. Johnson Center for Philanthropy at Grand Valley State University. Tera serves as an adjunct professor of nonprofit administration in the School of Public, Nonprofit, and Health Administration at Grand Valley, where she teaches introduction to nonprofits and volunteerism for undergraduate students.

In her role at the Dorothy A. Johnson Center for Philanthropy, Tera had the opportunity to work with thousands of philanthropic organizations, providing capacity-building and technical assistance in the areas of volunteerism, generational dynamics, governance, marketing and communications, human resources, evaluation, and strategic planning.

As a community member, Tera believes in the power of volunteerism for improving communities. For that reason, she has volunteered in various roles in her community and nationally. Her roles include the Kids' Food Basket Expansion Task Force, the Young Nonprofits Professional Network National Board, Independent Sector's NGen Committee, the League of Women Voters Grand Rapids, Grand Rapids GiveCamp, Project Blueprint Advisory Committee, and The Rapidian Steering Committee.

In 2007, she founded the Young Nonprofit Professionals Network of Greater Grand Rapids, the first professional organization specifically for young nonprofit professionals in the city. Dedicated to the development of young professionals and to improving the sector in Grand Rapids, Tera led the organization for four years. During her time at the head of the organization, she built it to over two hundred paid members, two yearly signature events, monthly professional development, and hosting the YNPN national conference in Grand Rapids. To further her belief in strong professional development, Tera led succession planning of her board to allow other young city leaders to take the reins after her four years leading the organization.

For her volunteer efforts and work at the Johnson Center, Tera has been recognized by the prestigious Grand Rapids Business Journal's 40-Under-40, as an ATHENA Young Professional Award Finalist, 2011; featured in "My NP Times Top 50: The Next Generation of Nonprofit Leaders You Should Know" from Nonprofit Leadership 601; and featured in "Top 10 Young Nonprofit Professionals on Twitter" from Perspectives from the Pipeline.

Since 2004, Tera has blogged professionally about the issues of young nonprofit professionals and generational shifts in the sector. Her writing includes Social Citizen, where her blogs are now housed at teraqualls.com; various blogs for Independent Sector's NGen Program; blogging for Idealist.org's Nonprofit Career Month; and an article titled "Beyond Succession Planning: Strategies to Engage the Next Generation" for the Michigan Nonprofit Association's monthly membership publication.

THE
TALENT
DEVELOPMENT
PLATFORM

Introduction

Now is the time to harness your people for a greater impact. Let ideas flow, and failure happen. Learn from that failure, let your people take a bet on you, and gather those voices that believe in your cause more than you do. Through giving people these opportunities, you will get a return on your investment that ultimately affects your organization's impact. Your people impact can be greater, but you have to give your people a chance.

Throughout this book, we are asking you to take a risk on your ideas, your people, and your structures. Some organizations are already doing it—making big waves with new structures of working and with strong learning cultures—but many have a long way to go. We will show you how to create organizational structures that allow you to make greater impacts simply through reorganizing your people and providing them the space for learning.

This book is for the employees, volunteers, and directors of organizations that are making positive change in the world, in communities—social change organizations. Organizations interested in social change can be 501(c) nonprofit organizations, foundations, for-profit organizations (such as regular corporations and LLCs) doing social good, and hybrid organizations like L3Cs and B corporations that blur the lines between nonprofit organizations and corporations.

Smart people work and volunteer in social change organizations. They address some of our world's biggest social problems and connect people to new ways of changemaking. They are giving their lives for their cause, raising money relentlessly, evaluating programs to fund, volunteering extra hours to make sure the people they are serving get what they need. But many are forgetting the most important rule of thumb for addressing social problems: taking care of the people who do the work! It's easy to structure your work for those you serve, but how about addressing your own development or the development of your team so they are equipped to keep on working smart?

In the last ten years, the social change sector has seen employment growth, where other sectors have seen a decline (Salamon, Sokolowsi, & Geller, 2012). Despite the huge growth, the sector falls behind when it comes to talent development. The sector is very good at engaging people with their cause but does a poor job of engaging staff and dedicated volunteers to keep engaged and excited about their work while also improving their performance in that work. Research backs this up and shows that social change organizations devote 2 percent or less of the budget to funding staff development (Carpenter, Clarke, & Gregg, 2013; Stahl, 2013). Many social change organizations are vulnerable to losing staff and key volunteers due to a lack of strategic talent development. Turnover of top talent costs the sector time and money on a regular basis. Turnover costs social change organizations millions in lost revenues yearly. You can avoid the costs related to recruiting, interviewing, and training new staff and volunteers if you are proactive about developing and keeping your talent.

We want you to think back to when you were just starting out your career; maybe you are there now. Who invested in you? How did you get to where you are? How do you think you can get where you want to be? Without personal support, passion will get you nowhere. Someone has to believe in you. Someone has to train you. We have been lucky in our careers to be surrounded by leaders who cared about our professional development, who invested in us, and with whom we were able to troubleshoot problems. We want the same for you and your employees and volunteers.

The type of support we are asking you to give to your employees and volunteers, to your organization, really, hasn't been natural in the life cycle of how social change organizations work. History and experience shows us that social change organizations tend to put their cause first. Additionally, donors and the general public require many social change organizations to do well at the lowest possible cost. This puts a strain on the internal cultures of many organizations; so at times the culture does not provide adequate space for talent development or adequate time to make collaborative decisions, which results in crisis mode. Many organizations work from one funding source to another; focus solely on programs; and may ignore staff, volunteers, and operations. This is when a strong leader must step in and decide to exercise leadership with the organization's staff and volunteers. You are that person!

As an organizational leader, it is up to you to champion the important organizational system of intentional talent development. If you aren't technically a leader in your organization, don't sell yourself short. You are a leader by picking up this book. Work with your leadership to convince them that this is important work. We provide data and the rationale for change throughout the book: use it. Why do we think this will work for you as a leader? Because we believe in the relational leadership model, which involves people working together to accomplish common good (Komives, Lucas, & McMahon, 2006). Originally, Komives, Lucas, and McMahon developed the relational leadership model for college students; however, social change organizations can use it under specific circumstances. Successful relational leadership incorporates five components:

- Inclusive—respectful of all people and diverse points of view
- Empowering—encourages others involved in work
- Purposeful—individual commitment and common purpose
- Ethical—driven by moral leadership
- Process oriented—intentional about being a group and accomplishing the group's purpose (Komives, Lucas, & McMahon, 2006, p. 74)

Groups that meet all five conditions can agree on the common good. Unfortunately, many social change organizations do not make the time to follow these steps, and the executive director ends up dictating the common good, which creates further disagreement among staff and volunteers. However, under the right circumstances, if the organization is ready, and the executive director and board are strong enough, the organization can challenge the existing system and provide a space for relational leadership, which has the goal of putting people first, to occur.

We have devoted this book to helping social change organizations do just that: put people first. We truly believe in the power of a developed and motivated talent pool. People who volunteer and work in the social change sector are serving some of the most vulnerable populations in the world, advocating for causes that are structuring the future of our country, and enhancing and uplifting the melting pot of cultures our country has to offer. They are also pursuing their passions and life's work. Now is the time for us all to harness their passion and power, and support them in any way we can. We believe in structured social change, and we know you do too. Together let's make that happen more effectively.

Make the Investment Now

This process does take a huge lift at the front end, but it is worth it, and frankly it is imperative for sustainability. By implementing these tools, you will give your organization one more chance to be competitive in the future, with top talent and effective programs. We want you to ask yourself the question, What's the harm in stepping back now to do this work? Is it loss of productivity while it's happening? What do using the hours for this really do to staff? The process does cost money in staff hours, but how much is that compared to the return? Your staff is asking for these changes and will be much better off with intentional learning systems in place. Really, there's more harm in not doing it.

According to the *2013 Nonprofit Employment Trends Survey,* 70 percent of nonprofit organizations say they will be or may be hiring in the near future. The number of jobs available is astounding; however, the pool of individuals available for these jobs is low (Nonprofit HR Solutions, 2013). Many social change organizations aren't competitive for top talent even though they have positions available. Yes, they attract individuals who will work for their passion over any other benefit, but many get burned out working in these organizations; not everyone will do that for the long haul. Invest in your employees now so that you are competitive over the long haul.

It is not lost on us that you have to fight the hard balance of keeping your doors open and managing the day-to-day operations, often with unpredictable clients. We've worked in these organizational settings. However, our research and experience shows us that organizations reap monetary and nonmonetary benefits when they take the time to support the people who serve their clients, so the clients can do their jobs better. In chapter 1, we'll talk real numbers—the tangible and intangible benefits your organization will reap from this process. In reality, *all* organizations have to make these tough decisions. You are always taking time out of your day to make systemic decisions; they might not always be intentional. You can develop your staff and keep your doors open if you have the right people in the right places. Best practices are important, but people doing the work are essential. You need strong, supported people to be competitive and to keep your lights on. Now is the time to get the right people and develop those you already have. **The greatest risk you are taking by not implementing these tools is losing top talent in the future.**

Social Change Organizations

When we first created these tools, we focused solely on nonprofit organizations, specifically those that meet the requirements of the Internal Revenue Service tax code 501(c), but as we began working with the tools and sifting through literature about the competencies we had identified, we realized the tools in this book are transferrable to all social change organizations. Many scholars, organizations, and authors have used this term to describe the sector in different ways. In our definition, social change organizations include nonprofit organizations, all types of foundations, voluntary organizations, newly designed organizations that blur the lines between corporations and nonprofit organizations, and regular corporations that are giving back to their communities. In plain terms, we believe our tools will work for any organization looking to make a positive impact on society by producing products, raising support, or informing and empowering individuals to make a change.

Changemakers are individuals who work or volunteer for organizations looking to make a social change. They are the lever for change; they are the "widgets" of the sector. Changemakers can be board members, trustees, volunteers, staff, leadership, program officers, or any other employee or volunteer working for a social change organization. When we refer to any of these roles throughout the book, we consider them all to be changemakers.

Due to this widened definition, providing accurate statistical information about whom this book is for is a bit tough. Numbers exist that show the breadth and depth of the nonprofit sector, but there are no true numbers to encompass those we define as social change organizations. With a sector so large and broad, some organizations just can't be counted. There are small voluntary organizations and churches that don't file for Internal Revenue Service status or formally organize. We will not count the unincorporated organizations here but will give some rough estimates. There are also no true numbers for small family foundations or corporations that serve the public good, many of which donate informally but have substantial impact. The social change sector is complex and growing and hard to pin down with numbers.

Here are some statistics we can tell you about. According to the National Center for Charitable Statistics, an estimated 2.3 million nonprofit organizations operate in the United States, and approximately 1.6 million nonprofits are registered with the Internal Revenue Service (IRS). This means the majority of social change organizations are super small and operate with less than $500,000 in annual revenues. The unregistered organizations are informal associations and faith-based charities that are not required to file according to tax law. The National Center for Charitable Statistics has done their best to estimate the number of organizations that do exist (National Center for Charitable Statistics, 2014). On the grantmaking side, there were 76,610 grantmaking foundations in the United States in 2010, a 35 percent increase from 2000 (National Center for Charitable Statistics, 2014).

The new types of organizations we have mentioned are often called social enterprises. Bromberger defines social enterprises as "any commercial activity or venture that is operated to achieve business and social goals simultaneously" (Bromberger, n.d., p. 1). Nonprofits, for-profits, and hybrid organizations can fall under that definition of a social enterprise. The key is these organizations are doing some sort of commercial activity and have a social mission or orientation. For example, we consider a nonprofit that runs a bakery and the YMCA social enterprises because they are working to achieve both a business and social good simultaneously. We also consider for-profit companies such as Tom's Shoes and Ben and Jerry's as social enterprises. These companies make a substantial profit, but they have purposely integrated their business practices with giving back and environmental consciousness. The number of social enterprises is growing. There are over 990 certified B corporations, for-profit companies that meet specific social and environmental standards, across sixty industries in twenty-seven countries (B Lab, 2014). As for L3Cs, low-profit limited liability corporations, the numbers are a bit lower, as not all states have the identified corporate tax model, but interSector Partners estimates approximately 1,050 organizations nationally (interSector Partners, 2014).

These organizations are a huge part of our economy in the United States. The 2.3 million nonprofit organizations contributed $804.8 billion to the U.S. economy in 2010, making up 5.5 percent of the country's gross domestic product. Foundation assets totaled $621.7 billion in 2010, a 1 percent increase from $615.5 billion in 2000 (National Center for Charitable Statistics, 2014). The nonprofit sector employs over 10.7 million workers, while close to 27 percent of the U.S. population, 64.3 million people, volunteered at least once in 2011 (National Center for Charitable Statistics, 2014). This employment in nonprofit organizations is distributed broadly across the country, with no one region having a significantly higher rate of employment in the sector, according to Salamon, Sokolowski, and Geller (2012). We don't have strong estimates for the number of employees in the other types of organizations, although when you consider their numbers and the potential size of B corporations, you can imagine they compound the numbers for social change organizations exponentially.

It is also important to note the diversity of individuals working in the social change sector. There are individuals with doctorates and with technical training in engineering and other fields. There are individuals with training in their faith and in the field of social work. There are individuals trained in anything from veterinary medicine to manufacturing, as well as those trained specifically to manage nonprofit organizations. In addition to those with formal training, there are individuals with a passion for a specific cause who get involved because they are interested in affecting a certain arena of their world. The diversity of potential employment options brings in a wide range of individuals of varying economic statuses, races, and ethnicities, and from the full range of generations able to work or volunteer in the United States.

Compounding the diversity of professional backgrounds in the sector is the wide age and racial diversity of the current United States workforce.

According to the Bureau of Labor Statistics there are 155,389,000 people in the United States over the age of sixteen who are eligible to work (Bureau of Labor Statistics, 2014). For the first time in our history that number is spread across four generations, including Millennials, Generation X, Baby Boomers, and the Silent Generation or Traditionalists. Millennials will soon represent the biggest chunk of the workforce, and that generation is bringing with it a new way of working. In addition to wanting to make the world a better place, Millennials want to be their own boss, work in a collaborative team environment, and have work-life integration, including flexible schedules (Asghar, 2014). Millennials also represent the most diverse and global generation, expanding the racial and ethnic diversity of our workforce. This combination of cultural factors demands that we change the way we work in many social change organizations, which have been running on a model developed by the very different Traditionalist generation.

Professional Development for Changemakers

The diversity of employees and volunteers in the sector and the demands of the next generation are forcing organizations to focus more heavily on effective talent development. The Millennials are coming of age during a time when innovation and entrepreneurship are the norm and anyone can make money as long as they have the right idea and way of achieving their goals. To keep this generation interested in the sector, social change organizations need to think differently about how they do business and keep employees in their organizations. A study by the Young Nonprofit Professionals Network titled "Good in Theory, Problems in Practice" (Dobin & Tchume, 2011) reiterates that nonprofits need to develop internal candidates in order to keep them in the sector: "compensation and lack of professional development were important reasons why Young Nonprofit Professionals Network members were considering a sector switch" (p. 12).

Over the past few years, major sector infrastructure organizations have been trying to answer the question, How do we become better at talent development to keep the next generation around? National organizations established the Nonprofit Workforce Coalition, the Next Generation Leadership Forum, and Independent Sector's NGen Program. Additionally, countless foundations funded programs like the Young Nonprofit Professionals Network, Net Impact, and Emerging Practitioners in Philanthropy to address this question as well. Beyond these established organizations and funding streams, recruitment agencies like Commongood Careers, Nonprofit HR Solutions, Talent Philanthropy, and the Nonprofit Professionals Advisory Group have led the way in identifying talent, developing talent growth strategies, and making a case for funding talent in the social change sector. Even though focusing on talent has become a prominent conversation for the sector, not much actual progress is being made.

Part of the reason these organizations and foundations created new infrastructure organizations was the realization that people involved in the social change sector needed to be engaged and encouraged at a level that helps them be more effective and satisfied with their work. In 2006, we became involved in the Nonprofit Workforce Coalition. The Nonprofit Workforce Coalition was composed of nearly seventy nonprofit organizations, associations, foundations, and academic centers focused on identifying and addressing issues facing the nonprofit sector workforce. The Coalition existed to connect talented, skilled, and diverse young people to nonprofit sector careers and to help nonprofit organizations recruit, retain, and cultivate diverse leadership (Nonprofit Workforce Coalition, 2009). During our time with the Workforce Coalition, we were on the forefront of discussions about the importance of talent development and creating solutions for staff and volunteer retention. We also learned about the vast number of organizations that don't understand the necessity of talent development and that use a lack of resources to explain why they don't support their talent intentionally. Unfortunately, funding dried up and infrastructure support for the Nonprofit Workforce Coalition and the Next Generation Leadership Forum dissolved. Initiatives like this don't ever seem to get traction, as they should, often because it is easy to talk about making change, but harder to generate the support from all stakeholders.

This book is the culmination of those many workforce discussions and the thought leadership we've been a part of over the last ten years. We attempt to take those conversations to the next level by providing organizations with the tools they need to make systemic changes and better support talent in social change organizations.

Who Is This Book For?

While writing this book, we had quite a bit of discussion about whether to write for nonprofit leaders, foundation leaders, or both. We decided to write for both, and then some. The depth and breadth of the types of organizations that could use our tools and structured competencies is endless. The social change sector is immeasurable. For those reasons this book is for any organization focused on social change or any business interested in creating systemic talent development practices that bring their organizations to the leading edge of impact. Our tools are structured specifically to enhance social change, and the tools are transferable to any organization size, type, or mission.

EXHIBIT I.1
Professional Development for Volunteers

Due to the huge number of social change organizations that do not have any formal staff members, we include information about supporting volunteers throughout the book. We understand that organizations functioning in this format have even less capacity and even more limited resources than small nonprofits. Providing professional development to volunteers increases satisfaction and reduces attrition. Organizations like Energize Inc., Board Source, Volunteer Match, and the Volunteer Management Association have created tools and literature to develop volunteers and board members and help organizations retain their volunteers. This book seeks to do the same by providing tools and resources that help volunteer-run organizations provide professional development to their board members and working volunteers at low or no cost.

Organization Leaders

Although the tools and lessons throughout the book are informative for changemakers in any position, we designed the process you are about to embark on to be implemented by your organization's leadership. These tools will provide you with the tools you need to structure the talent in your organization in the right ways and guide their learning to achieve your strategic mission and goals.

Human Resources Managers and Learning Officers

As the already established developers of talent, human resources managers and learning officers can use these tools to restructure their performance assessment process and justify including talent development and management discussions in all decision-making processes. Further, you can use these tools to enhance your already established systems of human resources management and professional development.

Individuals

Although most of the tools are written under the guise of organizational systems and culture, individual changemakers can use these tools to assess their own proficiency levels in important social change management areas and equip themselves with the tools they need to be active learners throughout their careers.

Board Members

Board members are those governing the organization in the best interests of the mission. For that reason alone they should be interested in ensuring that talent is developed intentionally for greater impact and that organizations are structured to be continually competitive and sustainable long into the future.

Focusing on Four Types of Organizations

While building the case for our tools, we asked thousands of changemakers if they would stand up to let us know their organization is doing professional development well. We did not get one response. To dig deeper, we asked consultants and large infrastructure organizations if they could identify any organizations doing professional development well. We again got no response for a model organization. Convinced there are some out there, we began asking more questions. We came across a few that have stellar practices for professional development in place, but even more that had only bits and pieces. Many organizations have part of what they need, but because of the perceived lack of urgency for structured learning in organizations, none of the practices were systemic. Instead, we highlighted organizations that had some processes in place and were interested in establishing stronger talent development practices.

We piloted the tools presented in this book with four organizations that represent typical social change organizations. Each pilot organization had unique talent development challenges. We use their real-life examples throughout the book, while keeping them anonymous. Each of these organizations piloted some or all of the tools we use in this book, and their cases will guide your learning and inform your implementation.

Volunteer-Run Organizations with One or Two Staff

The majority of social change organizations fall under this category, and they have the greatest need for focusing on their people. Many of these organizations are not officially incorporated. We've received a multitude of e-mails over the course of our careers from people who are starting and running these types of organizations. If you are a board member or the first staff member in a mostly volunteer-run organization, then you should receive huge kudos for picking up and reading this book. We've been told by critics to focus on midsize and larger social change organizations, but our passion is for start-ups and small organizations. We want you to start your organization out the right way, by putting your people first. You spend a countless number of hours addressing your cause, your mission; you should invest in yourself and your people too!

Small Grassroots Organizations with Under Five Staff

Next to volunteer-run organizations, the largest group of social change organizations consists of those with fewer than five staff members. These organizations typically have less than $500,000 in annual revenues and provide many of the social services in our country, including support of immigrants, food banks, childcare, animal care, and more. Organizations of this size often have an executive director and direct service staff who do the majority of the work, sometimes with an administrative staff or fundraising staff as resources allow. On the opposite end, some of the country's wealthiest family-run foundations operate with fewer than five staff. In both cases, professional development becomes more necessary because staff wear many hats regularly.

Midsized Organizations with Under Twenty Staff

There are far fewer social change organizations that fall into the midsize range. The organizations that do fall into this category are proven organizations that have shown they are able to scale and grow. These organizations typically have fewer than twenty staff and have under $2 million in annual revenues.

Grantmaking Organizations

This category covers a multitude of foundations (community, private, public, family, independent, and corporate). These organizations vary in size and scope and vary in their number of staff. Grantmaking organizations typically have more than $5 million in annual revenues.

Other Organizations Serving Social Change

We don't discuss hybrid social change organizations in the book although we have had the opportunity to work with some amazing B corporations and L3Cs that are large and deeply care about their employees.

What Is This Book About?

In short, this book is about results-driven talent development. We have developed a system for talent development, the Talent Development Platform, which gives your organization a strong foundation for keeping talent and driving results for your mission. We've structured each of the pieces of the Talent Development Platform intentionally to increase the results of your mission, whether it is increased funding, better volunteer management, more effective services, or larger outreach for advocacy campaigns. The Talent Development Platform provides you with all the tools you need to ready your organization, develop competencies for your staff and volunteers, manage a Talent Map to ensure that each employee and volunteer is in his or her right role, and evaluate the process to ensure

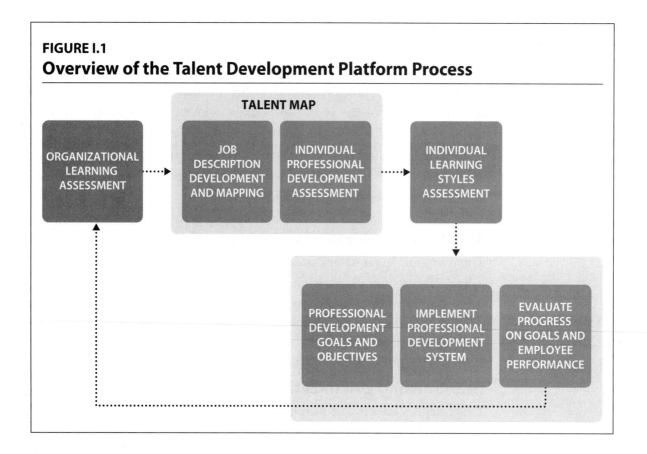

FIGURE I.1
Overview of the Talent Development Platform Process

that you've implemented each piece effectively. Figure I.1 provides you with an overview of the Talent Development Platform and the tools that are included in this book.

Each chapter in the book deals with different aspects of furthering the professional development of your staff and volunteers, using the Talent Development Platform.

Chapter 1, "Why Talent Development?," provides a foundation of what talent and professional development are and a snapshot of the social change sector today. In this chapter we walk through the Talent Development Platform extensively and provide you with the information you need to set a baseline for the return on investment for talent.

Chapter 2, "The Organizational Learning Assessment," guides your organization through determining whether you are ready to establish your own Talent Development Platform and assessing your organizational capacity to create and administer a professional development program. Staff and volunteers will take the Organizational Learning Assessment to provide a readiness score for implementing the Platform and a view of the organization's learning culture.

Chapter 3, "Social Change Competencies," summarizes the key social change competencies we established. We tested the competencies through a national professional development survey, organizations piloting the Talent Development Platform, and interviews with experts and practitioners in the social change sector. The ten competencies are as follows:

- Advocacy and Public Policy

- Communications, Marketing, and Public Relations

- Financial Management and Social Entrepreneurship

- Fundraising and Resources Development

- Grantmaking or Direct Service

- Human Resources Management and Volunteerism

- Information Management

- Leadership and Governance

- Legal and Regulatory

- Planning and Evaluation

The chapter also guides your organization through creating sub-competencies specific to the needs of your organization. You can use the sub-competencies during the Individual Professional Development Assessment process, described in chapter 6.

Chapter 4, "Creating Job Descriptions," examines the main components of job descriptions and the process of creating and revising them so that staff and volunteers understand their organizational roles. The chapter also provides sample job responsibilities based on social change competencies.

Chapter 5, "Mapping Competencies and Proficiency Levels to Job Descriptions," explains how social change organizations can create and then map job descriptions to proficiency levels within each of the ten competencies and organizational sub-competencies.

Chapter 6, "The Individual Professional Development Assessment," describes a tool that assesses employee and volunteer professional development needs based on the social change competencies. The questionnaire provides employees and volunteers with a list of competencies that are essential behaviors and duties within their jobs. Employees and volunteers then rate their proficiency level in each competency.

Chapter 7, "The Individual Learning Styles Assessment," provides a questionnaire for employees and volunteers to assess their learning styles and learning format preferences. We developed the questionnaire based on Riechmann and Grasha's (1974) learning styles assessment and general classroom preferences of collaborative, participant, independent, competitive, avoidant, and dependent learners. The assessment is also available in electronic format at talent4socialchange.org.

Chapter 8, "Developing Organizational Goals and Setting Objectives," guides organizations through creating organizational professional development goals. The professional development goals should be connected to the organization's strategic plan, annual plan, individual job descriptions, and competency mapping. Also, this chapter guides you through the process of identifying your professional development objectives through on-the-job learning, mentors, and training. The objectives connect to the professional development needs, learning styles, and goals of the employees and the organization.

Chapter 9, "Setting Individual Goals and Objectives," guides organizations through setting goals and objectives for their employees and volunteers. The chapter provides a process for connecting goals and objectives to performance assessment and developing a process for assessing employee and volunteer progress toward their goals.

Chapter 10, "Implementing the Plan," discusses how your organization can implement the Talent Development Platform. There are sample budgets and timelines as well as strategies to overcome barriers of implementation.

Chapter 11, "Organizational Evaluation and Performance Assessment," explains how to use the Individual Professional Development Assessment to evaluate employee performance. Employees and managers work together to set objectives for further years based on the employees' and volunteers' performance. The chapter also explains how you can develop processes to evaluate professional development exercises and delivery methods.

Guide 1, "Third-Party Professional Development Options," is a national directory of organizations, universities, and other providers offering professional development services to nonprofit organizations. The directory is organized geographically so you can identify the professional development offerings available in your geographic area.

Guide 2, "Talent Investing: Raising and Granting Funds to Develop Social Change Leadership," outlines ideas, both for grantseekers and for grantmakers, for effectively funding talent development within nonprofit organizations and foundations that rely on third-party funding for operational tasks. Rusty Stahl, founder of the Talent Philanthropy Initiative wrote this section.

Guide 3, "A Practical Guide on Intercultural Competence for Nonprofit Managers," is a standalone guide on developing a cultural competency program. It is easy to rely on our own biases when developing programs for our organization, but to succeed it is essential that we allow individuals to guide the process. Culturally competent practices make an organization's professional development program even more effective. Alexis S. Terry wrote this section.

Throughout the book you will come across worksheets, tools, and assessments to support your work on the Talent Development Platform. All of these tools are available for download at talent4 socialchange.org.

Terms Used in This Book

Throughout the book, we borrow concepts from the corporate sector. Many of these terms originated in Fortune 500 companies and have already seeped into the social change sector, but we want to take it a step further because these concepts are fully transferrable if sized in the right way. We do our best throughout the book to funnel these concepts down to fit our smaller budgets and light staff while staying true to the original theory behind each of them. Here are some terms related to professional development that are used throughout the book:

- *Capacity building*: According to Blumenthal (2003), capacity building consists of "actions that improve nonprofit effectiveness." If capacity building is successful, organizations gain skills and resources to support their missions in new ways.

- *Coaching*: A profession in which experts provide individuals with career support through direct reflection and discussion in an environment outside their workplace.

- *Competencies*: The knowledge, skills, abilities, and other characteristics that people need to possess in order to perform their job (Pynes, 2009). This term is common in the human resources management field.

- *Consulting*: A profession in which experts in a particular management function (e.g., strategic planning or fundraising) or a particular issue provide insight into and support for the improvement or development of a specific department, program, or project. (Not to be confused with coaching.)

- *Infrastructure organization*: An institution dedicated to affecting the way the social change sector works and the way individual organizations function. Infrastructure organizations support the sector with state and federal advocacy, training on best practices, and through connecting organizations to better the sector.

- *Leadership development*: The development of individuals specifically for leadership, often done through structured third-party programs, mentoring, or coaching.

- *Professional development*: Structured learning for career and skill building often targeted to specific employees for developing job-related skills.

- *Social change sector*: The entirety of organizations looking to serve the public good, whether they are voluntary associations, incorporated nonprofit organizations, grantmaking institutions, or corporations. These encompass a wide range of 501(c) nonprofits and foundations, but we use this general term intentionally to also include emergent, hybrid organization types focused on social change, such as benefit corporations (B corporations), L3Cs, and other social enterprises.

- *Strategic human resources*: The practice of examining all aspects of human resources and developing them for effectiveness, including recruitment and hiring, staff orientation, salary and benefits, training and learning, talent management, and structured work teams. The structures and functions of this type of human resources management make for the most successful talent management systems and professional development. If your organization doesn't practice strategic human resources management, the tools in this book will give you an opportunity to restructure your system and become more strategic.

- *Systemic talent development*: The organizational practice of looking at the talent—the people—as part of the organization's strategic planning process and including plans for talent movement and growth in all organization system decisions. Systemic talent management makes conversations about your people an intentional part of your strategic plan.

- *Technical assistance*: The work of consultants and infrastructure organizations targeted at learning a specific topic or helping a particular department. Examples include supporting the development of an organization's marketing plan, or working with the development team to increase the effectiveness of their annual giving program.

- *Training and development*: According to Aguinis and Kraiger (2009), training is "the systematic approach to affecting individuals' knowledge, skills, and attitudes in order to improve individual, team, and organizational effectiveness," and development is "systematic efforts affecting individuals' knowledge or skills for purposes of personal growth or future jobs and/or roles" (p. 452).

As you navigate the rest of this book, keep these terms in mind and refer back to this list as necessary.

Chapter 1
Why Talent Development?

Systematic talent management is vital to organizational impact. We made the case in the introduction about why you should take on the tools and systems in this book. You already know talent development is important, and now you understand why it's vital. In chapter 1, we take it a step further and describe the intricacies of what makes a strong talent development system tick and explain the research behind why we believe it's so vital to the sustainability and competitiveness of the social change sector.

The Case for Talent Development in Social Change

Due to the very nature of how social change organizations came to exist—individuals supporting others because of a moral or religious compass—professionalism hasn't always been seen as necessary. In the past, it was okay to simply help those you thought were in need because you believed it was the right thing to do. Yes, it is still okay to help people because it's the right thing to do; however, the true severity of the need demands more formal organizational structures to make a greater impact in serving vulnerable populations. And let's be honest with ourselves: as we serve others, it is in our human nature to want to do it better. We want to serve more and give more of ourselves. As the social change sector has grown, it has become clear that a moral compass is no longer the only predictor of the right person for the job.

Our society has come to rely on social change organizations to do work traditionally done by the government or through personal networks. Social change organizations have now become integral to the functioning of our society and thus can no longer rely on simply having good intentions. With this continued growth as well as the increase of hybrid organizations, professionalism is becoming even more important. With increased professionalism comes the need for professional development and growth opportunities.

Professionalism and strategic thinking have become prevalent in order to do good more efficiently and effectively. The social change sector has become professionalized through formalized education, professional development, and the formation of infrastructure organizations (O'Neill, 2005). But even with increased education and professionalism, professional development has fallen short. There has been discussion of a potential leadership deficit, and experts have emphasized the importance of training and development in the sector (Light & Light, 2006). What we've found through research and working directly with social change organizations is that professional development alone isn't enough; rather, talent development needs to become a systematic part of all social change organizations.

Organizations need to move away from the mentality of sending an employee to a training and instead integrate training across the entire organization (Ronquillo, Hein, & Carpenter, 2013). Consistently, changemakers are craving learning and growth opportunities in their current positions. Because changemakers often do their work because it is meaningful to them, their need to feel purposeful is greater. A recent report by Net Impact surveyed over 1,700 college students about what they wanted out of a job, and 72 percent of respondents indicated they want a job where they can make an impact (Heldrich, Zukin, & Szeltner, 2012). All the individuals who have taken the Organizational Learning Assessment indicated they believe their work is "extremely" meaningful, but they could not see themselves staying in their positions for very long. We can hypothesize about why that might be, but the assessment showed that the same individuals also indicated signs of burnout (for example, no time for learning or reflection, and lack of effective professional development systems in their organizations).

The desire for a meaningful career path, an increase in academic programs for changemakers, and changemakers' need for purposeful work make talent development even more important. Social change organizations can provide an environment for changemakers if they do it with intentionality and make learning and talent development part of the organizational culture. This is where strategic human resources management comes in.

Strategic human resources management is playing "an increasingly important role in enhancing the effectiveness and efficiency of [social change] organizations. As employees are viewed as an indispensable resource to achieve the organization's mission, investments in human resource practices that enhance employees skills, participation in decisions, and motivation are seen as a means of coping with the aforementioned challenges" (Ridder, Piening, & Baluch, 2012). Human resources management is still in the early stages of development in the social change sector, but as organizations grow and professionalize, and more Millennials join the ranks of leadership, human resources management will become more and more important.

Strategic human resources management consists of various components that provide holistic support to staff and volunteers, connecting skills to strategic planning and mission attainment:

- Organizational culture: the collection of values, working norms, habits and beliefs of staff and volunteers in the organization

- Planning for change: support for staff and volunteers to plan for and manage change as the organization's external and internal environments shift

- Training and development: structured learning and skill building for staff and volunteers

- Health and safety: ensuring the workplace meets federal and state safety and health laws and is an environment all can work in without harm

- Recruitment and retention: finding the right talent for the organization's work and keeping them interested and satisfied with their work

- Strategic talent development: ensuring staff and volunteers are in right fit positions

- Policies and procedures: managing legal policies and systems that help staff and volunteers know the rules, follow protocols, and stay safe from potential harm

In this book we focus on two of these major components: strategic talent development systems and training and development. You already know people are important for your long-term sustainability; now is the time to develop systematic functions that show your people are important to your organization.

There have been many efforts to develop systematic forms of talent development for the social change sector. Many organizations have studied the professional development that currently exists in the sector and have explored and tested efforts to fund professional development. In addition, organizations like the Young Nonprofit Professionals Network and Emerging Practitioners in Philanthropy have popped up to provide professional development to young professionals. None of the efforts, however, have been holistic. Rusty Stahl, author of the article "Talent Philanthropy: Investing in Nonprofit People to Advance Nonprofit Performance" (2013), states that the problem is vast and gives three important reasons for the lack of desired results:

- The flawed "leadership deficit" premise continues to dominate the discourse.
- Participants have to spend energy arguing for the legitimacy of the problem rather than developing viable solutions.
- It is extremely challenging to identify levers of change for this meta-issue from which many suffer but for which no one is entirely responsible. (p. 39)

Additionally, research by Genis (2008) stated that most professional development focuses on basic managerial concepts. Researchers argue "there is a need for training and development that is integrated across many programs and agencies, [and] that is blended and includes the use of technology, and development programs should be structured part-time and 'self-authoring' to be more geared towards the promotion of leadership in adults" (Ronquillo, Hein, & Carpenter, 2013, p. 105).

The argument of whether professional development is necessary for changemakers has dominated conversations thus far in the social change sector. However, the process of talent development has to be done one organization at a time. As more and more organizations, like yours, take on strategic human resources and strong talent development systems, the sector will increase its hunger for learning and growth and make talent development solutions much more attainable.

The Return on Your Investment

The implementation of the Talent Development Platform is a heavy lift for all organizations, but it will give you the tools you need to invest in this top talent. Your organization will receive tangible benefits in the form of lower turnover and greater output (without the burnout) from your team, as well as intangible benefits that make your organization more attractive to top talent.

Tangible Returns

One of the greatest impacts you will get from this book is a decrease in staff turnover. If implemented successfully, employees, volunteers, and board members will have more reason to stay and grow with your organization. According to the *2013 Nonprofit Employment Trends Survey*, "Organizations should continue to monitor their turnover rates with the understanding that as the U.S. economy continues to rebound, employees will more likely begin to seek new career opportunities outside of their current organizations" (Nonprofit HR Solutions, 2013, p. 10). With a down economy employees are more likely to stay, but with a better economy they have options. In the current rebounding economy, social change organizations have to become more competitive for top talent. "Not giving employees proper recognition and failing to pay competitively may lead to higher levels of dissatisfaction and subsequent turnover" (Nonprofit HR Solutions, 2013, p.13). Because most social change organizations are not able to provide the highest paying salaries, they need to provide other benefits, such as strong professional development and a healthy learning culture, which will keep staff around longer. Don't get us wrong; we believe all staff in the sector should be paid at more competitive rates, but we do understand that most social change organizations operate with limited monetary resources; therefore, you will absolutely have to build a stronger holistic talent development system to be sustainable.

Another effect that bad turnover rates and lack of professional development systems have on organizations is the inability to create proper succession plans. According to the *2013 Nonprofit Employment Trends Survey*, "Sixty-nine percent of nonprofits surveyed reported not having a formal succession plan for senior leadership. As the baby boom generation of nonprofit leaders retire the lack of a formal succession plan may endanger nonprofits' ability to effectively prepare for leadership transition and organizational sustainability will be at risk" (p. 1). And further, "the lack of sufficient professional development investment at the entry- and mid-level staff levels will likely continue to contribute to organizations' inabilities to retain individuals at these levels" (Nonprofit HR Solutions, 2013, p. 19). The length of time it takes to fill positions ranges from thirty-one to ninety days for most positions. Although that doesn't seem like a long time, consider the amount of money you will lose in staff productivity and the time spent recruiting and filling those positions. Researchers estimate that each lost position costs anywhere from 75 to 150 percent of that position's annual salary (Krause, 2014; Nonprofit HR Solutions, 2013).

To evaluate your return on investment, we recommend calculating your current turnover rate prior to beginning the Platform. We recommend measuring turnover in three different ways: staff and volunteer turnover, new hire turnover, and functional turnover (loss of productive workers). Staff and volunteer turnover measures your overall turnover. The new hire turnover determines if all your staff are leaving at the three- or six-month mark or if they are staying longer. The former is a sign that staff members recognize that no growth opportunities or professional development will be available to them at the organization. New staff often get excited about learning their new roles, but once they realize their future role will be stagnant, they leave. The functional turnover determines if you have a higher number of top performers leaving the organization compared to lower performers. This ratio is important, because if, on the one hand, your organization is losing employees that aren't very productive, this may be a good sign your culture is strong. On the other hand, if you are losing top performers, you have some culture and structures to fix in order to keep top talent in your organization. Just having warm bodies in seats isn't a good way of measuring turnover and effectiveness. You want to keep the right people. Exhibit 1.1 shows you how to calculate each of these turnover rates.

Intangible Returns

Organizations gain many intangible benefits from strong talent development systems. "Investing in talent development strengthens nonprofits

---

EXHIBIT 1.1

Turnover Ratios

Staff (or Volunteer) Turnover Rate

$$(\text{\# of terminations per year}/\text{avg. \# of active employees in the same year}) \times 100$$

This calculation determines your overall turnover rate without any other factors in mind.

New Hire Turnover Rate

$$(\text{\# of terminations within first year}/\text{\# of hires}) \times 100$$

This calculation gives you an idea of the number of employees you are losing within their first year in your organization. If new hire turnover is high, it is a sign that your learning culture is negative and new hires are seeing no room for growth.

Functional Turnover Rate

$$(\text{\# of poor performers who leave} - \text{\# of good performers who leave})/\text{total \# who leave}$$

This ratio is a bit subjective; however, it provides a good view of whether or not you are losing top performers. If you are losing more good performers than poor performers, this is a sign of an unsatisfactory organizational culture. There are many possible reasons for this, however, so use the assessments and the time spent working on the Talent Development Platform to determine what might be the core reasons top performers are leaving your organization (O'Connell & Kung, 2007).

and motivates and empowers employees. Specifically, we see that stronger organizations prioritize training, coaching and mentoring, and prepare for leadership transition, and that staff on the receiving end of these practices are more content with their work and more likely to stay for the long haul" (Colorado Nonprofit Association and Pathfinders Solutions, 2012, p. 15).

The investment you make through this process will give you an opportunity to decrease the intangible factors that lead to staff members' poor performance. Factors such as lower morale and errors made by overburdened staff are just a few of them (O'Connell & Kung, 2007).

These benefits aren't as easy to calculate as turnover, but they will allow you to assess improvements after your first year of implementation and on a longer-term basis:

- The first benefit is increased satisfaction among staff and volunteers. With intentional support, staff members and volunteers will be more satisfied with their roles, and those who are not satisfied will move on, which will reflect positively on your functional turnover ratio.

- The second benefit is the new skills learned and higher proficiency levels of staff and volunteers. The increased proficiency levels will give you a greater return on your mission.

- The third intangible benefit is a stronger learning culture, which is further reciprocated by increased staff and volunteer satisfaction and more effective services. A learning culture is one where staff feel safe to learn and grow and where innovation and effectiveness are at their finest.

We will talk more about each of these intangibles and how to measure them throughout the book.

The goals set for professional development will provide you with some insight on your return on investment. The process we provide in the book gives you the tools you need to meet your strategic goals, structure staff and volunteer roles, and set goals for proficiency level increases that will directly influence your mission return.

How Adults Learn and Why It Matters

One of the reasons talent development is so important has to do with how adults learn. At the core of all adults is their need to be intrinsically motivated. Part of this need is the desire to do purposeful work, which targets intrinsic or internal motivations. This means that the more purposeful and supported adults feel, the more they will learn. Doing meaningful work gives changemakers some intrinsic motivation, but they need to also feel supported. Adult learning theory, otherwise known as andragogy, explains that when adults are intrinsically motivated, there is a positive reciprocation for doing better work. Therefore, professional development is only successful if leadership taps the intrinsic motivations of staff, and it has to be done through more than supporting passion.

The Center for Creative Leadership states that all professional development systems should include the following:

- An opportunity for the participants to pursue goals with personal meaning

- An environment that piques curiosity

- Participant control over themselves and what they pursue

- Satisfaction over helping others

- Opportunity to compare personal performance favorably to others

- Recognition of accomplishments (Rabin, 2014)

This list suggests that the staff and volunteers in your organization want to manage their own learning and do it through supporting others and feeling supported themselves. These concepts seem basic, but implementing them can be tough in a fast-moving environment. It is common to forget to step back and relinquish a bit of control. However, employees learn and work more effectively if they are helping with decision making.

Knowles's theory on andragogy explores more of what adults need in their learning and provides insight on the best learning environments for adults:

- Adults need to know the reason for learning something.

- Experience provides the basis for learning activities.

- Adults need to be responsible for their decisions on education.

- Adults are most interested in learning subjects that have immediate relevance to their work.

- Adult learning is problem centered rather than content oriented.

- Adults respond better to internal versus external motivators (Merriam, 2001).

We have developed a model for talent development that integrates adult learning theories and makes learning and professional development intentional. Our model builds upon recommendations by previous consultants, researchers, and experts in the field (Genis, 2008; Paton, Mordaunt, & Cornforth, 2007).

Throughout the book, we explore tools and resources that encourage and support learning for the betterment of your mission. Our model includes information about how to shift culture, develop a map of your talent, and create an environment where learning happens regularly on the job and through formal and informal peer-to-peer interactions. According to the Center for Creative Leadership (Rabin, 2014), informal learning is often haphazard and triggered by external events. But you can support and enhance informal learning significantly. Leaders can engage in more-critical reflection to surface tacit knowledge. Tacit knowledge is learning that takes place by doing. In this book, we give you the tools to help your employees and volunteers develop their proficiency levels through learning on the job.

Further, we borrow from the Center for Creative Leadership's 70–20–10 model as we walk you through building your Talent Development Platform and setting goals and objectives for your organization. As the 70–20–10 name implies, the learning model calls for 70 percent of the staff member's time spent on professional development to consist of on-the-job learning, supported by 20 percent spent on coaching and mentoring, and 10 percent spent in classroom training (Bridgespan Group, 2013). It's easy for managers to jump right into hiring a trainer; spending money directly is easier than calculating the return on learning done on-the-job or through mentoring. Time spent in training is more tangible. However, as the model states, money spent on training will not support the full array of learning that adults need to grow in a specific competency area. The Center for Creative Leadership has found that although most organizations acknowledge formal training alone can be limited in impact, most of their training budget is for classroom events and e-learning assets (Rabin, 2014).

Implementing the tools in this book saves your organization money in the long run and makes you money in the future. The practices in this book make talent development part of the systems and culture of how your organization runs. Employees and volunteers take on learning opportunities willingly, are more open to and better at sharing feedback, and give themselves the space they need to provide innovative solutions to meet your mission. The Talent Development Platform provides you with the tools and guidelines you need in order to ensure the adults in your organization are learning and growing effectively.

The Talent Development Platform Overview

The Talent Development Platform process, shown in figure 1.1, provides your organization with a system for talent development. The Platform involves steps at the organizational and individual levels. Each

FIGURE 1.1
The Talent Development Platform Process

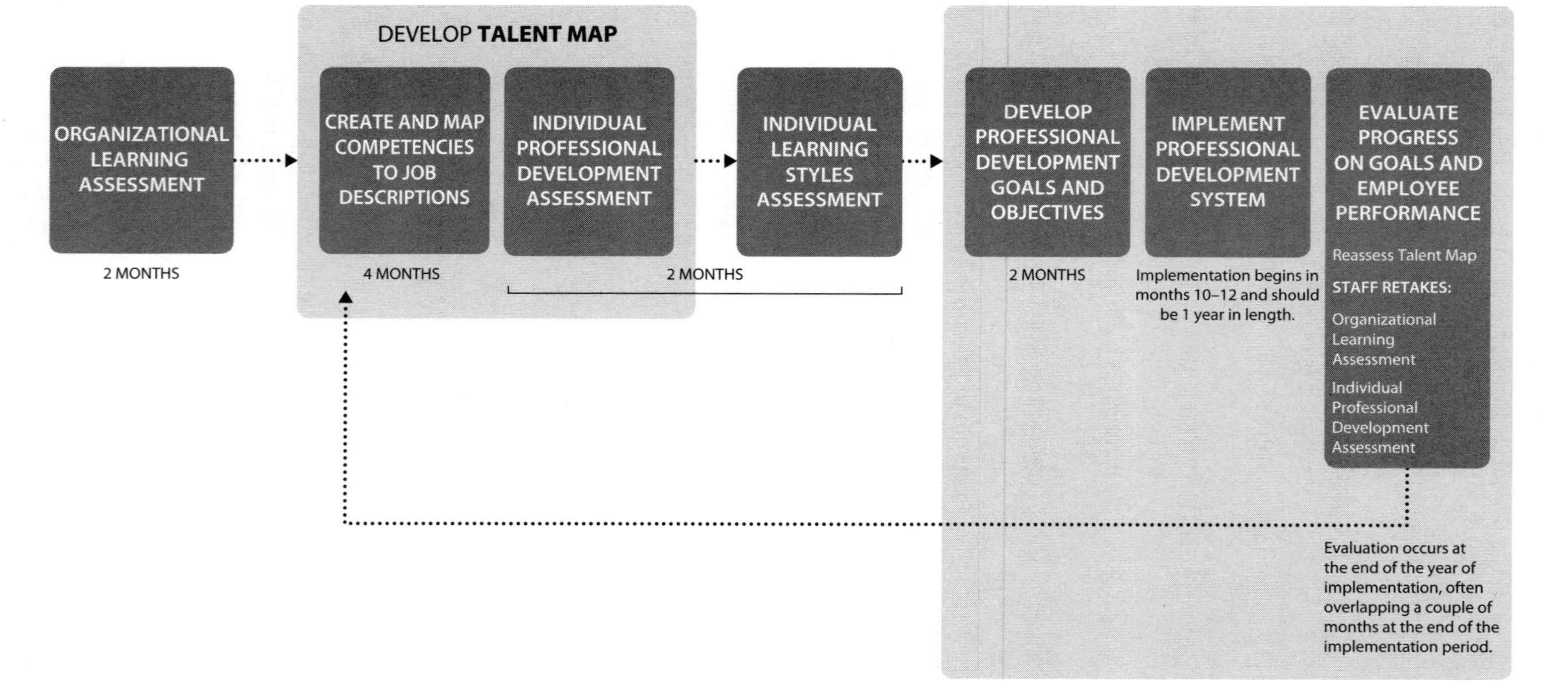

ORGANIZATIONAL LEARNING ASSESSMENT

2 MONTHS

DEVELOP TALENT MAP

CREATE AND MAP COMPETENCIES TO JOB DESCRIPTIONS

4 MONTHS

INDIVIDUAL PROFESSIONAL DEVELOPMENT ASSESSMENT

2 MONTHS

INDIVIDUAL LEARNING STYLES ASSESSMENT

DEVELOP PROFESSIONAL DEVELOPMENT GOALS AND OBJECTIVES

2 MONTHS

IMPLEMENT PROFESSIONAL DEVELOPMENT SYSTEM

Implementation begins in months 10–12 and should be 1 year in length.

EVALUATE PROGRESS ON GOALS AND EMPLOYEE PERFORMANCE

Reassess Talent Map

STAFF RETAKES:

Organizational Learning Assessment

Individual Professional Development Assessment

Evaluation occurs at the end of the year of implementation, often overlapping a couple of months at the end of the implementation period.

step enhances the learning culture and development systems within your organization. The Platform integrates seamlessly in your strategic-planning and decision-making processes. Each tool can stand alone or be integrated into your current talent management systems; however, the Platform in its entirety provides a strong foundation for holistic talent development.

Undertake the Organizational Learning Assessment

The Organizational Learning Assessment process takes approximately two months to implement and encompasses taking the assessment, gathering the results, and discussing the results with your team. This assessment provides a look at how your employees and volunteers feel about learning, how they feel about their need for development and how safe they feel sharing and failing at work.

Develop the Talent Map

Developing your Talent Map includes three steps:

1. Writing and revising accurate and clear job descriptions for each role in your organization

2. Assessing the competencies and proficiency levels needed for each job or volunteer role in your organization

3. Having staff and volunteers take the Individual Professional Development Assessment to identify their own competencies and proficiency levels based on their job descriptions

These steps provide staff and volunteers with a clear understanding of their role, so they can set their objectives for learning accordingly. These steps also provide you with a clear understanding of the roles your staff play on a daily basis, of whether employees and volunteers are in the right roles, and whether new positions are needed or some positions are no longer relevant. These job descriptions coupled with the Individual Professional Development Assessment results will give you a view of whether your employees and volunteers are in the right role or if they can take on more.

Administer the Learning Styles Assessment

The Learning Styles Assessment gives each employee and volunteer a view of how he or she learns most effectively and gives the organization a map of how everyone learns. This information is imperative when setting goals and objectives to ensure the learning objectives you set will be effective.

Develop Goals and Objectives

During this component of the Platform, you will utilize information gathered from each of the previous components to structure overall learning goals and three objectives tied to each. Your goals will be tied directly to the organization's strategic goals and take into account staff and volunteers' learning needs. During this stage you will also develop objectives tied to each goal that align with learning opportunities on the job, mentoring opportunities, and professional development and training. Staff members and volunteers participating in the process will utilize the organization's goals and objectives to set their own objectives for the year as well.

Implement Professional Development

During this stage of the process, you will plan for implementation of your goals and objectives. Implementation includes the development of a budget and timeline, as well as tools for participants to use to reflect on learning activities, evaluate their learning progress, and set action plans following trainings.

Evaluate Goals and Employee Performance

The evaluation stage of the Platform involves assessing the progress of staff and volunteers toward their objectives and the increases in their proficiency levels, as well as the organization's progress toward goals and objectives. During this stage you will assess any changes in your organization's learning culture and evaluate the process you have used throughout the year.

Your Organization's Talent Development Platform

As you navigate the Talent Development Platform process, you will be adding to your organization's own comprehensive Talent Development Platform as shown in figure 1.2. Using scoring averages from each of the tools in the process, the document provides you with a quick overview of your organization's learning culture and readiness for the process, the professional strengths and weaknesses and the learning styles of your staff and volunteers, and your organization's goals and objectives. Display your Platform prominently and bring it to decision-making and personnel meetings.

To integrate a commitment to learning in your organization the goals and objectives from your organization's Talent Development Platform will be transferred to an individual platform for each individual. Individuals will map their Individual Professional Development Assessment scores, their top learning styles, and individual goals and objectives alongside those goals for use year-to-year (figure 1.3). All individuals should display their Platforms where they can assess their progress and next steps regularly.

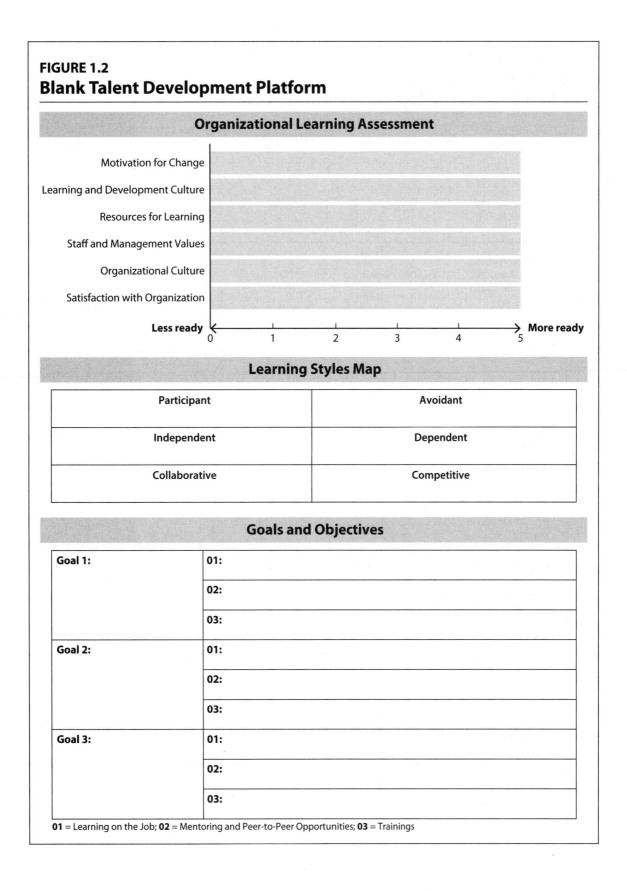

FIGURE 1.2
Blank Talent Development Platform

Organizational Learning Assessment

- Motivation for Change
- Learning and Development Culture
- Resources for Learning
- Staff and Management Values
- Organizational Culture
- Satisfaction with Organization

Less ready ← 0 — 1 — 2 — 3 — 4 — 5 → **More ready**

Learning Styles Map

Participant	Avoidant
Independent	Dependent
Collaborative	Competitive

Goals and Objectives

Goal 1:	01:
	02:
	03:
Goal 2:	01:
	02:
	03:
Goal 3:	01:
	02:
	03:

01 = Learning on the Job; **02** = Mentoring and Peer-to-Peer Opportunities; **03** = Trainings

FIGURE 1.2
Blank Talent Development Platform, Cont'd

Talent Map		1	2	3	4	5
Advocacy and Public Policy	Position Proficiency Level					
	Current Proficiency Level					
	Desired Proficiency Level					
Communications, Marketing, and Public Relations	Position Proficiency Level					
	Current Proficiency Level					
	Desired Proficiency Level					
Financial Management and Social Entrepreneurship	Position Proficiency Level					
	Current Proficiency Level					
	Desired Proficiency Level					
Fundraising and Resource Development	Position Proficiency Level					
	Current Proficiency Level					
	Desired Proficiency Level					
Grantmaking or Direct Service	Position Proficiency Level					
	Current Proficiency Level					
	Desired Proficiency Level					
Human Resources Management and Volunteerism	Position Proficiency Level					
	Current Proficiency Level					
	Desired Proficiency Level					
Information Management	Position Proficiency Level					
	Current Proficiency Level					
	Desired Proficiency Level					
Leadership and Governance	Position Proficiency Level					
	Current Proficiency Level					
	Desired Proficiency Level					
Legal and Regulatory	Position Proficiency Level					
	Current Proficiency Level					
	Desired Proficiency Level					
Planning and Evaluation	Position Proficiency Level					
	Current Proficiency Level					
	Desired Proficiency Level					

FIGURE 1.3
Blank Individual Talent Development Platform

Individual Professional Development Assessment						
		1	2	3	4	5
Advocacy and Public Policy	Position Proficiency Level					
	Current Proficiency Level					
	Desired Proficiency Level					
Communications, Marketing, and Public Relations	Position Proficiency Level					
	Current Proficiency Level					
	Desired Proficiency Level					
Financial Management and Social Entrepreneurship	Position Proficiency Level					
	Current Proficiency Level					
	Desired Proficiency Level					
Fundraising and Resource Development	Position Proficiency Level					
	Current Proficiency Level					
	Desired Proficiency Level					
Grantmaking or Direct Service	Position Proficiency Level					
	Current Proficiency Level					
	Desired Proficiency Level					
Human Resources Management and Volunteerism	Position Proficiency Level					
	Current Proficiency Level					
	Desired Proficiency Level					
Information Management	Position Proficiency Level					
	Current Proficiency Level					
	Desired Proficiency Level					
Leadership and Governance	Position Proficiency Level					
	Current Proficiency Level					
	Desired Proficiency Level					
Legal and Regulatory	Position Proficiency Level					
	Current Proficiency Level					
	Desired Proficiency Level					
Planning and Evaluation	Position Proficiency Level					
	Current Proficiency Level					
	Desired Proficiency Level					

Top Three Learning Styles

1. _____

2. _____

3. _____

FIGURE 1.3
Blank Individual Talent Development Platform, Cont'd

Organizational Goals and Objectives

Goal 1:	O1:
	O2:
	O3:
Goal 2:	O1:
	O2:
	O3:
Goal 3:	O1:
	O2:
	O3:

O1 = Learning on the Job; **O2** = Mentoring and Peer-to-Peer Opportunities; **O3** = Trainings

Individual Professional Development Goals and Objectives

	Learning on the Job	Mentoring and Peer-to-Peer	Trainings
Goal 1:			
Goal 2:			
Goal 3:			

Creating an Effective Talent Development System

To implement an effective talent development system—to implement the tools in this book successfully—you need to have the following guidelines in place:

- All goals, objectives, and planning should be linked directly back to your organization's mission and strategic goals.

- Employee- and volunteer-level objectives should be structured around their learning needs and styles.

- All staff members and key volunteers should be included in the Platform process. Investing in talent at all levels makes the process more systematic and effective. It is not just "leaders" who need development; all employees need learning opportunities to increase effectiveness.

- The process should be interculturally competent so that the needs of everyone are met, no matter their race, ethnicity, gender, sexual orientation, economic status, or any other factor that affects how they work (see Guide 3 for more information).

- All leadership should champion the efforts; this is a sign of a healthy learning culture, and trust us, staff will notice.

- Talk about and evaluate the Platform regularly to ensure the process is working well and can be adapted as necessary.

EXHIBIT 1.2

Professional Development for Volunteers and Boards

Intentional professional development for volunteers and boards is much less prevalent than professional development for employees of social change organizations. This makes sense considering the environment many social change organizations function in (low resources and high volume of output) and the fact that we are asking volunteers and board members to give us their time and knowledge for free. We ask that you flip the switch on this common ideal. In the case of volunteers and board members, professional development may be more hyperfocused to their particular role, but it equips them with the tools they need to do their particular role better, such as direct service, supporting yearly budget planning, or managing the organization's strategic vision.

In order to make professional development probable for volunteers and board members, you also have to get beyond the idea that board members and volunteers are more skilled than your employees at something. You did ask them to represent the organization because they are excellent at a particular skill, but in most cases they have a lot to learn about how their particular skills work in the social change sector and how the functions and culture of your organization may affect their work. You have plenty to teach them too; don't forget that.

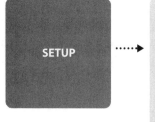

FIGURE 1.4
Setup Checklist

SETUP

- Meet with your team to discuss process and purpose for work.
- Plan process for implementation of Platform.
- Calculate turnover rates and current costs associated with hiring, turnover, and contractors.
- Determine process for reward and improvement planning for employees and volunteers (e.g., salary increases as a result of growth and meeting goals).
- Review strategic plan and determine whether employees and volunteers have clear goals and objectives for their work.

Conclusion

In this chapter, we discussed the intricacies of what makes a strong talent development system tick and explained the research behind why we believe it is so vital to the sustainability and competitiveness of the social change sector. Now it is time for you to get started in your organization with the Organizational Learning Assessment. Before you do that, though, run through the checklist in figure 1.4 to set up your Talent Development Platform process.

Chapter 2
The Organizational Learning Assessment

Before implementing the Talent Development Platform, it is important to assess your organization's readiness for implementation. Using the Organizational Learning Assessment, your organization can get a good sense of how leadership, staff, and volunteers perceive their need for professional development and whether your organization's culture is conducive to learning. Setting the right foundation gives your organization a step up in implementing a successful and sustainable professional development system and a chance to evaluate progress on a regular basis.

When learning is part of your organization's culture, professional development systems seem second nature. However, if your organization's culture doesn't make learning or professional development safe, the talent development system may do more harm than good. The Organizational Learning Assessment is meant to give you an opportunity to be honest about whether staff have the freedom to admit they need support, whether teams learn and grow together in healthy ways, and whether leadership supports intentional learning. If your organization does all these things, then you are ready to jump into implementation. If not, you need to take extra time to discuss the results and implement necessary interventions. Full implementation can begin after you've seen improvement using this assessment.

The Organizational Learning Assessment will give you a good idea of your organizational culture, and implementation of this work should be done carefully. Change is hard, so ensure that everyone in the organization is involved in the process, understands why they are taking the assessments, and sees the assessments being utilized. A strong learning culture depends on all those factors. Figure 2.1 provides you with an Organizational Learning Assessment checklist.

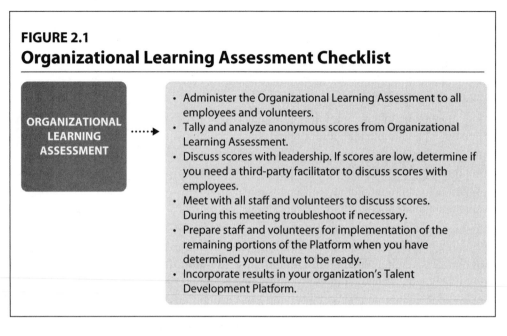

FIGURE 2.1
Organizational Learning Assessment Checklist

ORGANIZATIONAL LEARNING ASSESSMENT

- Administer the Organizational Learning Assessment to all employees and volunteers.
- Tally and analyze anonymous scores from Organizational Learning Assessment.
- Discuss scores with leadership. If scores are low, determine if you need a third-party facilitator to discuss scores with employees.
- Meet with all staff and volunteers to discuss scores. During this meeting troubleshoot if necessary.
- Prepare staff and volunteers for implementation of the remaining portions of the Platform when you have determined your culture to be ready.
- Incorporate results in your organization's Talent Development Platform.

Creation of the Organizational Learning Assessment

We created the Organizational Learning Assessment through the comparison of assessments corporations use for assessing their organizational culture for readiness, learning environment, and change management. We analyzed and compared assessments from Lehman, Greener, and Simpson (2002); Lerch et al. (2011); Garvin, Edmondson, and Gino (2008); Marsick and Watkins (2003); and Bess, Perkins, and McCown (2011). Our comparison led to six domains containing common themes from each of these very different assessments.

The six domains cover the range of cultural aspects your organization needs to have in place in order to implement a change strategy in the way the Talent Development Platform presents. We also chose these domains and assessments specifically because they support change management in the form of creating a stronger learning environment specifically:

1. Motivation for Change: Do the staff, volunteers, and leadership of the organization want and perceive a need to change?

2. Learning and Development Culture: Does the organization embrace learning and learn from failure?

3. Resources for Learning: Are employees and volunteers provided time and monetary support for professional development?

4. Staff and Management Values: Do staff, volunteers, and leadership value learning and professional growth?

5. Organizational Culture: Are employees safe to fail and are they able to ask for help? Does leadership publically support individuals who have taken risks and failed, and do they actively learn themselves?

6. Staff and Volunteer Satisfaction: Are staff and volunteers satisfied with the organization, and do they intend to stay with the organization?

These domains are applicable for all organizations, whether you are a grantmaking institution, a nonprofit social service agency, or a volunteer-run membership organization.

It is important for organizations to score high (4 or higher) on the spectrum of readiness for all six of these domains before implementing the Talent Development Platform. Scoring high on all the domains indicates that leadership, staff, and volunteers will all have a better chance of embracing the new structure of learning and that the talent development system will be more effective and sustainable. If your organization scores low on some or all of the domains, we offer guidance later in this chapter on how to prepare your organization.

The Importance of Being Ready

The basic definition of readiness is being prepared. Readiness for learning means having an organizational culture that supports learning and new systems. Organizational culture plays a huge role in whether staff and leadership will be open to new information, knowledge, and systems. Having employees and volunteers on board from the beginning will support implementation later on. You need structured talent systems in place, such as job descriptions, time off for professional development, performance assessment, a system for salary adjustments, and strategic human resources management. Being prepared in both culture and systems will give your talent development system the boost it needs to be successful and sustainable.

Although you may feel ready for implementation, it is important to be sure that your organization is ready for a new talent development system. Preparing for the process will make it more successful in the end. Retroactive learning doesn't work; once a staff member is gone, you can't train that person anymore. Begin now. Build a learning culture or support your current culture to keep top talent in your organization and your employees and volunteers satisfied and effective. There is strong evidence,

EXHIBIT 2.1
Organizational Learning Environment Domains

Motivation to Change

The Motivation to Change domain measures the staff member's or volunteer's belief in his or her need to change. This domain includes an assessment of

- the extent to which employees and volunteers are pessimistic or cynical about the organization's ability to change;
- whether staff and volunteers believe they and their counterparts have training needs;
- the level of pressure the organization receives from leadership and external stakeholders regarding the need to change; and
- staff and volunteer perception of the appropriateness of change and whether employees and volunteers believe a change is necessary.

Learning and Development Culture

The Learning and Development Culture domain assesses the organization's current perception of learning and whether staff and volunteers feel safe within the environment to share failures and learn together. This domain includes an assessment of

- the current culture of communication and feedback—whether employees and volunteers share information well and provide each with other constructive feedback;
- whether the organization is intentional in discussing improvements and learning from failure;
- the level at which staff and volunteers feel empowered to make decisions and learn;
- the intangible support that staff and volunteers are provided for professional development; and
- the ability of staff and volunteers to meet their own professional development needs.

Resources for Learning

The Resources for Learning domain assesses staff and volunteer knowledge and the availability of tangible learning assets. This domain includes an assessment of

- whether the organization has human resources policies in place for professional development and whether staff members are aware of the policies;
- the availability of rewards for improvement in proficiency levels;

- whether the organization has a budget for professional development, and whether staff and volunteers are aware of the budget and feel that it is sufficient for their needs; and
- the comfort level staff and volunteers have with taking time for professional development based on the capacity of their team and the rules of leadership.

Staff and Management Values

The Staff and Management Values domain assesses how the organization values learning. This domain includes an assessment of

- whether staff and volunteers feel they have regular learning and growth opportunities;
- the confidence that staff and volunteers have in their own skills and abilities;
- the level at which staff and volunteers believe they can be flexible and adapt to changing conditions;
- whether staff and volunteers are committed to the organization; and
- whether staff and volunteers believe their managers support professional development.

Organizational Culture

The Organizational Culture domain assesses the dynamics of the daily operations and whether staff and volunteers believe their current environment is open to change and whether their team works well together. This domain includes an assessment of

- the awareness and regular discussion of the organization's mission and strategic goals;
- staff and volunteer cohesiveness;
- the level at which staff and volunteers feel strain and have time to reflect on their work;
- the openness of staff and volunteers to change;
- whether a collective vision exists among all team members; and
- whether staff and volunteers appreciate the differences that exist within their team.

Staff and Volunteer Satisfaction

The Staff and Volunteer Satisfaction domain is a bit different from the others. This domain is meant to provide a comparison to the other domains. It gives you a sense of whether success or challenges in the other domains are causing staff and volunteers to be more or less satisfied with their work. This score is a good place to ask the question, Why aren't staff satisfied with their roles?

as we mentioned in previous chapters, that learning organizations are more likely to keep top performers and be competitive in the future. Be that organization!

We ask you to enlist new systems that evaluate your employees' and volunteers' positions. We know that this will give your organization the competitiveness it needs for top talent, but a new bit of scrutiny can scare those working and volunteering for your organization. The Organizational Learning Assessment gives you the information you need to ensure that you are implementing the system in the right way. The process we ask you to take enlightens full organizational transformation. A complete organizational transformation refers to a simultaneous realignment in organizational values, behaviors, structures, and outcomes. The assessment provides you with the baseline of where your staff and volunteers believe you are in each of these arenas.

As you are discussing the results and implementation of this assessment, we ask that you "look beyond prescribed flows and connections to informal structures and processes" (Cullen, Palus, & Appaneal, 2014). It's the informal processes, the unseen workings of the organization that represent the bulk of the culture. These are the hardest things to find but the most important to know when establishing a learning culture. In a culture of unsafe risk taking and where individuals can't fail, talent development systems could be hazardous. It's important to know the underlying support culture of your organization to avoid harmful results.

Why Organizational

Having a few employees who believe in learning and personal growth doesn't mean your organization has a culture of learning and growth. A learning organization is one where learning is part of the culture, where risk is acceptable, where failure is discussed, and where learning occurs from both success and failure. All staff and regular volunteers (which can include board members) should take the Organizational Learning Assessment in order to get a true picture of the culture of learning in your organization.

All staff and all volunteers who work in your organization on a regular basis (defined as at least once a month) should take the Organizational Learning Assessment. These are board members, volunteers who run your front desk, volunteers who have participated in capacity-building work, interns, and volunteers you've had for an extended period of time. Volunteers are just as valuable as employees and can provide great insight on culture. Just because they aren't in the office forty hours a week doesn't mean they don't see and feel the culture when they are there. Board members are on this list too. The board is an integral part of your talent pool. Having board members take the assessment is especially important for small nonprofit organizations. If you have only one or two staff members, the board becomes an extension of your staff. If you work in a larger organization, have the board take the survey separately, so you can compare and contrast results. Board and staff may have different views that may present challenges if the board is unaware of staff perceptions.

If you have a large organization with distinct departments, you might consider asking each department to take the assessment separately. Be sure to keep the assessments anonymous, taking care not to divide the groups in a way that eliminates anonymity. Dividing the assessments into departments will give you a good idea of whether the culture is different in each department and whether some managers provide or need more support than others.

If you have only two or three staff members, there may be less differentiation between responses; however, getting anonymous insight is a good way to assess the cohesiveness of your learning culture. If one person in a small organization doesn't feel the same way others do about the environment, it will be visible in the assessment results. In larger organizations outliers may become more hidden, but results will show trends in either culture direction. If only a few staff or volunteers take the assessment, your organization could miss out on important trends or outliers.

No matter how many employees or volunteers you have, do not use the assessment to enforce consequences. Staff should feel comfortable to answer truthfully, without a threat to their position. If your first thought is, "I want to know who said that," or "Who doesn't want to be here for the next five years," then you need to step out of this process and assess your own leadership as well as your own individual development. Your thoughts (as a leader) turn into cultural norms that hurt the learning environment of your organization.

Benefits of the Assessment

After your employees and volunteers take the assessment, leadership gets the opportunity to have crucial conversations about your organization's systems and employees' awareness and satisfaction with those systems. Components of the assessment provide insight on various workings in your office that may affect other functions of your organization. The assessment scores, even if they are on the higher end, may bring up staff and volunteer challenges regarding roles or different systems in the organization. Staff may be unaware of policies or may be completely dissatisfied with the organization. Whichever the outcome, the assessment provides a basis for conversations and allows solutions to arise for challenges staff may be facing.

To recap, implementing the assessment provides you with insight on

- the motivations of your staff and volunteers;

- whether staff and volunteers feel safe to take accountability for their actions;

- staff members' and volunteers' satisfaction with their work;

- whether staff and volunteers are aware of the resources available to them for learning; and

- the values your staff and volunteers have for personal growth.

Administering the Assessment

We have already mentioned this, but would like to reiterate the importance of anonymity in the assessment process. It is of the utmost importance for staff to feel safe, knowing that they cannot be targeted for answering the questions in any particular way. If staff and volunteers feel safe, they are more likely to answer honestly. Having an honest picture of your culture will make the implementation of the entire process that much more successful.

Tread carefully when scoring the survey. The assessment isn't the be-all and end-all. You want to use it as a conversation starter with your staff. Ask yourself *why* for each of the results and discuss how you might be able to positively affect in the future the components you scored low on or maintain the progress you have made in all the domains. This tool isn't meant to be a decision maker on its own; it's the discussions you have about the results that matter. Use this tool for learning.

Once you prepare leadership and staff for the assessment, send the assessment to staff and volunteers via e-mail. We have provided a template invitation for you to customize (exhibit 2.2).

Allow staff and volunteers three weeks to take the survey, and each week send a reminder e-mail. It is important to be persistent with reminding busy staff and volunteers to take the survey (exhibit 2.3).

Scoring the Assessment

Each employee and volunteer who has taken the assessment uses the Organizational Learning Assessment Scoring sheet to score his or her own

---

EXHIBIT 2.2

Organizational Learning Assessment E-mail Introduction Template

Dear _____,

As you are aware, _____ [name of organization] is in the process of assessing our learning culture and your professional development preferences so that we can be more strategic and systematic in our professional development offerings.

Please set aside 10–15 minutes to take the Organizational Learning Assessment. This assessment will gather information on how you feel about our organization's culture and the resources you are provided for learning.

The assessment is completely anonymous and you should answer as truthfully as possible. The responses will in no way be used for any type of assessment of staff members.

We will be able to use the summary data to determine the process for which we want to implement some new learning and talent initiatives in the organization.

Again, please be as honest as possible when taking the assessment.

Take the survey here: [Insert Link]

Please let us know if you have any questions about the survey.

Thank you.

---

assessment results. Then, scores are averaged for an overall organizational score. We recommend you include all employees and volunteers who took the assessment in the scoring process and share the results with them.

Scoring Individual Assessments

Exhibit 2.5 shows the full scoring sheet for the assessment. To begin scoring, have participants go through their assessment, with the scoring sheet side by side. Each response for a question has been designated a score from 1 to 5 based on whether the score indicates the individual is ready for the new system (5), or not ready (1), and the spectrum in between. Exhibit 2.4 shows the scores from two employees of a small grassroots organization for Domain 1 as an example.

Tallying Results for the Full Staff

Once all employees and volunteers have tallied the results for each of their domains, you can calculate your organization's score in each domain. If you have an organization with more than thirty staff or with departments that serve very different functions in the organization, you should tally scores

EXHIBIT 2.3

The Organizational Learning Assessment

In this assessment, you will be asked several questions about your organization's current culture and infrastructure for learning and training. Please answer each question truthfully and from your own perspective. The data will be used to determine your organization's readiness for implementing an in-house professional development training system.

If you are working in an all-volunteer organization or are the sole staff member answer the questions about your team with your board and all key volunteers in mind.

Rate your agreement with the following statements.

	Strongly Agree	Agree	Neutral	Disagree	Strongly Disagree
1. I believe all staff, leadership, and volunteers, including me, need some sort of professional development.					
2. Our organization has a comprehensive professional development system in place.					
3. Our organization has a professional development system in place that works for me.					

Please answer the following questions based on the frequency for which they occur in your organization.

	Frequently (monthly or more often)	Sometimes (quarterly, biannually)	Never
4. How often do your external stakeholders (donors, clients, and/or grantees) ask how your organization is improving its programs and expect feedback reports?			
5. How often does your organization's leadership talk about training and/or professional development?			

EXHIBIT 2.3
The Organizational Learning Assessment, Cont'd

Rate your agreement with the following statements.

	Strongly Agree	Agree	Neutral	Disagree	Strongly Disagree
6. Our organization views mistakes as an opportunity to learn.					
7. When a team member shares a new idea, we all discuss it and encourage them to think it through.					
8. I feel comfortable asking for support when I am unable to complete a task.					

Please answer the following questions based on the frequency of which they occur in your organization.

	Frequently (monthly or more often)	Sometimes (quarterly, biannually)	Never
9. How often does your team encourage feedback and open communication?			
10. How often are you provided with resources specifically allocated for learning?			
11. How often do you have the opportunity to create your own professional development plans?			

EXHIBIT 2.3

The Organizational Learning Assessment, Cont'd

Rate your agreement with the following statements.

	Strongly Agree	Agree	Neutral	Disagree	Strongly Disagree
12. Our organization has a formal performance evaluation process.					
13. Our organization's job or position descriptions are current.					
14. If I meet my professional development goals for the year, I am rewarded.					
15. My organization allows me to use paid time off or scheduled volunteer time for trainings.					
16. There are enough people on my team that I feel comfortable taking time away from my duties for trainings or workshops.					

Please answer the following questions based on the frequency of which they occur in your organization.

	Frequently (monthly or more often)	Sometimes (quarterly, biannually)	Never
17. How often does your organization conduct formal performance evaluations?			
18. How often are you provided time for professional development?			
19. How often do you get one-on-one performance feedback from your manager or fellow team members?			

EXHIBIT 2.3
The Organizational Learning Assessment, Cont'd

Rate your agreement with the following statements.

	Strongly Agree	Agree	Neutral	Disagree	Strongly Disagree
20. I believe I have the right skills to do my work or volunteer assignments.					
21. If a challenge arises, I am able to adapt to the new conditions.					
22. I am supportive of our organization.					
23. I hope to be working or volunteering in this organization three years from now.					

Please answer the following questions based on the frequency of which they occur in your organization.

	Frequently (monthly or more often)	Sometimes (quarterly, biannually)	Never
24. How often does leadership share information from books and articles to help improve your organization?			
25. How often does your supervisor or team leader encourage you to read books and articles that may help improve your role?			
26. How often does leadership check on the progress toward your organization's strategic goals?			

EXHIBIT 2.3
The Organizational Learning Assessment, Cont'd

Rate your agreement with the following statements.

	Strongly Agree	Agree	Neutral	Disagree	Strongly Disagree
27. I understand our strategic plan.					
28. I know the mission of our organization.					
29. I work in an organization that supports and encourages team collaboration.					
30. My team works really well together.					

Please answer the following questions based on the frequency of which they occur in your organization.

	Daily	Sometimes (one or two times a week)	Never
31. In a typical week, how often can you take time to reflect on your work or volunteer activities?			
32. In a typical week, how often do you have to do anything outside of your role-specific work?			

Please answer the following questions based on your level of agreement with each statement.

	Extremely	Somewhat	Not at All
33. Overall how satisfied are you with your experience at the organization as a staff member or volunteer?			
34. How meaningful do you feel the work you do for the organization is?			

EXHIBIT 2.4

Sample Score Sheet

Employee 1: Motivation for Change

1.	5 – Strongly Agree	2 – Disagree		
	4 – Agree	1 – Strongly Disagree		
	3 – Neutral		Score:	5
2.	1 – Strongly Agree	4 – Disagree		
	2 – Agree	5 – Strongly Disagree		
	3 – Neutral		Score:	3
3.	1 – Strongly Agree	4 – Disagree		
	2 – Agree	5 – Strongly Disagree		
	3 – Neutral		Score:	2
4.	5 – Frequently	1 – Never		
	3 – Sometimes		Score:	3
5.	5 – Frequently	1 – Never		
	3 – Sometimes		Score:	5

(add questions 1–5 / 5)   18/5

Motivation for Change Score: **3.6**

Employee 2: Motivation for Change

1.	5 – Strongly Agree	2 – Disagree		
	4 – Agree	1 – Strongly Disagree		
	3 – Neutral		Score:	4
2.	1 – Strongly Agree	4 – Disagree		
	2 – Agree	5 – Strongly Disagree		
	3 – Neutral		Score:	4
3.	1 – Strongly Agree	4 – Disagree		
	2 – Agree	5 – Strongly Disagree		
	3 – Neutral		Score:	4
4.	5 – Frequently	1 – Never		
	3 – Sometimes		Score:	5
5.	5 – Frequently	1 – Never		
	3 – Sometimes		Score:	5

(add questions 1–5 / 5)   22/5

Motivation for Change Score: **4.4**

EXHIBIT 2.5

Organizational Learning Assessment Scoring

Each question in the assessment has a corresponding score. Using the indicated scores listed, identify your score for each question and the average for each domain. The score for each domain should be the total of all the scores for the questions in that domain divided by the number of questions in that domain.

Domain 1: Motivation for Change

1.	5 – Strongly Agree	2 – Disagree	Score: _____
	4 – Agree	1 – Strongly Disagree	
	3 – Neutral		
2.	1 – Strongly Agree	4 – Disagree	Score: _____
	2 – Agree	5 – Strongly Disagree	
	3 – Neutral		
3.	1 – Strongly Agree	4 – Disagree	Score: _____
	2 – Agree	5 – Strongly Disagree	
	3 – Neutral		
4.	5 – Frequently	1 – Never	Score: _____
	3 – Sometimes		
5.	5 – Frequently	1 – Never	Score: _____
	3 – Sometimes		

(add scores for questions 1–5 / 5)   /5 =

Motivation for Change Score: _____

EXHIBIT 2.5
Organizational Learning Assessment Scoring, Cont'd

Domain 2: Learning and Development Culture

6.	5 – Strongly Agree	2 – Disagree	Score: _____
	4 – Agree	1 – Strongly Disagree	
	3 – Neutral		
7.	5 – Strongly Agree	2 – Disagree	Score: _____
	4 – Agree	1 – Strongly Disagree	
	3 – Neutral		
8.	5 – Strongly Agree	2 – Disagree	Score: _____
	4 – Agree	1 – Strongly Disagree	
	3 – Neutral		
9.	5 – Frequently	1 – Never	Score: _____
	3 – Sometimes		
10.	5 – Frequently	1 – Never	Score: _____
	3 – Sometimes		
11.	5 – Frequently	1 – Never	Score: _____
	3 – Sometimes		

(add scores for questions 6–11 / 6)   /6 = _____

Learning and Development
Culture Score: _____

EXHIBIT 2.5
Organizational Learning Assessment Scoring, Cont'd

Domain 3: Resources for Learning

12.   5 – Strongly Agree   2 – Disagree   Score: _____

4 – Agree   1 – Strongly Disagree

3 – Neutral

13.   5 – Strongly Agree   2 – Disagree   Score: _____

4 – Agree   1 – Strongly Disagree

3 – Neutral

14.   5 – Strongly Agree   2 – Disagree   Score: _____

4 – Agree   1 – Strongly Disagree

3 – Neutral

15.   5 – Strongly Agree   2 – Disagree   Score: _____

4 – Agree   1 – Strongly Disagree

3 – Neutral

16.   5 – Strongly Agree   2 – Disagree   Score: _____

4 – Agree   1 – Strongly Disagree

3 – Neutral

17.   5 – Frequently   1 – Never   Score: _____

3 – Sometimes

18.   5 – Frequently   1 – Never   Score: _____

3 – Sometimes

19.   5 – Frequently   1 – Never   Score: _____

3 – Sometimes

(add scores for questions 12–19 / 8)   /8 =

Resources for Learning Score: _____

EXHIBIT 2.5
Organizational Learning Assessment Scoring, Cont'd

Domain 4: Staff and Management Values

20.   5 – Strongly Agree   2 – Disagree   Score: _____

     4 – Agree   1 – Strongly Disagree

     3 – Neutral

21.   5 – Strongly Agree   2 – Disagree   Score: _____

     4 – Agree   1 – Strongly Disagree

     3 – Neutral

22.   5 – Strongly Agree   2 – Disagree   Score: _____

     4 – Agree   1 – Strongly Disagree

     3 – Neutral

23.   5 – Strongly Agree   2 – Disagree   Score: _____

     4 – Agree   1 – Strongly Disagree

     3 – Neutral

24.   5 – Frequently   1 – Never   Score: _____

     3 – Sometimes

25.   5 – Frequently   1 – Never   Score: _____

     3 – Sometimes

26.   5 – Frequently   1 – Never   Score: _____

     3 – Sometimes

(add scores for questions 20–26 / 7)   /7 =

Staff and Management Values Score: ——

EXHIBIT 2.5
Organizational Learning Assessment Scoring, Cont'd

Domain 5: Organizational Culture

27.	5 – Strongly Agree	2 – Disagree	Score:	_____
	4 – Agree	1 – Strongly Disagree		
	3 – Neutral			

28.	5 – Strongly Agree	2 – Disagree	Score:	_____
	4 – Agree	1 – Strongly Disagree		
	3 – Neutral			

29.	5 – Strongly Agree	2 – Disagree	Score:	_____
	4 – Agree	1 – Strongly Disagree		
	3 – Neutral			

30.	5 – Strongly Agree	2 – Disagree	Score:	_____
	4 – Agree	1 – Strongly Disagree		
	3 – Neutral			

31.	5 – Frequently	1 – Never	Score:	_____
	3 – Sometimes			

32.	5 – Frequently	1 – Never	Score:	_____
	3 – Sometimes			

(add scores for questions 27–32 / 6)   /6 =

Organizational Culture Score: _____

Domain 6: Staff and Volunteer Satisfaction

33.	5 – Extremely	1 – Not At All	Score:	_____
	3 – Somewhat			

34.	5 – Extremely	1 – Not At All	Score:	_____
	3 – Somewhat			

(add scores for questions 33–34 / 2)   /2 =

Staff and Volunteer Satisfaction Score: _____

for each department separately as well. The following example shows an average score for Domain 1, Motivation to Change, in the small grassroots organization.

Staff 1	Staff 2	Staff 3	Staff 4	Staff 5	Staff 6	Staff 7	Total for all Staff
3.6	4.4	4.4	3.8	3.8	3.8	3.8	27.6

Average Score for Domain = Total for all Staff / # of Staff
Example: 27.6 / 7 = 3.94

The average score in this example is on the high end of the learning readiness scale. Figure 2.2 provides an explanation of the implementation readiness scale and what your score may mean, whether it is low, middle range, or high. A score in the beginning of the high end in this example indicates that the employees in the small grassroots organization are motivated for change. Yes, there may be an opportunity to increase their motivation a bit, but the small change needed will come with implementation of the new talent development system as employees become more aware of their needs and how to manage their learning.

Figure 2.3 shows the average scores for each domain for the small grassroots organization.

According to the assessment, the small grassroots organization scored high in all six domains. The scores indicate they have a very strong learning

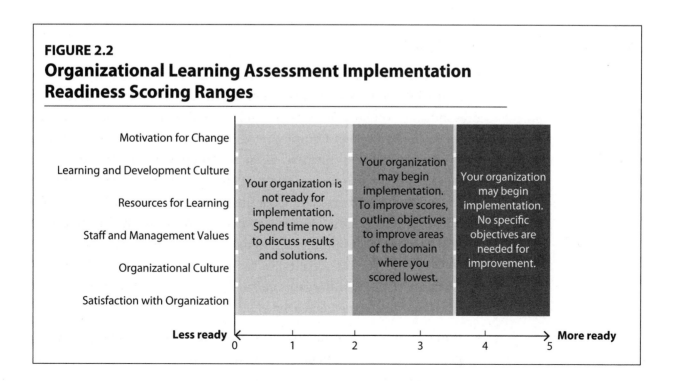

FIGURE 2.2
Organizational Learning Assessment Implementation Readiness Scoring Ranges

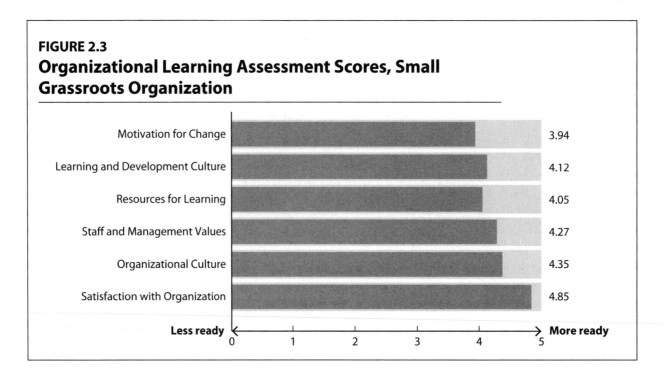

FIGURE 2.3
Organizational Learning Assessment Scores, Small Grassroots Organization

Motivation for Change	3.94
Learning and Development Culture	4.12
Resources for Learning	4.05
Staff and Management Values	4.27
Organizational Culture	4.35
Satisfaction with Organization	4.85

Less ready ⟵ 0   1   2   3   4   5 ⟶ **More ready**

culture. With scores this high, it is clear the organization should move forward with full system implementation. Even with strong scores, however, it is important to have a team conversation regarding the results. Conversations about the results are more important than simply reading the results. If your scores are high, have discussions about what is working well. If your scores are low, discuss challenges you may be having and how you can turn those challenges into opportunities.

What If You Aren't Ready?

Ultimately, you will need to decide if your organization should move forward with the Talent Development Platform. If your organizational domain scores indicate you are not ready to implement the Platform, take the time now to discuss scores and employ potential interventions. Developing a strong learning culture is the first step in a talent development system, and you should spend the time ensuring that your learning culture is healthy. If you do land in the "not ready" area of the spectrum, you may have to push back the timing of the launch of the next steps in the Talent Development Platform. The length of time you should spend on readiness preparation depends on how much time it takes to improve your organizational culture. Here are potential interventions you can implement prior to moving on to the next step in the Platform:

- Bring in an external facilitator to lead discussions among staff and potentially do some smaller group discussions to investigate your culture challenges.

- Focus on goals and objectives that help individuals with change management. Examples include holding healthy conversations and supporting team members with constructive feedback. Enhancing these areas will make your team more open to learning and teaching.

When we piloted the Talent Development Platform, we had one organization, a midsized nonprofit, begin the process but stop after having their staff take the Organizational Learning Assessment. The organization had scores in both the low and middle ranges of the readiness spectrum. It was apparent, though, during the assessment scoring and the team discussions that the mid-range scores were a result of a divide between the staff's and the leadership's views of the organization. As a result, the organization decided not to move forward with the rest of the process right away. Here is a description of their scores and the potential challenges the organization had in domains where they scored lower:

Motivation for Change: (3.53) The score indicates that some staff feel change is necessary, while others may not feel as strongly about the need for change. The score is not too low, though, which means the organization could implement the Talent Development Platform but would need to ensure that all employees feel empowered to participate (including leadership).

Learning and Development Culture: (3.94). The score shows that the organization's current perception of learning is close to the high range. This could indicate that employees and volunteers feel safe within the environment to share failures and learn together.

Resources for Learning: (2.85). The score shows employees' and volunteers' knowledge and the availability of tangible learning assets. The score is the lowest of all the domain scores for this organization. The low score indicates there is not enough time or money for staff to participate in professional development. This is a common experience in social change organizations. This organization should focus on providing resources for learning and shifting employees to allow time for learning and reflection.

Staff and Management Values: (3.88). The Staff and Management Values domain shows how learning is valued within the organization. This score is in the middle range, which indicates that some of the individuals who took the assessment are neutral about their need for learning and growth and some believe in their need for learning and growth. Considering the other domain scores, the latter seems to be closer to the truth. An organization with a score in this range should spend some time discussing learning values with employees and leadership prior to implementation.

Organizational Culture: (3.83). This domain indicates whether employees and volunteers believe their current environment is open to change and their team works well together. This mid-range score indicates that most employees feel safe communicating their learning needs within their team and that leadership is intentionally providing a safe environment. During the discussion of this domain, the organization did realize that leadership gave the higher scores in this range and employees felt they needed more support.

Staff and Volunteer Satisfaction: (4.00). This score is the highest of the six domain scores. A high score in satisfaction indicates that employees and volunteers are satisfied with their roles in the organization. Considering the lower scores in the other domains, the organization needs to work on maintaining or increasing scores in order to keep the Staff and Volunteer Satisfaction domain score high. If scores in the other domains slip or if challenges brought up during their conversations are not resolved, scores in this domain may decrease over time.

The Organizational Learning Assessment in Practice

The results from the four pilot organizations' Organizational Learning Assessments show that most of the organizations are in the mid- to high range. All four of the organizations were able to continue with implementation. We've described a few of their challenges in the following sections and discussed many of the differences in the scores.

Volunteer-Run Organization

Figure 2.4 shows the average scores of the seven board members of the volunteer-run organization who took the Organizational Learning Assessment.

The volunteer-run organization scored high in almost every domain, which indicates that they are ready to implement the Talent Development Platform. The results revealed that the board focuses strongly on learning—in their case often learning from organizations similar to theirs. The organization scored low, however, in the Resources for Learning domain. As a volunteer-run organization they do not have monetary resources allocated specifically for learning. In this organization all learning happens outside the boardroom and on each volunteer's own time.

When implementing the Talent Development Platform, the board will need to set aside resources (time and money) for learning.

Small Grassroots Organization

The small grassroots organization had its five staff members take the Organizational Learning Assessment, and their average scores are presented again in figure 2.5.

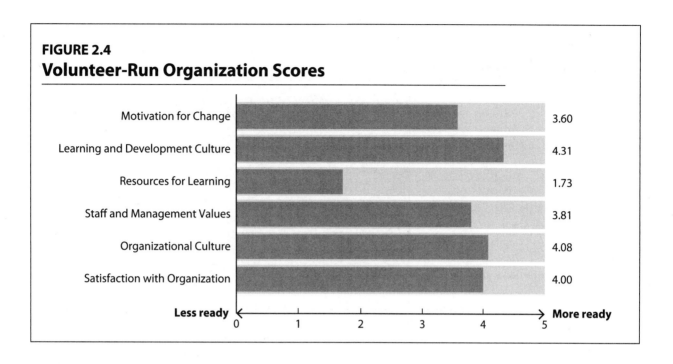

FIGURE 2.4
Volunteer-Run Organization Scores

Motivation for Change	3.60
Learning and Development Culture	4.31
Resources for Learning	1.73
Staff and Management Values	3.81
Organizational Culture	4.08
Satisfaction with Organization	4.00

Less ready ← → More ready
0 1 2 3 4 5

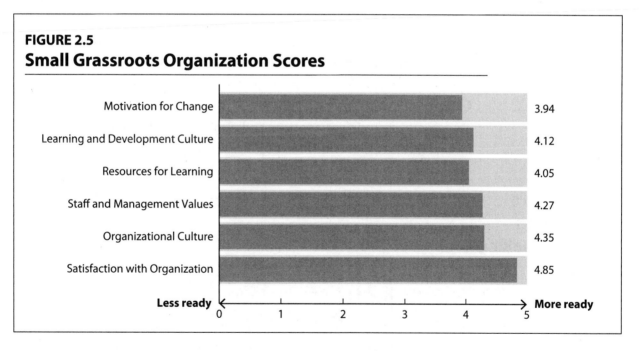

FIGURE 2.5
Small Grassroots Organization Scores

Motivation for Change	3.94
Learning and Development Culture	4.12
Resources for Learning	4.05
Staff and Management Values	4.27
Organizational Culture	4.35
Satisfaction with Organization	4.85

Less ready ← → More ready
0 1 2 3 4 5

As we saw earlier, the small grassroots organization scored high in every learning domain. This organization is ready to implement the Talent Development Platform. To ensure the numbers stay high, they will have to continue to practice strong learning-culture activities.

Midsized Organization

The Organizational Learning Assessment average scores of the midsized organization's eleven staff members are shown in figure 2.6.

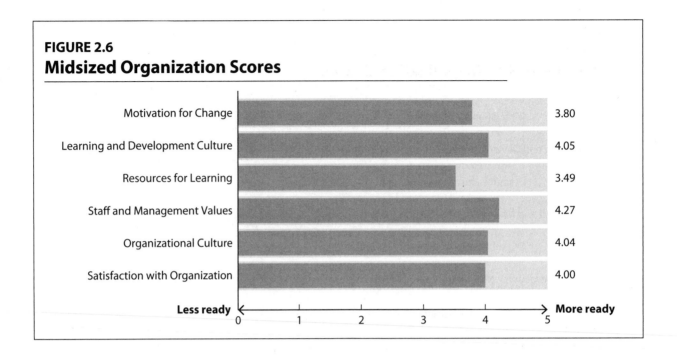

FIGURE 2.6
Midsized Organization Scores

	Score
Motivation for Change	3.80
Learning and Development Culture	4.05
Resources for Learning	3.49
Staff and Management Values	4.27
Organizational Culture	4.04
Satisfaction with Organization	4.00

Less ready ← 0 1 2 3 4 5 → More ready

The midsized organization also scored high in each domain. Just like the small grassroots organization, they are ready for implementation and should focus on keeping their learning culture intentional.

Grantmaking Organization

The grantmaking organization had four staff take the Organizational Learning Assessment, and their scores are shown in Figure 2.7.

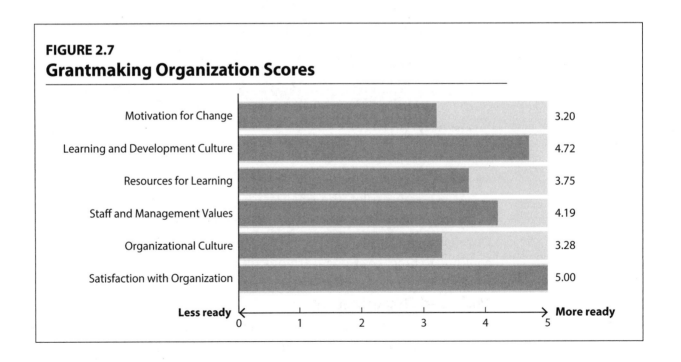

FIGURE 2.7
Grantmaking Organization Scores

	Score
Motivation for Change	3.20
Learning and Development Culture	4.72
Resources for Learning	3.75
Staff and Management Values	4.19
Organizational Culture	3.28
Satisfaction with Organization	5.00

Less ready ← 0 1 2 3 4 5 → More ready

The grantmaking organization's scores were on the higher end of the spectrum for four domains and somewhat lower for two. The two lower domains (motivation for change and organizational culture) indicate that the grantmaking organization may need some work on team culture and self-efficacy. The organization can move on with implementation but should include self-efficacy or team culture objectives in everyone's individual goals and objectives. In future chapters we will be discussing options for managing your organization's learning culture and integrating activities in the process to enhance your learning culture in the areas you may be at a deficit. For more tools and to download the assessment for your team, visit talent4socialchange.org.

Conclusion

In this chapter we discussed the Organizational Learning Assessment and the importance of having a strong learning culture and what that could look like in your organization. The information in this chapter is very important to set the basis for an effective talent development system in your organization. Use the concepts you've learned in this chapter and the knowledge you get from discussions with your team as you implement the rest of the tools in the Platform.

Chapter 3
Social Change Competencies

In this chapter we summarize ten core social change competencies and the steps you will use to create organizational specific sub-competencies. We define social change competencies and describe why competencies are important.

What Are Competencies and Why Are They Important?

Competencies aren't sexy, but they are crucial for ensuring success in a social change organization. They are popular in the human resources management profession and important for all employees and volunteers to understand. Extensive research has been conducted on the benefits of using competencies to assess the knowledge, skills, abilities, and other characteristics needed within a job (Pynes, 2009; Shippmann et al., 2000). The use of competencies has helped organizations recruit and select high-performing employees, increase workforce efficiency, and improve organizational performance (Gangani, McLean, & Braden, 2006; Lucia & Lepsinger, 1999; Rodriguez, Patel, Bright, Gregory, & Gowing, 2002). Table 3.1 describes the meaning behind each competency component as the Office of Personnel Management defines them (Shippmann et al., 2000).

Although the human resources management field widely accepts competencies and the federal government has used them for some time, they are largely unknown to nonprofit professionals. The National Institutes of Health (2014) is well known for its competency program and explains competencies that are helpful to

- identify hiring needs based on competency gaps;

- map job descriptions to your current talent pool;

- utilize the pool of talent within organizations appropriately; and

- clarify realistic expectations of a position.

TABLE 3.1
Competency Components and Definitions

Competency Component	Definition
Knowledge	Level of information obtained to perform job
Skills	Observable expertise obtained to perform job (something that can be learned)
Abilities	Innate quality or behavior of an individual to perform the job
Other Characteristics	Other attributes of a person needed for the job, for example, personality, mental, or physical traits

The social change competencies are the foundation of our professional development assessment process and an important tool for organizations to fully understand what a job or volunteer position needs to be successful. But up until now there hasn't been an agreed-upon set of common competencies in the social change sector. Few organizations have the time and expertise to create their own competencies, therefore we conducted extensive research to identify and create a core set of social change competencies you can use in your talent development and planning process.

We developed and tested the social change competencies through an extensive literature review, a statewide survey and then national professional development survey, interviews with experts and practitioners in the nonprofit sector, and organizations who piloted the Talent Development Platform. In the following section, we explain the process we took to identify and define the social change competencies.

Our Competency Development Process

In Tera's work as a trainer with the Dorothy A. Johnson Center for Philanthropy, she noticed nonprofits would continually request the same types of assistance (e.g., governance, financial management, marketing, and fundraising assistance). Likewise, Heather's review of literature showed that the same type of training needs came up over and over. Our experiences led us to believe that all individuals working in and volunteering for social change organizations were in need of similar skills and abilities in their work. They needed a common set of competencies or language to grow from.

However, there is a challenge to the competency identification process in the nonprofit academic community. Scholars hesitate to identify a core set of social change competencies due to the variety of nonprofit, for-profit, and hybrid organizations pursuing social change. Due to this hesitancy, organizations are left to their own devices, and many small social change organizations are struggling to identify the skills and personnel needed for their work. Through the following process, we identified ten core social change competencies.

Step 1: Literature review

We dug deeper into both the management consulting (a.k.a. practitioner) and scholarly literature. We reviewed studies about nonprofit management competencies, nonprofit capacity building, and nonprofit training needs. Based on the literature review we coded and conducted a network analysis of the data. We used Gephi (an open-source social network analysis software) to map commonalities of the terms within nonprofit capacity building measures, nonprofit management competencies, and nonprofit managers' training needs. Figure 3.1 shows the common terms network map we created.

From this research, twelve competencies emerged: leadership, planning, public relations, volunteer management, financial management, communications, marketing, governance, data utilization, human resources, fundraising, and information technology.

Step 2: Michigan Survey

With support from the School of Public, Nonprofit and Health Administration and the Dorothy A. Johnson Center for Philanthropy at Grand Valley State University, we surveyed 138 nonprofits in Michigan about their professional development needs. The three most crucial training needs that emerged from the study were board of directors training; program evaluation and data-based decision making; and technology, marketing, communications, and social media (Carpenter, Clarke, & Gregg, 2013).

Step 3: National Survey

In September 2013, we also conducted a nationwide survey of nonprofit and philanthropic professionals about their professional development needs. The survey presented respondents with a list and descriptions of the social change competencies and asked them to identify the frequency (monthly, a few times a year, and never) in which they perform these competencies in their job. The most frequently performed competencies were leadership; communications, marketing, and public relations; and program organizational and strategic planning and management. These competencies are similar to the competencies that emerged during the

FIGURE 3.1
Competency Network Map

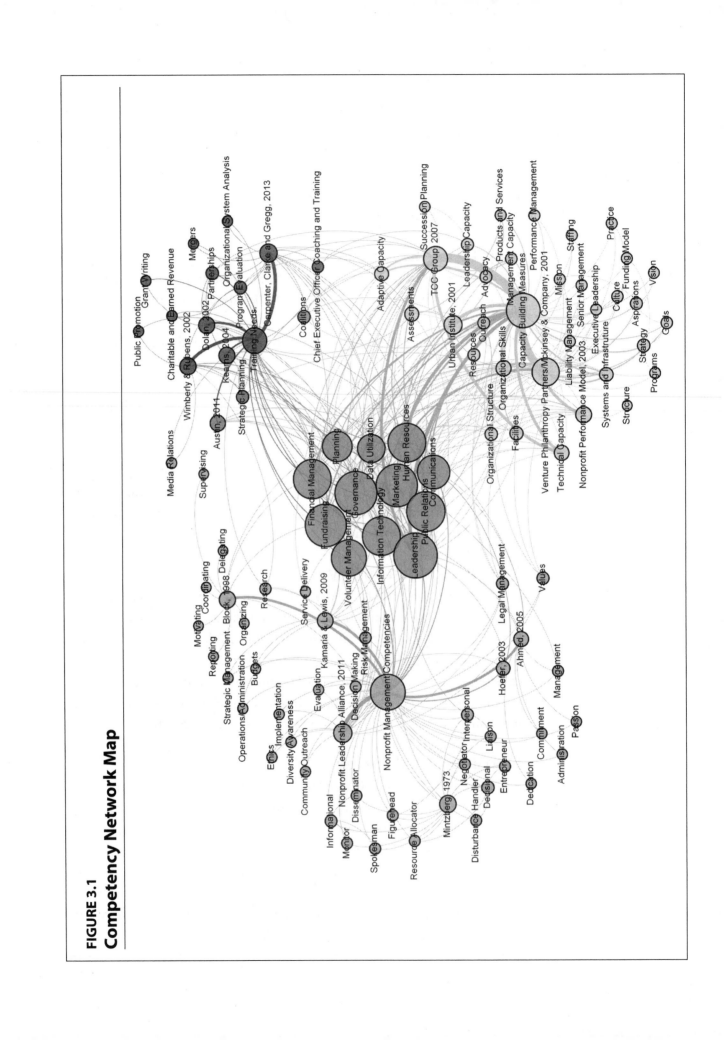

statewide survey and during the review of literature. Similar to the competencies performed on the job, the majority of participants were likely to pursue professional development in leadership as well as program, organizational, and strategic planning and management.

Step 4: Survey of Experts

We also sought advice from twenty experts who serve in various professional roles and asked them what competencies are important for social change.

We compared their responses with the competencies identified in the literature review and the state and national surveys, and we came up with a set of ten core social change competencies and descriptions.

The Ten Core Social Change Competencies

Based on our literature review and surveys, we identified ten core social change competencies:

- *Advocacy and Public Policy.* Effectively using community organizing, public education, policy research, and lobbying to educate government officials, organize community support, garner social change, and influence public policy.

- *Communications, Marketing, and Public Relations.* Demonstrating principles and techniques that provide transparency and accountability, while understanding and communicating specifically to various constituents—including internal stakeholders—using communications, general and social media marketing, and public relations that develop financial and nonfinancial support for the organization.

- *Financial Management and Social Entrepreneurship.* Applying critical financial concepts and generally accepted accounting principles (GAAP) practices to establish and maintain realistic budgets, internal controls, financial statements, cash flow maintenance, audits, and tax reporting. Creating and maintaining sustainable business models, impact and/or social investment strategies, hybrid organizational forms, and innovative revenue structures.

- *Fundraising and Resource Development.* The ability to develop a diversified fund development strategy that is proactive and integrated into the organization's long-term strategic plan and budget projections. Knowledge of and ability to execute several different fundraising strategies, including but not limited to stewardship and cultivation of donors, gift processing, developing new business, event planning, planned giving and major gifts campaigns, and grantwriting.

- *Grantmaking* or *Direct Service*. Grantmaking: Identifying and working with prospective and existing grantees, monitoring grantee progress, and exploring new grantmaking areas. Providing recommendation for funding and conducting grant reviews. In-depth knowledge of program area(s). Direct service: Effectively working with clients and/or constituents. Expertise in a specific field of service, client relations, and intercultural competency. We found employees and volunteers will exhibit direct service or grantmaking but not both competencies at the same time. Therefore, we combined these two competencies into one.

- *Human Resources Management and Volunteerism*. Ability to apply knowledge of employment laws and practices for nonprofit recruitment and selection; for managing employees and volunteers; and for monitoring performance, diversity and intercultural competency, compensation and benefits, training and development, labor relations, and health and safety.

- *Information Management*. Development, maintenance, and application of information technology, including planning, budgeting, staffing and training, evaluation, and selecting hardware and software, social media, and website capabilities and use.

- *Leadership and Governance*. Understanding of the relationship between leadership and management in establishing and attaining mission and long- and short-term organizational goals. Ability to look within self and team members in order to understand how personal backgrounds and experience shape the leadership experience. Demonstrated ability to lead effectively and manage the governing board of the organization.

- *Legal and Regulatory*. Understanding of the influences of external and internal stakeholders in creating and maintaining legal compliance, ethical and risk management practices, and professional standards in the appropriate settings.

- *Planning and Evaluation*. Understanding of the external and internal influences of program and organizational development, as well as organizational life cycles. Ability to create logic models, data-based decision making, program feasibility, and continuous improvement plans for effective management. Ability to develop a theory of change and apply various methods of evaluation to comprehensively evaluate performance measurement and program and organizational effectiveness.

We provide these competencies as resources for organizations and to help you identify the important skills, abilities, and other characteristics

---

EXHIBIT 3.1
Competency Research

Extensive research has been conducted about the general competencies individuals must possess to succeed in life and the workplace. Psychologists have determined there are five components of personality (openness, extroversion, agreeableness, emotional stability, and neuroticism), and each of the five components provides different predictors of success (Tupes & Christal, 1961). Additionally, general cognitive abilities (for example, verbal, quantitative and problem-solving abilities) have been found to predict proficiency and training success (Hunter, 1986). Although personality components and cognitive abilities are key components within the ten social change competencies we identified, you may decide to highlight certain personality components or cognitive abilities that are important to your organization.

---

needed in your organization. We do not consider these competencies to be all encompassing, but they are an important step forward for organizations wanting to effect social change.

Creating Sub-competencies for Your Organization

We recognize the social change competencies we identified are broad. There will be specific knowledge, skills, abilities, and other characteristics that are important for positions within your organization that aren't listed in the core competencies. This is why it is important to go through the process of creating sub-competencies that reflect the funding needs as well as the mission, vision, values, and culture of your organization (Gangani et al., 2006).

Organizational Sub-competencies

Organizational sub-competencies are connected directly to your organization's values and mission. When developing sub-competencies, you should also determine what other specific interpersonal and intrapersonal characteristics your employees and volunteers need that are unique to your organizational culture.

You may choose to prescribe an organizational sub-competency related to cultural competency or one focused on the quality of service you want staff to provide your clients. Sub-competencies are very organization specific, but here are a few examples created by four types of social change organizations.

EXHIBIT 3.2
Emotional Intelligence & Inter-cultural Competence

Salovey and Mayer define emotional intelligence as "the ability to monitor one's own and others' feelings and emotions, to discriminate among them and use this information to guide one's thinking and actions" (Salovey & Mayer as cited by Tan, 2012, p. 10). There are four quadrants of emotional intelligence (Boyatzis, Goleman, & Rhee, 2000; Goleman, 2005; Watson, 2009):

- Self-awareness: knowing one's internal states, preferences, and intuitions
- Self-management: managing one's internal states, impulses, and resources
- Social awareness: awareness of others' feelings, needs, and concerns
- Social skills: adeptness at inducing desirable responses in others

The National Center for Cultural Competence defines *cultural competence* as "having the capacity to value diversity, conduct self-assessment, manage the dynamics of the difference, acquire and institutionalize cultural knowledge, and adapt to diversity and cultural contexts of individuals and communities served" (Rouson, 2009, p. 148).

Volunteer-Run Organizations

In a volunteer-run organization, typical sub-competencies might include initiative, crisis management, and mentoring. In volunteer-run organizations, volunteers need to be self-starters who are able to handle the flux of a new organization and mentor other leaders to take over the organization in the future:

- *Initiative.* Starting new projects with little to no supervision.

- *Crisis Management.* Calmly handling challenging scenarios and implementing changes quickly.

- *Mentoring.* Developing, supporting, and building relationships with colleagues and constituents.

Small Grassroots Organization

In a small grassroots organization (with a few staff members), typical sub-competencies might include adaptability, community organizing, and multitasking workload management. Because there are few staff members within small organizations, employees and volunteers often must take on roles with which they are unfamiliar and must have a willingness to connect with community members:

- *Adaptability.* Flexibility and willingness to change within the organization's context and situation.

- *Community organizing.* Passion and willingness to implement strategies that create change in an entire community or neighborhood, and that engage community members to connect with the organization's purpose.

- *Multitasking workload management.* Ability to take on multiple activities and projects at once.

Midsized Organization

In a midsized organization, sub-competencies might include collaboration and strategic thinking and doing:

- *Collaboration.* Working together to achieve a common goal.

- *Strategic thinking and doing.* Making decisions based on critical thinking and research, ensuring that interactive dialogue occurs for all organizational decisions.

Grantmaking Organization

In a grantmaking organization, typical sub-competencies might include collaboration and community building and donor engagement:

- *Collaboration and community building.* Using interpersonal understanding to build relationships, connect, and engage diverse groups of people.

- *Donor engagement.* Building deep and sustainable relationships with current and prospective donors.

- *Investment Practices.* Effectively managing investment assets and/or overseeing outside investment managers.

Here are a few more examples from organizations that have developed competencies for their employees or their work.

Emerging Practitioners in Philanthropy (2013), an organization that promotes and provides professional development for young professionals in grantmaking institutions, created a set of sub-competencies for their members:

- *Strategic and analytical skills.* Anticipating future needs and trends; creating competitive strategies and plans; thinking broadly when analyzing an issue or presented with a challenge.

- *Leadership and management skills.* Directing individuals or groups to accomplish desired results; delegating appropriately and allocating resources as needed; emulating exemplary individual behavior and ethics.

- *Communication skills.* Communicating ideas and concepts clearly, persuasively and dynamically; expressing ideas clearly through both verbal and written means.

- *Decision-making skills.* Displaying ability to make timely, well-considered decisions.

- *Innovation and problem-solving skills.* Thinking unconventionally while inspiring others to as well; soliciting diverse perspectives to aid problem solving; analyzing problems, creating solutions and solving problems quickly; integrating new technology and data analysis into problem solving.

- *Social justice and racial analysis skills.* Embracing diversity based on race, ethnicity, gender, sexual orientation, disability, and age; understanding the historical origins of long-standing structural problems; ensuring equitable and just outcomes for all people.

- *Influencing and fundraising skills.* Inspiring and influencing others; influencing funding partners to join collaborative projects; raising resources for community organizations they support.

Well-known, successful corporations, such as Google and Toyota have also created sub-competencies to provide their employees with clear guidance on the skills and knowledge they should have to perform their jobs effectively. Liker, Convis, and Meskimen (2012, p. 53) outline Toyota's competencies:

- Active and open-mindedly observing the work of the organization

- Active listening to hear what people are really saying

- Systems thinking

- Understanding the actual strengths and weaknesses of each person

- Clearly defining problems and identifying the root cause

- Planning

- Creatively identifying countermeasures to the true root causes

- Translating plans into action with clear accountability

- Taking the time and energy for deep reflection to identify further opportunities for improvement

- Motivating and influencing people across the organization (with no direct authority) toward common objectives

- Being able to teach others all the above

Google's self-care competencies include attention training, self-knowledge and self-mastery, and creating useful mental habits (Tan, 2012, p. 7).

In each of these examples, you can see the culture of the organization and their purposes coming through in their sub-competencies. Sub-competencies related to each of the core social change competencies should do the same for your organization. As you develop sub-competencies, keep in mind both the organizational mission and each individual's role in achieving the mission. In some organizations, creating sub-competencies means developing departmental sub-competencies. In the next section we show examples of departmental sub-competencies for four types of social change organizations.

Departmental Sub-competencies
Volunteer-Run Organization

Even though there are no departments in a volunteer-run organization, there may be sub-competencies for volunteers that serve on different committees. For example, many organizations struggle with financial management and social entrepreneurship. The board members can decide if they want to develop their proficiency level within this category. The board sub-competency, therefore, would be *reading, understanding, and interpreting financial statements*. The board could assign this sub-competency to a small group of board members working on a finance committee or come together in an ad hoc committee to build their skills and knowledge in this category. Additionally, our research shows that many boards desire professional development in strategic planning. Therefore, a sub-competency for the executive committee of the board would be *understanding and identifying the internal and external forces that affect an organization*.

Small Grassroots Organization

Small grassroots organizations with few staff members do not have departments per se; however, staff within these organizations may be part of specific focus areas or teams such as the administrative, development, and program teams. Therefore, they could set sub-competencies for each focus area and team. A department sub-competency for the administrative team might be *understanding profitability and sustainability*. A sub-competency for the development team might be *consistency in messaging and branding of organizational materials*. And a sub-competency for the program team might be *client dedication and commitment*.

Midsized Organization

Within a midsized organization, administration department sub-competencies might be *implementing policies and procedures and database management.* The development department sub-competencies might be *donor engagement and prospect research.* And the program department sub-competencies might be *client data tracking and program outcome analytics.*

Grantmaking Organization

Within a grantmaking organization, an executive department sub-competency might be *investment portfolio strategies.* A finance department sub-competency might be *market fluctuation and risk.* And a program or grantmaking department competency might be *income disparities awareness.* If the grantmaking organization is a small foundation, such as a private family foundation or corporate foundation with only one or two staff members, each staff member may have his or her own sub-competencies depending on the person's role. Next, we provide some examples of position-specific sub-competencies.

Position Sub-competencies

In the next chapter, we go more in depth on how to write job descriptions. In order to create sub-competencies, you'll want to view each employee's or volunteer's job description (or if no job description exists, use the job analysis form provided in chapter 4) as you create the sub-competencies. Here are a few position-specific sub-competencies to get you started for a variety of roles:

- Board Chair
    - Leads the board in fiscal, governance, and legal responsibilities.
    - Oversees and supports the recruitment and selection of board members.
- Board Treasurer
    - Provides financial oversight of the organization, including overseeing the annual budgeting and monthly financial reports of budgets to actuals.
    - Conducts long-term financial planning, cash flow analysis, and risk analysis.
- Executive Director
    - Leads and manages staff to execute the organization's mission.
- Chief Operating Officer/Operations Manager
    - Oversees and directs all financial and administrative activities of the organization, including accounting, budgeting, financial planning and reporting, internal audits, operations, human resources,

and information systems. (Many small to midsized social change organizations do not have a separate CFO position and have a COO responsible for the finances and administration.)

- Human Resources Manager
  - Manages, develops, and implements personnel procedures related to applications, examinations, eligibility, promotion, demotion, transfer, dismissal, resignation, layoff, reemployment, vacation, leave of absence, compensation, licensing, and certification.

- Development Director/Donor Advisor
  - Oversees the research, identification, solicitation, and stewardship of potential foundation, corporate, and individual donors.
  - Plans, manages, and coordinates designated fundraising events and programs.

- Development Coordinator
  - Assists in the research, identification, solicitation, and stewardship of potential foundation, corporate, and individual donors.

- Program Manager
  - Oversees and administers programs.
  - Manages the planning and evaluation of programmatic activities and ensures that all program elements are followed.

- Volunteer Coordinator
  - Recruits, trains, and retains volunteers for assigned area of service.
  - Coordinates the recruitment, retention, and support of volunteers.
  - Ensures that volunteers and staff are adhering to agency volunteer policies.

- Administrative Assistant
  - Completes a broad variety of administrative tasks for the leadership team.
  - Assists in scheduling meetings and takes minutes at all meetings.

- Marketing Coordinator
  - Updates social media pages to add or change information as needed.
  - Writes, edits, and tracks the production of publications including e-newsletters, fundraising materials, brochures, special invitations, annual reports, and other print and electronic publications.

- Program Officer
  - Coordinates multiple grantmaking programs simultaneously.
  - Conducts grant proposal reviews, including assessing organizational goals, plans, and capacity.
- Program Coordinator/Program Associate
  - Works proactively to facilitate effective communications about and management of grantmaking processes and portfolio reviews.
  - Assists with monitoring grantee performance against established grant terms and agreements.
- Director of Donor Services
  - Reviews and improves the donor recognition levels and donor award programs.
  - Designs and implements an annual integrated donor relations plan that includes acknowledgment processes and donor recognition events.
- Evaluator
  - Works closely with staff to build on existing evaluation tools to create a strategic evaluation plan that measures progress and success for both internal program improvement purposes as well as for external reporting purposes.
  - Independently, or with external vendors, designs and implements evaluation tools to support the strategic evaluation plan, using both quantitative and qualitative methods as appropriate.

Sub-competencies per Competency Category

To further give you some idea of sub-competencies that may apply to the ten social change competencies, the experts that we spoke to provided us a list of knowledge, skills, and abilities needed within each competency category. The following list is not comprehensive but provides examples of what sub-competencies might be included in each competency category:

Advocacy and Public Policy

- Knowledge of current events, social movement history, and the access gaps that exist for the issues you are working on.
- Identifying which policy makers would be receptive to your message (e.g., who should be the targets to carry your bill, such as a senator or congress member, or other representative?).

- Developing relationships and demonstrating strong communication techniques with policy makers.

- Synthesizing and presenting research in such a way that policy makers understand the scope of the problem, the solution that you propose, and whom you represent (e.g., the members of your coalition).

- Analyzing and understanding the context in which one is making a request (e.g., what are the financial implications, if any, for your request and where would the government secure funding for this effort?).

- Attracting other stakeholders (ideally, a diverse group of organizations and individuals) to your effort or cause to advocate for the issue you wish to advance.

- Educating members of your organization, members of coalition groups, and members of the public on your issue in such a way that nonprofessionals feel comfortable advocating for the issue.

- Using social and mainstream media to publicize your efforts.

- Raising funds for advocacy efforts.

Communications, Marketing, and Public Relations

- Creating end-user awareness and preference for your brand.

- Maintaining unique and differentiated value propositions, positioning statements, and key messages.

- Mastering the use of marketing and communications tools, including social media, networks, electronic, print, promotions, advertising, events, direct mail.

- Using simplified writing.

- Using crisp, attention-getting speaking.

- Creating visual content, including infographics.

- Developing integrated, clear, and cohesive communications (marketing/public relations/branding) plans.

- Strong people and project management skills.

- Effectively working with the press.

Financial Management and Social Entrepreneurship

- Understanding how money moves through an organization.

- Telling a story with financial statements—making sure everybody understands what they are looking at.

- Knowing when to effectively use earned income strategies.

- Creating or managing L3Cs, B corps, or other hybrid organizations.

- Selecting appropriate investment strategies and managing the organization's investment portfolio.

- Interpreting liability risk and managing assets.

- Following FAS 116 and 117 in the financial management and oversight of the organization.

- Knowing when to conduct a compilation, review, or an audit.

- Reviewing and submitting clear and accurate necessary tax forms.

- Conducting a financial analysis and interpreting results.

- Setting internal controls that safeguard the organization.

Fundraising and Resource Development

- Creating a culture of philanthropy throughout the organization.

- Identifying, selecting, and implementing appropriate individual, corporate, foundation, major, and planned giving strategies for the organization.

- Cultivating relationships with potential and current donors.

- Determining organizational investment risk and portfolio management.

- Managing endowment and understanding endowment/investment policies and procedures.

Grantmaking or Direct Service

- Reviewing proposals and recommending grantmaking decisions.

- Analyzing budgets and determining appropriate grant amounts.

- Involvement in peer networks.

- Understanding of issue areas related to programmatic activities.

Human Resources Management and Volunteerism

- Actively recruiting, selecting, evaluating, and training employees.

- Implementing retention strategies and solutions.

- Coaching employees through challenging work situations.

- Specializing is employee benefits, including health and wellness.

- Knowledge of all pertinent employment laws that are applicable to the organization.

- Serving as the mediator between union and management in negotiations and disputes.

- Creating an interculturally competent workplace.

Information Management

- Providing hardware, software, website, data, and all necessary information technology training.

- Maintaining system and computer operations.

- Navigating the Internet and web.

- Developing web applications.

- Skillful implementation of e-mail backup and organization.

- Creating and maintaining organizational databases.

- Designing and editing visually appealing images, designs, and presentations.

- Promoting organizational brand through social media.

- Analyzing and troubleshooting network.

- Accurately identifying and discerning data issues.

Leadership and Governance

- Recognizing and respecting the functional differences between management and governance.

- Thinking strategically and engaging in future-oriented discussion and planning.

- Accepting, analyzing, and then discerning between divergent sets of information and experiences.

- Engaging respectfully with a wide range of personalities and worldviews.

- Seeking out information, asking provocative questions, and using the result of that learning to drive thoughtful decision making (intellectual curiosity).

- Understanding and accepting the fiduciary/accountability responsibilities of governance.

- Advocating for the mission and programs with others, from one-on-one to group settings.

- Sharing knowledge, expertise, and experience to expand the board's collective capacity to govern.

- Engaging as part of a leadership team.

- Setting aside personal agendas for the greater good.

- Showing self-awareness, social awareness, self-management, and social skills that demonstrate full emotional intelligence.

- Supervising employees and volunteers appropriately in the right contexts and situations.

- Engaging in executive director recruitment, selection, and evaluation.

Legal and Regulatory

- Understanding and responding to watchdog organization regulations.

- Preparing for accreditation standards.

- Following risk management policies and procedures.

- Ensuring the organization has the appropriate amount of insurance to cover liabilities.

Planning and Evaluation

- Engaging in logic model development.

- Leading strategic planning and strategic positioning efforts.

- Familiarity with various types of evaluation methods.

- Knowledge of appropriate data collection and analysis techniques to adequately track outputs and report on outcomes.

Developing Sub-competencies for Your Organization

We have provided you with some examples of sub-competencies. Now it is your turn to identify the sub-competencies within your organization. Here is a sub-competency worksheet to get you started (exhibit 3.3). All individuals should fill out their own worksheet and then spend time with their supervisor confirming and finalizing the list. If you have regular work teams or people who work in similar positions, each team or department should identify sub-competencies and then compare notes so that everyone

---

EXHIBIT 3.3

Sub-competency Worksheet

Organizational sub-competencies

_____

_____

_____

Departmental sub-competencies

_____

_____

_____

Position-specific sub-competencies

_____

_____

_____

---

is on the same page. If you create a common list of organizational sub-competencies, provide it to staff and volunteers before they fill out their worksheet.

Conclusion

In this chapter, we discussed the process we took to create ten social change competencies, including: advocacy and public policy; communications, marketing, and public relations; financial management and social entrepreneurship; fundraising and resource development; grantmaking or direct service; human resources management and volunteerism; information management; leadership and governance; legal and regulatory; and planning and evaluation. We also discussed the process by which you can create organizational, departmental, and position sub-competencies. The competencies and sub-competencies you have identified in this chapter will be used in the next step of the process to develop holistic job descriptions for your employees, board members, and volunteers.

Chapter 4
Creating Job Descriptions

This chapter and the next explain how you can create and maintain job descriptions relevant to your employees' and volunteers' current responsibilities. In this chapter we provide sample job descriptions for the four types of social change organizations and describe the components of a job description. We also provide sample job responsibilities for several positions within each type of social change organization.

Nonprofits have a history of piling on responsibilities to volunteers and employees (Nonprofit HR Solutions, 2013). This pile-on effect causes stress, burnout, and ultimately turnover (Opportunity Knocks, 2010). By creating clear job descriptions—revised on an annual basis—employees and management can stay on track and avoid the pile-on effect.

There are different philosophies on how to create job descriptions. Some organizations create separate internal job descriptions and external position announcements. Or some organizations create one job description that is used for both purposes. In this chapter, we focus on what recruitment experts call the internal job description.

The internal job description is an important part of the entire talent development process. It provides employees with a clear understanding of their role and responsibilities within the organization and helps employers track employee and volunteer performance and success. We'll discuss the performance and success pieces in later chapters.

Strong job descriptions describe the organization, work environment, the position, educational requirements, other qualifications, and salary information. Figure 4.1 provides you with a job description mapping checklist. Here we look at four different job descriptions, one for each type of social change organization (exhibits 4.1, 4.2, 4.3, and 4.4). These are actual job descriptions created by the social change organizations before they conducted proficiency mapping, which we discuss in the next chapter.

FIGURE 4.1
Job Description Mapping Checklist

CREATING AND MAPPING JOB DESCRIPTIONS ······▶

- Identify necessary job roles and descriptions.
- Complete job analysis forms to identify activities employees and volunteers perform regularly.
- Meet with employees and volunteers to confirm job description activities.
- Compare current activities to job description and adjust as necessary.
- Map job description activities to competencies.
- Analyze all job descriptions and set proficiency levels for each role.
- Rewrite job descriptions based on proficiency levels using action words.
- Identify organizational, departmental, and individual sub-competencies based on process and discussions.

EXHIBIT 4.1
Sample Job Description (Before Proficiency Mapping)

President/Board Chair, Volunteer-Run Organization

Job Title: President/Board Chair

Status: Volunteer

Salary Range: None

Reports to: None

Supervisory Responsibilities: Board of Directors

About the Organization

The goal of the Music Festival is to produce a quality festival that enhances the community through entertainment, tourism, education, and philanthropy. The Music Festival is 100 percent volunteer driven and has continued to offer an outstanding event in September each year. With 2,000 attendees the first year, the Music Festival has grown into a much larger than regional draw for the community over the years.

About the Position

The president/board chair is responsible for directing the festival and leading the board of directors. The festival expects each board member to attend monthly meetings, three days of the festival, volunteer orientation, the board of directors' retreat, and the volunteer kick-off party and to participate in the conversation and planning of making a better event.

EXHIBIT 4.1
Sample Job Description (Before Proficiency Mapping), Cont'd

Responsibilities

Communications, Marketing, and Public Relations

- Responds to all community requests.
- Orders all signs.
- Leads correspondence for festival as needed.

Financial Management and Social Entrepreneurship

- Works with treasurer to establish and implement budget.

Fundraising and Resource Development

- Recruits, renews, and develops partners and sponsors for festival.

Direct Service

- Oversees all areas of the festival.
- Works with beverage directors to ensure beverage services.

Human Resources Management and Volunteerism

- Conducts interviews as needed.
- Presents at volunteer kick-off and orientation.
- Schedules all beer volunteers.

Information Management

- Updates website as needed (shared with Marketing and IT).

Leadership and Governance

- Develops agendas for all meetings and conducts meetings.
- Supports all directors and team leads as needed.

Legal and Regulatory

- Works with insurance provider(s) for all insurance.

EXHIBIT 4.1
Sample Job Description (Before Proficiency Mapping), Cont'd

Qualifications

- At least two years of previous nonprofit board experience.

Educational Requirements

- Bachelor's degree required.

Work Environment

- Because this is a volunteer position, you will work in your own home setting. Board meetings take place at various locations throughout the community.
- The position requires access to transportation to visit festival site and vendors; exposure to heat, cold, inclement weather conditions; and standing for periods of time during the festival.
- Must be able to lift 30 pounds.

EXHIBIT 4.2
Sample Job Description (Before Proficiency Mapping)

Executive Director, Small Grassroots Organization

Job Title: Executive Director

Status: Exempt / Full-time

Salary Range: $45,000–$55,000

Reports to: Board of Directors

Supervisory Responsibilities: All Program Managers, Office Staff

About the Organization

Our vision is that every young refugee will have the opportunity to fully contribute to the local and global community. Our mission is to provide exemplary wrap-around services to prepare young refugees to succeed in school and in life.

Position Information

The executive director develops and manages all program activities of the agency in accordance with its stated purpose and within the general policies as formulated by the board of directors. The executive director appropriately uses the agency's financial resources, staff, and volunteers in providing overall

EXHIBIT 4.2
Sample Job Description (Before Proficiency Mapping), Cont'd

direction, leadership, and coordination of organizational activities. The executive director also ensures that staff and volunteers carry out the mission and vision of the agency in daily operations.

Responsibilities

Advocacy and Public Policy

- Nurtures and develops collaborative relationships between the organization and other congregations, agencies, and groups concerned with the public welfare within the communities it serves.
- Conducts in-services/seminars with community institutions to bring community awareness to refugee issues.

Communications, Marketing, and Public Relations

- Ensures that the organization and its mission, programs, and services are consistently presented with a strong, positive image to relevant stakeholders.
- Provides information, publicity, and marketing designed to increase community understanding of the organization, its goals, and its services.
- Maintains active involvement in community organizations to establish the organization's identity within the community.

Financial Management and Social Entrepreneurship

- Recommends the yearly budget for board approval.
- Ensures that all financial, tax, risk, and facilities requirements for the organization are fully met and executed according to current laws and regulations.
- Develops and maintains sound financial practices, resulting in annual audits with no exceptions.
- Practices open and timely communication about financial issues with the board.
- Performs ongoing budget review.
- Ensures the development of monthly, annual, and other periodic statements, budgets, and reports.
- Administers agency salary and benefits policy.
- Acts as the chief financial agent for the agency in ensuring the proper use of budgeted funds and maintenance of sound accounting procedures to safeguard the assets of the organization.

EXHIBIT 4.2
Sample Job Description (Before Proficiency Mapping), Cont'd

- Develops and presents budget requests to community funding organizations.
- Monitors contracts with other public or private organizations as authorized by the board of directors.

Fundraising and Resource Development

- Works in a mutually supportive manner with the board and staff in identifying resource requirements, researching funding sources, and establishing strategies to approach funders.
- Participates in fund development activities, including hosting events, making asks, authoring proposals, identifying funding sources, and undertaking other tasks required by the fundraising plan.
- Ensures the appropriate management of donor and fundraising documentation.
- Ensures the appropriate management of funds raised in accordance with the wishes of the donors.
- Ensures compliance with the reporting requirements of donors.

Direct Service

- Develops programs and services that reflect the strategic direction for the organization.
- Observes professional confidentiality at all times; protects the rights of clients and their families.

Human Resources Management and Volunteerism

- Ensures the selection, supervision, and evaluation of quality staff to deliver services.
- Follows all authorized personnel policies and procedures that fully conform to current laws and regulations.
- Sees that an effective management team, with appropriate provision for succession, is in place.
- Oversees staff orientation, training, and development.

Information Management

- Ensures that the organization maintains all necessary records.

Leadership and Governance

- Supports board members in their communications with relevant organizations.
- Provides administrative support to the board.
- Keeps the board informed about key aspects of the functioning of the organization.
- Responds to information requests from the board.

EXHIBIT 4.2
Sample Job Description (Before Proficiency Mapping), Cont'd

- Openly provides all information the board requires to conduct its governance role.
- Acts as advisor to the board of directors in the carrying out of its policy-making responsibility.
- Serves as ex officio member of all board committees.
- Meets regularly with the board and the executive committee.
- Positively accepts and responds to direction and feedback from the board.
- Provides the interface between the board and staff, ensuring that information is exchanged between the two groups.
- Facilitates staff meetings.
- Welcomes constructive feedback from staff and clients and works to provide an environment of openness and compassion.
- Conducts oneself in a manner that models professional behavior at all times.

Legal and Regulatory

- Oversees the translation and implementation of board policies into effective action.
- Ensures that the organization obtains and keeps current all required licenses related to its work.

Planning and Evaluation

- Works collaboratively with the board to ensure that a sound annual fundraising plan is established and implemented.
- Develops procedures for assessing the organization's effectiveness in achieving its goals.
- Establishes goals and objectives for each program and service.
- Implements an effective and cohesive management system to achieve these goals and objectives.

Qualifications

- At least five years of experience working in a nonprofit setting.

Educational Requirements

- Bachelor's degree required.

Work Environment

- Office environment with occasional meetings at various community organization locations.

EXHIBIT 4.3

Sample Job Description (Before Proficiency Mapping)

Development Coordinator, Midsized Organization

Job Title: Development Coordinator

Department: Development

Status: Exempt / Full-time

Salary Range: $30,000–$42,000

Reports to: Development Director

Supervisory Responsibilities: Development Assistant, Development Interns

About the Organization

For twelve years, the Community Food Bank has been a force for attacking hunger to help young people live well. Hunger is a community problem, with a community solution.

Our organization is an equal opportunity employer. Our policy is to provide equal employment opportunity to all qualified persons without regard to race, creed, color, religious belief, gender, age, national origin, ancestry, sexual orientation, gender identity, qualifying physical or mental disability, height, weight, marital status, or veteran status.

Position Information

This position coordinates annual fundraising for the organization, specifically working with individuals, corporations, and community groups, including but not limited to semi-annual appeals, stewardship, major donor support, corporate matches, monthly donors, direct mailings, and third-party events. The development coordinator will support the development director and supervise the development assistant in these efforts.

Responsibilities

Advocacy and Public Policy

- Maintains awareness of how advocacy efforts may bring in prospective donors.

Communications, Marketing, and Public Relations

- Coordinates appeal mailings in-house and communicates with printers.

Financial Management and Social Entrepreneurship

- Ensures that gifts are posted for accountant review.

Fundraising and Resource Development

- Coordinates donor recognition programs and thank-you process.

EXHIBIT 4.3

Sample Job Description (Before Proficiency Mapping), Cont'd

- Cultivates volunteer groups.
- Prepares letters of appreciation to be sent to contributors in collaboration with the development assistant.
- Understands fund development, stewardship, and community outreach.

Human Resource Management and Volunteerism

- Supervises Fund Development assistant and interns.

Information Management

- Pulls data reports from database system and prepares reports for the development director.
- Assists in maintaining records of contributions and grants.

Leadership and Governance

- Interfaces and establishes rapport with key board members and donors.

Legal and Regulatory

- Understands the fundraising solicitation regulations and how they apply in the organizational setting.

Planning and Evaluation

- Works with the development director to establish strategy to meet annual fund goals for the organization.

Other Responsibilities

Youth Cultural Competency

- Effectively interacts with a diverse population of youth and college-age volunteers from a variety of ethnic and socioeconomic backgrounds.

Public Speaking

- Has experience speaking in front of groups, making presentations and leading groups of five to three hundred, consisting of all ages and backgrounds.

Flexibility and Adaptability

- Is organized and has the ability to work in a fast-paced, ever-changing work environment. Possesses skills in project and time management. Can work independently as well as collaboratively.

EXHIBIT 4.3

Sample Job Description (Before Proficiency Mapping), Cont'd

Problem Solving

- Demonstrates the ability to solve problems, analyze systems and data, and make suggestions for improvement.

Work Environment

- A minimum of 40 hours per week—this includes two nontraditional work shifts each week with some level of flexibility (e.g., three traditional 9 a.m. to 5 p.m. shifts and then maybe noon to 8 p.m. one weekday and perhaps a daytime shift on Saturday or Sunday).
- Physical requirements include a typical office environment with periods of sitting at a computer screen and being able to lift up to 25 pounds.
- The job entails duties offsite including local travel, exposure to heat, cold, inclement weather conditions, and standing for periods of time.

Compensation Package

- The organization provides medical, dental, and vision insurance, 401k plan, flexible spending account, paid time off (PTO), and paid holidays. Details available upon request.

EXHIBIT 4.4

Sample Job Description (Before Proficiency Mapping)

Program Associate, Grantmaking Organization

Job Title: Program Associate

Department: Economic and Community Benefit

Status: Exempt / Full-time

Salary Range: $50,000–$55,000

Reports to: Director of Grants and Nonprofit Services

Supervisory Responsibilities: None

About the Organization

The mission of the Regional Area Community Foundation is to improve and enhance the quality of life in the regional area by

- serving as a leader, catalyst, and resource for philanthropy;
- building and holding a permanent and growing endowment for the community's changing needs and opportunities;

EXHIBIT 4.4
Sample Job Description (Before Proficiency Mapping), Cont'd

- striving for community improvement through strategic grantmaking in such areas as arts and culture, economic and community betterment, education, the environment, and health and human services; and

- providing a flexible and cost-effective way for donors to improve their community now and in the future.

Position Information

The program associate is a full-time position at the foundation. The program associate works with grantees to develop effective strategies around economic and community benefit and assists in tracking the work of the grantees, identifying areas in which technical assistance would be beneficial and helping the grantees in their efforts to promote policy and practice improvements that will benefit the community.

Responsibilities

Advocacy and Public Policy

- Stays current on relevant issues, policies, exemplary programs, resources, and information in the work that supports economic and community benefit.

- Develops policy and practice recommendations for new strategies and programs based on research of effective models for hard-to-employ populations.

- Works with officials from the private and public sectors, as well as with other nonprofits, to develop programs and strategies that create public benefit access programs and policies for low-income populations.

Communications, Marketing, and Public Relations

- Represents and supports the work at meetings and conferences, and assists in organizing and participating in meetings, conferences, and site visits.

- Has experience in working with community groups performing outreach related to free tax preparation and/or access to public benefits.

Grantmaking

- Assists in the development, management, and monitoring of grantmaking and investment strategies, which involves reviewing and analyzing proposals and budgets, preparing correspondence in response, handling grant letters and payments, and maintaining records on grantees.

- Reviews the progress of selected grantees, with a particular emphasis on program development and capacity building, assisting with management of technical assistance to the grantee, and facilitating communication and the exchange of information among grantees in the program portfolio.

EXHIBIT 4.4
Sample Job Description (Before Proficiency Mapping), Cont'd

- Organizes and provides direct technical assistance to grantees in order to strengthen their program implementation and strategy development; has proven ability to troubleshoot service delivery methods in order to achieve desired results.
- Has in-depth knowledge and experience working with low-income communities.
- Has experience conducting work support programs for hard-to-employ individuals.

Information Management

- Uses the Internet and basic software applications such as the Microsoft Office suite and translates raw data into meaningful management information.

Leadership and Governance

- Exhibits sensitivity to and respect for diversity in personal, professional, and business relationships on behalf of the foundation.
- Performs administrative duties in support of grantmaking work.
- Shows flexibility, maturity, and the ability to work as a team with managing directors, consultants, and persons outside the foundation who have varying backgrounds and styles.
- Demonstrates ability to develop working relationships with organizations and community groups that contribute to implementing strategies.
- Outstanding judgment, initiative, and motivation.

Planning and Evaluation

- Assists with strategic and program planning, organizational development and management, continuous quality improvement techniques, market research, and business planning.
- Demonstrates skill in the areas of strategic and program planning, organizational development and management, continuous quality improvement techniques, market research, and business planning.

Other Responsibilities

Field Building

- Has experience building a field around a content area (e.g., research, policy, practice, infrastructure, nonprofit collaboration, government and private sector partnerships).

Multitasking

- Able to work on multiple tasks and deadlines.

EXHIBIT 4.4
Sample Job Description (Before Proficiency Mapping), Cont'd

Communications Skills

- Excellent written and verbal communication skills.

Research and Analytic Skills

- Ability to prepare reports and conduct literature reviews.

Mission Commitment

- Commitment to improving outcomes for disadvantaged children and families.

Educational Requirements

- Minimum requirement includes bachelor's degree in human services, social work, business, or related field. The ideal candidate for this position holds a graduate degree (MMP, MPA, MNA, MBA, MPH, MSW, JD) and has relevant pre- or postgraduate work experience.
- Candidates should also have five to seven years of practitioner experience working directly with community-based organizations and/or policy organizations focused on low-income families.

Work Environment

- The work is performed primarily in an office setting with extensive overnight travel required (40 percent of the time).
- Must occasionally lift and move up to 30 pounds.

Job Description Components

Now that you've seen examples, we'll go into detail about what components should be included in a job description. Each component described in table 4.1 makes the job description clearer to the employee or volunteer.

To develop accurate job descriptions, you should start with job analysis. We recommend employees and volunteers list the activities they perform on a daily, weekly, monthly, and annual basis. This can be done on a form such as the one provided in exhibit 4.7.

Once all employees and volunteers have identified their job activities, they should categorize these activities by competency category. Alternatively, if you have a brand-new position, you can pull from sample job responsibilities later on in the chapter.

TABLE 4.1
Job Description Components

Job Title: Executive, Director, Associate, Assistant, etc.	
Department	Administrative, Development, Research, etc.
Status	• *Exempt/Nonexempt:* Exempt means that the position meets the requirements of the Fair Labor Standards Act and is not entitled to overtime pay. Employees who meet this requirement make over a certain amount of money, or fall under the "executive," "professional," or "administrative" job categories. Nonexempt means that a position is entitled to overtime pay if the position works over 8 hours in one day and more than 40 hours in one week (FLSA, n.d.). • *Full-time/Part-time:* The Fair Labor Standards Act does not define full-time or part-time employment but leaves the decision up to each employer. Best practice suggests you should consider employees that work over 30 hours a week full-time.
Salary Range	• Best practices in determining compensation: Look up similar organizations using www.guidestar.org and researching 990 Forms. Many different compensation studies are available through the library or nonprofit state associations and foundation regional associations. Be sure to consider the cost of living in your city also.
Reports to/ Supervisory Responsibilities	Job descriptions should include the title of the position that supervises the employee/volunteer and the titles of the positions that the employee supervises. This can include multiple employees and volunteers. This section gives the employee/volunteer an understanding of their management and supervisory roles, as well as their position level within the organization.
Information about the Organization	This section should be a one to two paragraph overview of your organization. Typically, organizations include the mission and a brief history. Information about the organization also includes the location of the position.

TABLE 4.1
Job Description Components, Cont'd

Position Information	This is a one to two paragraph summary of the position. This section should include an accurate portrayal of the day-to-day activities of this position.
Responsibilities Mapped to Social Change Competencies	This section is where you will categorize each job responsibility within the ten core social change competencies discussed in the previous chapter.
Qualifications	You must indicate what levels of experience are required for the position, as well as how many prior years of experience in a similar type of position or a lower-level position are required.
Educational Requirements	Does this job or volunteer position require a bachelor's degree or master's degree? Often people put bachelor's as a standard for entry-level nonprofit jobs, but is a bachelor's degree really necessary for a job where the employee is minimally paid? The accurate level of education the position truly demands will prevent turnover (e.g., hiring overqualified people who will leave in several months when they get a "better fit" position).
Work Environment	It is also important to include information about the work environment. Is your organization located in an office or a warehouse? How many employees are there? How many volunteers are there? Is outdoor work required?

EXHIBIT 4.5
Our Philosophy on Compensation

There has been a lot of discussion about compensation in social change organizations. Workers in social change organizations should make a living wage comparable to that offered by organizations of similar size, type, and mission, and considering their geographic location. This salary practice is in alignment with putting people first. Many small grassroots organizations start paying their staff very little money, often less than minimum wage. We've seen that although employees have chosen to work in social change organizations for mission-related reasons, many decide to switch jobs and move to the for-profit sector due to lack of compensation (Preston, 1994; Solomon & Sandahl, 2007). As stated previously, it costs an organization up to 150 percent of an employee's salary to replace him or her. Even though organizations believe they are saving money by providing low compensation, in reality the organization is spending more money because of the turnover costs of replacing an employee. Paying your staff more costs you less in the long run. You can calculate the amount of savings from turnover and salary payments using calculations in chapter 1 and during evaluation of the Platform.

EXHIBIT 4.6

Do We Have to Do This in a Volunteer-Run Organization Too?

You should provide clear job descriptions in volunteer-run organizations too. Board members and other key volunteers in the organization should have job descriptions just like paid employees. In volunteer-run organizations, volunteers often have the same responsibilities as paid employees. The job descriptions will also help when the time comes for the organization to hire paid employees.

Social Change Competencies within Job Descriptions

The hardest part of the process of developing strong job descriptions is separating responsibilities into specific social change competency categories. You can do this by identifying social change competency words within each job responsibility. For example, the small grassroots nonprofit had a list of all the job responsibilities for the executive director. Then they looked for words that could be associated with the core social change competencies. Table 4.2 shows the job responsibilities for the executive director, the italicized word that was associated with a competency category, and the identified competency category.

We reviewed job descriptions from many job sites for social change professionals, including Idealist.org, Opportunity Knocks, Craigslist, Indeed.com, and many others, and then identified common responsibilities tied to each social change competency. We've provided these sample responsibilities separated by each social change competency category as a resource for you to create and revise your job descriptions. Start categorizing the job responsibilities using the samples in the exhibits in this chapter and the job analysis forms completed by employees and volunteers.

Before we get into the sample responsibilities, let's clarify position levels. Even though many social change organizations operate under a flat organizational structure, with few levels of hierarchy, it is important to understand the levels that do exist. Understanding position levels clarifies the level of responsibility and the proficiency level each employee or volunteer needs to have for his or her specific role. Understanding position levels also helps avoid the pile-on effect discussed earlier in the chapter.

Assistant and coordinator positions. These tend to be positions at the entry level and require little background or prior experience; for example, development coordinator, administrative assistant, or program assistant. These positions may have increased responsibilities in smaller organizations.

EXHIBIT 4.7
Job Analysis Form

Name _____ Date _____

Position _____

Department _____

Daily Activities _____

_____

Weekly Activities _____

_____

Monthly activities _____

_____

Annual activities _____

_____

TABLE 4.2

Executive Director Job Responsibilities, by Competency Area

Job Responsibilities	Competency Category
Develop *programs and services* that reflect the strategic direction for the organization.	Direct Service
Establish *goals and objectives* for each program and service.	Planning and Evaluation
Work in a mutually supportive manner with the board and staff in identifying resource requirements, *researching funding sources*, and establishing strategies to approach funders.	Fundraising and Resource Development
Participate in *fund development activities*, including hosting events, making asks, authoring proposals, identifying funding sources, and undertaking other tasks required by the fundraising plan.	Fundraising and Resource Development
Ensure that the organization and its mission, programs, and services are consistently *presented with a strong, positive image* to relevant stakeholders.	Communications, Marketing, and Public Relations
Provide for information, *publicity, and marketing* designed to increase community understanding of the organization, its goals, and its services.	Communications, Marketing and Public Relations
Act as *advisor to the board of directors* in the carrying out of its policy-making responsibility.	Leadership and Governance
Meet regularly with the board and the executive committee	Leadership and Governance
Oversee the translation and *implementation of board policies* into effective action.	Legal and Regulatory
Recommend the *yearly budget* for board approval.	Financial Management and Social Entrepreneurship
Ensure that all *financial, tax, risk, and facilities* requirements for the organization are fully met and executed according to current laws and regulations.	Financial Management and Social Entrepreneurship
Act as the chief financial agent for the agency in ensuring the *proper use of budgeted funds* and maintenance of sound accounting procedures to safeguard the assets of the organization.	Financial Management and Social Entrepreneurship
Ensure the *selection, supervision, and evaluation of quality staff* to deliver services.	Human Resources Management and Volunteerism

TABLE 4.2	
Executive Director Job Responsibilities, by Competency Area, Cont'd	
Job Responsibilities	**Competency Category**
Ensure that the organization obtains and keeps current all *required licenses* related to its work.	Legal and Regulatory
Welcome constructive feedback from staff and clients and work to *provide an environment of openness and compassion.*	Leadership and Governance
Conduct oneself in a manner that models *professional behavior* at all times.	Leadership and Governance

Manager and director positions. These positions tend to be mid- to executive level. Research shows that organizations tend to hire people from outside the organization to fill these positions (Nonprofit HR Solutions, 2013). This is because the majority of organizations do not develop talent from within—but you can change that statistic!

As you are picking competencies for each role from the samples, if you find you are choosing all the responsibilities for one specific sample position, it is likely that position is doing too much. Consider splitting the position into two positions or make it a higher-level position. The position descriptions provided in the rest of this chapter are as follows:

- Board Chair
- Board Treasurer
- Executive Director
- Chief Operating Officer/Operations Manager
- Human Resources Manager
- Development Director
- Development Coordinator
- Program Manager
- Volunteer Coordinator
- Administrative Assistant
- Marketing Coordinator
- Program Officer
- Program Associate
- Director of Donor Services
- Evaluator

The samples divide the responsibilities for each job description into the ten social change competencies. If a position does not require the competency, we do not include any responsibilities for that position.

EXHIBIT 4.8

Sample Responsibilities of a Board Chair

Advocacy and Public Policy

- Advances the organization's community outreach and advocacy efforts to further agency vision, mission, and goals and to maintain strong community values at the local, state, and national level.
- Supports advocacy efforts directed at public and private agencies in the local community and in the state and federal legislature.

Communications, Marketing, and Public Relations

- Develops relationships and maintains communication with funders, partners, and other stakeholders, and supports executive director in managing these relationships.
- Publicizes the activities of the organization, including its programs and goals.
- Establishes sound working relationships and cooperative arrangements with community groups and organizations.

Financial Management and Social Entrepreneurship

- As a board member approves the organization's annual budget, audit reports, and material business decisions.
- Ensures that the board and organization adhere to all legal and fiduciary responsibilities.
- In collaboration with the executive director generates substantial annual revenue and fosters the organization's overall financial health.

Fundraising and Resource Development

- Personally treats the organization as a top philanthropic priority reflected in an annual financial gift.
- Ensures that 100 percent of the organization's board members make an annual contribution commensurate with their capacity.
- Identifies, qualifies, cultivates, solicits, and stewards major individual donors, and corporate and foundation gifts.

EXHIBIT 4.8
Sample Responsibilities of a Board Chair, Cont'd

Grantmaking or Direct Service

- Oversees all grantmaking decisions.
- Sets grantmaking direction.

Human Resources Management and Volunteerism

- Assists the executive director and board nominating committee in recruiting board members.
- Ensures that the organization's commitment to a diverse board and staff reflects the communities the organization serves.

Information Management

- Ensures that technology purchases or donations are made to support the organizational infrastructure.
- Oversees information transmission throughout the organization.

Leadership and Governance

- Fully informs the board on the condition of the organization and all important factors influencing it.
- Leads the board in its fiscal, governance, and legal responsibilities.
- Oversees and supports the recruitment and selection of board members.
- Periodically consults with board members on their roles and in helping them assess their performance.

Legal and Regulatory

- Reports appropriate information to watchdog and regulatory organizations.
- Ensures compliance with all applicable laws and regulations.

Planning and Evaluation

- Reviews outcomes and metrics created by the organization for evaluating its impact, and regularly measures its performance and effectiveness using those metrics.
- Coordinates an annual performance evaluation of the executive director.
- Ensures the organization conducts annual and strategic planning.
- Plans, presides over, and facilitates board and committee meetings; partners with the executive director to ensure that board resolutions are carried out.

EXHIBIT 4.9
Sample Responsibilities of a Board Treasurer

Advocacy and Public Policy
- Supports the advocacy activities of the organization.

Communications, Marketing, and Public Relations

- Ensures that the organization communicates financial information to constituents, regulators, and the public.

Financial Management and Social Entrepreneurship

- Establishes accounting procedures and internal control processes.
- Assists executive director and staff with long-term financial planning, cash-flow analysis, and risk analysis.
- Selects a bank, reviews cash disbursements, and effectively invests excess funds. (In a volunteer-run organization)
- Assists accounting staff to develop cash-flow management systems.
- Oversees financial transactions and ensures that employees record transactions properly. (In a volunteer-run or other small organization)
- Advises the executive director as she or he develops the annual budget and then reviews monthly financial reports of budgets to actuals.
- Ensures that the organization completes required financial reports on time and makes these reports available to the board.
- Presents financial data at monthly board meetings.
- Works with the executive director to ensure that the board sees appropriate financial reports on a timely basis.
- Oversees investment decisions.
- Presents the annual budget to the board for approval.

Fundraising and Resource Development

- Personally treats the organization as a top philanthropic priority reflected in an annual financial gift.
- Oversees the creation of policies regarding gift acceptance and other financial donation transactions.
- Processes donations and donor receipts. (In a volunteer-run organization)
- Advises the organization on its fundraising strategy.

EXHIBIT 4.9
Sample Responsibilities of a Board Treasurer, Cont'd

Grantmaking or Direct Service

- Ensures the organization keeps grantmaking recordkeeping up to date.
- Ensures client transactions are in compliance with laws and internal control procedures.
- Prepares sponsorship and grant proposals. (In a volunteer-run organization)

Human Resources Management and Volunteerism

- Trains or informs staff and board members on fiscal oversight, internal controls, and financial reporting.
- Oversees the recruitment and selection of an outside CPA.

Information Management

- Identifies, selects, and oversees the organization's secure financial recordkeeping and payroll system.

Leadership and Governance

- Keeps the board informed of key financial events, trends, concerns, and assessments of fiscal health.
- Trains or informs board members on their fiscal responsibility.
- Oversees the development and observance of the organization's financial policies and procedures.
- Leads the board and executive director in long-term financial planning and analyzing financial risks.
- Manages, along with the board finance committee, the board's review of an action related to the board's financial responsibilities.
- Serves as the chair of the finance committee.

Legal and Regulatory

- Ensures the organization files Form 990 and other financial reports with external regulators and watchdog organizations.
- Oversees the organization's adherence to all financial policies.

Planning and Evaluation

- Integrates financial implications in annual and strategic planning sessions.
- Reviews the annual audit and answers board members' questions about the audit.
- Prepares and disseminates quarterly financial reports.

EXHIBIT 4.10

Sample Responsibilities of an Executive Director

Advocacy and Public Policy

- Coordinates fundraising and events with advocacy efforts.

- Establishes and maintains strong relationships with consumers, government, business, funders, and volunteers.

- Advances the organization's community outreach and advocacy efforts to further agency vision, mission, and goals.

- Maintains strong relationships with policy makers at the local and state level.

- Responsible for advocacy efforts directed at public and private agencies in the local community and in the state and federal legislature.

- Works with elected officials, agencies, and organizations to develop and promote legislation and programs that will benefit the organization's clients and constituents.

Communications, Marketing, and Public Relations

- Ensures the organization and its mission, programs, and services are consistently presented by a strong positive brand image to relevant stakeholders.

- Publicizes the activities of the organization, its programs, and goals.

- Establishes sound working relationships and cooperative arrangements with community groups and organizations.

- Represents the point of view of the organization to agencies, organizations, and the public.

- Produces regular publications, web-based products, annual reports, newsletters, and other marketing and communication materials (or in larger organization—oversees staff who produce regular publication, web-based products, annual reports, newsletters and other marketing and communication materials).

- Works with staff to produce daily high-quality social media postings (or in larger organization—oversees staff who produces high-quality social media postings).

- Engages entities, organizations, and businesses to increase public awareness.

- Serves as liaison to local, federal, and state entities; acts as the primary contact with community funding agents, civic groups, and the public.

- Participates in appropriate community initiatives and activities that support the organization's mission, as well as initiates and coordinates all public relations efforts and represents the organization at public and professional meetings.

- Serves as primary contact for all media relations.

EXHIBIT 4.10
Sample Responsibilities of an Executive Director, Cont'd

- Develops and maintains relationships with key media contacts within local media outlets.
- Develops and maintains community networking relationships with assistance of staff.
- Utilizes technology for outreach and social media communication.
- Raises the visibility of the organization through the development and implementation of sustainable marketing efforts geared to its various constituencies as well as the public.

Financial Management and Social Entrepreneurship

- Oversees, develops, and maintains sound organizational financial practices.
- Works with the staff, finance committee, and the board in preparing a budget; sees that the organization operates within budget guidelines.
- Ensures that adequate funds are available to permit the organization to carry out its work.
- Provides ongoing, accurate financial accounting including maintenance of the financial management system.
- Recommends yearly budget for board approval and prudently manages organization's resources within those budget guidelines according to current laws and regulations.
- Oversees the yearly budget in conjunction with the board finance committee.
- Authorizes expenditures requisitioned within the confines of the budget and as set forth in the financial policies; signs checks and contracts.
- Ensures timely compliance of the organization's contractual, financial, and legal obligations.
- Oversees facilities and asset management.
- Ensures adequate facilities and equipment are in place to carry out the programs and operations of the organization.
- Works with staff and the board to efficiently and effectively oversee cash, liabilities, and organizational assets.

Fundraising and Resource Development

- Identifies, solicits, and manages current and potential donors, including maintenance of effective communication and ongoing relationships with donors regarding the use of their funds. (Or in a larger organization—oversees fundraising staff in identifying, soliciting, and managing current and potential donors, including maintenance of effective communication and ongoing relationships with donors regarding the use of their funds.)
- Seeks, develops, and negotiates new contracts, grants, and other funding with public and private sources.
- Oversees the development, implementation, and evaluation of fundraising activities.

EXHIBIT 4.10
Sample Responsibilities of an Executive Director, Cont'd

Grantmaking or Direct Service

- Establishes grantmaking and investment strategy.
- Establishes rigorous grantmaking guidelines and processes that raise the bar for impact philanthropy.
- Establishes and leverages a strong network of leading philanthropists, impact investors, and foundation partners.
- Continually innovates, tests new models, and develops best practices in philanthropy and impact investing.
- Sets programmatic direction for the organization and ensures client needs are being met.
- Participates in community activities.

Human Resources Management and Volunteerism

- Recruits, selects, and releases all personnel, both paid staff and volunteers. (Or in larger organizations—oversees human resources management and volunteer management staff that conducts recruitment, selection, and release of all personnel, both paid staff and volunteers.)
- Ensures that job descriptions are developed, that regular performance evaluations are held, and that sound human resources practices are in place.
- Sees that an effective management team, with appropriate provision for succession, is in place.
- Encourages staff development and education, and assists staff in relating their specialized work to the organizational mission.
- Maintains a climate that attracts, keeps, and motivates a diverse staff of top quality people.

Information Management

- Oversees the information management systems within the organization ensuring that staff and volunteers have access to computers and technology to effectively carry out their jobs.
- Ensures that adequate organizational databases are identified, selected, and implemented and that staff or volunteers are trained on using the databases.

Leadership and Governance

- Provides leadership in developing program, organizational, and financial plans with the board of directors and staff, and carries out plans and policies authorized by the board.
- Sees that the board is kept fully informed on the condition of the organization and all important factors influencing it.

EXHIBIT 4.10
Sample Responsibilities of an Executive Director, Cont'd

- Effectively implements the organization's programs. (In larger organizations: oversees the program staff who will implement the organization's programs.)
- Leads and manages staff to execute the organization's mission.

Legal and Regulatory

- Maintains official records and documents and ensures compliance with federal, state, and local regulations.
- Ensures compliance with all applicable laws and regulations.
- Monitors contract compliance.
- Maintains a working knowledge of significant developments and trends in the field.
- Reports to third-party regulators as mandated by the law or undertakes voluntary completion of nonprofit oversight and accountability.

Planning and Evaluation

- Develops well-designed research studies to measure program outcomes.
- Ensures that the organization has a long-range strategy that achieves its mission, and toward which it makes consistent and timely progress.
- Presents results of research or program activities with evidence-based criteria in a variety of public and private venues and provides for dissemination in scholarly journals as well as in-house publications.
- Oversees the monitoring and evaluation of all programs.

EXHIBIT 4.11
Sample Responsibilities of a Chief Operating Officer / Operations Manager

Advocacy and Public Policy

- Supports executive director in advocacy efforts.
- Develops organizational culture that embodies organization's core values.

EXHIBIT 4.11
Sample Responsibilities of a Chief Operating Officer / Operations Manager, Cont'd

Communications, Marketing, and Public Relations

- Promotes the organization in various forms of media and communications.
- Ensures that all activities operate consistently and ethically within the mission and values of our organization.
- Provides strategic input to staff regarding communications and public relations aspects of projects.

Financial Management and Social Entrepreneurship

- Liaises with the external auditors for annual audits and timely execution of all annual tax and government filings.
- Manages the financial operations of the organization, providing monthly financial reports to the board and works with all departments on planning and managing their budgets.
- Partners with program services to develop and refine the annual budgeting process.
- Defines organizational budget reporting needs and proposes annual operating budget and allocations to the executive director.

Fundraising and Resource Development

- Ensures that efficient and effective donation tracking is in place.
- Supports development efforts as needed.
- Promotes operational and infrastructure components as part of fund development efforts.

Grantmaking or Direct Service

- Develops plans for the cost-effective maintenance, development, and implementation of services, systems, and management tools that support grantmaking and administrative operations and contribute to organizational effectiveness.
- Assists in grantmaking and oversight.

Human Resources Management and Volunteerism

- Responsible for human resources activities including payroll and benefits and employment contracts.
- Manages and trains the team of employees.

Information Management

- Oversees technology operations, including financial databases, hardware and software purchases, upgrades and maintenance, staff technology training, and technology vendor contracts.

EXHIBIT 4.11

Sample Responsibilities of a Chief Operating Officer / Operations Manager, Cont'd

---

- Oversees maintenance and ongoing development of all database systems.
- Manages and supports IT infrastructure, including network and software needs.

Leadership and Governance

- Oversees and directs all financial and administrative activities of the organization, including accounting, budgeting, financial planning and reporting, internal audits, operations, human resources, and information systems.
- Guides day-to-day operations for the organization including financial oversight, human resources, and governance issues.
- Provides executive leadership for the development, implementation, and maintenance of processes, policies, and procedures across all operational functions.
- Oversees the operational management of facilities, meetings and travel, food, mail, copy services, and records and archives.
- Manages and nurtures relationships with financial advisors, board members, corporate partners, attorneys, members of the media, and other nonprofit organizations.

Legal and Regulatory

- Works closely with staff and the executive director in ensuring that the organization operates in a fiscally responsible fashion in compliance with all legal and regulatory requirements.

Planning and Evaluation

- Ensures that evaluation systems, processes, and practices are in place to accomplish the goals and objectives of the organization.

EXHIBIT 4.12

Sample Responsibilities of a Human Resources Manager

Advocacy and Public Policy

- N/A

Communications, Marketing, and Public Relations

- Markets and recruits a talented pool of job candidates.
- Communicates the organizational culture in organizational training materials.

EXHIBIT 4.12
Sample Responsibilities of a Human Resources Manager, Cont'd

Financial Management and Social Entrepreneurship

- Understands financial implications of staffing increases.
- Involved in staff budgeting process.
- Manages staffing costs and is in tune with employment taxes, fringe benefits, and retirement costs.
- Administers benefits and processes payroll and workers compensation claims in an accurate and timely manner.

Fundraising and Resource Development

- N/A

Grantmaking or Direct Service

- Acts as a liaison between grant officials, program staff, and the evaluation team.

Human Resources Management and Volunteerism

- Provides HR support to managers on issues such as presentation and review of measures and metrics, employee onboarding and separation, salary administration, performance management, reasonable accommodation, leaves of absence, and investigation and resolution of employee complaints.
- Provides advice, recommendations, and coaching to leaders on employee issues.
- Creates employee engagement and morale-boosting activities.
- Plans and directs a program for recruitment, selection, and assignment of the best-qualified staff that demonstrate the ability and desire to perform the essential job functions.
- Provides overall management of human resources functions within the organization.
- Manages, develops, and implements personnel procedures related to applications, examinations, eligibility, promotion, demotion, transfer, dismissal, resignation, layoff, reemployment, vacation, leave-of-absence, compensation, licensing, and certification.
- Supervises and evaluates the performance of assigned staff on a regular basis and provides clear, constructive feedback to improve staff effectiveness.
- Interviews and selects highly qualified employees and recommends transfers, reassignments, terminations, and disciplinary actions.
- Provides counseling to employees regarding their rights, classification, benefits, requirements, retirement, compensation, and other related items.

EXHIBIT 4.12
Sample Responsibilities of a Human Resources Manager, Cont'd

Information Management

- Trains and supervises managers in employee recordkeeping and the collection of performance management data.
- Analyzes data and maintains employee records.

Leadership and Governance

- Supports staff and volunteers in their personal and professional successes and challenges.
- Communicates and collaborates with managers to resolve issues and conflicts and to exchange information.
- Serves as key talent management partner for executive leaders, providing advice and counsel on a broad range of talent management issues.
- Maintains collaborative relationships and continued communications with staff, volunteers, and constituents.

Legal and Regulatory

- Ensures compliance with regulatory requirements while performing duties such as recruiting, interviewing, hiring, and training of staff.
- Assists supervisors with employee relations and legal issues.
- Provides input and assistance in development of policies, procedures, and guidelines.
- Conducts collective negotiations with one or more bargaining units as assigned.
- Advises managers on and ensures compliance with HR policies, procedures and practices, and assists in the management of day-to-day employee and labor relations.
- Coordinates grievance procedures.
- Administers programs in accordance with union contracts and ensures that inappropriate assignments are corrected.

Planning and Evaluation

- Plans, coordinates, and arranges for appropriate training of staff in support of professional learning.
- Oversees managers in conducting annual performance appraisals.
- Provides support for strategic planning and insight for long-term staff sustainability and growth.
- Assists with developing staff evaluation protocols in grant applications as time allows.

EXHIBIT 4.13

Sample Responsibilities of a Development Director

Advocacy and Public Policy

- Cultivates relationships with potential donors through advocacy-related activities.

Communications, Marketing, and Public Relations

- Develops and maintains ongoing relationships with major donors.
- Oversees the organization of special events.
- Represents the organization at media-related functions on an as-needed basis.
- Ensures that marketing and communications efforts include a donation component.
- Develops compelling written correspondence to support investment opportunities.

Financial Management and Social Entrepreneurship

- Oversees the financial health of the organization in regards to the development plan.
- Establishes various donor-advised funds including endowments.
- Produces grant financial reports.

Fundraising and Resource Development

- Oversees the research, identification, solicitation, and stewardship of potential foundation, corporate, and individual donors.
- Plans, manages, and coordinates designated fundraising events and programs.
- Creates and executes a strategy for a large, sustained base of annual individual donors.
- Develops and tracks proposals and reports for all foundation and corporate fundraising.

Grantmaking or Direct Service

- Ensures that funds raised support grantmaking initiatives and commitments.

Human Resources Management and Volunteerism

- Recruits and supervises the development staff team.
- Works with the volunteer coordinator to recruit and train fundraising volunteers.
- Provides training and support to development team as they evolve in their roles.

Information Management

- Selects and oversees fundraising database and donor tracking.
- Researches new funding prospects and development trends.
- Serves as fundraising database expert and advocate.

EXHIBIT 4.13

Sample Responsibilities of a Development Director, Cont'd

Leadership and Governance

- Works with the executive director and board to create a culture of philanthropy throughout the organization.
- Professionally and assertively represents the values of the organization through words, actions, and decisions.

Legal and Regulatory

- Establishes donor policies.
- Understands solicitation rules and regulations.
- Ensures that the organization follows specific laws on donor restrictions.

Planning and Evaluation

- Develops and executes the organization's annual fundraising plan.
- Ensures that fundraising is integrated in annual and strategic plans.
- Evaluates fundraising activities.
- Assesses the development program, makes recommendations, and implement plans to grow the organization.
- Establishes and realizes goals to increase yearly contributions.

EXHIBIT 4.14

Sample Responsibilities of a Development Coordinator

Advocacy and Public Policy

- Maintains awareness of how advocacy efforts may bring in prospective donors.

Communications, Marketing, and Public Relations

- Assists in cultivating individuals and companies for the direct purpose of sponsorship.
- Assists with the creation, design, and production of event-related collateral including, but not limited, to PowerPoint presentations, brochures, flyers, invitations (physical and electronic), newsletters, and other fundraising publications. (In small organizations, will be responsible for creating these items.)

EXHIBIT 4.14

Sample Responsibilities of a Development Coordinator, Cont'd

- Supports social media platforms and outreach and assists with website maintenance. (In small organizations, this position may have full responsibility for coordinating these efforts).
- When needed, assists with mailings and general administrative tasks.
- Interfaces with departments and outside vendors to coordinate all aspects of fundraising events.
- Represents organization at designated events and outside meetings on an as-needed basis.
- Interfaces with media representatives in the absence of the development director or executive director.
- Provides support with event coordination.

Financial Management and Social Entrepreneurship

- Maintains and monitors contributions through data input into Excel or internal constituent databases.
- Understands the expenses associated with fundraising activities.
- Assists with producing grant financial reports.

Fundraising and Resource Development

- Under supervisory guidance and direction plans, manages, and coordinates designated fundraising events and programs.
- Assists in the research, identification, solicitation, and stewardship of potential foundation, corporate, and individual donors.
- Supports with grant identification, writing, and reporting.

Grantmaking or Direct Service

- N/A

Human Resources Management and Volunteerism

- Assists with recruiting, selecting, managing, and evaluating fundraising volunteers. (In small organizations, may coordinate volunteer program.)

Information Management

- Categorizes and logs all contributions received in donor database.
- Assists with mailings and general administrative tasks.

EXHIBIT 4.14
Sample Responsibilities of a Development Coordinator, Cont'd

Leadership and Governance

- Interfaces and establishes rapport with key board members and donors.

Legal and Regulatory

- Understands the fundraising solicitation regulations and how they apply in the organizational setting.

Planning and Evaluation

- Identifies areas of improvement and provides new ideas for fundraising opportunities.
- Assists with annual fundraising planning and evaluation of fundraising-related activities.

EXHIBIT 4.15
Sample Responsibilities of a Program Manager

Advocacy and Public Policy

- Remains abreast of best practices, sector trends, and policy implications for the programmatic issue area.

Communications, Marketing, and Public Relations

- Provides effective communication to inform the community about the programmatic issue area through in-person, written, and online forums.
- Actively participates in relevant affinity and professional groups as a thought leader and a knowledgeable resource on the programmatic issue area.
- Develops collaborative relationships with a diverse cross-section of multisector agencies and leaders.

Financial Management and Social Entrepreneurship

- Oversees petty cash and all administrative expenses for the program(s).
- Constructs program budget(s) and ensures the provision of quality program services within established budget(s).
- Ensures that timesheets are monitored and approved within each pay period.

EXHIBIT 4.15
Sample Responsibilities of a Program Manager, Cont'd

Fundraising and Resource Development

- Raises money for new program activities on an as-needed basis.

Grantmaking or Direct Service

- Oversees and administers program.

Human Resources Management and Volunteerism

- Audits, organizes, and ensures that attendance reports and timesheets are turned in per agreed schedule.
- Ensures that all program staff are correctly paid and addresses any payroll issues with the appropriate staff member.
- Onboards volunteers, ensuring their smooth transition into the organization. (Or supports volunteer coordinator in onboarding program volunteers.)
- Effectively recruits and manages successful volunteers. (Or supports volunteer coordinator in recruiting and managing program volunteers.)
- Conducts orientations for new programmatic staff.
- Provides progressive disciplinary action for employee performance improvement, when necessary.
- Provides appropriate response to requests for time off, in accordance with human resources policy.

Information Management

- Manages the program's communications and technology platforms.
- Advises information technology staff on developing and maintaining client database.

Leadership and Governance

- Develops and maintains good relations with community stakeholders.
- Maintains and communicates up-to-date programmatic policies and partners as needed with other staff members in these implementations.
- Oversees program staff and volunteers.

Legal and Regulatory

- Provides all documentation to comply with contractual agreements.
- Ensures compliance with grants and funders, including overseeing the collection of documentation and data tracking.

EXHIBIT 4.15
Sample Responsibilities of a Program Manager, Cont'd

Planning and Evaluation

- Manages the evaluation of programmatic activities and ensures that all program elements are followed.
- Ensures the regular tracking of qualitative and quantitative client data.
- Ensures that progress reports are completed and sent out to funding agencies.
- Ensures that program goals, objectives, and outcomes are met.
- Evaluates program impact and outcomes.
- Completes monthly, quarterly, and annual reports for funding sources and the board of directors.

EXHIBIT 4.16
Sample Responsibilities of a Volunteer Coordinator

Advocacy and Public Policy

- Involves volunteers in advocacy efforts.
- Supports coordination of advocacy activities.

Communications, Marketing, and Public Relations

- Works with various staff and board members to determine volunteer requirements.
- Networks with community resources and represents the organization within the community.
- Serves as a liaison to facilitate communication between the volunteers and staff.
- Increases the organization's volunteer visibility through traditional and nontraditional media outlets.
- Develops and cultivates relationships with local media, including newspapers and television and radio stations in order to promote volunteer opportunities.
- Maintains volunteer opportunities and updates through social media.
- Collects and maintains volunteer activities and promotion, including articles and samples of volunteer success.
- Represents the organization in the community to promote volunteer activities, such as special events, receptions, and community resource fairs.

EXHIBIT 4.16
Sample Responsibilities of a Volunteer Coordinator, Cont'd

Financial Management and Social Entrepreneurship

- Manages volunteer budget and any expenses related to the volunteer management program, including volunteer recognition events.

Fundraising and Resource Development

- Works with executive director and development staff to cultivate relationships with volunteers and turn volunteers into donors.

Grantmaking or Direct Service

- Ensures that direct service volunteers adhere to client policies and procedures.

Human Resources Management and Volunteerism

- Develops and distributes volunteer training materials.
- Schedules and leads volunteer training sessions.
- Schedules volunteers and ensures (through positive confirmations) that volunteers are aware of assignments and are committed to appearing as scheduled.
- Recruits, trains, and retains volunteers for assigned area of service.
- Coordinates the recruitment, retention, and support of volunteers.
- Ensures that volunteers and staff are adhering to agency volunteer policies.

Information Management

- Develops and manages the database of volunteer information.
- Ensures that all volunteers are recorded and tracked.

Leadership and Governance

- Represents the volunteer program in team meetings while encouraging use of volunteers.

Legal and Regulatory

- Updates volunteer policies as needed.
- Ensures that the organization adheres to the portions of the Federal Labor Standards Act that are applicable to volunteers.
- Keeps up with necessary volunteer regulations.

Planning and Evaluation

- Ensures that the recruitment, selection, management, and professional development of volunteers are included in annual and strategic planning efforts.

EXHIBIT 4.17

Sample Responsibilities of an Administrative Assistant

Advocacy and Public Policy

- Assists with advocacy event preparation.

Communications, Marketing, and Public Relations

- Directs public relations issues to the appropriate person.
- Assists in scheduling meetings and takes minutes at all meetings.
- Edits and completes first drafts of written communications, which could include e-mails, memos, proposals, and reports.
- Maintains extremely active calendar of appointments.
- Composes and prepares correspondence that is sometimes confidential.

Financial Management and Social Entrepreneurship

- Completes expense requests and expense reports.
- Follows appropriate procedures for incoming financial mail.

Fundraising and Resource Development

- Supports fundraising efforts.

Grantmaking or Direct Service

- Processes incoming grantfunding requests.
- Channels grantee inquiries to the appropriate person.

Human Resources Management and Volunteering

- Documents volunteer inquiries.

Information Management

- Maintains strict confidentiality of personal data, proprietary information, and sensitive materials as required.

Leadership and Governance

- Builds relationships crucial to the success of the organization and manages a variety of special projects for the leadership team, some of which may have organizational impact.
- Assists in coordinating the agenda of all staff meetings.

EXHIBIT 4.17
Sample Responsibilities of an Administrative Assistant, Cont'd

- Completes a broad variety of administrative tasks for the leadership team.
- Arranges complex and detailed travel plans, itineraries, and agendas.
- Compiles documents for travel-related meetings.

Legal and Regulatory

- Supports legal and regulatory compliance efforts.

Planning and Evaluation

- Supports annual planning and evaluation efforts.

EXHIBIT 4.18
Sample Responsibilities of a Marketing Coordinator

Advocacy and Public Policy

- Supports advocacy- and policy-related activities with promotions.

Communications, Marketing, and Public Relations

- Produces diverse written products, including speeches, blog posts, press releases, and newsletter content.
- Provides editing services on important public documents (reports, correspondence with board members, grant proposals, etc.).
- Assists in shaping communications and collateral development for press conferences and events.
- Understands and translates the organization's mission, strategy, current operating plan, and event calendar into a strong communications plan with clear, achievable deliverables.
- Updates social media pages to change or add new information as needed.
- Develops and implements program and organizational marketing tactics and action plans, with measurable results as assigned.
- Maintains the marketing calendar and action plan.
- Develops and implements an editorial calendar and production schedule for e-newsletters for consultants, clients, and funders.

EXHIBIT 4.18

Sample Responsibilities of a Marketing Coordinator, Cont'd

- Writes, edits, and tracks the production of publications including e-newsletters, fundraising materials, brochures, special invitations, annual reports, and other print and electronic publications.
- Helps to create and implement a media plan to increase organizational visibility of target markets.
- Works to extend and protect the brand.

Financial Management and Social Entrepreneurship

- Assists with developing and managing budget for marketing and communications efforts.

Fundraising and Resource Development

- Supports fundraising staff by researching leads and cold-calling potential donors.
- Assists with fundraising-related activities.

Grantmaking or Direct Service

- Supports promotion of the organization's grantmaking initiatives.

Human Resources Management and Volunteerism

- Recruits and manages marketing and communications volunteers.
- Oversees contracts and projects with communications vendors such as designers and photographers or videographers, as well as media consultants.

Information Management

- Tracks and analyzes web traffic and the success of online campaigns and makes changes in strategy.
- Analyzes programmatic trends and adjusts marketing efforts accordingly.
- Mines the client database for relevant marketing data to refine marketing targets and messages.
- Supports information technology staff in the administration and maintenance of the website.
- Recommends and manages social media activities that support marketing and development strategies, with measurable results.

Leadership and Governance

- Facilitates marketing and communications across the organization.
- Builds and maintains relationships with journalists, producers, and bloggers.

EXHIBIT 4.18
Sample Responsibilities of a Marketing Coordinator, Cont'd

Legal and Regulatory

- N/A

Planning and Evaluation

- Conducts an assessment of all marketing initiatives, measuring and reporting results and recommendations as requested.
- Plays a central role in the planning and execution of fundraising events and follow-up.

EXHIBIT 4.19
Sample Responsibilities of a Program Officer

Advocacy and Public Policy

- Develops and tracks knowledge of trends across social change issues.

Communications, Marketing, and Public Relations

- Builds strategic relationships with other funders and organizations and promotes collaboration and coordination between entities.
- Organizes meetings of grantees, experts, and practitioners.
- Attends key meetings and conferences in the sector across a variety of disciplines and perspectives. Participates in cross-foundation learning sessions, planning activities, and knowledge exchange.
- Assists in the Foundation's external communications, including assistance in developing website content, blogs, articles, and Twitter feeds as appropriate.
- Represents the Foundation at appropriate meetings, conferences, and site visits. This includes public speaking and the preparation of presentations and written materials.
- Maintains strong relationships with trustees, grantees, and colleagues.

Financial Management and Social Entrepreneurship

- Ensures that grant proposals include accurate budgets and financial information.
- Manages financial portfolio of grants.

EXHIBIT 4.19
Sample Responsibilities of a Program Officer, Cont'd

Fundraising and Resource Development

- N/A

Grantmaking or Direct Service

- Manages a roster of active grants.
- Identifies prospective grantees and counsels grant seekers.
- Analyzes grant requests and determines the relevance of the request within the Foundation's areas of interest.
- Conducts grant proposal reviews, including assessing organizational goals, plans, and capacity.
- Works with grantees to develop and refine grant proposals and define outcomes.
- Prepares written analysis, summary materials, and presentations for board meetings.
- Monitors progress of grantees through personal contact, site visits, and review of progress reports.
- Provides guidance and assistance to grantees as needed.
- Designs and implements special grant initiatives.
- Monitors and evaluates funded grant implementation and arranges for consultation and technical assistance as appropriate.

Human Resources Management and Volunteerism

- Recruits, selects, and manages program staff.

Information Management

- Manages grant and reporting calendars, including maintaining databases and files.
- Conducts a detailed tracking and management of grants, with timely attention to all internal tracking systems.

Leadership and Governance

- Coordinates multiple grantmaking programs simultaneously.
- Plans and implements learning opportunities for grantees, staff, and board that contribute to the understanding of new approaches, best practices, and trends.
- Effectively manages consultants to help the Foundation to accomplish its work.

Legal and Regulatory

- N/A

EXHIBIT 4.19
Sample Responsibilities of a Program Officer, Cont'd

Planning and Evaluation

- Develops and manages an implementation plan to achieve the Foundation's goals within one or more of its priority initiatives.
- Participates in planning and evaluation activities related to the Foundation's programs in general.
- Collaborates with staff in planning and facilitating discussions.

EXHIBIT 4.20
Sample Responsibilities of a Program Associate

Advocacy and Public Policy

- Supports advocacy efforts around Foundation issue areas.

Communications, Marketing, and Public Relations

- Works proactively with staff to facilitate effective communications about and management of grantmaking processes and portfolio reviews.
- Attends quarterly grantmaking discussions and discusses grants in progress.
- Organizes, compiles, and ensures timely delivery of a monthly electronic newsletter.

Financial Management and Social Entrepreneurship

- Assists with maintaining grantmaking programmatic budget.
- Supports program officer in reviewing grant proposal budgets and financial reports.

Fundraising and Resource Development

- Observes current programmatic trends and best practices, the funding landscape, and potential partners.

Grantmaking or Direct Service

- Supports the program officer in organizing and executing meetings, briefings, learning communities, or other events that engage stakeholders around programmatic issues and priorities.

EXHIBIT 4.20
Sample Responsibilities of a Program Associate, Cont'd

- Develops and maintains calendar of grantmaking deadlines and communicates with staff about expectations and status.
- Serves as an initial point of contact, addressing grantseeker inquiries knowledgably and punctually.
- Assists program officer in grantmaking efforts.
- Participates in the cultivation, review, and preparation of proposals for strategic and responsive grants.

Human Resources Management and Volunteerism

- Observes discussions, trainings, and exchanges of best practices between staff and other foundations in order to assist grantmaking staff.

Information Management

- Works with staff to maintain key data points about grantmaking.
- Maintains calendar of portfolio reviews, stays abreast of new developments regarding portfolio reviews, and organizes discussions to recap lessons learned.
- Sets up and manages technology needs for online programs and meetings.

Leadership and Governance

- Exhibits sensitivity to and respect for diversity in personal, professional, and business relationships on behalf of the Foundation.
- Develops working relationships with organizations and community groups that contribute to implementing strategies.

Legal and Regulatory

- Serves as intermediary and tracker on proposals and eligibility assessments that have been submitted for review and approval.

Planning and Evaluation

- Discusses and recommends ways to improve our grantmaking processes.
- Assists with monitoring grantee performance against established grant terms and agreements, and formats reported data of milestones and outcomes for internal program dashboards.
- Contributes to the planning and development process for the long-term strategy, including the evolution of systems for capturing evidence of deeper impact.

EXHIBIT 4.21

Sample Responsibilities of a Director of Donor Services

Advocacy and Public Policy

- Meets with local, state, and national legislators to promote issues of the foundation.

Communications, Marketing, and Public Relations

- Establishes and manages information-tracking processes regarding acknowledgment, recognition, and ongoing communications.
- Continues cultivation of past and current major donors to enhance their relationship with the organization and increase the likelihood of continued contributions.
- Maintains contact with donors and family members who have established endowed funds, providing them with yearly endowment reports.
- Recommends and facilitates publicity of major gifts.
- Advises on and facilitates the recognition of donors in both print and web-based publications.
- Contributes donor and gift information for the organization's annual report.
- Assists with the planning and execution of donor recognition and cultivation events.

Financial Management and Social Entrepreneurship

- Decides appropriate investment strategies for donor-advised funds.
- Reviews and maintains financial portfolio of grants.

Fundraising and Resource Development

- Designs and implements an annual integrated donor relations plan that includes acknowledgment processes and donor recognition events.

Grantmaking or Direct Service

- Advises donors on grantmaking opportunities within the foundation.
- Oversees and directs grant procurement and administration, supervising and coordinating staff as assigned and contracted.
- Provides guidance and imagination to the creation, development, and execution of special initiatives and funding opportunities across the larger region.

Human Resources Management and Volunteerism

- Identifies regional development training needs and coordinates appropriate opportunities for professional growth amongst staff, including workshops, webinars, conference calls, etc.

EXHIBIT 4.21

Sample Responsibilities of a Director of Donor Services, Cont'd

Information Management

- Devises and uses consistent, accurate, and appropriate information-sharing mechanisms for stewarding prospects and donors.

Leadership and Governance

- Supervises staff engaged in stewardship, events, and communications.
- Provides leadership in the design and development of initiatives and partnerships while promoting collaboration initiatives between organizational teams.

Legal and Regulatory

- N/A

Planning and Evaluation

- Reviews and improves the donor recognition levels and donor award programs.

EXHIBIT 4.22

Sample Responsibilities of an Evaluator

Advocacy and Public Policy

- N/A

Communications, Marketing, and Public Relations

- Works with senior leadership team to effectively communicate evaluation results both internally and externally.
- Disseminates and translates research and evaluation findings to a variety of constituencies.
- Produces publications, presentations, research resources, and briefings or white papers designed to inform the policy makers about evaluation results.
- Represents the organization publicly and regularly presents on the organization's evaluation and performance management work to a variety of audiences (existing and potential funders, government officials, foundations, etc.).
- Disseminates evaluation results to organizational partners, including federal and municipal agencies, foundations, community organizations, and constituents.

EXHIBIT 4.22
Sample Responsibilities of an Evaluator, Cont'd

Financial Management and Social Entrepreneurship

- Manages all administrative aspects of research and evaluation, including budget, staffing, data collection logistics, and other related duties as necessary.

Fundraising and Resource Development

- Works closely with the organization's development office to provide outcome information for proposal writing and to author text for evaluation plans and logic models.

Grantmaking or Direct Service

- Coordinates evaluation findings with the foundation's grantmaking and investment strategy.

Human Resources Management and Volunteerism

- Manages evaluation staff.
- Oversees volunteers involved in the data collection process.

Information Management

- Coordinates with IT staff on the development and implementation of a centralized assessment database.
- Consolidates all current tools and practices for measuring impact to ensure cohesive, consistent, high-quality data collection and analysis.
- Creates systems for using data to provide ongoing feedback and support to providers for the improvement of program practices.
- Designs or modifies specific data collection instruments for each organizational program such as pre- and posttests, surveys, assessments, interview guides, and focus group protocols.
- Analyzes collected output and outcome data and prepares reports for internal use and external distribution summarizing analyzed results.

Leadership and Governance

- Supervises evaluation staff and ensures smooth operation of evaluating activities, including identifying and overseeing professional development opportunities.
- Acts as liaison between the organization and all external evaluation projects and organizations.
- Works with external stakeholders, including funders and partners, to ensure best practices and transparency.

EXHIBIT 4.22
Sample Responsibilities of an Evaluator, Cont'd

Legal and Regulatory

- Ensures that evaluations are in compliance with applicable laws and regulations.
- Produces evaluations that meet necessary regulatory bodies' requests.

Planning and Evaluation

- Builds capacity for, implements, and manages internal systems for conducting ongoing outcomes measurement and assessment.
- Manages the design and implementation of the strategic evaluation plan.
- Works closely with staff to build on existing evaluation tools to create a strategic evaluation plan that measures progress and success for both internal program improvement purposes as well as for external reporting purposes.
- Independently, or with external vendors, designs and implements evaluation tools to support the strategic evaluation plan including both quantitative and qualitative methods as appropriate.
- Oversees the use of evaluation as a tool in accomplishing program or project objectives and ensures that data is being collected accurately, analyzed appropriately, and adapted as needed.
- Manages a portfolio of strategic evaluations, working closely with the program staff to ensure that the evaluations provide high-quality, useful, and timely information.

Conclusion

In this chapter we discussed the importance of creating and maintaining job descriptions. We described the key components of a job description, and we provided sample job descriptions and responsibilities. The next chapter covers how to map social change competencies to each job description and assign a proficiency level to each job responsibility.

Chapter 5
Mapping Competencies and Proficiency Levels to Job Descriptions

In the last chapter, we provided a list of ten core social change competencies and encouraged you to create sub-competencies personalized to your organization, departments, and positions. We also showed you how to create job descriptions for each staff and volunteer position. Now we'll show you how to map the social change competencies to job descriptions and how to realign job descriptions based on the proficiency mapping.

The Importance of Accurate Job Descriptions

We cannot express enough the importance of keeping accurate and up-to-date job descriptions. We recognize you have limited time and many of you are overworked, but you will lose many employees and volunteers because they are using an outdated job description or don't have one at all. Remember the motto—people first. By putting your people first, you are making the time to create and revise their job descriptions on an annual basis.

Accurate job descriptions have been proven to help organizations with performance management, staff planning, and training and development (Hassad, 2005; Tyler, 2013). Keeping job responsibilities up to date also ensures that responsibilities fit the overall purpose of the position and match the proficiency level of the employee or volunteer. The job description realignment process increases employee morale, and reduces employee burnout and turnover. The process we describe in this chapter enables you to separate the job responsibilities into specific competency categories, identify the appropriate proficiency level for each job responsibility, and realign the responsibility description based on specific action words.

Proficiency Level Descriptions and Action Words

Proficiency levels show at what level each staff member or volunteer needs to perform a specific skill in order to be successful in his or her role. Understanding and identifying proficiency levels is key to the job description realignment process. The National Institutes of Health (NIH) has developed five proficiency levels:

- 1 = fundamental awareness
- 2 = novice
- 3 = intermediate
- 4 = advanced
- 5 = expert

We chose NIH proficiency levels because they are well established, tested within NIH, and similar to Dreyfus and Dreyfus (1986) and *shu ha ri* cycle of learning (Tan, 2012). We've provided the definitions for each proficiency level and common action words associated with each proficiency level. For example, most job responsibilities at the fundamental awareness level involve observing and viewing; at the novice level, assisting and supporting; at the intermediate level, performing and conducting; at the advanced level, leading and creating; and at the expert level, synthesizing and analyzing. In table 5.1 you will find the proficiency level name, description, and common action words associated with each proficiency level.

EXHIBIT 5.1
Bloom's Learning Taxonomy

We used Bloom's learning taxonomy (Bloom, Engelhart, Furst, Hill, & Krathwohl, 1956) and the sample job responsibilities from chapter 4 to identify common action words for each proficiency level. Action words associated with proficiency levels allow employees and managers to correctly identify the proficiency levels needed for each job responsibility and, subsequently, each position. The action words clarify roles and ensure that staff and volunteer proficiency levels match organization expectations, or that there is a professional development plan to move an employee or volunteer into a position that fits his or her proficiency level. Some recruiters include measurable results.

TABLE 5.1
Proficiency Scale

Score	Proficiency Level	Description	Common Action Words
N/A	*Not Applicable*	This position does not need to apply or demonstrate this competency.	
1	*Fundamental Awareness* (basic knowledge)	This role requires a common knowledge or an understanding of basic techniques and concepts.	defines, observes, recalls, relates, seeks, sees
2	*Novice* (limited experience)	This role demands a level of experience gained in a classroom, in experimental scenarios, or as a trainee on the job. A person in this role is expected to need help when performing this skill.	accepts, assists, documents, engages, follows, helps, recognizes, reports, responds, reviews, shares, supports, takes, welcomes
3	*Intermediate* (practical application)	A person in this role should be able to successfully complete tasks in this competency. The person may require help from an expert from time to time but can usually perform the skill independently.	acts, arranges, assesses, authors, categorizes, channels, collects, communicates, completes, conducts, consolidates, contributes, coordinates, delivers, distributes, executes, exhibits, handles, hosts, interacts, interfaces, keeps, lists, locates, maintains, markets, meets, monitors, organizes, participates, performs, plays, practices, processes, promotes, provides, publicizes, pulls, raises, remains, represents, researches, retains, schedules, serves, shows, solicits, stays, submits, tracks, treats, undertakes, uses, works, writes

TABLE 5.1
Proficiency Scale, Cont'd

Score	Proficiency Level	Description	Common Action Words
4	**Advanced** (applied theory)	This role demands performing actions associated with this skill without assistance. A person in this role should be recognized within the immediate organization as "a person to ask" when difficult questions arise regarding this skill.	administers, advances, advises, approves, assures, audits, authorizes, builds, collaborates, compiles, composes, connects, constructs, consults, creates, demonstrates, designs, determines, develops, directs, disseminates, edits, encourages, ensures, establishes, facilitates, formulates, generates, guides, identifies, implements, increases, interviews, involves, leads, liaises, makes, manages, mines, models, negotiates, networks, nurtures, onboards, orders, oversees, partners, plans, prepares, presents, prioritizes, produces, qualifies, recruits, releases, renews, selects, sets, starts, stewards, supervises, translates, understands, updates, utilizes; experienced, responsible
5	**Expert** (recognized authority)	This role demands an expert in this area. A person in this role can provide guidance, troubleshoot, and answer questions related to this area of expertise and the field where this competency is used.	analyzes, compares, cultivates, debates, educates, evaluates, examines, improves, innovates, integrates, interprets, masters, measures, presides, protects, recommends, safeguards, solves, synthesizes, tests, trains, troubleshoots, values, visualizes

Source: Adapted from Competencies Proficiency Scale, National Institutes of Health, http://hr.od.nih.gov/workingatnih/competencies/proficiencyscale.htm

The Proficiency Mapping Process

The proficiency mapping process involves four steps:

1. Separating job responsibilities by competency category, which the last chapter demonstrated

2. Filling in job responsibilities for missing competency categories

3. Identifying proficiency levels based on job responsibility action words

4. Realigning action words to competency proficiency level

Before we describe each step in detail, it is important to note that managers or supervisors should complete the proficiency mapping process for each position they oversee. Individual employees and volunteers can assist with the mapping process, but managers should ensure that competencies and proficiency levels are identified for each position and not identified on the sole basis of the individual holding that position.

Separate the Job Responsibilities by Competency Category

In chapter 4 we explained how to separate job responsibilities by competency category, but here is a review: we searched for words that were used to describe each job responsibility that fit within each competency category. For example, the job responsibilities that had the words *community awareness and public welfare* were separated into the Advocacy and Public Policy competency. Table 5.2 shows an example of the job responsibilities that were separated into the Advocacy and Public Policy competency category for the executive director of the small grassroots organization.

In table 5.3 you can see all the job responsibilities separated by competency category for the executive director's job description, which we first showed you in exhibit 4.2.

TABLE 5.2

Advocacy and Public Policy Job Responsibilities: Executive Director, Small Grassroots Organization

Competency Category	Job Responsibilities
Advocacy and Public Policy	Nurtures and develops collaborative relationships between the organization and other congregations, agencies, and groups concerned with the public welfare within the communities it serves. Conducts in-services/seminars with community institutions to bring community awareness to refugee issues.

TABLE 5.3

Job Responsibilities Separated by Social Change Competency Category: Executive Director, Small Grassroots Organization

Competency Category	Job Responsibilities
Advocacy and Public Policy	Nurtures and develops collaborative relationships between the organization and other congregations, agencies, and groups concerned with the public welfare within the communities it serves.
	Conducts in-services/seminars with community institutions to bring community awareness to refugee issues.
Communications, Marketing, and Public Relations	Ensures that the organization and its mission, programs, and services are consistently presented with a strong, positive image to relevant stakeholders.
	Provides for information, publicity, and marketing designed to increase community understanding of the organization, its goals, and its services.
	Maintains active involvement in community organizations to establish the organization's identity within the community.
Direct Service	Develops programs and services that reflect the strategic direction for the organization.
	Observes professional confidentiality at all times; protects the rights of clients and their families.
Financial Management and Social Entrepreneurship	Recommends the yearly budget for board approval.
	Ensures that all financial, tax, risk, and facilities requirements for the organization are fully met and executed according to current laws and regulations.
	Develops and maintains sound financial practices, resulting in annual audits with no exceptions.
	Practices open and timely communication about financial issues with the board.
	Performs ongoing budget review
	Ensures the development of monthly, annual, and other periodic statements, budgets, and reports.
	Administers agency salary and benefits policy.
	Acts as the chief financial agent for the agency in ensuring the proper use of budgeted funds and maintenance of sound accounting procedures to safeguard the assets of the organization.
	Develops and presents budget requests to community funding organizations.
	Monitors contracts with other public or private organizations as authorized by the board of directors.

TABLE 5.3

Job Responsibilities Separated by Social Change Competency Category: Executive Director, Small Grassroots Organization, Cont'd

Competency Category	Job Responsibilities
Fundraising and Resource Development	Works in a mutually supportive manner with the board and staff in identifying resource requirements, researching funding sources, and establishing strategies to approach funders.
	Participates in fund development activities, including hosting events, making asks, authoring proposals, identifying funding sources, and undertaking other tasks required by the fundraising plan.
	Ensures the appropriate management of donor and fundraising documentation.
	Ensures the appropriate management of funds raised in accordance with the wishes of the donors.
	Ensures compliance with the reporting requirements of donors.
Human Resources Management and Volunteerism	Ensures the selection, supervision, and evaluation of quality staff to deliver services.
	Follows all authorized personnel policies and procedures that fully conform to current laws and regulations.
	Sees that an effective management team, with appropriate provision for succession, is in place.
	Oversees staff orientation, training, and development.
Information Management	Ensures that the organization maintains all necessary records.
Leadership and Governance	Supports board members in their communications with relevant organizations.
	Provides administrative support to the board.
	Keeps the board informed about key aspects of the functioning of the organization.
	Responds to information requests from the board.
	Openly provides all information the board requires to conduct its governance role.
	Acts as advisor to the board of directors in the carrying out of its policy-making responsibility.
	Serves as ex officio member of all board committees.
	Meets regularly with the board and the executive committee.
	Positively accepts and responds to direction and feedback from the board.
	Provides an information interface between the board and staff.
	Facilitates staff meetings.

TABLE 5.3
Job Responsibilities Separated by Social Change Competency Category: Executive Director, Small Grassroots Organization, Cont'd

Competency Category	Job Responsibilities
	Welcomes constructive feedback from staff and clients and works to provide an environment of openness and compassion.
	Conducts oneself in a manner that models professional behavior at all times.
Legal and Regulatory	Oversees the translation and implementation of board policies into effective action.
	Ensures that the organization obtains and keeps current all required licenses related to its work.
Planning and Evaluation	Works collaboratively with the board to ensure that a sound annual fundraising plan is established and implemented.
	Develops procedures for assessing the organization's effectiveness in achieving its goals.
	Establishes goals and objectives for each program and service.
	Implements an effective and cohesive management system to achieve these goals and objectives.

Fill in Job Responsibilities for Missing Competency Categories

After you separate job responsibilities by competency category, you may find that you are missing some job responsibilities for key competency categories. You can use the online competency-mapping supplement to fill in the job responsibilities for the missing competency categories (exhibit 5.2).

Identify Proficiency Levels Based on Action Words

Next, you'll identify action words within each job responsibility (exhibit 5.3). Then, you'll identify the proficiency level of each job responsibility (use table 5.1 as a guide for action words tied to each proficiency level). Remember, having the right action words clarifies roles and ensures that staff and volunteer proficiency levels match organization expectations.

Realign Action Words to Proficiency Level

Once you have identified proficiency levels for each responsibility, review the action words in the proficiency map to see if you need to realign action words, which will allow you to change the proficiency level for each competency category (exhibit 5.4). The proficiency level may need to be increased

EXHIBIT 5.2

Adding Job Responsibilities

When conducting the mapping exercise for the executive director of the small grassroots organization, the board noticed that the Information Management competency only included one job responsibility, but it was an important competency for the executive director to have. Therefore, they added another job responsibility for the Information Management competency using the examples provided in the online competency mapping supplement.

Added Job Responsibility: Executive Director, Small Grassroots Organization

Competency Category	Job Responsibility
Information Management	Ensures that all necessary records are maintained.
	ADDED: Oversees the information management systems within the organization, ensuring that staff and volunteers have access to computers and technology to carry out their jobs effectively.

EXHIBIT 5.3

Identifying Action Words

In the small grassroots organization, the board started with the Advocacy and Public Policy competency category and action words associated with that competency area. In the following table, action words in the executive director's position are shown in bold. The board identified the words *nurtures* and *develops* at the advanced proficiency level (4) and the action word *conducts* at the intermediate proficiency level (3).

Action Words and Associated Proficiency Level Identified

Competency Category	Job Responsibilities	Proficiency Levels
Advocacy and Public Policy	**Nurtures** and **develops** collaborative relationships between the organization and other congregations, agencies, and groups concerned with the public welfare within the communities it serves.	4, 4
	Conducts in-services/seminars with community institutions to bring community awareness to refugee issues.	3

EXHIBIT 5.4

Realigning the Proficiency Level

In the small grassroots organization, the board would like the executive director to demonstrate the advanced proficiency level in the Advocacy and Public Policy competency category, so the board must realign the action word *conducts* to an action word at the advanced proficiency level. The board selects the action word *leads*.

Realigned Proficiency Levels

Competency Category	Job Responsibilities Realigned	Proficiency Level
Advocacy and Public Policy	**Nurtures** and **develops** collaborative relationships between the organization and other congregations, agencies and groups concerned with the public welfare within the communities it serves.	4, 4
	Leads in-services/seminars with community institutions to bring community awareness to refugee issues.	4

---

or decreased depending on the level of responsibility you would like the employee or volunteer to have. You can use the action words provided in table 5.1 to realign the job responsibilities.

During the realignment process, the board realized it needed to revise the action words in the executive director's job description significantly. Table 5.4 shows the job responsibilities, highlighted action words, and proficiency levels before and after the realignment process within each competency category. As a reminder, the proficiency levels are 1 = fundamental awareness; 2 = novice; 3 = intermediate; 4 = advanced; 5 = expert.

At the end of the job description proficiency mapping and realignment process, you will have a proficiency map in the form of a table for each role in your organization. You will then use the proficiency maps to compare staff members' and volunteers' current and desired proficiencies later, during the Individual Professional Development Assessment and the process of creating an organizational Talent Map.

Table 5.5 shows the executive director's proficiency map for each competency category, based on the realigned job description. Each proficiency level shown is a rounded average of the levels of each responsibility in that category, rounded to the nearest whole number.

TABLE 5.4

Realigned Job Responsibilities: Executive Director, Small Grassroots Organization

Competency Category	Job Responsibilities Before	Proficiency Level Before	Job Responsibilities Realigned	Proficiency Level Realigned
Advocacy and Public Policy	**Nurtures** and **develops** collaborative relationships between the organization and other congregations, agencies, and groups concerned with the public welfare within the communities it serves.	4, 4	**Nurtures** and **develops** collaborative relationships between the organization and other congregations, agencies, and groups concerned with the public welfare within the communities it serves.	4, 4
Advocacy and Public Policy	**Conducts** in-services/seminars with community institutions to bring community awareness to refugee issues.	3	**Leads** in-services/seminars with community institutions to bring community awareness to refugee issues.	4
Communications, Marketing, and Public Relations	**Ensures** that the organization and its mission, programs, and services are consistently presented with a strong, positive image to relevant stakeholders.	4	**Ensures** that the organization and its mission, programs, and services are consistently presented with a strong, positive image to relevant stakeholders.	4

TABLE 5.4
Realigned Job Responsibilities: Executive Director, Small Grassroots Organization, Cont'd

Competency Category	Job Responsibilities Before	Proficiency Level Before	Job Responsibilities Realigned	Proficiency Level Realigned
Communications, Marketing, and Public Relations	**Provides** information, publicity, and marketing designed to increase community understanding of the organization, its goals, and its services.	3	**Creates** information, publicity, and marketing designed to increase community understanding of the organization, its goals, and its services.	4
Communications, Marketing, and Public Relations	**Maintains** active involvement in community organizations to establish the organization's identity within the community.	3	**Establishes** the organization's identity within the community by **maintaining** active involvement in community organizations.	4, 3
Financial Management and Social Entrepreneurship	**Recommends** the yearly budget for board approval.	5	**Recommends** the yearly budget for board approval.	5
Financial Management and Social Entrepreneurship	**Ensures** that all financial, tax, risk, and facilities requirements for the organization are fully met and executed according to current laws and regulations.	4	**Analyzes** all financial, tax, risk, and facilities requirements for the organization according to current laws and regulations.	5
Financial Management and Social Entrepreneurship	**Develops** and **maintains** sound financial practices, resulting in annual audits with no exceptions.	4, 3	**Develops** and **maintains** sound financial practices, resulting in annual audits with no exceptions.	4, 3

TABLE 5.4

Realigned Job Responsibilities: Executive Director, Small Grassroots Organization, Cont'd

Competency Category	Job Responsibilities Before	Proficiency Level Before	Job Responsibilities Realigned	Proficiency Level Realigned
Financial Management and Social Entrepreneurship	**Practices** open and timely communication about financial issues with the board.	3	**Facilitates** open and timely communication about financial issues within the board.	4
Financial Management and Social Entrepreneurship	**Performs** ongoing budget review.	3	**Leads** ongoing budget review.	4
Financial Management and Social Entrepreneurship	**Ensures** the development of monthly, annual, and other periodic statements, budgets, and reports.	4	**Synthesizes** monthly, annual, and other periodic statements, budgets, and reports.	5
Financial Management and Social Entrepreneurship	**Administers** agency salary and benefits policy.	4	**Administers and evaluates** agency salary and benefits policy.	4, 5
Financial Management and Social Entrepreneurship	**Acts** as the chief financial agent for the agency in **ensuring** the proper use of budgeted funds and **maintenance** of sound accounting procedures to safeguard the assets of the organization.	3, 4, 3	As chief financial agent, **safeguards** the assets of the organization **ensuring** the proper use of budgeted funds and **maintenance** of sound accounting procedures.	5, 4, 3
Financial Management and Social Entrepreneurship	**Develops** and **presents** budget requests to community funding organizations.	4, 4	**Develops, presents, and evaluates** budget requests to community funding organizations.	4, 4, 5

TABLE 5.4

Realigned Job Responsibilities: Executive Director, Small Grassroots Organization, Cont'd

Competency Category	Job Responsibilities Before	Proficiency Level Before	Job Responsibilities Realigned	Proficiency Level Realigned
Financial Management and Social Entrepreneurship	**Monitors** contracts with other public or private organizations as authorized by the board of directors.	3	**Establishes** contracts with other public or private organizations as authorized by the board of directors.	4
Fundraising and Resource Development	**Works in a mutually supportive manner** with board and staff in **identifying** resource requirements, **researching** funding sources, and **establishing** strategies to approach funders.	3, 4, 3, 4	**Trains** board and staff in identifying resource requirements, researching funding sources, and establishing strategies to approach funders.	5
Fundraising and Resource Development	**Participates** in fund development activities, including **hosting** events, **making** asks, **authoring** proposals, **identifying** funding sources, and **undertaking** other tasks required by the plan.	3, 3, 4, 3, 4, 3	**Facilitates** fund development activities, including **hosting** events, **making** asks, **authoring** proposals, **identifying** funding sources, and **undertaking** other tasks required by the plan.	4, 3, 4, 3, 4
Fundraising and Resource Development	**Ensures** the appropriate management of donor and fundraising documentation.	4	**Compares** and **selects** the appropriate management of donor and fundraising documentation.	5, 4

TABLE 5.4

Realigned Job Responsibilities: Executive Director, Small Grassroots Organization, Cont'd

Competency Category	Job Responsibilities Before	Proficiency Level Before	Job Responsibilities Realigned	Proficiency Level Realigned
Fundraising and Resource Development	**Ensures** the appropriate management of funds raised in accordance with the wishes of the donors.	4	**Recommends** the appropriate management of funds raised in accordance with the wishes of the donors.	5
Fundraising and Resource Development	**Ensures** compliance with the reporting requirements of donors.	4	**Masters** compliance reporting requirements of donors.	5
Direct Service	**Develops** programs and services that reflect the strategic direction for the organization.	4	**Develops** programs and services that reflect the strategic direction for the organization.	4
Direct Service	**Observes** professional confidentiality at all times; **protects** the rights of clients and their families, and **ensures** that confidentiality is maintained.	1, 5, 4	**Demonstrates** professional confidentiality at all times; **protects** the rights of clients and their families, and **ensures** that confidentiality is maintained.	4, 5, 4
Human Resources Management and Volunteerism	**Ensures** the selection, supervision, and evaluation of quality staff to deliver services.	4	**Ensures** the selection, supervision, and evaluation of quality staff to deliver services.	4

TABLE 5.4
Realigned Job Responsibilities: Executive Director, Small Grassroots Organization, Cont'd

Competency Category	Job Responsibilities Before	Proficiency Level Before	Job Responsibilities Realigned	Proficiency Level Realigned
Human Resources Management and Volunteerism	**Follows** all authorized personnel policies and procedures that fully conform to current laws and regulations.	2	**Implements** personnel policies and procedures and **ensures** that they fully conform to current laws and regulations.	4, 4
Human Resources Management and Volunteerism	**Sees** that an effective management team, with appropriate provision for succession, is in place.	1	**Leads** an effective management team and **ensures** that appropriate provision for succession is in place.	4, 4
Human Resources Management and Volunteerism	**Oversees** staff orientation, training, and development.	4	**Oversees** staff orientation, training, and development.	4
Information Management	**Ensures** that the organization maintains all necessary records.	4	**Ensures** that the organization maintains all necessary records.	4
Information Management	(Only one responsibility was originally designated in this category.)		**Oversees** the information management systems within the organization, **ensuring** that staff and volunteers have access to computers and technology to effectively carry out their jobs.	4, 4

TABLE 5.4
Realigned Job Responsibilities: Executive Director, Small Grassroots Organization, Cont'd

Competency Category	Job Responsibilities Before	Proficiency Level Before	Job Responsibilities Realigned	Proficiency Level Realigned
Leadership and Governance	**Supports** board members in their communications with relevant organizations.	2	**Advises** board members in their communications with relevant organizations.	4
Leadership and Governance	**Provides** administrative support to the board.	3	**Provides** administrative support to the board by **preparing** information about key aspects of the functioning of the organization.	3, 4
Leadership and Governance	**Keeps** the board informed about key aspects of the functioning of the organization.	3	**Prepares** information for the board about key aspects of the functioning of the organization.	4
Leadership and Governance	**Responds** to information requests from the board.	2	(Combined with responsibility above)	
Leadership and Governance	Openly **provides** all information the board requires to conduct its governance role.	3	(Combined with responsibility above)	
Leadership and Governance	**Acts** as advisor to the board of directors in the carrying out of its policy-making responsibility.	3	**Leads** the board of directors in the carrying out of its policy-making responsibility.	4

TABLE 5.4

Realigned Job Responsibilities: Executive Director, Small Grassroots Organization, Cont'd

Competency Category	Job Responsibilities Before	Proficiency Level Before	Job Responsibilities Realigned	Proficiency Level Realigned
Leadership and Governance	**Serves** as ex officio member of all board committees.	3	**Serves** as ex officio member of all board committees.	3
Leadership and Governance	**Meets** regularly with the board and the executive committee.	3	**Meets** regularly with the board and the executive committee.	3
Leadership and Governance	Positively **accepts** and **responds** to direction and feedback from the board.	2, 2	**Responds** to direction and feedback from the board in a positive way.	2
Leadership and Governance	**Provides** the interface between the board and staff, **ensuring** that information is exchanged between the two groups.	3, 4	**Provides** the interface between the board and staff, **ensuring** that information is exchanged between the two groups.	3, 4
Leadership and Governance	**Facilitates** staff meetings.	4	**Facilitates** staff meetings.	4
Leadership and Governance	**Welcomes** constructive feedback from staff and clients and **works to provide** an environment of openness and compassion.	2, 3	**Demonstrates** an environment of openness and compassion with staff and clients.	4
Leadership and Governance	**Conducts** oneself in a manner that models professional behavior at all times.	3	**Models** professional behavior at all times.	4

TABLE 5.4

Realigned Job Responsibilities: Executive Director, Small Grassroots Organization, Cont'd

Competency Category	Job Responsibilities Before	Proficiency Level Before	Job Responsibilities Realigned	Proficiency Level Realigned
Legal and Regulatory	**Oversees** the translation and implementation of board policies into effective action.	4	**Oversees** the translation and implementation of board policies into effective action.	4
Legal and Regulatory	**Ensures** that the organization obtains and keeps all required licenses related to its work.	4	**Ensures** that the organization obtains and keeps all required licenses related to its work.	4
Planning and Evaluation	**Works** collaboratively with the board to **ensure** that a sound annual fundraising plan is established and implemented.	3, 4	**Collaborates** with the board and **advises** the staff in establishing and implementing a sound annual fundraising plan.	4, 4
Planning and Evaluation	**Develops** procedures for assessing the organization's effectiveness in achieving its goals.	4	**Compares and selects** procedures for assessing the organization's effectiveness in achieving its goals.	5, 4
Planning and Evaluation	**Establishes** goals and objectives for each program and service.	4	**Evaluates** goals and objectives created for each program and service.	5
Planning and Evaluation	**Implements** an effective and cohesive management system to achieve these goals and objectives.	4	**Implements** and **integrates** an effective management system to achieve these goals and objectives.	4, 5

TABLE 5.5
Position Proficiency Levels: Executive Director, Small Grassroots Organization

Competency Category	Position Proficiency Level
Advocacy and Public Policy	4
Communications, Marketing, and Public Relations	4
Financial Management and Social Entrepreneurship	5
Fundraising and Resource Development	5
Direct Service	4
Human Resources Management and Volunteerism	4
Information Management	4
Leadership and Governance	4
Legal and Regulatory	4
Planning and Evaluation	5

Revising Job Descriptions

Proficiency mapping is an important part of revising organizational job descriptions. You may find that you need to revise the language in job descriptions to match the required proficiency levels of the position. In the example we provided in table 5.4, the executive director needed to be at the advanced proficiency level in the Human Resources Management and Volunteerism competency category; however the before job description reads, "**Follows** all authorized personnel policies and procedures that fully conform to current laws and regulations." In order to increase the proficiency level of the human resources management job responsibility, the board needed to revise the word *follows*. The sentence in the job description was revised to read "**Implements** personnel policies and procedures and **ensures** that they fully conform to current laws and regulations."

During the mapping process, you may find that there are competency categories that are important to a position but missing from the job description. In the example in exhibit 5.2, we demonstrated that by separating the executive director's responsibilities by competency category, the Information Management competency only had one responsibility listed and needed one more.

If there are discrepancies in job descriptions, such as in a situation where an employee is doing far more than what their job description portrays, you will need to update the job description. If an employee is doing more than what is in their job description, consider a raise or an increase in title. If you find a situation where an employee is doing far fewer activities than what is listed in their job description, the employee may need a performance improvement discussion. In the second situation (where the employee is doing far fewer activities), it may be the case that the activities the employee is performing are far more demanding than previously thought. Be sure to assess all the potential reasons why an employee's or volunteer's responsibilities are not in alignment with his or her job description. After the work the board did in the small grassroots organization, they were able to write a more accurate job description for the executive director. Exhibit 5.5 shows the new, realigned description that was originally presented in exhibit 4.2.

EXHIBIT 5.5

Sample Job Description (Realigned)

Executive Director, Small Grassroots Organization

Job Title: Executive Director

Status: Exempt / Full-time

Salary Range: $45,000–$55,000

Reports to: Board of Directors

Supervisory Responsibilities: All Program Managers, Office Staff

About the Organization

Our vision is that every young refugee will have the opportunity to fully contribute to the local and global community. Our mission is to provide exemplary, wrap-around services to prepare young refugees to succeed in school and in life.

Position Information

The executive director develops and manages all program activities of the agency in accordance with its stated purpose and within the general policies as formulated by the board of directors. The executive director appropriately uses the agency's financial resources, staff and volunteers in providing overall direction, leadership, and coordination of organizational activities. The executive director also ensures that staff and volunteers carry out the mission and vision of the agency in its daily operations.

Responsibilities

Advocacy and Public Policy

- Nurtures and develops collaborative relationships between the organization and other congregations, agencies, and groups concerned with the public welfare within the communities it serves.

- Leads in-services/seminars with community institutions to bring community awareness to refugee issues.

EXHIBIT 5.5
Sample Job Description (Realigned), Cont'd

Communications, Marketing, and Public Relations

- Ensures the organization and its mission, programs, and services are consistently presented with a strong, positive image to relevant stakeholders.
- Creates information, publicity, and marketing designed to increase community understanding of the organization, its goals, and its services.
- Establishes the organization's identity within the community by maintaining active involvement in community organizations.

Financial Management and Social Entrepreneurship

- Recommends the yearly budget for board approval.
- Analyzes all financial, tax, risk, and facilities requirements for the organization according to current laws and regulations.
- Develops and maintains sound financial practices, resulting in annual audits with no exceptions.
- Facilitates open and timely communication about financial issues with the board.
- Leads ongoing budget review.
- Synthesizes monthly, annual, and other periodic statements, budgets, and reports.
- Administers and evaluates agency salary and benefits policy.
- As chief financial agent, safeguards the assets of the organization ensuring the proper use of budgeted finds and maintenance of sound accounting procedures.
- Develops, presents, and evaluates budget requests to community funding organizations.
- Establishes contracts with other public or private organizations as authorized by the board of directors.

Fundraising and Resource Development

- Trains board and staff in identifying resource requirements, researching funding sources, and establishing strategies to approach funders.
- Facilitates fund development activities, including hosting events, making asks, authoring proposals, identifying funding sources, and undertaking other tasks required by the plan.
- Compares and selects the appropriate management of donor and fundraising documentation.
- Recommends the appropriate management of funds raised in accordance with the wishes of the donors.
- Masters compliance reporting requirements of donors.

EXHIBIT 5.5
Sample Job Description (Realigned), Cont'd

Direct Service

- Develops programs and services that reflect the strategic direction for the organization.
- Demonstrates professional confidentiality at all times; protects the rights of clients and their families, and ensures that confidentiality is maintained.

Human Resources Management and Volunteerism

- Ensures the selection, supervision, and evaluation of quality staff to deliver services.
- Implements personnel policies and procedures and ensures they fully conform to current laws and regulations.
- Leads an effective management team and ensures that appropriate provision for succession is in place.
- Oversees staff orientation, training, and development.

Information Management

- Ensures that the organization maintains all necessary records.
- Oversees the information management systems within the organization ensuring that staff and volunteers have access to computers and technology to effectively carry out their jobs.

Leadership and Governance

- Advises board members in their communications with relevant organizations.
- Provides administrative support to the board by preparing information about key aspects of the functioning of the organization.
- Prepares information for the board about key aspects of the functioning of the organization.
- Leads the board of directors in the carrying out of its policy-making responsibility.
- Serves as ex officio member of all board committees.
- Meets regularly with the board and the executive committee.
- Responds to direction and feedback from the Board in a positive way.
- Provides the interface between the board and staff, ensuring that information is exchanged between the two groups.
- Facilitates staff meetings.
- Demonstrates an environment of openness and compassion with staff and clients.
- Models professional behavior at all times.

EXHIBIT 5.5
Sample Job Description (Realigned), Cont'd

Legal and Regulatory

- Oversees the translation and implementation of board policies into effective action.
- Ensures that all required licenses are obtained and kept current related to the organization's work.

Planning and Evaluation

- Collaborates with the board and advises the staff in establishing and implementing a sound annual fundraising plan.
- Compares and selects procedures for assessing the organization's effectiveness in achieving its goals.
- Evaluates goals and objectives created for each program and service.
- Implements and integrates an effective and cohesive management system to achieve these goals and objectives.

Qualifications

- At least five years of experience working in a nonprofit setting.

Educational Requirements

- Bachelor's degree required.

Work Environment

- Office environment with occasional meetings at various community organization locations.

Proficiency Mapping in Practice

We've looked in detail at the proficiency mapping process using the job description of an executive director of a small grassroots organization. We'll now provide some sample proficiency maps for positions within the other three types of social change organizations: volunteer-run, midsized, and grantmaking. We will also provide examples of organization-wide proficiency mapping results for all four types of organizations. Please remember that these examples and proficiency levels vary based on the size of the organization, the type of organization, and the responsibilities tied to the position. In addition, for demonstration purposes, we included at least one responsibility from every competency category in the sample job descriptions. There is also an online resource at talent4socialchange.org for sample proficiency maps of the following positions:

- Board Chair

- Board Treasurer

- Executive Director

- Chief Operating Officer/Operations Manager

- Human Resources Manager

- Development Director

- Development Coordinator

- Program Manager

- Volunteer Coordinator

- Administrative Assistant

- Marketing Coordinator

- Program Officer

- Program Associate

- Director of Donor Services

- Evaluator

Proficiency Mapping: Volunteer-Run Organization

The president/board chair of the volunteer-run organization completed proficiency mapping for his seven board members. He first separated the job responsibilities by competency category, filled in job responsibilities for the missing competency categories, identified proficiency levels based on job responsibility action words, and realigned action words in the job descriptions to reflect the role's required proficiency level for each competency. Table 5.6 shows the proficiency mapping results for the entire organization (1 = fundamental awareness; 2 = novice; 3 = intermediate; 4 = advanced; 5 = expert).

Table 5.7 shows the job responsibilities, highlighted action words, and proficiency levels before and after the realignment process within each competency category for the president/board chair. The before job description is shown in exhibit 4.1.

The board believed that some of the job responsibilities were in alignment with the proficiency levels the board president should possess, and these were not revised or were revised slightly. Thirteen of the eighteen

TABLE 5.6 Proficiency Mapping Results: Volunteer-Run Organization

	President/ Board Chair	Treasurer	Site Director (2 positions)	Marketing Director	Volunteer Director	IT Director
Advocacy and Public Policy	4	3	3	3	5	1
Communications, Marketing, and Public Relations	4	3	3	5	4	4
Financial Management and Social Entrepreneurship	5	5	3	3	3	1
Fundraising and Resource Development	4	3	3	3	3	1
Direct Service	4	3	4	4	4	2
Human Resources Management and Volunteerism	4	3	4	3	5	2
Information Management	4	5	4	5	4	5
Leadership and Governance	4	4	4	3	4	3
Legal and Regulatory	5	4	3	3	4	3
Planning and Evaluation	4	4	5	5	4	4

TABLE 5.7
Proficiency Mapping: President/Board Chair, Volunteer-Run Organization

Competency Category	Job Responsibilities Before	Proficiency Level Before	Job Responsibilities Realigned	Proficiency Level Realigned
Advocacy and Public Policy	(No responsibilities were originally designated in this category)		**Advances** the organization's community outreach and advocacy efforts to further the awareness and cultural traditions of music.	4
Communications, Marketing, and Public Relations	**Responds** to all community requests.	2	**Identifies** and **responds** to all community requests.	4, 2
	Orders all signs.	4	**Orders** all signs.	4
Communications, Marketing, and Public Relations	**Leads** correspondence for festival as needed.	4	**Leads** correspondence for festival as needed.	4
Financial Management and Social Entrepreneurship	**Works** with treasurer to establish and implement budget.	3	**Analyzes** and **troubleshoots** budget.	5, 5
Fundraising and Resource Development	**Recruits, renews,** and **develops** partners and sponsors for festival.	4, 4, 4	**Recruits** partners and sponsors for festival.	4

TABLE 5.7

Proficiency Mapping: President/Board Chair, Volunteer-Run Organization, Cont'd

Competency Category	Job Responsibilities Before	Proficiency Level Before	Job Responsibilities Realigned	Proficiency Level Realigned
Direct Service	**Oversees** all areas of the festival.	4	**Oversees** all areas of the festival.	4
Direct Service	**Works** with beverage directors to ensure beverage services.	3	**Advises** beverage directors to ensure beverage services.	4
Human Resources Management and Volunteerism	**Conducts** interviews as needed.	3	**Leads** volunteer interviews as needed.	4
Human Resources Management and Volunteerism	**Presents** at volunteer kick-off and orientation.	4	**Presents** at volunteer kick-off and orientation.	4
Human Resources Management and Volunteerism	**Schedules** all beer volunteers.	3	**Selects** all beer volunteers.	4
Information Management	**Updates** website as needed (shared with Marketing and IT).	4	**Prepares** updates for website as needed (shared with Marketing and IT).	4
Leadership and Governance	**Develops** agendas for all meetings and **conducts** meetings.	4, 3	**Develops** agendas for all meetings and **conducts** meetings.	4, 3
Leadership and Governance	**Supports** all directors and team leads as needed.	2	**Advises** all directors and team leads.	4
Leadership and Governance	(Only two responsibilities were originally designated in this category.)		**Leads** the board in their fiscal, governance, and legal responsibilities (NEW).	4

TABLE 5.7

Proficiency Mapping: President/Board Chair, Volunteer-Run Organization, Cont'd

Competency Category	Job Responsibilities Before	Proficiency Level Before	Job Responsibilities Realigned	Proficiency Level Realigned
Leadership and Governance			**Oversees** the recruitment and selection of board members (NEW).	4
Legal and Regulatory	**Works** with insurance provider(s) for all insurance.	3	**Evaluates** all insurance options and **troubleshoots** risks with insurance provider.	5, 5
Planning and Evaluation	(No responsibilities were originally designated in this category.)		**Ensures** that annual and strategic planning are conducted on an ongoing basis.	4
Sub-competencies				
Initiative	(No sub-competencies were originally included in the job description.)		**Starts** new projects with little to no supervision.	4
Crisis Management			Calmly **handles** worst-case scenarios and **implements** changes quickly.	3, 4
Mentoring			**Develops, supports,** and **builds** relationships with colleagues and constituents.	4, 2, 4

responsibilities were realigned. For example, both the Financial Management and the Legal and Regulatory proficiency levels were too low and needed to be increased during the realignment process. Also, there were no Advocacy and Public Policy or Planning and Evaluation competencies in the first job description and there were no sub-competencies; therefore, these job responsibilities were added at the advanced proficiency level. After the proficiency mapping process was complete, the board chair added realigned job responsibilities from table 5.7 to his before job description shown in exhibit 4.1, to create the realigned job description shown in exhibit 5.6.

EXHIBIT 5.6
Sample Job Description (Realigned)

President/Board Chair, Volunteer-Run Organization

Job Title: President/Board Chair

Status: Volunteer

Salary Range: None

Reports to: None

Supervisory Responsibilities: Board of Directors

About the Organization

The goal of the Music Festival is to produce a quality music festival that enhances the community through entertainment, tourism, education, and philanthropy. The Music Festival is 100 percent volunteer driven and has continued to offer an outstanding event in September each year. With 2,000 attendees the first year, the Music Festival has grown into a much larger than regional draw for the community over the years.

About the Position

The president/board chair is responsible for directing the festival and leading the board of directors. Each board member is expected to attend monthly meetings, three days of the festival, volunteer orientation, the board of directors' retreat, and the volunteer kick-off party and to participate in the conversation and planning of making a better event.

Responsibilities

Advocacy and Public Policy

- Advances the organization's community outreach and advocacy efforts to further the awareness and cultural traditions of music.

EXHIBIT 5.6
Sample Job Description (Realigned), Cont'd

Communication, Marketing, and Public Relations

- Identifies and responds to all community requests.
- Orders all signs.
- Leads correspondence for festival as needed.

Financial Management and Social Entrepreneurship

- Analyzes and troubleshoots budget with treasurer.

Fundraising and Resource Development

- Recruits partners and sponsors for festival.

Direct Service

- Oversees all areas of the festival.
- Advises beverage directors to ensure beverage services.

Human Resources Management and Volunteerism

- Leads volunteer interviews as needed.
- Presents at volunteer kick-off and orientation.
- Selects all beer volunteers.

Information Management

- Prepares updates for website as needed (shared with Marketing and IT).

Leadership and Governance

- Develops agendas for all meetings and conducts meetings.
- Advises all directors and team leads.
- Leads the board in their fiscal, governance, and legal responsibilities.
- Oversees the recruitment and selection of board members.

Legal and Regulatory

- Evaluates all insurance options and troubleshoots risks with insurance provider.

EXHIBIT 5.6
Sample Job Description (Realigned), Cont'd

Planning and Evaluation

- Ensures that annual and strategic planning are conducted on an ongoing basis.

Initiative

- Starts new projects with little to no supervision.

Crisis Management

- Calmly handles worst-case scenarios and implements changes quickly.

Mentoring

- Develops, supports, and builds relationships with colleagues and constituents.

Qualifications

- At least two years of previous nonprofit board experience.

Educational Requirements

- Bachelor's degree required.

Work Environment

- Because this is a volunteer position, you will work in your own home setting. Board meetings take place at various locations throughout the community.
- The position requires access to transportation to visit festival site and vendors; exposure to heat, cold, inclement weather conditions; and standing for periods of time during the festival.
- Must be able to lift 30 pounds.

Proficiency Mapping: Small Grassroots Organization

The executive director of the small grassroots organization completed the proficiency mapping process for her five employees. She first separated the job responsibilities by competency category, filled in job responsibilities for the missing competency categories, identified proficiency levels based on job responsibility action words, and realigned action words to their competency proficiency levels. Table 5.8 shows the proficiency mapping results for the entire organization (1 = fundamental awareness; 2 = novice; 3 = intermediate; 4 = advanced; 5 = expert).

TABLE 5.8 Proficiency Mapping Results: Small Grassroots Organization

	Executive Director	Community Worker	Program Coordinator	Community Engagement Supervisor	Education Supervisor
Advocacy and Public Policy	4	3	4	4	2
Communications, Marketing, and Public Relations	4	3	3	4	2
Financial Management and Social Entrepreneurship	5	1	2	2	2
Fundraising and Resource Development	5	1	2	4	1
Direct Service	4	4	5	3	5
Human Resources Management and Volunteerism	4	3	4	5	4
Information Management	4	1	1	1	2
Leadership and Governance	4	1	3	1	2
Legal and Regulatory	4	2	2	3	2
Planning and Evaluation	5	4	4	4	4

To review the proficiency mapping process for the executive director of the small grassroots organization, see table 5.4, and to review the realigned job description for the position, see exhibit 5.5.

Proficiency Mapping: Midsized Organization

The executive director of the midsized organization worked with her senior staff, including the development director and office manager, to complete proficiency mapping for her eleven employees. They separated the job responsibilities by competency category; then they filled in job responsibilities for the missing competency category. Next, they identified proficiency levels based on job responsibility action words, and last they revised action words to align more effectively with each of her competency's proficiency levels. Table 5.9 shows the proficiency mapping results for the entire organization (1 = fundamental awareness; 2 = novice; 3 = intermediate; 4 = advanced; 5 = expert).

We'll now walk you through the proficiency mapping for the development coordinator's position. In exhibit 4.3 we provided the development coordinator's job description. The development director (the coordinator's direct supervisor) followed the steps we've described and quickly noticed that the development coordinator's job description included higher proficiency levels than needed. In fact, the proficiency levels identified in the job description were, in many cases, at the same level as those of the development director. Table 5.10 shows the proficiency levels of the development coordinator position before the realignment process, compared to the development director's proficiency levels after the alignment process.

Therefore, during the alignment process, the development director made sure to realign the job responsibilities to lower proficiency levels. Table 5.11 shows the development coordinator's job responsibilities and proficiency levels before and after the realignment process.

Then the development director revised the development coordinator's job description based on the realignment (shown in exhibit 5.7). The development director reviewed the proficiency mapping results and revised job description with the development coordinator.

Proficiency Mapping: Grantmaking Organization

The president of the grantmaking organization completed proficiency mapping for her four employees. She first separated the job responsibilities by competency category, filled in job responsibilities for the missing competency categories, identified proficiency levels based on job responsibility action words, and realigned action words in the job descriptions to the role's required proficiency level for each competency. Table 5.12 shows the proficiency map for the grantmaking organization (1 = fundamental awareness; 2 = novice; 3 = intermediate; 4 = advanced; 5 = expert).

TABLE 5.9 Proficiency Mapping Results: Midsized Organization

	Outreach Manager	Volunteer Coordinator	Program Coordinator	Development Director	Outreach Director	Special Projects Manager	Operations Manager	Office Manager/HR	Development Coordinator	Program Assistant	Operations Assistant
Advocacy and Public Policy	4	3	3	3	3	3	3	3	2	1	2
Communications, Marketing, and Public Relations	3	4	3	4	5	3	3	3	2	2	2
Financial Management and Social Entrepreneurship	3	2	4	4	4	3	3	3	3	2	2
Fundraising and Resource Development	3	2	4	5	3	3	3	2	3	1	2
Direct Service	4	3	4	2	2	4	4	2	1	3	3
Human Resources Management and Volunteerism	3	4	4	3	3	4	4	4	3	2	3
Information Management	3	4	3	3	4	3	3	3	4	3	3
Leadership and Governance	3	3	3	4	3	3	3	2	2	2	2
Legal and Regulatory	3	2	3	3	3	3	3	4	2	1	2
Planning and Evaluation	3	3	3	4	4	3	3	3	3	3	2

TABLE 5.10

Proficiency Level Comparisons between Development Coordinator and Development Director

Competency Category	Proficiency Mapping Before Alignment (Dev. Coordinator)	Proficiency Mapping After Alignment (Dev. Director)
Advocacy and Public Policy	3	3
Communications, Marketing, and Public Relations	3	4
Financial Management and Social Entrepreneurship	4	4
Fundraising and Resource Development	3, 5, 3, 4	5
Direct Service	(No responsibilities were originally designated in this category.)	2
Human Resources Management and Volunteerism	4	3
Information Management	3, 4, 2	3
Leadership and Governance	4, 4	3
Legal and Regulatory	4	4
Planning and Evaluation	3	4

We'll focus on the proficiency map and job description realignment process more specifically for the program associate position within the grantmaking organization. The president followed the proficiency mapping steps we've described, and table 5.13 shows the program associate's job responsibilities before and after realignment.

The competency mapping process revealed that the program associate's job description (originally shown in exhibit 4.4) was lacking key competency categories such as Financial Management and Social Entrepreneurship, Fundraising and Resource Development, Human Resources Management and Volunteerism, and Legal and Regulatory. The mapping process allowed the president to add several new job responsibilities to the program associate's job description. The president increased the proficiency levels of some competency categories and reduced the proficiency levels of less important responsibilities. The president then put all the realigned job responsibilities into a revised job description, shown in exhibit 5.8.

TABLE 5.11
Proficiency Mapping: Development Coordinator, Midsized Organization

Competency Category	Job Responsibilities Before	Proficiency Level Before	Job Responsibilities Realigned	Proficiency Level Realigned
Advocacy and Public Policy	**Maintains** awareness of how advocacy efforts may bring in prospective donors.	3	**Recognizes** how advocacy efforts may bring in prospective donors.	2
Communications, Marketing, and Public Relations	**Coordinates** appeal mailings in-house and **communicates** with printers.	3, 3	**Assists** with appeal mailings in-house and **communicates** with printers.	2, 3
Financial Management and Social Entrepreneurship	**Ensures** that gifts are posted for accountant review.	4	**Keeps** gift postings current for accountant review.	3
Fundraising and Resource Development	**Coordinates** donor recognition programs and thank-you process.	3	**Coordinates** donor recognition programs and thank-you process.	3
Fundraising and Resource Development	**Cultivates** volunteer groups.	5	**Creates** volunteer groups.	4
Fundraising and Resource Development	**Prepares** letters of appreciation to be sent to contributors in collaboration with the development assistant.	4	**Prepares** letters of appreciation to be sent to contributors in collaboration with the development assistant.	4
Fundraising and Resource Development	**Understands** fund development, stewardship, and community outreach.	4	**Exhibits** proficiency in fund development, stewardship, and community outreach.	3

TABLE 5.11
Proficiency Mapping: Development Coordinator, Midsized Organization, Cont'd

Competency Category	Job Responsibilities Before	Proficiency Level Before	Job Responsibilities Realigned	Proficiency Level Realigned
Direct Service	None		**Observes** food insecurities to better understand organizational mission.	1
Human Resources Management and Volunteerism	**Supervises** fund development assistant and interns.	4	**Monitors** fund development assistant and interns.	3
Information Management	**Pulls** data **reports** from database system and prepares reports for development director.	3, 2	**Identifies** data reports from database system and **prepares** reports for development director.	4, 4
Information Management	**Assists** in maintaining records of contributions and grants.	2	**Oversees** the maintenance records of contributions and grants.	4
Leadership and Governance	**Interfaces** and **establishes** rapport with board members and donors.	3, 4	**Recognizes** organizational values and represents them to board members and donors.	2
Legal and Regulatory	**Understands** the fundraising solicitation regulations and how they apply in the organizational setting.	4	**Supports** fundraising solicitation regulations and how they apply in the organizational setting.	2

TABLE 5.11

Proficiency Mapping: Development Coordinator, Midsized Organization, Cont'd

Competency Category	Job Responsibilities Before	Proficiency Level Before	Job Responsibilities Realigned	Proficiency Level Realigned
Planning and Evaluation	**Works** with development director to establish strategy to meet annual fund goals for the organization.	3	**Works** with development director to establish strategy to meet annual fund goals for the organization.	3
Sub-competencies				
Youth Cultural Competency	Effectively **interacts** with a diverse population of youth and college-age volunteers from a variety of ethnic and socioeconomic backgrounds.	3	Effectively **interacts** with a diverse population of youth and college-age volunteers from a variety of ethnic and socioeconomic backgrounds.	3
Public Speaking	Has experience speaking in front of groups, **making** presentations and **leading** groups of 5 to 300 consisting of all ages and backgrounds.	4, 4	Has experience speaking in front of groups, **making** presentations and **leading** groups of 5 to 300 consisting of all ages and backgrounds.	4, 4
Flexibility and Adaptability	Is organized and has the ability to **work** in a fast-paced, ever-changing work environment. Possesses skills in project and time management.	3	Is organized and has the ability to **work** in a fast-paced, ever-changing work environment. Possesses skills in project and time management.	3

TABLE 5.11
Proficiency Mapping: Development Coordinator, Midsized Organization, Cont'd

Competency Category	Job Responsibilities Before	Proficiency Level Before	Job Responsibilities Realigned	Proficiency Level Realigned
Flexibility and Adaptability	Can **work** independently as well as collaboratively.	3	Can **work** independently as well as collaboratively.	3
Problem Solving	**Demonstrates** the ability to solve problems, **analyzes** systems and data, and **makes** suggestions for improvement.	4, 5, 4	**Solves** problems, **analyzes** systems and data, and **makes** suggestions for improvement.	5, 5, 4

EXHIBIT 5.7
Sample Job Description (Realigned)

Development Coordinator, Midsized Organization

Job Title: Development Coordinator

Department: Development

Status: Exempt / Full-time

Salary Range: $30,000–$42,000

Reports to: Development Director

Supervisory Responsibilities: Development Assistant, Development Interns

About the Organization

For twelve years, the Community Food Bank has been a force for attacking hunger to help young people live well. Hunger is a community problem, with a community solution.

Our organization is an equal opportunity employer. Our policy is to provide equal employment opportunity to all qualified persons without regard to race, creed, color, religious belief, gender, age,

EXHIBIT 5.7
Sample Job Description (Realigned), Cont'd

national origin, ancestry, sexual orientation, gender identity, qualifying physical or mental disability, height, weight, marital status, or veteran status.

Position Information

This position coordinates annual fundraising for the organization, specifically working with individuals, corporations, and community groups, including but not limited to semi-annual appeals, stewardship, major donor support, corporate matches, monthly donors, direct mailings, and third-party events. The development coordinator will support the development director and supervise the development assistant in these efforts.

Responsibilities

Advocacy and Public Policy

- Recognizes how advocacy efforts may bring in prospective donors.

Communications, Marketing, and Public Relations

- Assists with appeal mailings in-house and communicates with printers.

Financial Management and Social Entrepreneurship

- Keeps gift postings current for accountant review.

Fundraising and Resource Development

- Coordinates donor recognition programs and thank-you processes.
- Creates volunteer groups.
- Prepares letters of appreciation to be sent to contributors in collaboration with the development assistant.
- Exhibits proficiency in fund development, stewardship, and community outreach.

Direct Service

- Observes food insecurities to better understand organizational mission.

Human Resources Management and Volunteerism

- Monitors fund development assistant and interns.

Information Technology

- Identifies data reports from database system and prepares reports for development director.
- Oversees the maintenance records of contributions and grants.

EXHIBIT 5.7
Sample Job Description (Realigned), Cont'd

Leadership and Governance

- Recognizes organizational values and represents them to board members and donors.

Legal and Regulatory

- Supports fundraising solicitation regulations and how they apply in the organizational setting.

Planning and Evaluation

- Works with development director to establish strategy to meet annual fund goals for the organization.

Youth Cultural Competency

- Effectively interacts with a diverse population of youth and college-age volunteers from a variety of ethnic and socioeconomic backgrounds.

Public Speaking

- Has experience speaking in front of groups, making presentations and leading groups of five to three hundred consisting of all ages and backgrounds.

Flexibility and Adaptability

- Is organized and has the ability to work in a fast-paced, ever-changing work environment.
- Possesses skills in project and time management.
- Can work independently as well as collaboratively.

Problem Solving

- Demonstrates the ability to solve problems, analyze systems and data, and make suggestions for improvement.

Work Environment

- A minimum of 40 hours per week—this includes two nontraditional work shifts each week with some level of flexibility (e.g., work three traditional 9 a.m. to 5 p.m. shifts and then maybe noon to 8 p.m. one weekday, and perhaps a daytime shift on Saturday or Sunday).
- Physical requirements include a typical office environment with periods of sitting at a computer screen and being able to lift up to 25 pounds.
- The job entails duties offsite including local travel, exposure to heat, cold, inclement weather conditions, and standing for periods of time.

EXHIBIT 5.7
Sample Job Description (Realigned), Cont'd

Compensation Package

- The organization provides medical, dental, and vision insurance, 401k plan, flexible spending account, paid time off (PTO), and paid holidays. Details available upon request.

TABLE 5.12
Proficiency Mapping Results: Grantmaking Organization

	President	Program Associate	Director of Finance	Director of Grants and Nonprofit Services
Advocacy and Public Policy	4	2	3	4
Communications, Marketing, and Public Relations	5	3	3	4
Financial Management and Social Entrepreneurship	4	2	5	4
Fundraising and Resource Development	4	1	3	2
Grantmaking	5	3	5	5
Human Resources Management and Volunteerism	5	1	3	2
Information Management	4	3	4	3
Leadership and Governance	5	2	4	4
Legal and Regulatory	4	2	5	4
Planning and Evaluation	5	4	3	4

TABLE 5.13
Proficiency Mapping: Program Associate, Grantmaking Organization

Competency	Job Responsibilities Before	Proficiency Level Before	Job Responsibilities Realigned	Proficiency Level Realigned
Advocacy and Public Policy	**Stays** current on relevant issues, policies, exemplary programs, resources, and information in the work that supports economic and community benefit.	3	**Follows** current issues, policies, exemplary programs, resources, and information in the fields of work supports, benefits access, and family self-sufficiency.	2
Advocacy and Public Policy	**Develops** policy and practice rec-ommendations for new strategies and programs based on research of effective models for hard-to-employ populations.	4	**Reviews** policy and practice rec-ommendations for new strategies and programs based on research recom-mendations of effective models for hard-to-employ populations.	2

TABLE 5.13

Proficiency Mapping: Program Associate, Grantmaking Organization, Cont'd

Competency	Job Responsibilities Before	Proficiency Level Before	Job Responsibilities Realigned	Proficiency Level Realigned
Advocacy and Public Policy	**Works** with officials from the private and public sectors, as well as with other nonprofits, to **develop** programs and strategies that create public benefit access programs and policies for low-income populations.	3, 4	**Assists** officials from the private and public sectors, as well as with other nonprofits, to **support** programs and strategies that create public benefit access programs and policies for low-income populations.	2, 2
Communications, Marketing, and Public Relations	**Represents** and **supports** the organization at meetings and conferences, and **assists** in organizing and participating in meetings, conferences, and site visits.	3, 2, 2	**Represents** the organization at meetings and conferences, and **participates** in organizing meetings, conferences, and site visits.	3, 3
Communications, Marketing, and Public Relations	Has experience in **working** with community groups **performing** outreach related to free tax preparation and/or access to public benefits.	3, 3	Has experience in **working** with community groups **performing** outreach related to free tax preparation and/or access to public benefits.	3, 3

TABLE 5.13
Proficiency Mapping: Program Associate, Grantmaking Organization, Cont'd

Competency	Job Responsibilities Before	Proficiency Level Before	Job Responsibilities Realigned	Proficiency Level Realigned
Financial Management and Social Entrepreneurship	(No responsibilities were originally designated in this category)		**Assists** the executive director with **ensuring** that appropriate financial reports are made available to the board on a timely basis.	2, 4
Fundraising and Resource Development	(No responsibilities were originally designated in this category)		**Observes** current programmatic trends and best practices, the funding landscape, and potential partners.	1
Grantmaking	**Assists** in the development, management, and monitoring of grantmaking and investment strategies, which involves **reviewing** and **analyzing** proposals and budgets, **preparing** correspondence in response, **handling** grant letters and payments, and **maintaining** records on grantees.	2, 2, 5, 4, 3, 3	**Provides** development, management, and monitoring of grantmaking and investment strategies, which involves **analyzing** proposals and budgets, **preparing** correspondence in response, **handling** grant letters and payments, and **maintaining** records on grantees.	3, 5, 4, 3, 3

TABLE 5.13

Proficiency Mapping: Program Associate, Grantmaking Organization, Cont'd

Competency	Job Responsibilities Before	Proficiency Level Before	Job Responsibilities Realigned	Proficiency Level Realigned
Grantmaking	**Reviews** the progress of selected grantees, with a particular emphasis on program development and capacity building, assisting with management of technical assistance to the grantee, and facilitating communication and the exchange of information among grantees in the program portfolio.	2	**Monitors** the progress of selected grantees, with a particular emphasis on program development and capacity building, assisting with management of technical assistance to the grantee, and facilitating communication and the exchange of information among grantees in the program portfolio.	3
Grantmaking	**Organizes** and **provides** direct technical assistance to grantees in order to strengthen their program implementation and strategy development; has proven ability to **troubleshoot** service delivery methods in order to achieve desired results.	3, 3, 5	**Conducts** and **provides** direct technical assistance to grantees in order to strengthen their program implementation and strategy development; has proven ability to **troubleshoot** service delivery methods in order to achieve desired results.	3, 3, 5

TABLE 5.13

Proficiency Mapping: Program Associate, Grantmaking Organization, Cont'd

Competency	Job Responsibilities Before	Proficiency Level Before	Job Responsibilities Realigned	Proficiency Level Realigned
Grantmaking	Has in-depth **knowledge** and experience working with low-income communities.	4	Has experience **working** with the Earned Income Tax Credit (EITC) program, Temporary Assistance to Needy Families (TANF), Medicaid, and/or earned benefits/public access programs.	3
Grantmaking	Has experience **developing** work support programs for hard-to-employ individuals.	4	Has experience **conducting** work support programs for hard-to-employ individuals.	3
Human Resources Management and Volunteerism	(No responsibilities were originally designated in this category)		**Observes** discussions, trainings, and exchanges of best practices between staff and other foundations in order to assist staff.	1
Information Management	**Uses** the Internet and basic software applications such as the Microsoft Office suite and **translates** raw data into meaningful management information.	3, 4	**Uses** the Internet and basic software applications such as the Microsoft Office suite. **Translates** raw data into meaningful management information.	3, 4

TABLE 5.13

Proficiency Mapping: Program Associate, Grantmaking Organization, Cont'd

Competency	Job Responsibilities Before	Proficiency Level Before	Job Responsibilities Realigned	Proficiency Level Realigned
Leadership and Governance	**Exhibits** sensitivity to and respect for diversity in personal, professional, and business relationships on behalf of the Foundation.	3	**Welcomes** and **encourages** diversity in personal, professional, and business relationships on behalf of the Foundation.	2, 4
Leadership and Governance	**Performs** administrative duties in support of grantmaking work.	3	**Supports** grantmaking work in an administrative role.	2
Leadership and Governance	**Shows** flexibility, maturity, and the ability to work as a team with managing directors, consultants, and persons outside the Foundation who have varying backgrounds and styles.	3	**Supports** managing directors, consultants, and persons outside the Foundation who have varying backgrounds and styles..	2
Leadership and Governance	**Demonstrates** ability to develop working relationships with organizations and community groups that contribute to implementing strategies.	4	**Assists** development director in developing working relationships with organizations and community groups that contribute to implementing strategies.	2

TABLE 5.13
Proficiency Mapping: Program Associate, Grantmaking Organization, Cont'd

Competency	Job Responsibilities Before	Proficiency Level Before	Job Responsibilities Realigned	Proficiency Level Realigned
Legal and Regulatory	(No responsibilities were originally designated in this category)		**Assists** the director with tracking proposals and eligibility assessments that have been submitted for review and approval.	2
Planning and Evaluation	**Assists** with strategic and program planning, organizational development and management, continuous quality improvement techniques, market research, and business planning.	2	**Provides** strategic and program planning, organizational development and management, continuous quality improvement techniques, market research, and business planning.	3
Planning and Evaluation	**Demonstrates** skill in the areas of strategic and program planning, organizational development and management, continuous quality improvement techniques, market research, and business planning.	4	Demonstrates skill in the areas of strategic and program planning, organizational development and management, continuous quality improvement techniques, market research, and business planning.	

TABLE 5.13
Proficiency Mapping: Program Associate, Grantmaking Organization, Cont'd

Competency	Job Responsibilities Before	Proficiency Level Before	Job Responsibilities Realigned	Proficiency Level Realigned
Field Building	Has experience **building** a field around a content area (e.g., research, policy, practice, infrastructure, nonprofit collaboration, government and private sector partnerships).	4	Has experience **building** a field around a content area (e.g., research, policy, practice, infrastructure, nonprofit collaboration, government and private sector partnerships).	4
Multitasking	Able to **work** on multiple tasks and deadlines.	3	Able to **work** on multiple tasks and deadlines.	3
Multitasking	**Demonstrates** excellent written and verbal communication skills.	4	**Exhibits** excellent written and verbal communication skills.	3
Research and Analytic Skills	Ability to **prepare** reports and **conduct** literature reviews.	4, 3	Ability to **prepare** reports and **conduct** literature reviews.	4, 3
Mission Commitment	Commitment to **improving** outcomes for disadvantaged children and families.	5	Commitment to **improving** outcomes for disadvantaged children and families.	5

EXHIBIT 5.8

Sample Job Description (Realigned)

Program Associate, Grantmaking Organization

Job Title: Program Associate

Department: Economic and Community Benefit

Status: Exempt / Full-time

Salary Range: $50,000–$55,000

Reports to: Director of Grants and Nonprofit Services

Supervisory Responsibilities: None

Responsibilities

Advocacy and Public Policy

- Follows current issues, policies, exemplary programs, resources, and information in the fields of work supports, benefits access, and family self-sufficiency.

- Reviews policy and practice recommendations for new strategies and programs based on research of effective models for hard-to-employ populations.

- Assists officials from the private and public sectors, as well as other nonprofits to support programs and strategies that create public benefit access programs and policies for low-income populations.

Communications, Marketing, and Public Relations

- Represents the organization at meetings and conferences, and participates in organizing meetings, conferences, and site visits.

- Has experience in working with community groups performing outreach related to free tax preparation and/or access to public benefits.

Financial Management and Social Entrepreneurship

- Assists the executive director to ensure that appropriate financial reports are made available to the board on a timely basis.

Fundraising and Resource Development

- Observes current programmatic trends and best practices, the funding landscape, and potential partners.

EXHIBIT 5.8
Sample Job Description (Realigned), Cont'd

Grantmaking

- Provides development, management, and monitoring of grantmaking and investment strategies, which involves analyzing proposals and budgets, preparing correspondence in response, handling grant letters and payments, and maintaining records on grantees.

- Monitors the progress of selected grantees, with a particular emphasis on program development and capacity building, assisting with management of technical assistance to the grantee, and facilitating communication and the exchange of information among grantees in the program portfolio.

- Conducts and provides direct technical assistance to grantees in order to strengthen their program implementation, and strategy development; has proven ability to troubleshoot service delivery methods in order to achieve desired results.

- Has experience working with the Earned Income Tax Credit (EITC) program, Temporary Assistance to Needy Families (TANF), Medicaid, and/or earned benefits/public access programs as well.

- Has experience conducting work support programs for hard-to-employ individuals.

Human Resources Management and Volunteerism

- Observes discussions, trainings, and exchanges of best practices between staff and other foundations in order to assist grantmaking staff.

Information Management

- Uses the Internet and basic software applications such as the Microsoft Office suite and translates raw data into meaningful management information.

Leadership and Governance

- Welcomes and encourages diversity in personal, professional, and business relationships on behalf of the foundation.

- Supports grantmaking work in an administrative role.

- Supports managing directors, consultants, and persons outside the foundation who have varying backgrounds and styles.

- Assists development director in developing working relationships with organizations and community groups that contribute to implementing strategies. Has outstanding judgment, initiative, and motivation.

EXHIBIT 5.8
Sample Job Description (Realigned), Cont'd

Legal and Regulatory

- Assists the director with tracking proposals and eligibility assessments that have been submitted for review and approval.

Planning and Evaluation

- Provides strategic and program planning, organizational development and management, continuous quality improvement techniques, market research, and business planning.
- Demonstrates skill in the areas of strategic and program planning, organizational development and management, continuous quality improvement techniques, market research, and business planning.

Field Building

- Has experience building a field around a content area (e.g., research, policy, practice, infrastructure, nonprofit collaboration, government and private sector partnerships).

Multitasking

- Able to work on multiple tasks and deadlines.

Communication Skills

- Exhibits excellent written and verbal communication skills.

Research and Analytic Skills

- Able to prepare reports and conduct literature reviews.

Mission Commitment

- Is committed to improving outcomes for disadvantaged children and families.

Educational Requirements

- Minimum requirement includes bachelor's degree in human services, social work, business, or related field. The ideal candidate for this position holds a graduate degree (MMP, MPA, MNA, MBA, MPH, MSW, JD) and has relevant pre- or postgraduate work experience.

EXHIBIT 5.8
Sample Job Description (Realigned), Cont'd

- Candidates should also have five to seven years of practitioner experience working directly with community-based organizations and/or policy organizations focused on low-income families.

Work Environment

- The work is performed primarily in an office setting with extensive overnight travel required (40 percent of the time).

- Must occasionally lift and move up to 30 pounds.

Resources

Exhibits 5.9 and 5.10 contain forms you can use during the proficiency mapping process. You can use the form in exhibit 5.9 to identify the competencies and proficiency levels for each position. The form in exhibit 5.10 allows you to view the proficiency mapping scores for multiple positions across a department or an organization. Exhibit 5.10 is very useful when you are identifying goals and objectives for a team or identifying employees for specific positions or roles.

EXHIBIT 5.9

Position Mapping Form

Please identify the desired competencies that are essential behaviors and duties within each job or volunteer role. Then rate the proficiency level required for each competency

(* = Required)

1. Name of Organization* _____

2. Job Title or Volunteer Role* _____

Social Change Competencies and Descriptions

Advocacy and Public Policy: Uses community organizing, public education, policy research, and lobbying effectively to educate government officials, organize community support, garner social change, and influence public policy.

Communications, Marketing, and Public Relations: Demonstrates principles and techniques that provide transparency and accountability, while understanding and communicating specifically to various constituents—including internal stakeholders—using communications, general and social media marketing, and public relations that develop financial and nonfinancial support for your organization.

Financial Management and Social Entrepreneurship: Applies critical financial concepts and GAAP practices to establish and maintain realistic budgets, internal controls, financial statements, cash flow maintenance, audits, and tax reporting. Creates and maintains sustainable business models, impact and/or social investment strategies, hybrid organizational forms, and innovative revenue structures.

Fundraising and Resource Development: Demonstrates ability to develop a diversified fund development strategy that is proactive and integrated into the organization's long-term strategic plan and budget projections. Is familiar with and able to execute several different fundraising strategies, including but not limited to stewardship and cultivation of donors, gift processing, developing new business, event planning, planned giving and major gifts campaigns, and grant writing.

Grantmaking: Identifies and works with prospective and existing grantees, monitors grantee progress, and explore new grantmaking areas. Provides recommendation for funding and conducts grant reviews. Has in-depth knowledge of program area(s).

Direct Service: Effectively work with clients and/or constituents. Has expertise in specific field of service, client relations, and intercultural competency.

Human Resources Management and Volunteerism: Applies knowledge of employment laws and practices for recruitment and selection, for managing employees and volunteers, and for monitoring performance, diversity and intercultural competency, compensation and benefits, training and development, labor relations, and health and safety.

EXHIBIT 5.9
Position Mapping Form, Cont'd

Information Management: Supports the development, maintenance, and application of information technology planning, budgeting, staffing and training, evaluation, and selecting hardware and software, social media, and website capabilities and use.

Leadership and Governance: Appreciates the relationship between leadership and management in establishing and attaining mission and long- and short-term organizational goals. Is able to look within self and team members in order to understand how personal backgrounds and experience shape the leadership experience. Demonstrates ability to lead effectively and manage the governing board of the organization.

Legal and Regulatory: Understands influences of external and internal stakeholders in creating and maintaining legal compliance, ethical and risk management practices, and professional standards in the appropriate settings.

Planning and Evaluation: Understands external and internal influences of program and organizational development, as well as organizational life cycles. Creates logic models, data-based decision making, program feasibility, and continuous improvement plans for effective management. Is able to develop a theory of change and apply various methods of evaluation to comprehensively evaluate performance measurement and program and organizational effectiveness.

Proficiency Level Scores and Descriptions

Fundamental Awareness (basic knowledge): You have a common knowledge or an understanding of basic techniques and concepts.

Novice (limited experience): You have the level of experience gained in a classroom, in experimental scenarios, or as a trainee on the job. You are expected to need help when performing this skill.

Intermediate (practical application): You are able to successfully complete tasks in this competency as requested. Help from an expert may be required from time to time, but you can usually perform the skill independently.

Advanced (applied theory): You can perform the actions associated with this skill without assistance. You are certainly recognized within your immediate organization as "a person to ask" when difficult questions arise regarding this skill.

Expert (recognized authority): You are known as an expert in this area. You can provide guidance, troubleshoot, and answer questions related to this area of expertise and the field where the skill is used.

3. Using the competency descriptions, rate the desired proficiency level with the essential duties of the job or volunteer role.*

Check only one box per row.

EXHIBIT 5.9
Position Mapping Form, Cont'd

	Fundamental Awareness	Novice	Intermediate	Advanced	Expert
Advocacy and Public Policy					
Communications, Marketing, and Public Relations					
Financial Management and Social Entrepreneurship					
Fundraising and Resource Development					
Grantmaking or Direct Service					
Human Resources Management and Volunteerism					
Information Technology					
Leadership and Governance					
Legal and Regulatory					
Planning and Evaluation					

4. Please create specific competencies for the organizational, department, and position and list them below. Please be as specific as possible. For example: The first organizational competency is _____. Our first departmental competency is _____.

Organizational Sub-competencies _____

_____

_____

_____

Department Sub-competencies _____

_____

_____

_____

Position Sub-competencies _____

_____

_____

_____

EXHIBIT 5.9
Position Mapping Form, Cont'd

5. Using the sub-competency list above, rate the desired proficiency level with the essential duties of the job or volunteer role.

Check only one box per row.

	Fundamental Awareness	Novice	Intermediate	Advanced	Expert
Organizational Competency 1					
Organizational Competency 2					
Organizational Competency 3					
Organizational Competency 4					
Organizational Competency 5					
Department Competency 1					
Department Competency 2					
Department Competency 3					
Department Competency 4					
Department Competency 5					
Position Competency 1					
Position Competency 2					
Position Competency 3					
Position Competency 4					
Position Competency 5					

EXHIBIT 5.10

Proficiency Mapping Worksheet across a Department or an Organization

	Position _____	Position _____	Position _____	Position _____
Advocacy and Public Policy				
Communications, Marketing, and Public Relations				
Financial Management and Social Entrepreneurship				
Fundraising and Resource Development				
Grantmaking or Direct Service				
Human Resources Management and Volunteerism				
Information Management				
Leadership and Governance				
Legal and Regulatory				
Planning and Evaluation				

Conclusion

In this chapter we described how to map social change competencies to job responsibilities by identifying action words and proficiency levels. We also showed you how to realign job descriptions and provided proficiency maps for the four social change organizations. The next chapter discusses the Individual Professional Development Assessment, which allows you to compare employees' and volunteers' current proficiency levels to the position proficiency levels you identified during the proficiency mapping process.

Chapter 6
The Individual Professional Development Assessment

In chapters 4 and 5 you identified competencies for each job or role within your organization and created sub-competencies important for your organization and various departments. In this chapter, you will learn about the Individual Professional Development Assessment (IPDA) and how to administer this assessment to your staff and volunteers. In this chapter we also discuss how to overcome the challenges that may come up during the IPDA administration process and how to analyze results. Figure 6.1 provides you with an IPDA checklist.

About the Individual Professional Development Assessment

Shippmann et al. (2009) and Pynes (2009) define competencies as the knowledge, skills, abilities, and other characteristics people need to possess in order to perform their job. Research has also discussed the benefits of competencies and the importance of using competencies within organizations. We created the IPDA to provide social change organizations a way of using competencies to their advantage. The IPDA assesses employee and volunteer proficiency levels against the social change competencies and your organization's identified sub-competencies. The IPDA also identifies proficiency strengths, deficiencies, and gaps. We validated the assessment through a survey of over eight hundred nonprofit and philanthropic staff members located across the United States.

The assessment, shown in exhibit 6.1, contains three sections. In the first section (questions 1–4), employees and volunteers identify their position and the general functions of their job. This section also allows employees and volunteers to identify competencies they perform regularly in their job (never, occasionally, frequently). In the second section

FIGURE 6.1
IPDA Checklist

INDIVIDUAL PROFESSIONAL DEVELOPMENT ASSESSMENT

- Take Individual Professional Development Assessments with additional sub-competencies as created during job description process.
- Tally scores for each individual, department (if applicable), and the full organization.
- Map scores along side proficiency levels on the organization's Talent Development Platform.
- Identify proficiency strengths, deficiencies, and gaps for each employee.
- Assess roles for salary level, and assess each employee or volunteer for role placement based on proficiency.

(questions 5–6), employees and volunteers identify their proficiency level in each competency category. (This information will be compared with the position mapping you completed for each position in chapter 5.) The third section (questions 7–9) allows you to include the sub-competencies you created specific to your organization, department, and individual positions. In the second and third sections, employees and volunteers also rate their Desired Proficiency Levels in each competency one year from the time of taking the assessment.

The benefits of implementing this assessment are at both the organization and individual level. The organization can assess the proficiency strengths and deficiencies for the organization (or department). And individuals get the opportunity to see their own proficiency strengths, deficiencies, and gaps. Combined, the information helps the organization utilize talent more effectively and offer the right types of professional development based on the employees and volunteers proficiency gaps.

Administering the Assessment

Preparing and Administering the Assessment

If you've already done the work outlined in chapters 4 and 5, you will have official job descriptions for each of your employees or volunteers mapped against the core social change competencies. We recommend that you also identify the organizational, department, and position-specific sub-competencies and include them in this assessment.

EXHIBIT 6.1

The Individual Professional Development Assessment

Please identify the competencies that are essential behaviors and duties within your job or volunteer role. Then rate your proficiency level in each competency and what proficiency level you hope to obtain. The data will be used to determine common proficiency levels within core competencies across the organization.

Participation in this survey is entirely voluntary; you can choose to opt out at any time. The information collected in this survey will be shared with your organization and will be used for research purposes. There are no risks for you to participate in this survey that exceed the risks encountered in everyday life.

(* = Required)

I have read and understand this form, and consent to the process and research it describes to me.*

❑　Yes

❑　No

1. Name of Organization* _____

2. Job Title or Volunteer Role* _____

3. Please indicate your essential job function(s) or volunteer role(s).*

Check all that apply.

❑　Accounting and Finance

❑　Administration

❑　Advocacy/Lobbying

❑　Communications

❑　Community Organizing

❑　Counseling

❑　Direct Service

❑　Education

❑　Event Planning

❑　Facilities and Property Management

❑　Food Services and Housing

❑　Fundraising

❑　Grants Management

❑　Information Technology

❑　Human Resources

❑　Legal—Law Services

EXHIBIT 6.1
The Individual Professional Development Assessment, Cont'd

- ❏ Medical and/or Health
- ❏ Program Management
- ❏ Public Relations
- ❏ Other:

Social Change Competencies and Descriptions

Read the descriptions below and use the information to answer question 4.

Advocacy and Public Policy: Uses community organizing, public education, policy research, and lobbying effectively to educate government officials, organize community support, garner social change, and influence public policy.

Communications, Marketing, and Public Relations: Demonstrates principles and techniques that provide transparency and accountability, while understanding and communicating specifically to various constituents—including internal stakeholders—using communications, general and social media marketing, and public relations that develop financial and nonfinancial support for your organization.

Financial Management and Social Entrepreneurship: Applies critical financial concepts and GAAP practices to establish and maintain realistic budgets, internal controls, financial statements, cash flow maintenance, audits and tax reporting. Creates and maintains sustainable business models, impact and/or social investment strategies, hybrid organizational forms, and innovative revenue structures.

Fundraising and Resource Development: Demonstrates ability to develop a diversified fund development strategy that is proactive and integrated into the organization's long-term strategic plan and budget projections. Is familiar with and able to execute several different fundraising strategies, including but not limited to stewardship and cultivation of donors, gift processing, developing new business, event planning, planned giving and major gifts campaigns, and grantwriting.

Grantmaking: Identifies and works with prospective and existing grantees, monitors grantee progress, and explore new grantmaking areas. Provides recommendation for funding and conducts grant reviews. Has in-depth knowledge of program area(s).

Direct Service: Effectively work with clients and/or constituents. Has expertise in specific field of service, client relations, and intercultural competency.

Human Resources Management and Volunteerism: Applies knowledge of employment laws and practices for nonprofit recruitment and selection, for managing employees and volunteers, and for monitoring performance, diversity and intercultural competency, compensation and benefits, training and development, labor relations, and health and safety.

Information Management: Supports the development, maintenance, and application of information technology planning, budgeting, staffing and training, evaluation, selecting hardware and software, social media, and website capabilities and use.

EXHIBIT 6.1
The Individual Professional Development Assessment, Cont'd

Leadership and Governance: Appreciate the relationship between leadership and management in establishing and attaining mission and long- and short-term organizational goals. Is able to look within self and team members in order to understand how personal backgrounds and experience shape the leadership experience. Demonstrates ability to lead effectively and manage the governing board of the organization.

Legal and Regulatory: Understands influences of external and internal stakeholders in creating and maintaining legal compliance, ethical and risk management practices, and professional standards in the appropriate settings.

Planning and Evaluation: Understands external and internal influences of program and organizational development, as well as organizational life cycles. Creates logic models, data-based decision making, program feasibility, and continuous improvement plans for effective management. Is able to develop a theory of change and apply various methods of evaluation to comprehensively evaluate performance measurement and program and organizational effectiveness.

4. Using the descriptions provided, please select the frequency with which you perform the ESSENTIAL duties in your job or volunteer role.*

Check only one box per row.

	Never	Occasionally (several times a year)	Frequently (at least once a month)
Advocacy and Public Policy			
Communications, Marketing, and Public Relations			
Financial Management and Social Entrepreneurship			
Fundraising and Resource Development			
Grantmaking or Direct Service			
Human Resources Management and Volunteerism			
Information Management			
Leadership and Governance			
Legal and Regulatory			
Planning and Evaluation			

EXHIBIT 6.1
The Individual Professional Development Assessment, Cont'd

Proficiency Level Scores and Descriptions

Read the descriptions below and use the information to answer questions 5, 6, 8, and 9.

Fundamental Awareness (basic knowledge): You have a common knowledge or an understanding of basic techniques and concepts.

Novice (limited experience): You have the level of experience gained in a classroom, in experimental scenarios, or as a trainee on the job. You are expected to need help when performing this skill.

Intermediate (practical application): You are able to successfully complete tasks in this competency as requested. Help from an expert may be required from time to time, but you can usually perform the skill independently.

Advanced (applied theory): You can perform the actions associated with this skill without assistance. You are certainly recognized within your immediate organization as "a person to ask" when difficult questions arise regarding this skill.

Expert (recognized authority): You are known as an expert in this area. You can provide guidance, troubleshoot, and answer questions related to this area of expertise and the field where the skill is used.

5. Using the descriptions provided, rate your proficiency level in the essential duties of your job or volunteer role.*

Check only one box per row.

	Fundamental Awareness	Novice	Intermediate	Advanced	Expert
Advocacy and Public Policy					
Communications, Marketing, and Public Relations					
Financial Management and Social Entrepreneurship					
Fundraising and Resource Development					
Grantmaking or Direct Service					
Human Resources Management and Volunteerism					
Information Management					
Leadership and Governance					
Legal and Regulatory					
Planning and Evaluation					

EXHIBIT 6.1
The Individual Professional Development Assessment, Cont'd

6. Using the descriptions provided, rate the proficiency level you would like to be at in one year in the essential duties of your job or volunteer role.

Check only one box per row.

	Fundamental Awareness	Novice	Intermediate	Advanced	Expert
Advocacy and Public Policy					
Communications, Marketing, and Public Relations					
Financial Management and Social Entrepreneurship					
Fundraising and Resource Development					
Grantmaking or Direct Service					
Human Resources Management and Volunteerism					
Information Management					
Leadership and Governance					
Legal and Regulatory					
Planning and Evaluation					

Organizational, Department, and Position Competencies

7. If your organization has created specific competencies for your organization, department, and position, please list them below, being as specific as possible. For example: Our first organizational competency is _____. Our first department competency is _____.

Organizational Sub-competencies _____

_____

_____

_____

EXHIBIT 6.1
The Individual Professional Development Assessment, Cont'd

Department Sub-competencies _____

_____

_____

_____

Position Sub-competencies _____

_____

_____

_____

8. Please rate your proficiency level in the organizational, department, and/or position competencies you listed in #7.

Check only one box per row.

	Fundamental Awareness	Novice	Intermediate	Advanced	Expert
Organizational Competency 1					
Organizational Competency 2					
Organizational Competency 3					
Organizational Competency 4					
Organizational Competency 5					
Department Competency 1					
Department Competency 2					
Department Competency 3					
Department Competency 4					
Department Competency 5					
Position Competency 1					
Position Competency 2					
Position Competency 3					
Position Competency 4					
Position Competency 5					

EXHIBIT 6.1
The Individual Professional Development Assessment, Cont'd

9. Please rate the proficiency level you would like to be at in one year in the organizational, department, and/or position competencies you marked in question 8.

Check only one box per row.

	Fundamental Awareness	Novice	Intermediate	Advanced	Expert
Organizational Competency 1					
Organizational Competency 2					
Organizational Competency 3					
Organizational Competency 4					
Organizational Competency 5					
Department Competency 1					
Department Competency 2					
Department Competency 3					
Department Competency 4					
Department Competency 5					
Position Competency 1					
Position Competency 2					
Position Competency 3					
Position Competency 4					
Position Competency 5					

Thank you for taking the time to fill out the Individual Professional Development Assessment. Data collected in this survey will be used to understand common competency preferences across the organization.

We recommend that a manager or someone within the organization fill in the proficiency mapping form (covered in chapter 5) to clarify the proficiency levels each role demands. The process of comparing the employees' or volunteers' proficiency levels with those their role demands is called a gap analysis. Gap analysis work helps employees and volunteers identify competencies they want or need to improve upon based on the job description (Gangani, McLean, & Braden, 2006). We'll talk more in later sections of this chapter about how to perform a gap analysis.

Once you have prepared the assessment, send the survey out to staff, allowing them three weeks to complete it. We've provided a template invitation for you to customize (exhibit 6.2), or you can use the online resources to send out the invitation and assessment. Send out a reminder several times within the three weeks to be sure to get responses from each employee and volunteer.

EXHIBIT 6.2
Administering the IPDA: Sample E-mail Template

Dear _____,

As you are aware _____ [your organization] is in the process of assessing our learning culture and your professional development preferences so that we can be more strategic and systematic in our professional development offerings.

Please set aside 10–15 minutes to take the Individual Professional Development Assessment. This assessment will gather information about your proficiency levels within ten core competencies.

We've also identified the following organizational, department, and job-specific competencies for your position:

[List Specific Sub-competencies Here]

We will be able use the summary data to determine common proficiency levels across the organization and areas we can target our professional development efforts toward.

Please be as honest as possible when taking the assessment.

Take the survey here: [Insert Link]

Please let us know if you have any questions about the survey.

Potential Errors

As with any assessment tool there is a potential for errors. Research shows that employees and volunteers will rate their proficiency levels either lower or higher than they really are (Fiske & Taylor, 2009). It is important to emphasize that employees and volunteers need to be as accurate as possible and not overstate their proficiency levels.

Another error has to do with organizational culture. Employees or volunteers may rate themselves higher if they feel the culture is less accepting of mistakes or of lower proficiency levels. We've seen entry-level employees rate themselves advanced and expert in the majority of the competencies, so they won't disappoint their boss. This is where a safe environment for administering a survey becomes the most important. All leadership should be trained in talking about the assessment and use language that makes staff feel comfortable answering the questions honestly.

The last common error occurs when employees rates themselves lower than their position requires. This error happens the most often when job descriptions are not in alignment with the employees' proficiency level. This is why it is critical to keep job descriptions up to date, revised on an annual basis, so that employees and volunteers can rate themselves accurately.

Interpreting IPDA Results and Creating the Talent Map

Once employees and volunteers have taken the IPDA, the executive director or department manager should review and compare the results across the department or organization (or both) and create a Talent Map. This process involves identifying the Position Proficiency Level scores for each role and comparing them to the Current Proficiency Level and Desired Proficiency Level scores that employees and volunteers identified in their assessments. To help with analysis, map the averages for the organization on the organization's Talent Development Platform; and each individual can map theirs on an individual Platform as well.

Calculating Proficiency Levels

To start calculating results, compile the IPDA scores for all your employees and volunteers in each of the three mapping categories (Position Proficiency Level, Current Proficiency Level, and Desired Proficiency Level). Next, calculate the average scores for each competency category. Table 6.1 shows the individual and average scores for each competency category in the three mapping areas for the small grassroots organization.

Table 6.2 shows the final calculations in a more simplified format for each competency category.

Once you have calculated the combined average scores, you can now plot those scores on your Talent Map located on the Talent Development Platform. Figure 6.2 shows the Talent Map for the small grassroots organization in its final format. The competencies are located on the left side of

TABLE 6.1
IPDA Scores: Small Grassroots Organization

Position Proficiency Level	Executive Director	Community Worker	Program Coordinator	Community Engagement	Education Supervisor	Avg.
Advocacy and Public Policy	4	3	4	4	2	3.4
Communications, Marketing, and Public Relations	4	3	3	4	2	3.2
Financial Management and Social Entrepreneurship	5	1	2	2	2	2.4
Fundraising and Resource Development	5	1	2	4	1	2.6
Direct Service	4	4	5	3	5	4.2
Human Resources Management and Volunteerism	4	3	4	5	4	4
Information Management	4	1	1	1	2	1.8
Leadership and Governance	4	1	3	1	2	2.2
Legal and Regulatory	4	2	2	3	2	2.6
Planning and Evaluation	5	4	4	4	4	4.2
Current Proficiency Level	**Executive Director**	**Community Worker**	**Program Coordinator**	**Community Engagement**	**Education Supervisor**	**Avg.**
Advocacy and Public Policy	2	3	3	3	1	2.4
Communications, Marketing, and Public Relations	2	3	3	4	1	2.6

TABLE 6.1
IPDA Scores: Small Grassroots Organization, Cont'd

Current Proficiency Level	Executive Director	Community Worker	Program Coordinator	Community Engagement	Education Supervisor	Avg.
Financial Management and Social Entrepreneurship	3	1	1	2	1	**1.6**
Fundraising and Resource Development	3	1	2	3	1	**2**
Direct Service	4	4	4	5	3	**4**
Human Resources Management and Volunteerism	3	2	1	5	1	**2.4**
Information Management	3	3	4	3	1	**2.8**
Leadership and Governance	3	3	4	3	1	**2.8**
Legal and Regulatory	2	1	2	3	1	**1.8**
Planning and Evaluation	4	3	4	4	3	**3.6**

Desired Proficiency (1 Year from Now)	Executive Director	Community Worker	Program Coordinator	Community Engagement	Education Supervisor	Avg.
Advocacy and Public Policy	3	3	3	4	2	**3**
Communications, Marketing, and Public Relations	4	3	3	5	2	**3.4**
Financial Management and Social Entrepreneurship	4	3	3	4	3	**3.4**
Fundraising and Resource Development	4	3	3	5	3	**3.6**

TABLE 6.1
IPDA Scores: Small Grassroots Organization, Cont'd

Desired Proficiency (1 Year from Now)	Executive Director	Community Worker	Program Coordinator	Community Engagement	Education Supervisor	Avg.
Direct Service	5	5	4	4	4	**4.4**
Human Resources Management and Volunteerism	4	3	2	5	4	**3.6**
Information Management	3	3	4	4	2	**3.2**
Leadership and Governance	4	3	4	5	3	**3.8**
Legal and Regulatory	3	3	3	4	3	**3.2**
Planning and Evaluation	4	4	5	5	4	**4.4**

the map and the proficiency levels are across the top. Results are shown in three columns: Position Proficiency Level, Current Proficiency Level, and Desired Proficiency Level. As a recap, the proficiency levels range from 1 to 5. 1 = novice; 2 = fundamental awareness; 3 = intermediate; 4 = advanced; 5 = expert.

Reviewing and Interpreting IPDA Results

Now that you have created your organization's Talent Map, take the following three steps to review and interpret the organizational data.

Organizational Strengths, Deficiencies, and Gaps

1. Identify organizational proficiency strengths: areas where most staff or volunteers scored advanced or expert proficiency levels (4 or 5).

2. Identify organizational proficiency deficiencies: areas where most employees or volunteers scored novice or fundamental awareness proficiency levels (1 or 2).

3. Identify organizational position proficiency gaps: areas where most employees or volunteers scored lower in their Current Proficiency Levels compared to their Position Proficiency Levels.

TABLE 6.2 Combined Average Proficiency Scores: Small Grassroots Organization

	Advocacy and Public Policy	Communications, Marketing, and Public Relations	Financial Management and Social Entrepreneurship	Fundraising and Resource Development	Direct Service	Human Resources Management and Volunteerism	Information Management	Leadership and Governance	Legal and Regulatory	Planning and Evaluation
Position Proficiency Level	3.4	3.2	2.4	2.6	4.2	4	1.8	2.2	2.6	4.2
Current Proficiency Level	2.4	2.6	1.6	2	4	2.4	2.8	2.8	1.8	3.6
Desired Proficiency Level	3	3.4	3.4	3.6	4.4	3.6	3.2	3.8	3.2	4.4

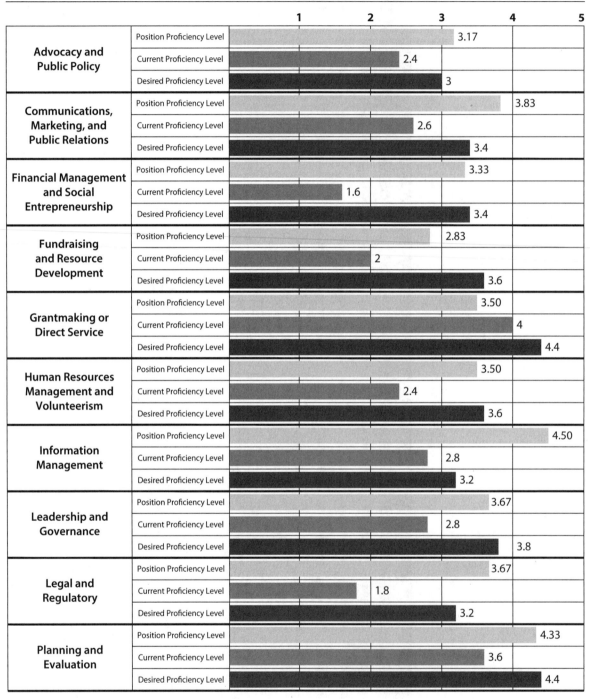

FIGURE 6.2
Talent Map: Small Grassroots Organization

These three steps will you help identify the competency categories where your employees and volunteers will need professional development.

After reviewing the organizational results, review individual results for each employee and volunteer. In a volunteer-run organization the board chair or a small committee of the board should review assessment results. In a small grassroots organization, the board chair should review the executive director's assessment results, and the executive director should review assessment results for all staff. In a midsized organization, the executive director and directors should review assessment results. In a grantmaking organization, the executive director and vice presidents should review assessment results. More information about how to discuss IPDA results with individual employees is included in chapter 9.

Similar to the organizational Talent Map review, the board or manager should review the following individual IPDA results.

Individual Strengths, Deficiencies, and Gaps

1. *Individual proficiency strengths*. Identify and applaud expert and advanced proficiency levels. Identify one to two ways the employee can utilize their advanced and expert proficiency levels to advance the professional development of the organization.

2. *Individual proficiency deficiencies*. Identify fundamental awareness and novice proficiency levels.

3. *Individual position proficiency gaps and examples*. Identify competency categories where the position requires higher proficiency levels but the employee's Current Proficiency Level is lower. Then identify examples of why the position requires specific proficiency levels.

4. *Individual desired proficiency gaps and examples*. Identify where employee's Desired Proficiency Level is higher than Position Proficiency Level. Then identify examples to justify Position Proficiency Levels.

The information collected in the IPDA will aid in professional development goal setting, which we'll discuss further in chapter 9. Before we discuss this goal setting in detail, let's look at a few examples of the Talent Map and IPDA results from our four pilot organizations.

The Talent Map and IPDA in Practice

Volunteer-Run Organization

All board members within the volunteer-run organization took the IPDA. After the board members took the IPDA, the board chair calculated the responses and identified the organizational proficiency strengths, organizational proficiency deficiencies, and organizational position proficiency gaps. In figure 6.3, you can see there were no proficiency strengths for the organization (in which case most board members score a 4 or 5 for the Current Proficiency Level).

Additionally, the proficiency deficiencies (where most board members scored a 2 or lower in Current Proficiency Level) were in Legal and Regulatory. Moreover, there were position proficiency gaps (where most staff scored lower in their Current Proficiency Level than their Position Proficiency Level) in all categories except Fundraising and Resource Development, and Leadership and Governance. The Talent Map review is shown in table 6.3.

Because the volunteer-run organization needed a lot of professional development, it focused on the largest organizational proficiency gaps, which were in the Information Management, Legal and Regulatory, and Planning and Evaluation categories.

In reviewing the Talent Map, the board then turned their attention to the individual results. We'll specifically discuss the IPDA results for the president/board chair shown in figure 6.4. The board first identified the president/board chair's proficiency strengths; second, his proficiency deficiencies; third, his position proficiency gaps; and last, the desired proficiency gaps.

The president/board chair demonstrated expert and advanced proficiency levels in most competencies. He showed advanced proficiency (with a score of 4 in Current Proficiency Level) in five categories and expert proficiency level (with a score of 5 in Current Proficiency Level) in four categories. The president/board chair had no proficiency deficiencies. Table 6.4 summarizes the president/board chair's proficiency strengths.

Next, comparisons were made between Position Proficiency Levels and Current Proficiency Levels to identify the position proficiency gap analysis (shown in Table 6.5).

TABLE 6.3	
Talent Map Review: Volunteer-Run Organization	
Proficiency Strengths	None
Proficiency Deficiencies	Legal and Regulatory
Position Proficiency Gaps	Advocacy and Public Policy; Communications, Marketing, and Public Relations; Financial Management and Social Entrepreneurship; Direct Service; Human Resources Management and Volunteerism; Information Management; Legal and Regulatory; and Planning and Evaluation

FIGURE 6.3
Talent Map: Volunteer-Run Organization

		1	2	3	4	5
Advocacy and Public Policy	Position Proficiency Level			3.14		
	Current Proficiency Level		2.43			
	Desired Proficiency Level		2.71			
Communications, Marketing, and Public Relations	Position Proficiency Level				3.71	
	Current Proficiency Level				3.43	
	Desired Proficiency Level					4.14
Financial Management and Social Entrepreneurship	Position Proficiency Level				3.29	
	Current Proficiency Level		2.43			
	Desired Proficiency Level				3.57	
Fundraising and Resource Development	Position Proficiency Level			2.86		
	Current Proficiency Level			3.14		
	Desired Proficiency Level				3.43	
Grantmaking or Direct Service	Position Proficiency Level				3.57	
	Current Proficiency Level				3.5	
	Desired Proficiency Level				3.29	
Human Resources Management and Volunteerism	Position Proficiency Level				3.57	
	Current Proficiency Level				3.29	
	Desired Proficiency Level				3.86	
Information Management	Position Proficiency Level					4.43
	Current Proficiency Level			3.00		
	Desired Proficiency Level				3.57	
Leadership and Governance	Position Proficiency Level				3.71	
	Current Proficiency Level				3.71	
	Desired Proficiency Level					4.29
Legal and Regulatory	Position Proficiency Level				3.57	
	Current Proficiency Level		1.86			
	Desired Proficiency Level		2.71			
Planning and Evaluation	Position Proficiency Level					4.43
	Current Proficiency Level				3.43	
	Desired Proficiency Level					4.43

FIGURE 6.4
IPDA Results: President/Board Chair, Volunteer-Run Organization

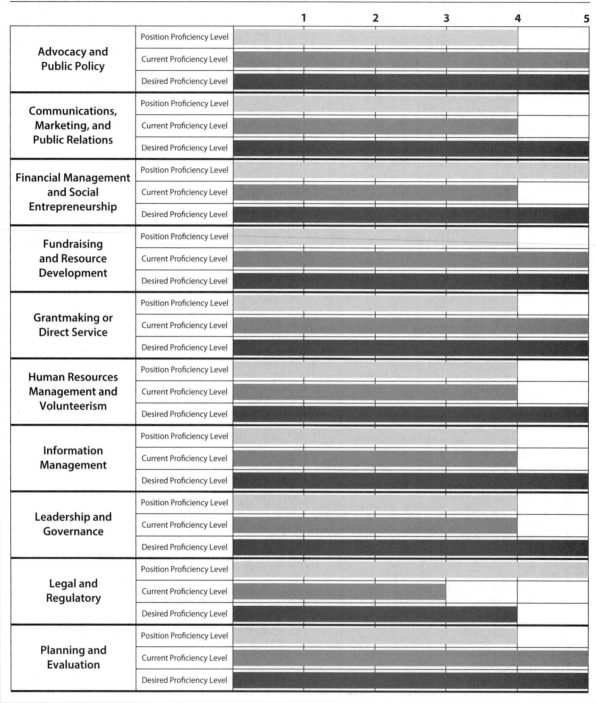

TABLE 6.4
Proficiency Strengths: President/Board Chair, Volunteer-Run Organization

Competencies	Current Proficiency Level	Specific Examples/Justification for Rating
Advocacy and Public Policy	5	Recommends community outreach and advocacy efforts to further the awareness and cultural traditions of music.
Communications, Marketing, and Public Relations	4	Leads correspondence for festival.
Financial Management and Social Entrepreneurship	4	Collaborates with treasurer to establish, implement, and troubleshoot budget.
Fundraising and Resource Development	5	Cultivates partners and sponsors for festival.
Direct Service	5	Troubleshoots all areas of the festival.
Human Resources and Volunteerism	4	Leads volunteer interviews.
Information Management	4	Prepares updates for website.
Leadership and Governance	4	Advises all directors and team leads.
Planning and Evaluation	5	Facilitates annual and strategic planning on an ongoing basis.

TABLE 6.5
Position Proficiency Gap Analysis: President/Board Chair, Volunteer-Run Organization

Competencies	Current Proficiency Level	Position Proficiency Level	Job Responsibility Examples
Financial Management and Social Entrepreneurship	4	5	Needs to take financial leadership.
Legal and Regulatory	3	5	Needs to evaluate all insurance options and troubleshoot risks with insurance provider.

The position proficiency gap analysis revealed the president/board chair had proficiency gaps in Financial Management and Social Entrepreneurship and in Legal and Regulatory. The board also used the president/board chair's job description to identify proficiency level examples required by the position.

The board chair/president's Desired Proficiency Levels compared to his Position Proficiency Levels (desired proficiency gap analysis) are shown in table 6.6.

TABLE 6.6
Desired Proficiency Gap Analysis: President/Board Chair, Volunteer-Run Organization

Competencies	Desired Proficiency Level	Position Proficiency Level	Job Responsibility Examples
Advocacy and Public Policy	5	4	Needs to continue to advance the organization's community outreach and advocacy efforts to further the awareness and cultural traditions of music.
Communications, Marketing, and Public Relations	5	4	Needs to continue to lead correspondence for festival as needed.
Fundraising and Resource Development	5	4	Needs to continue to recruit partners and sponsors for festival.
Direct Service	5	4	Needs to oversee all areas of the festival.
Human Resources Management and Volunteerism	5	4	Needs to continue to lead volunteer interviews as needed.
Information Management	5	4	Needs to continue to prepare updates for website as needed (shared with Marketing and IT).
Leadership and Governance	5	4	Needs to continue to advise all directors and team leads.
Legal and Regulatory	4	5	Needs to evaluate all insurance options and troubleshoots risks with insurance provider.
Planning and Evaluation	5	4	Needs to continue to facilitate annual and strategic planning on an ongoing basis.

The board chair discussed his results with the executive committee during the professional development goal setting process, which we discuss in chapter 8.

Small Grassroots Organization

As you saw in the Talent Map example for the small grassroots organization in table 6.1 and figure 6.2, the proficiency strengths (where most staff scored a 4 or 5 in their Current Proficiency Level) were in Direct Service and in Planning and Evaluation.

Additionally, the proficiency deficiencies (where most staff scored a 2 or lower in their Current Proficiency Level), were in the Financial Management and Social Entrepreneurship, Fundraising and Resource Development, and Legal and Regulatory categories. Moreover, there were position proficiency gaps (where most staff scored lower in their Current Proficiency Level compared to their Position Proficiency Level) in eight categories. The Talent Map review is shown in table 6.7.

Because the small grassroots organization needed a lot of professional development, it focused on the largest organizational proficiency gaps, which were in Advocacy and Public Policy and in Human Resources Management and Volunteerism.

In reviewing the Talent Map, the board then turned their attention to the individual results. We'll specifically discuss the IPDA results for the executive director shown in figure 6.5.

Following the steps we've described, the board first identified where the executive director showed expert and advanced proficiency levels. The executive director showed advanced proficiency levels (scored 4 in Current Proficiency Level) in Direct Service and in Planning and Evaluation. Then the board identified proficiency deficiencies, where the executive director

TABLE 6.7 Talent Map Review: Small Grassroots Organization	
Proficiency Strengths	Direct Service; Planning and Evaluation
Proficiency Deficiencies	Financial Management and Social Entrepreneurship; Fundraising and Resource Development; Legal and Regulatory
Position Proficiency Gaps	Advocacy and Public Policy; Communications; Marketing, and Public Relations; Financial Management and Social Entrepreneurship; Fundraising and Resource Development; Human Resources Management and Volunteerism; Legal and Regulatory; and Planning and Evaluation

FIGURE 6.5
IPDA Results: Executive Director, Small Grassroots Organization

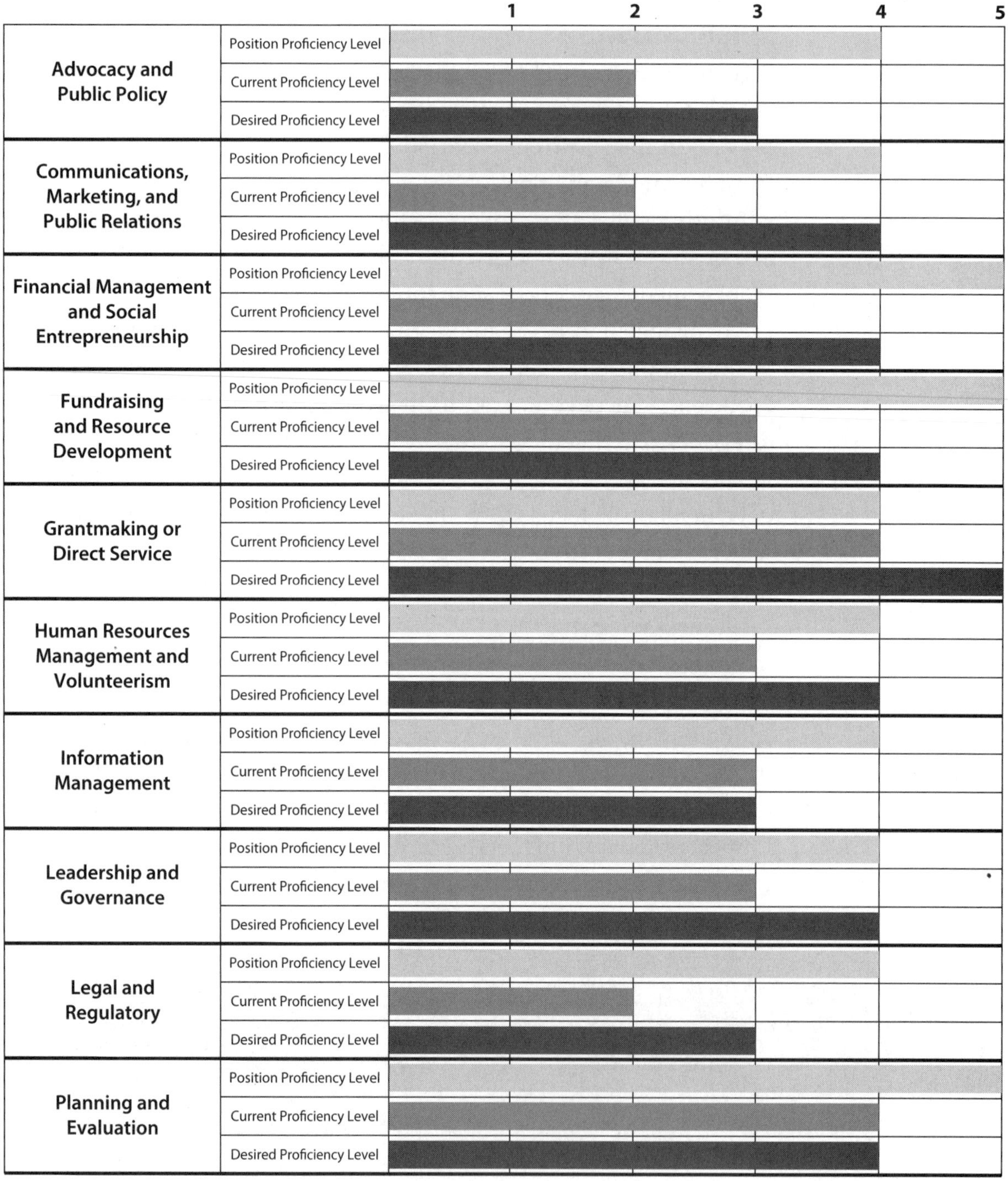

scored a 1 or 2 Current Proficiency Level. Tables 6.8 and 6.9 show the executive director's proficiency strengths and deficiencies.

Next, the board compared the executive director Position Proficiency Levels and Current Proficiency Levels to identify position proficiency gaps. This comparison revealed the executive director had proficiency gaps within all competencies except for Direct Service. The board also identified examples for the Position Proficiency Levels required of the job (shown in table 6.10). The board brought in specific responsibilities from the job description.

TABLE 6.8
Proficiency Strengths: Executive Director, Small Grassroots Organization

Competencies	Current Proficiency Level	Specific Examples / Justification for Rating
Direct Service	4	Develops programs and services that reflect the strategic direction for the organization.
Planning and Evaluation	4	Leads planning efforts to move the organization into the future.

TABLE 6.9
Proficiency Deficiencies: Executive Director, Small Grassroots Organization

Competencies	Current Proficiency Level	Specific Examples/Justification for Rating
Advocacy and Public Policy	2	Needs to nurture and develop collaborative relationships between the organization and other congregations, agencies, and groups concerned with the public welfare within the communities it serves.
Communications, Marketing, and Public Relations	2	Needs to ensure that the organization and its mission, programs, and services are presented consistently with a strong, positive image to relevant stakeholders.
Legal and Regulatory	2	Needs to ensure that all required licenses are obtained and kept current related to the organization's work.

TABLE 6.10
Position Proficiency Gap Analysis: Executive Director, Small Grassroots Organization

Competencies	Current Proficiency Level	Position Proficiency Level	Job Responsibility Examples
Advocacy and Public Policy	2	4	Needs to nurture and develop collaborative relationships between the organization and other congregations, agencies, and groups concerned with the public welfare within the communities it serves.
Communications, Marketing, and Public Relations	2	4	Needs to ensure that the organization and its mission, programs, and services are consistently presented with a strong, positive image to relevant stakeholders.
Financial Management and Social Entrepreneurship	3	5	Needs to solve all financial, tax, risk, and facilities requirements for the organization according to current laws and regulations.
Fundraising and Resource Development	3	5	Needs to facilitate fund development activities, including hosting events, making asks, authoring proposals, identifying funding sources, and undertaking other tasks required by the plan.
Human Resources Management and Volunteerism	3	4	Needs to ensure the selection, supervision, and evaluation of quality staff to deliver services.
Information Management	3	4	Needs to oversee the information management systems within the organization, ensuring that staff and volunteers have access to computers and technology to effectively carry out their jobs.
Leadership and Governance	3	4	Needs to advise the board of directors in the carrying out of its policy-making responsibility.
Legal and Regulatory	2	4	Needs to ensure that all required licenses are obtained and kept current related to the organization's work.
Planning and Evaluation	4	5	Needs to compare procedures for assessing the organization's effectiveness in achieving its goals.

The fact that the executive director had so many proficiency gaps could mean that there are too many advanced and expert proficiency levels required for this small organization. The board decided to focus on the largest proficiency gaps (where the executive director Current Proficiency Level scores were 2 levels below the Position Proficiency Level scores). Therefore, the position gap analysis was narrowed to five categories: Advocacy and Public Policy; Marketing, Communications, and Public Relations; Financial Management and Social Entrepreneurship; Fundraising and Resource Development; and Legal and Regulatory. Then the board compared the Desired Proficiency Levels, that is, where the executive director wants to be in the Position Proficiency Levels within one year. Table 6.11 shows the desired proficiency gap analysis.

Table 6.11 shows there is some disconnect with what is expected in the position and where the employee wants to be. These results were discussed with the executive director, and she came up with three professional development goals and objectives (to be discussed in chapter 9).

Midsized Organization

All staff members within the midsized organization took the IPDA, and the executive director calculated the responses and identified the organizational proficiency strengths, organizational proficiency deficiencies, and organizational position proficiency gaps. In figure 6.6, you can see there were no proficiency strengths for the organization (in which, most employees scored a 4 or 5).

Additionally, there were proficiency deficiencies (where most employees scored a 2 or lower) in five categories and position proficiency gaps (where most staff scored lower in their Current Proficiency Level than their Position Proficiency Level) in the same five categories, as well as in Planning and Evaluation. The Talent Map review is shown in table 6.12.

Because the midsized organization needed a lot of professional development, it focused on the largest organizational proficiency gaps, which were in three categories: Advocacy and Public Policy, Information Management, and Legal and Regulatory. In reviewing the Talent Map, the executive director then turned her attention to the individual results. We'll specifically discuss the IPDA results for the development coordinator shown in figure 6.7. The development coordinator had proficiency strengths in six categories (with a score of 4 in Current Proficiency Level) and had no proficiency deficiencies.

Table 6.13 shows the development coordinator's proficiency strengths.

TABLE 6.11

Desired Proficiency Gap Analysis: Executive Director, Small Grassroots Organization

Competencies	Desired Proficiency Level	Position Proficiency Level	Job Responsibility Examples
Advocacy and Public Policy	3	4	Needs to lead in-services/seminars with community institutions to bring community awareness to refugee issues.
Financial Management and Social Entrepreneurship	4	5	Needs to solve all financial, tax, risk, and facilities requirements for the organization according to current laws and regulations.
Fundraising and Resource Development	4	5	Needs to facilitate fund development activities, including hosting events, making asks, authoring proposals, identifying funding sources, and undertaking other tasks required by the plan.
Direct Service	5	4	Needs to continue to develop programs and services that reflect the strategic direction for the organization.
Information Management	3	4	Needs to oversee the information management systems within the organization, ensuring that staff and volunteers have access to computers and technology to effectively carry out their jobs.
Legal and Regulatory	3	4	Needs to ensure that all required licenses are obtained and kept current related to the organization's work.
Planning and Evaluation	4	5	Needs to evaluate goals and objectives for each program and service.

Next, the executive director compared the program coordinator's Position Proficiency Levels and Current Proficiency Levels to identify position proficiency gaps. This comparison revealed the development coordinator had a proficiency gap in Information Management. The board also provided examples for the Position Proficiency Levels required of the job. The board brought in specific responsibilities from the job description. The position proficiency gap analysis is shown in table 6.14.

FIGURE 6.6
Talent Map: Midsized Organization

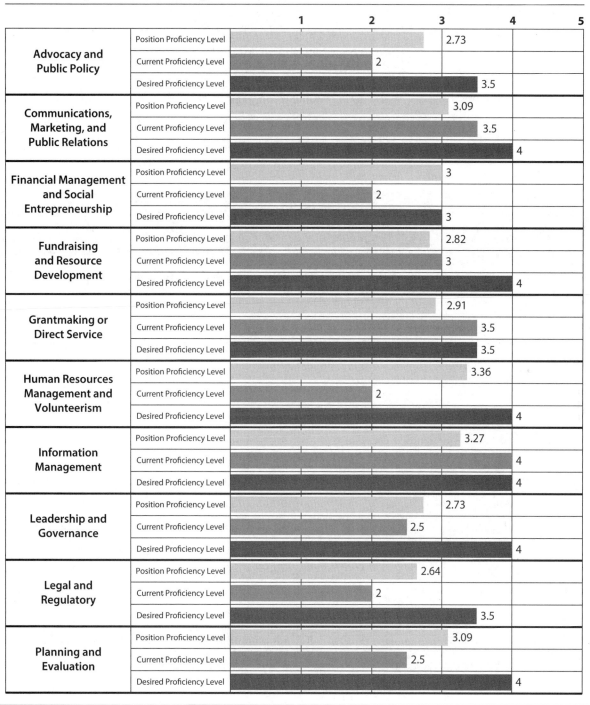

		1	2	3	4	5
Advocacy and Public Policy	Position Proficiency Level			2.73		
	Current Proficiency Level		2			
	Desired Proficiency Level			3.5		
Communications, Marketing, and Public Relations	Position Proficiency Level			3.09		
	Current Proficiency Level			3.5		
	Desired Proficiency Level				4	
Financial Management and Social Entrepreneurship	Position Proficiency Level			3		
	Current Proficiency Level		2			
	Desired Proficiency Level			3		
Fundraising and Resource Development	Position Proficiency Level			2.82		
	Current Proficiency Level			3		
	Desired Proficiency Level				4	
Grantmaking or Direct Service	Position Proficiency Level			2.91		
	Current Proficiency Level			3.5		
	Desired Proficiency Level			3.5		
Human Resources Management and Volunteerism	Position Proficiency Level			3.36		
	Current Proficiency Level		2			
	Desired Proficiency Level				4	
Information Management	Position Proficiency Level			3.27		
	Current Proficiency Level				4	
	Desired Proficiency Level				4	
Leadership and Governance	Position Proficiency Level			2.73		
	Current Proficiency Level		2.5			
	Desired Proficiency Level				4	
Legal and Regulatory	Position Proficiency Level		2.64			
	Current Proficiency Level		2			
	Desired Proficiency Level			3.5		
Planning and Evaluation	Position Proficiency Level			3.09		
	Current Proficiency Level		2.5			
	Desired Proficiency Level				4	

TABLE 6.12
Talent Map Review: Midsized Organization

Proficiency Strengths	None
Proficiency Deficiencies	Advocacy and Public Policy; Financial Management and Social Entrepreneurship; Direct Service; Information Management; Legal and Regulatory
Position Proficiency Gaps	Advocacy and Public Policy; Financial Management and Social Entrepreneurship; Direct Service; Information Management; Legal and Regulatory; Planning and Evaluation

TABLE 6.13
Proficiency Strengths: Development Coordinator, Midsized Organization

Competencies	Current Proficiency Level	Specific Examples/Justification for Rating
Communications, Marketing, and Public Relations	4	Develops appeal mailings and communicates with printers.
Financial Management and Social Entrepreneurship	4	Determines the expenses associated with fundraising activities. Creates grant financial reports.
Fundraising and Resource Development	4	Identifies, solicits, and stewards potential foundation, corporate, and individual donors.
Direct Service	4	Demonstrates awareness of client issues when participating in and planning client events.
Human Resources Management and Volunteerism	4	Supervises fundraising volunteers.
Planning and Evaluation	4	Identifies areas of improvement and provides new ideas for fundraising opportunities.

The executive director then compared the Desired Proficiency Levels, that is, where the development coordinator wants to be in one year with the position. Because the development coordinator already had advanced proficiency levels in the majority of the competency categories, the executive director realized through this process that the development coordinator

FIGURE 6.7
IPDA Results: Development Coordinator, Midsized Organization

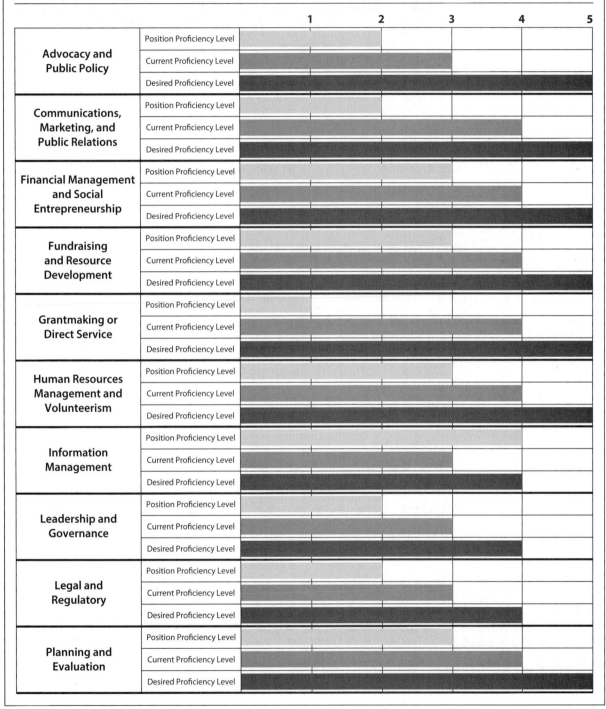

TABLE 6.14

Position Proficiency Gap Analysis: Development Coordinator, Midsized Organization

Competency Category	Current Proficiency Level	Position Proficiency Level	Job Responsibility Examples
Information Management	3	4	Needs to oversee the maintenance records of contributions and grants.

was overqualified for her position and should be promoted to development manager. The executive director then had a meeting and discussed the IPDA results and her promotion.

Grantmaking Organization

Four staff members from the grantmaking organization took the IPDA: the executive director, director of operations, director of grants and nonprofit services, and the program associate. The results are shown in figure 6.8. The executive director then identified the organizational proficiency strengths, organizational proficiency deficiencies, and organizational position proficiency gaps. There were no proficiency strengths in the organization (in which case most staff score a 4 or 5 in Current Proficiency Level).

There were also no proficiency deficiencies (in which case most staff score a 2 or lower in Current Proficiency Level). However, there were position proficiency gaps (where most staff scored lower in their Current Proficiency Level than their Position Proficiency Level) in all but two competency categories. The Talent Map review is shown in table 6.15.

TABLE 6.15

Talent Map Review: Grantmaking Organization

Proficiency Strengths	None
Proficiency Deficiencies	None
Position Proficiency Gaps	Advocacy and Public Policy; Communications, Marketing, and Public Relations; Grantmaking; Financial Management and Social Entrepreneurship; Human Resources Management and Volunteerism; Leadership and Governance; Legal and Regulatory; Planning and Evaluation

FIGURE 6.8
Talent Map: Grantmaking Organization

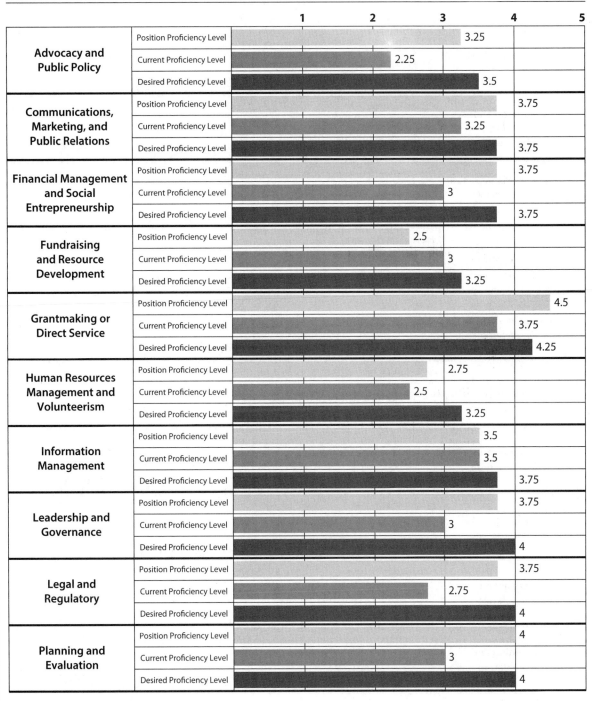

		1	2	3	4	5
Advocacy and Public Policy	Position Proficiency Level			3.25		
	Current Proficiency Level		2.25			
	Desired Proficiency Level			3.5		
Communications, Marketing, and Public Relations	Position Proficiency Level				3.75	
	Current Proficiency Level			3.25		
	Desired Proficiency Level				3.75	
Financial Management and Social Entrepreneurship	Position Proficiency Level				3.75	
	Current Proficiency Level			3		
	Desired Proficiency Level				3.75	
Fundraising and Resource Development	Position Proficiency Level		2.5			
	Current Proficiency Level			3		
	Desired Proficiency Level			3.25		
Grantmaking or Direct Service	Position Proficiency Level					4.5
	Current Proficiency Level				3.75	
	Desired Proficiency Level				4.25	
Human Resources Management and Volunteerism	Position Proficiency Level			2.75		
	Current Proficiency Level		2.5			
	Desired Proficiency Level			3.25		
Information Management	Position Proficiency Level			3.5		
	Current Proficiency Level			3.5		
	Desired Proficiency Level				3.75	
Leadership and Governance	Position Proficiency Level				3.75	
	Current Proficiency Level			3		
	Desired Proficiency Level				4	
Legal and Regulatory	Position Proficiency Level				3.75	
	Current Proficiency Level			2.75		
	Desired Proficiency Level				4	
Planning and Evaluation	Position Proficiency Level				4	
	Current Proficiency Level			3		
	Desired Proficiency Level				4	

FIGURE 6.9
IPDA Results: Program Associate, Grantmaking Organization

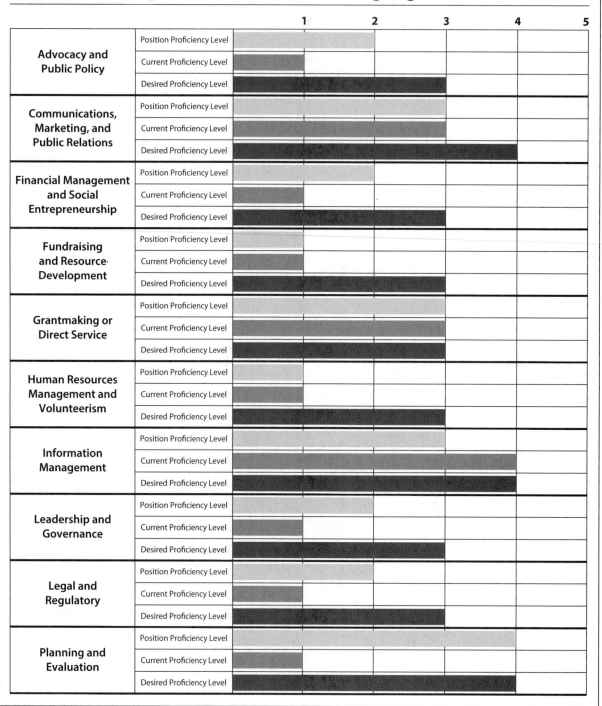

Because the grantmaking organization needed a lot of professional development, it focused on the largest organizational proficiency gaps, which were in Advocacy and Public Policy, Legal and Regulatory, and Planning and Evaluation.

In reviewing the Talent Map, the executive director then turned her attention to the individual results. We'll specifically discuss the IPDA results for the program associate shown in figure 6.9. The executive director identified the program associate's proficiency strengths, her proficiency deficiencies, her position proficiency gaps, desired proficiency gaps, and her professional development goals.

The program associate showed advanced proficiency (with a score of 4 in Current Proficiency Level) in Information Management. Then the executive director looked for proficiency deficiencies, where the program associate scored a 1 or 2 Current Proficiency Level. The program associate had several proficiency deficiencies. Table 6.16 shows the program associate's proficiency strengths, and table 6.17 shows the program associate's proficiency deficiencies.

Note that Human Resources is not a proficiency deficiency because the position requires only fundamental awareness (level 1).

Next, the executive director compared the program associate's Position Proficiency Levels and Current Proficiency Levels to identify position proficiency gaps. The executive director also identified examples for the Position Proficiency Levels from the job description. The position proficiency gap analysis is shown in table 6.18.

Then the executive director compared the Desired Proficiency Levels (where the program associate wants to be in one year with the Position Proficiency Levels). Table 6.19 shows the desired proficiency gap analysis.

The executive director reviewed the results of the IPDA with the program associate, and she came up with three professional development goals and objectives, which will be discussed in chapter 9.

TABLE 6.16
Proficiency Strengths: Program Associate, Grantmaking Organization

Competencies	Current Proficiency Level	Specific Examples/Justification for Rating
Information Technology	4	Translates raw data into meaningful management information.

TABLE 6.17

Proficiency Deficiencies: Program Associate, Grantmaking Organization

Competencies	Current Proficiency Level	Specific Examples/Justification for Rating
Advocacy and Public Policy	1	Needs to follow current issues related to grantmaking.
Financial Management and Social Entrepreneurship	1	Needs to assist the executive director to ensure that appropriate financial reports are made available to the board on a timely basis.
Leadership and Governance	1	Supports grantmaking staff to develop working relationships with organizations and community groups.
Legal and Regulatory	1	Need to assist the director with tracking proposals and eligibility assessments that have been submitted for review and approval.
Planning and Evaluation	1	Needs to provide strategic and program planning support.

TABLE 6.18

Position Proficiency Gap Analysis: Program Associate, Grantmaking Organization

Competencies	Current Proficiency Level	Position Proficiency Level	Job Responsibility Examples
Advocacy and Public Policy	1	2	Needs to support policy and practice recommendations for new strategies.
Financial Management and Social Entrepreneurship	1	2	Needs to assist the executive director to ensure that appropriate financial reports are made available to the board on a timely basis.
Leadership and Governance	1	2	Needs to help with developing working relationships with organizations and community groups that contribute to implementing strategies.
Legal and Regulatory	1	2	Needs to assist the director with tracking proposals and eligibility assessments that have been submitted for review and approval.
Planning and Evaluation	1	3	Needs to provide strategic and program planning support.

TABLE 6.19

Desired Proficiency Gap Analysis: Program Associate, Grantmaking Organization

Competencies	Desired Proficiency Level	Position Proficiency Level	Job Responsibility Examples
Advocacy and Public Policy	3	2	Needs to support policy and practice recommendations for new strategies and programs.
Communications, Marketing, and Public Relations	4	3	Needs to participate in organizing meetings, conferences, and site visits.
Financial Management and Social Entrepreneurship	3	2	Needs to assist the executive director to ensure that appropriate financial reports are made available to the board on a timely basis.
Fundraising and Resource Development	3	1	Needs to observe current programmatic trends and best practices, the funding landscape, and potential partners.
Human Resources Management and Volunteerism	3	1	Needs to observe discussions, trainings, and exchanges of best practices between staff and other foundations in order to assist staff.
Information Management	4	3	Needs to use the Internet and basic software applications.
Leadership and Governance	3	2	Needs to help with developing working relationships with organizations and community groups that contribute to implementing strategies.
Legal and Regulatory	3	2	Needs to assist the director with tracking proposals and eligibility assessments that have been submitted for review and approval.

Conclusion

In this chapter we described the Individual Professional Development Assessment, how to administer the IPDA to staff and volunteers, and how to interpret and review results. In the next chapter, we cover the next piece of the Talent Development Platform—the Individual Learning Styles Assessment. This assessment will help you create professional development opportunities that are specific to employees' and volunteers' learning styles and preferences.

Chapter 7
The Individual Learning Styles Assessment

Now that you've administered and scored the IPDA, it's time to administer one last assessment to your employees and volunteers, the Individual Learning Styles Assessment (ILSA). In this chapter we explain the ILSA, provide you a sample assessment, and show you how to score the assessment and interpret the results. We also provide you examples of ILSA results from our four pilot organizations. Figure 7.1 gives you an ILSA checklist.

About the Individual Learning Styles Assessment

There has been a lot of research about learning styles. We use the most popular definition to define learning styles as the basis for this assessment process: learning styles are "the way in which individuals characteristically approach different learning tasks" (Cassidy, 2004, p. 421). We believe that an individual possesses multiple learning styles and that these learning styles may change depending on the situation. Keeping these two beliefs in mind, there are over twenty learning styles assessment tools developed by various scholars over the years that we could have used in this book. In selecting a learning styles assessment for social change organizations, we knew we wanted to use an established tool that had been tested in a variety of organizational settings, was free to use, didn't have validity issues, and has been replicated in a variety of settings.

Heather has been using a popular learning styles assessment tool in the classroom setting for the past three years. The assessment is called the Styles of Learning Interaction model (Riechmann & Grasha, 1974). She picked the Styles of Learning Interaction model because the academic community has discussed it for years (e.g., Curry, 1987; Ferrell, 1983; Jonassen & Grabowski, 1993; Riding & Rayner, 1998), and it has been

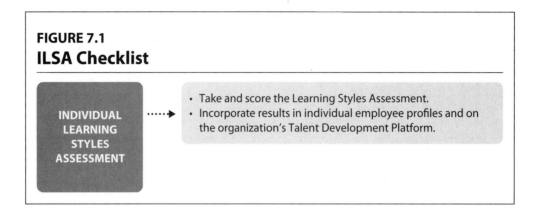

FIGURE 7.1
ILSA Checklist

INDIVIDUAL LEARNING STYLES ASSESSMENT

- Take and score the Learning Styles Assessment.
- Incorporate results in individual employee profiles and on the organization's Talent Development Platform.

tested for reliability and validity, which means that when the tool is used in a variety of settings, those who take the assessment will score similarly.

In the assessment, employees and volunteers indicate their level of agreement, from strongly disagree to strongly agree, to a series of questions about how they like to learn. This allows them to identify their preferred learning styles using six categories: participant, avoidant, independent, dependent, collaborative, and competitive. In addition, Heather added a series of questions to the Learning Styles Assessment so employees and volunteers can more specifically identify their preferences (strong, moderate, depends on training, and no) for their training location, format, time, day, duration, and how far they are willing to travel for training.

Benefits of Administering the Individual Learning Styles Assessment

The Learning Styles Assessment provides you with your employees' and volunteers' perspective on how they want to learn. As with any self-assessment, participants may perceive their learning needs one way, but they may actually need a different way of learning. If certain employees find out from the assessment that they are participatory learners, but they wish to set an objective where they work on a more independent project, then allow them to do that. Don't hold each employee and volunteer to his or her scores; the assessment is really an opportunity for them to get to know themselves a bit more, which will help them set their objectives more effectively in the future.

The assessment also allows employees to explore their learning style and learning preferences in an individualized way. Often when working with a team, the general preferences of the team become the perceived preferences by all of its members. The Learning Styles Assessment allows individuals to get a sense of how they learn most effectively apart from their team.

The ILSA results will present trends across the organization as well as discrepancies. Some employees will be outliers, with a particular learning style no one else has in the organization. In the small grassroots organization, there was one employee who scored as a competitive learning style, while the rest of the employees were participant, collaborative, or independent. In such a case, be sure the employee with a competitive style is able to select individual professional development goals and objectives when working through his or her objectives. When going through the assessment scores with staff, the identification of outliers within the full group is also important. If the staff knows that someone learns differently than they do, especially when the rest of the team has similar learning styles, that individual will feel safer to learn and less ostracized. Be sure to talk through all these differences with your team and what it means for how everyone interacts on a regular basis.

To further support outliers, we recommend following research on learning styles. For example, researchers have found that if the majority of the learners are participant with one or two avoidant learners, the executive director or manager can facilitate positive reinforcements to the avoidant learner and tie learning activities to the avoidant learner's life. If the majority of learners are independent, then the executive director or manager can support the dependent learner in self-identifying and recommending learning activities. If the majority of learners are collaborative, the executive director or manager can provide an opportunity where the competitive individual can lead the group to consensus (Jonassen & Grabowski, 1993).

Administering the Individual Learning Styles Assessment

Just like the Organizational Learning Assessment and the Individual Professional Development Assessment, we recommend that after you send out the Individual Learning Styles Assessment to your employees and volunteers, you send multiple e-mail reminders and provide a specific deadline to complete the assessment. We also recommend allowing three weeks to take the assessment, but no longer. This timeline allows for busy schedules but doesn't give participants the opportunity to put off taking the assessment. We've provided a template invitation for you to customize (exhibit 7.1). You can also administer the assessment online through talent4socialchange.org.

You might also consider having employees and volunteers take the assessment during a regularly scheduled staff meeting. You will most likely have one or two employees to catch after the meeting, but this could significantly reduce the time it takes to receive the completed surveys. This is the only survey suitable for administering and discussing as a group, so take advantage. The Individual Professional Development Assessment and the Organizational Learning Assessment both require more individual time to take in order for employees and volunteers to answer in a thoughtful manner.

EXHIBIT 7.1
ILSA E-mail Invitation Template

Dear _____,

As you are aware _____ [your organization] is in the process of assessing our learning culture and your professional development preferences so that we can be more strategic and systematic in our professional development offerings.

Please set aside 10–15 minutes to take the Individual Learning Styles Assessment. This assessment will gather information about how you learn. The survey will also ask about your training format preferences.

We will be able use the summary data to determine common learning styles across the organization and opportunities to create meaningful learning experiences based on specific learning styles.

Please be as honest as possible when taking the assessment.

Take the survey here: [Insert Link]

Please let us know if you have any questions about the survey.

The Individual Learning Styles Assessment

The Individual Learning Styles Assessment is split into two sections (exhibit 7.2). The first section consists of six questions, each of which focuses on a specific learning style. Each question asks respondents to rate five statements. Table 7.1 lists the question numbers and corresponding learning styles and provides a description of each style.

The second section of the assessment allows staff and volunteers to indicate their training preferences, which will help your organization develop more specific and customized training. The assessment covers the following types of training preferences:

- Training location
- Training format
- Training time

TABLE 7.1
Learning Styles and Descriptions

Question Number	Learning Style	Description
1	Participant	Good citizen in the work place. Enjoys learning and takes part in much of the learning activities as possible. Typically eager to do as much of the required learning activity and optional learning activities as possible.
2	Avoidant	Not enthusiastic about learning content. Does not like to participate in learning activities. Is uninterested in learning.
3	Independent	Likes to think for themselves and is confident in learning abilities.
4	Dependent	Shows little intellectual curiosity and only learns what is required. Views supervisors and managers as structure and support and as the providers of specific guidelines on what to do.
5	Collaborative	Enjoys working harmoniously with peers.
6	Competitive	Suspicious of peers, leading to competition for rewards and recognition.

Source: Adapted from Riechmann and Grasha (1974).

- Training day

- Training duration

- Travel to training

This information helps confirm the learning style of each employee or volunteer and provides more specific information about training preferences so that the organization can create meaningful professional development experiences.

EXHIBIT 7.2

The Individual Learning Styles Assessment

In this assessment, you will be asked a series of questions about how you learn. Data collected in this survey will be used to understand learning style preferences across the organization.

Participation in this survey is entirely voluntary; you can choose to opt out at any time. The information collected in this survey will be shared with your organization and will be used for research purposes. There are no risks for you to participate in this survey that exceed the risks encountered in everyday life.

EXHIBIT 7.2
The Individual Learning Styles Assessment, Cont'd

(* = Required)

I have read and understand this form, and consent to the process and research it describes to me.*

❏   Yes

❏   No

Name of Organization*_____

Job Title or Volunteer Role*_____

SECTION 1

For each of the questions in section 1, use the following scale: 1 = strongly disagree; 2 = disagree; 3 = unsure; 4 = agree; 5 = strongly agree.

1. Rate your agreement with the following statements.*

Mark only one box per row.

	Strongly Disagree	Disagree	Unsure	Agree	Strongly Agree
Training seminars are usually something worth attending.					
It is my responsibility to get as much as I can out of a training seminar.					
Training seminars are interesting.					
I try to participate as much as I can in all aspects of training.					
I complete work/volunteering assignments above and beyond what is required of me.					

EXHIBIT 7.2
The Individual Learning Styles Assessment, Cont'd

2. Rate your agreement with the following statements.*

Mark only one box per row.

	Strongly Disagree	Disagree	Unsure	Agree	Strongly Agree
Seminars/workshops are usually boring.					
I very seldom am excited about attending a training seminar or workshop.					
Paying attention in training seminars or workshops is very difficult for me to do.					
I learn just enough about my job or volunteer role to get by.					
I typically leave things to the last minute.					

3. Rate your agreement with the following statements.*

Mark only one box per row.

	Strongly Disagree	Disagree	Unsure	Agree	Strongly Agree
I learn a lot about how to do my job or volunteer role on my own.					
I feel very confident about my ability to learn on my own.					
If I like a topic, I try to find out more about it on my own.					
I like to learn at my own pace.					
When I don't understand something, I try to figure it out myself.					

EXHIBIT 7.2
The Individual Learning Styles Assessment, Cont'd

4. Rate your agreement with the following statements.*

Mark only one box per row.

	Strongly Disagree	Disagree	Unsure	Agree	Strongly Agree
I rely on managers to tell me what is important to learn.					
I only do what is required to do in my learning.					
I complete my assignments exactly how my manager tells me to complete them.					
I learn better when I am more closely supervised.					
I like it when managers are well organized.					

5. Rate your agreement with the following statements.*

Mark only one box per row.

	Strongly Disagree	Disagree	Unsure	Agree	Strongly Agree
Working with other coworkers or volunteers on projects is something I enjoy doing.					
I enjoy discussing my ideas and issues about the organization with my coworkers.					
Coworkers should be encouraged to share their ideas with one another.					
I think an important part of training is learning how to get along with other people.					
I am willing to help out other coworkers when they don't understand something.					

EXHIBIT 7.2
The Individual Learning Styles Assessment, Cont'd

6. Rate your agreement with the following statements.*

Mark only one box per row.

	Strongly Disagree	Disagree	Unsure	Agree	Strongly Agree
It is necessary to compete with other employees/volunteers for positive performance reviews.					
I like to solve problems before anyone else can.					
To stand out, I complete my assignments better than other employees/volunteers.					
I want my manager to give me more recognition for the work I do.					
Employees/volunteers have to be aggressive to do well in training situations.					

SECTION 2

In order for our organization to create and refer to relevant training, it is important we understand your training preferences.

7. In the question below, please rate your preference for training locations.*

Mark only one box per row.

	No Preference (1)	Depends on Training (2)	Moderate Preference (3)	Strong Preference (4)
Training on-site				
Training off-site				
Online training				

EXHIBIT 7.2
The Individual Learning Styles Assessment, Cont'd

8. In the question below, please rate your preference for training formats.*

Mark only one box per row.

	No Preference (1)	Depends on Training (2)	Moderate Preference (3)	Strong Preference (4)
One-on-one coaching or mentoring				
Workshops				
Conferences				
YouTube training				
Webinar				
Live chat / help desk				
Self-learning				
Computer directed				
Training manual				
Computer testing				
Increased community involvement				
Increased supervision				
Stretch assignment				
Other _____				
Other _____				

9. Please rate your preference for training time.*

Mark only one box per row.

	No Preference (1)	Depends on Training (2)	Moderate Preference (3)	Strong Preference (4)
Morning training time				
Afternoon training time				
Evening training time				

10. Please rate your preference for training day.*

Mark only one box per row.

EXHIBIT 7.2
The Individual Learning Styles Assessment, Cont'd

	No Preference (1)	Depends on Training (2)	Moderate Preference (3)	Strong Preference (4)
Weekday training				
Weekend training				

11. Please rate your preference for training duration.*

Mark only one box per row.

	No Preference (1)	Depends on Training (2)	Moderate Preference (3)	Strong Preference (4)
Less than 1 hour training				
Less than 3 hours training				
One half-day training				
One whole-day training				
More than one full day training				

12. Please rate your preference for travel time to training.*

Mark only one box per row.

	No Preference (1)	Depends on Training (2)	Moderate Preference (3)	Strong Preference (4)
0–25 miles travel to the training				
26–50 miles travel to the training				
51–75 miles travel to the training				
76–100 miles travel to the training				
100+ miles travel to the training				

Scoring and Interpreting Results

Once employees and volunteers take the ILSA, they can immediately calculate their scores. Scoring for each section of the assessment is straightforward and can be done quickly following delivery of the assessment.

Section 1 Scoring

Gather scores from each employee or volunteer and figure an average for each question. The scoring example we provide is from question 3 in the assessment, which focuses on the independent learning style. In this example, the executive director determined her average score for question 3. In table 7.2, the executive director's average score for question 3 was 4.

When an employee's or volunteer's average score is 4 or more for that question, the score indicates that the person prefers that learning style. The executive director clearly identified with the independent learning style (the focus of question 3). This scoring is repeated for every question in section 1. Employees and volunteers could potentially score high in three categories, although it is more likely they will show preference for one or two categories. Here are the learning styles preferences for the executive director of the small grassroots organization:

- Independent
- Collaborative
- Participant

Next, you'll want to get the average scores for each employee for each question in section 1. In table 7.3 we've provided responses to all statements in question 3 from all five staff in the small grassroots organization. The average scores for question 3 are shown in the far right column.

TABLE 7.2 **Learning Styles Assessment: Question 3 Scores, Executive Director**						
Job Title or Volunteer Role	I learn a lot about how to do my job or volunteer role on my own.	I feel very confident about my ability to learn on my own.	If I like a topic, I try to find out more about it on my own.	I like to learn at my own pace.	When I don't understand something, I try to figure it out myself.	Avg.
Executive Director	4	4	4	4	4	**4**

TABLE 7.3
Learning Styles Assessment: Question 3 Scores, Small Grassroots Organization

Job Title or Volunteer Role	I learn a lot about how to do my job or volunteer role on my own.	I feel very confident about my ability to learn on my own.	If I like a topic, I try to find out more about it on my own.	I like to learn at my own pace.	When I don't understand something, I try to figure it out myself.	Avg.
Executive Director	4	4	4	4	4	**4**
Community Worker	4	5	5	4	5	**4.6**
Program Coordinator	4	2	5	2	4	**3.4**
Community Engagement Coordinator	4	5	5	5	4	**4.6**
Education Supervisor	5	3	4	3	3	**3.6**

Looking further at the scores, the executive director, community worker and community engagement supervisor demonstrate they each prefer the independent learning style, having scored 4 or above.

Next, the organization can average the scores from each question to determine the common learning styles across the organization. Table 7.4 shows the average scores for each question in section 1 for the small grassroots organization.

After you have calculated each employee's score for each question, you need to put them on the Learning Styles Map. The Learning Styles Map visualizes the results of the ILSA and can be found on the Talent Development Platform. Put a dot or X where an employee scored a four or higher for that learning style. In the case of the small grassroots organization, shown in figure 7.2 and table 7.4, the main learning styles for their team were participant, independent, and collaborative. The education supervisor also preferred the competitive learning style.

TABLE 7.4
Learning Styles Assessment: Section 1 Combined Average Scores per Question

	Question 1 Participant	Question 2 Avoidant	Question 3 Independent	Question 4 Dependent	Question 5 Collaborative	Question 6 Competitive
Executive Director	3.8	1.8	4	2.4	4	2.6
Community Worker	4.4	1.8	4.6	3	4.6	2.6
Program Coordinator	4	2.6	3.4	2.8	4.2	2.6
Community Engagement Coordinator	3.8	3.4	4.6	3.4	4	2.8
Education Supervisor	4.2	2	3.6	3.6	4	4
Average	**4.04**	**2.32**	**4.04**	**3.04**	**4.16**	**2.92**

FIGURE 7.2
Learning Styles Map: Small Grassroots Organization

Participant ● ● ●	Avoidant
Independent ● ● ●	Dependent
Collaborative ● ● ● ● ●	Competitive ●

Section 2 Scoring

The second half of the assessment is scored differently. Staff and volunteers rate their training preferences on the following scale: 1 = no preference; 2 = depends on training; 3 = moderate preference; or 4 = strong preference. To score section 2, first have employees identify where they scored a 3 or a 4. This will allow them to see their preferences in each of the six training preference categories. Employees and volunteers can indicate more than one training preference within each category. Here are all the possible training preference categories:

- *Training Locations*: on-site, off-site, online

- *Training Formats*: one-on-one coaching, workshops, conferences, YouTube training, webinar, live chat/help desk, self-learning, computer directed, training manual, computer testing, increased community involvement, increased supervision, stretch assignment

- *Training Time*: morning, afternoon, evening

- *Training Day*: weekday, weekend

- *Training Duration*: less than 1 hour, less than 3 hours, one half-day, more than one full day

- *Travel to Training*: 0–25 miles, 26–50 miles, 51–75 miles, 76–100 miles, 100+ miles

In the small grassroots organization the executive director scored "depends on training" for the training location (as shown in table 7.5), and therefore is flexible when it comes to on-site versus off-site training locations.

This scoring is continued for each employee with each training preference. Here are all the individual training preferences for the executive director of the small grassroots organization:

- *Training Location*: Depends on training

- *Training Format*: Self-learning (strongest preference), one-on-one coaching, workshops, conferences, increased community involvement, increased supervision

- *Training Time*: Morning

- *Training Day*: Weekday

- *Training Duration*: Less than 3 hours, one half-day

- *Travel to Training*: 0–50 miles from office

Now that you know how to score individual training preferences, you'll need to determine the preferences of each individual in each of the six training categories. After that, you'll average the scores in each training

TABLE 7.5
Training Location Preferences: Executive Director, Small Grassroots Organization

Job Title	On-Site	Off-Site	Online
Executive Director	2	2	1

TABLE 7.6
Training Location Preferences: Small Grassroots Organization

	On-Site	Off-Site	Online
Community Worker	4	2	3
Program Coordinator	2	4	1
Community Engagement Coordinator	3	4	1
Education Supervisor	3	3	1
Average	**2.8**	**3**	**1.4**

preference category to get a sense of training preferences across the entire organization. Table 7.6 shows the individual preferences and the average scores of all employees within the small grassroots organization for the Training Location question.

As you can see in table 7.6, the training location preferences vary across the staff. However, training off-site has a higher average score by a bit, indicating it is moderately preferred by staff over on-site training. Due to this minimal difference in scoring, employees in the small grassroots organization should be offered training opportunities both on-site and off-site.

It is also important to consider location preferences for individual employees and volunteers. For example, the executive director indicated her location preference as "depends on training," whereas the community worker indicated "on-site" as the preferred training location. You can use employees' individual scores when setting their professional development goals and objectives for the year. Tables 7.7 through 7.11 show the remaining training preferences for the small grassroots organization.

After averaging all the scores, here is a summary of the training preferences for the small grassroots organization:

- *Training Location*: Off-site (moderate preference)

- *Training Format(s)*: Workshops, conferences, increased community involvement, one-on-one coaching, self-learning, and increased supervision

- *Training Time*: Evening or morning, depends on training

- *Training Day*: Weekday

- *Training Duration*: Less than 3 hours

- *Travel to Training*: 0–25 miles travel

TABLE 7.7 Training Format Preferences: Small Grassroots Organization

	One-on-One Coaching	Work-shops	Confer-ences	YouTube Training	Webinar	Live Chat/Help Desk	Self-Learning	Computer Training Directed	Manual	Computer Testing	Increased Community Involvement	Increased Supervision	Stretch Assignment
Executive Director	3	3	3	1	1	1	4	1	1	1	3	3	1
Community Worker	4	4	4	3	3	3	4	3	1	1	4	3	1
Program Coordinator	4	4	4	2	1	1	1	3	3	3	4	3	1
Community Engagement Coordinator	3	4	4	2	2	1	4	1	3	1	4	3	3
Education Supervisor	3	3	3	3	3	1	4	3	3	3	3	4	4
Average	3.4	3.6	3.6	2.2	2	1.4	3.4	2.2	2.2	1.8	3.6	3.2	2

TABLE 7.8 **Training Time Preferences: Small Grassroots Organization**			
	Morning Training Time	**Afternoon Training Time**	**Evening Training Time**
Executive Director	3	1	1
Community Worker	4	3	1
Program Coordinator	2	3	4
Community Engagement Coordinator	1	4	4
Education Supervisor	3	1	3
Average	**2.6**	**2.4**	**2.6**

TABLE 7.9 **Training Day Preferences: Small Grassroots Organization**		
	Weekday Training	**Weekend Training**
Executive Director	3	1
Community Worker	4	1
Program Coordinator	4	3
Community Engagement Coordinator	3	1
Education Supervisor	3	1
Average	**3.4**	**1.4**

Utilizing the Results

Once you've scored the Individual Learning Styles Assessment, it is important to identify what types of learning activities would be the most appropriate based on the types of learning styles and preferences within your organization. Employee and volunteer involvement is key during this process. Involvement can take place during individual or all-staff meetings. Research shows that having employees and volunteers involved in identifying their learning activities is empowering (Tough, 1979).

We've adapted the table provided by Riechmann and Grasha to identify the types of learning activities employees and volunteers may prefer based on their individual learning styles (table 7.12). It is important to keep these activities in mind when identifying professional development stretch assignments, mentoring, and training.

TABLE 7.10
Training Duration Preferences: Small Grassroots Organization

	Less than 1 hour training	Less than 3 hour training	One half-day training	One whole-day training	More than one full day training
Executive Director	1	3	3	1	1
Community Worker	3	4	2	2	2
Program Coordinator	3	2	4	4	4
Community Engagement Coordinator	4	4	1	1	3
Education Supervisor	3	3	3	1	1
Average	**2.8**	**3.2**	**2.6**	**1.8**	**2.2**

TABLE 7.11
Travel to Training Preferences: Small Grassroots Organization

	0–25 miles travel to training	26–50 miles travel to training	51–75 miles travel to training	76–100 miles travel to training	100+ miles travel to training
Executive Director	3	3	1	1	1
Community Worker	2	2	2	2	2
Program Coordinator	3	2	2	4	4
Community Engagement Coordinator	4	4	3	2	4
Education Supervisor	3	1	1	1	1
Average	**3**	**2.4**	**1.8**	**2**	**2.4**

Based on the learning styles and learning preference results, the small grassroots organization determined that they should implement the following types of professional development activities and training:

- Conferences*
- Weeklong trainings

TABLE 7.12 **Learning Activities Based on Learning Styles**	
Participant	**Avoidant**
• Conferences • Weeklong trainings • Service learning • Increased community involvement	• Mentoring • Coaching • YouTube videos • Self-learning
Independent	**Dependent**
• Self-learning • Computer directed • One-on-one coaching • Stretch assignment • Training manual	• Webinars • Workshops • Retreats • Increased supervision • Job shadowing
Collaborative	**Competitive**
• On-site trainings • Group learning • Role playing or modeling	• On-site trainings • Webinars • Computer testing

- Service learning
- Increased community involvement*
- On-site trainings*
- Group learning*
- Role playing or modeling*
- Self-learning*
- Computer directed*
- One-on-one coaching*

The items starred on the list also match the executive director's learning styles and preferences.

Make and use a similar list while creating professional development objectives for the organization.

The Learning Styles Assessment in Practice

Volunteer-Run Organization

All of the board members within the volunteer-run organization took the Learning Styles Assessment. Their learning styles are shown in figure 7.3.

FIGURE 7.3
Learning Styles Map: Volunteer-Run Organization

Participant	Avoidant
●	
Independent	Dependent
● ● ● ●	
Collaborative	Competitive
● ● ● ●	

TABLE 7.13
Learning Styles: President/Board Chair, Volunteer-Run Organization

Participant (1)	Avoidant
Independent (1)	Dependent
Collaborative (1)	Competitive

The president/board chair's learning styles were similar to those of the rest of the board members. His results are shown in table 7.13.

The training preferences results for the volunteer-run organization were as follows:

- *Training Location*: Off-site

- *Training Format(s)*: Conferences, workshops, training manual, increased community involvement

- *Training Time*: Evening

- *Training Day*: Weekend

- *Training Duration*: Depends on Training

- *Travel to Training*: 0–25 miles

Here are the individual training preferences for the president/board chair for the volunteer-run organization:

- *Training Location*: Off-site

- *Training Format*: Conferences (strong preference), workshops, increased community involvement

- *Training Time*: No preference

- *Training Day*: Weekend

- *Training Duration*: One half-day

- *Travel to Training*: 0–25 miles

Based on the learning styles results and the training preferences, the board of the volunteer-run organization determined it would benefit from the following learning activities:

- Self-learning

- Computer directed

- One-on-one coaching

- Stretch assignment

- Training manual

- Conferences

- Weeklong trainings

- Service learning

- Increased community involvement

- On-site trainings

- Group learning

- Role playing or modeling

Small Grassroots Organization

As we stated earlier, in the small grassroots organization, the main learning styles were collaborative, independent, and participatory. These results are shown again in figure 7.4.

Delving further into the individual results, we see that the executive director from the small grassroots organization has two primary learning styles: collaborative and independent, shown in table 7.14.

FIGURE 7.4
Learning Styles Map: Small Grassroots Organization

Participant ● ● ●	Avoidant
Independent ● ● ●	Dependent
Collaborative ● ● ● ● ●	Competitive ●

TABLE 7.14 **Learning Styles: Executive Director, Small Grassroots Organization**	
Participant	Avoidant
Independent (1)	Dependent
Collaborative (1)	Competitive

As shown in the earlier summary of tables 7.7 through 7.11, the training preferences for the small grassroots organization were as follows:

- *Training Location*: Off-site (moderate preference)

- *Training Format(s)*: Workshops, conferences, increased community involvement, one-on-one coaching, self-learning, and increased supervision

- *Training Time*: Evening and morning, depends on training

- *Training Day*: Weekday

- *Training Duration*: Less than 3 hours

- *Travel to Training*: 0–25 miles travel

In addition, the individual training preferences for the executive director of the small grassroots organization were as follows:

- *Training Location*: Depends on training

- *Training Format*: Self-learning (strongest preference), one-on-one coaching, workshops, conferences, increased community involvement, increased supervision

- *Training Time*: Morning

- *Training Day*: Weekday

- *Training Duration*: less than 3 hours, one half-day

- *Travel to Training*: 0–50 miles

Therefore, when planning learning activities for the entire organization, the executive director noted the following learning activities would be the most applicable to the organization:

- On-site trainings

- Group learning

- Role playing or modeling

- Self-learning

- Computer directed

- One-on-one coaching

Midsized Organization Learning Styles and Preferences

In the midsized organization, the top learning styles were collaborative, independent, and participative. The results from the learning assessment are shown in figure 7.5.

The development coordinator from the midsized organization scored similarly to the overall organization in his learning style, which you can see in table 7.15.

The training preferences for the midsized organization were as follows:

- *Training Location*: Depends on training

- *Training Format(s)*: Workshops, increased community involvement

- *Training Time*: Depends on training

- *Training Day*: Weekday

- *Training Duration*: Depends on training

- *Travel to Training*: 0–25 miles

FIGURE 7.5
Learning Styles Map: Midsized Organization

Participant	Avoidant
● ● ● ● ● ● ● ● ●	
Independent	**Dependent**
● ● ● ● ● ● ● ● ● ● ● ●	
● ● **Collaborative** ● ●	**Competitive**
● ● ● ● ● ● ● ● ● ● ● ●	

TABLE 7.15
Learning Styles: Development Coordinator, Midsized Organization

Participant (1)	Avoidant
Independent (1)	Dependent
Collaborative (1)	Competitive

Also, the individual training preferences for the development coordinator of the midsized organization were as follows:

- *Training Location*: On-site

- *Training Format*: Workshops, conferences, increased supervision

- *Training Time*: Morning

- *Training Day*: Weekday

- *Training Duration*: 1 hour, 3 hours

- *Travel to Training*: 0–25 miles

The HR/office manager determined the following learning activities would be most appropriate for the organization:

- Self-learning

- Computer directed

- One-on-one coaching

- Stretch assignment

- Training manual

- Conferences

- Weeklong trainings

- Service learning

- Increased community involvement

- On-site trainings

- Group learning

- Role playing or modeling

Grantmaking Organization

The grantmaking organization's employees scored similarly to the midsized organization with independent, collaborative, participant learning styles, as shown in figure 7.6.

The program associate's learning styles were similar to those of the entire grantmaking organization. Her results are shown in table 7.16.

The training preferences for the grantmaking organization were as follows:

- *Training Location*: Depends on training

- *Training Format(s)*: Workshops (strong preference), conferences, one-on-one coaching, self-learning, computer directed, increased community involvement

FIGURE 7.6
Learning Styles Map: Grantmaking Organization

Participant	Avoidant
●	
Independent	Dependent
● ●	
Collaborative	Competitive
● ●	

TABLE 7.16
Learning Styles: Program Associate, Grantmaking Organization

Participant	Avoidant
Independent (1)	Dependent
Collaborative (1)	Competitive

- *Training Time*: No preference
- *Training Day*: No preference
- *Training Duration*: One half-day
- *Travel to Training*: 26–50 miles

The individual training preferences for the program associate of the grantmaking organization were as follows:

- *Training Location*: Off-site
- *Training Formats*: Workshops, conferences, training manual, increased community involvement
- *Training Time*: No preference
- *Training Day*: Weekday
- *Training Duration*: Less than 3 hours, one half-day
- *Travel to Training*: 0–25 miles, 26–50 miles

Based on the learning styles results, the president of the grantmaking organization identified the following learning activities based on the employees' learning styles:

- Self-learning
- Computer directed

- One-on-one coaching

- Stretch assignment

- Training manual

- Conferences

- Weeklong trainings

- Service learning

- Increased community involvement

- On-site trainings

- Group learning

- Role playing or modeling

Conclusion

In this chapter we described the Individual Learning Styles Assessment and how it identifies employees' and volunteers' unique learning styles and learning preferences. Knowledge of individual learning styles, trends, and preferences across the organization should inform the process of setting professional development goals and objectives that we discuss in the next chapter.

Chapter 8
Developing Organizational Goals and Setting Objectives

During the first few chapters of the book, you assessed the learning culture of your organization, your employees' and volunteers' proficiency levels, and what roles you needed to meet your strategic goals. This chapter takes all the pieces of the Talent Development Platform and brings them together for goal setting. We will walk you through setting organizational goals and objectives for professional development utilizing the results from the Talent Development Platform assessments. Figure 8.1 provides you with an organizational goal and objectives checklist.

Preparing for Goal Setting

In order to create your organization's professional development goals you will need several tools finalized to inform your decisions:

- The results from your Organizational Learning Assessment

- Your organizational Talent Map

- The results from staff members' and volunteers' Individual Professional Development Assessments

- Staff members' and volunteers' learning styles

- Your strategic and business plans

After you complete this process, you will have a completed organizational Talent Development Platform and professional development objectives for the year, which can be used to inform the process of setting staff and volunteer professional development objectives.

To begin goal setting, you need to structure how the professional development goal-setting process is going to work for your organization. The

FIGURE 8.1
Organizational Goals and Objectives Checklist

ORGANIZATIONAL GOALS AND OBJECTIVES ······▶

- Analyze the organization's Talent Development Platform alongside organization's strategic goals. (Note: This process should be done alongside yearly strategic planning, if possible.)
- Discuss results and necessary staff changes to be made prior to finalizing goals.
- Discuss assessment results with full staff to develop professional development goals, with objectives for on-the-job learning mentoring opportunities, and training.
- Set department goals and objectives, if applicable.
- Pass organizational and department goals and objectives to all employees and volunteers to set individual goals.

most effective goal-setting processes include everyone on staff (board and volunteers too) and are championed by all leadership and influencers in your organization. You can easily fit professional development goal setting into your strategic planning process, which is the optimal way to set learning goals. Because of the varying sizes of social change organizations, there isn't an exact framework for goal setting. However, here are some ground rules that you should consider when devising your format.

The Ground Rules

1. **Tie professional development goals directly to strategic goals.** If you connect your learning goals directly to strategic goals, you will maximize your goal-setting efforts and increase your return on investment.

2. **Give all staff and volunteers the opportunity to be involved in goal setting in some way.** This does not mean they have to be in every goal-setting meeting, but they do have to participate in department goal setting and drive individual objectives. We've already discussed adult learning, but this is one of the pillars of how adults learn best. Adults need to be part of establishing their destiny in order to learn most effectively.

3. **Have your board sign off on your goals.** If the board signs off on your goals, they are more likely to champion learning and give you the room in the budget and programs for professional development.

4. **Create a safe and noncompetitive environment for goal setting.** Creating a safe environment for all individuals participating in goal setting is part of a strong learning culture. All change, no matter how big or small, makes people squirm, which makes it all the more important to keep the environment safe and transparent for all staff and volunteers involved.

5. **Don't take goal setting lightly.** Because the goal-setting stage may change staff roles or positions, tread lightly. Listen to everyone during the process, and confirm that leadership is listening to concerns. Don't ignore anxiety; listen and take everything into consideration for the best of the organization.

6. **Use "SMART" criteria.** All goals should be specific, measurable, agreed to, realistic, and time bound" or SMART (Doran, 1981). Keep this acronym in mind as you are setting goals for the organization and for staff members. SMART goals, no matter how audacious, feel more obtainable.

7. **Discuss results in a full staff meeting.** Discuss, as a group, what goals will best work for everyone in the organization. If you have a large organization, you may want discussions to be a part of a shorter full staff meeting and longer department meetings. Either way, be sure to get everyone together at the same time to talk about the results.

8. **Ensure that staff and volunteers confirm goals before they're written in stone.** Give staff members an opportunity to confirm goals before they are finalized in your Platform. This will give your employees and volunteers a moment to champion the goals as their own. Be sure to use language like "These goals are a culmination of all the work we've done thus far and the input you gave us" and "I would like to thank you again for all the work you did to help us structure these goals for what we need." These statements remind them that they have had plenty of opportunity to provide input and shape the goals. *Make sure they actually do!*

9. **Once goals are set, give staff the opportunity to draft their objectives to meet the goals.** Organization leadership can facilitate the goal-setting process, but employees and volunteers should 'lead' their own objective setting. We'll talk extensively in chapter 9 about how employees and volunteers should set their individual goals and objectives.

Keep each of these ground rules in mind as you read this chapter and determine your goal-setting process. Remember, the process needs to fit the flow of how your organization works, and if you spent the right amount of time assessing your organization's learning culture, you should know exactly what is the best flow for your people.

Reviewing Strategic Goals and Setting Professional Development Goals

To begin the goal-setting process, have your strategic goals and business plans available for all staff, volunteers, and board members. If you have scheduled a large meeting to begin this process, start with an overview of your strategic goals. Everyone should be on the same page with your organization's intentions and their expectations toward those goals as employees or volunteers in the organization. Keep your strategic goals and business plan at the forefront of all conversations.

Connecting Learning Goals to Organizational Goals

We've already said this a few times, but it's important and bears repeating: you must have a strategic plan and business plan completed prior to setting these goals. We're fans of the business model canvas (Business Model Foundry, 2014) and Bryson's strategic planning framework (2011), if you need some recommendations. Some organizations complete this professional development goal-setting process alongside their strategic planning process. We interviewed a vice president at a B corporation who mentioned, "This [professional development goal-setting] process will be easy to implement for us, because of the level of bureaucracy we already have in place and the breadth to which our strategic goals are embedded across the organization. This process would be impossible for any organization that doesn't have a strategic plan" (Kenyatta Brame, personal communication, May 2014). He's right! Having strategic goals for your organization is what sets the bedrock for the professional development goal-setting process. If you don't have strategic goals, how will you know which direction to send staff into learning?

After you have reviewed your strategic goals and ensured that employees and volunteers are ready for goal setting, review the results from *all* of the Talent Development Platform assessments and talent mapping. If you are completing the goal-setting process along with your strategic or business planning process, you may want to review assessments prior to decision making and then again following individual goal setting before you finalize your organizational goals.

Reviewing Your Talent Development Platform

In each of the previous chapters we provided tips and tools for analyzing your organization's assessments, using team discussions to further your learning culture, and mapping your talent to ensure that the right people are in the right positions. Your Talent Development Platform puts all those items in one space for you to use during the goal-setting process. Figure 8.2 shows the small grassroots organization's Platform filled in with their assessments.

Weigh the results of your Organizational Learning Assessment, Talent Map, and Learning Styles Map as a team. Lead the discussion of the Platform with the following questions. Play facilitator and go where the team needs to go, but use these questions as a basis to get started:

- What competency areas are our greatest strengths?

- What areas provide the greatest opportunity?

- Which areas do we need improvement in to meet our organizational goals more effectively?

- Are there challenges we may have in reaching our goals that we can use learning objectives to overcome?

- Through your own learning, which areas do you believe you could provide a boost in?

- Are there areas where more than one staff member is interested in learning or sharing together?

- Are there staff members interested in leading learning topics?

- What overlaps do we have in our learning styles?

- Can we find areas where we can share trainings or team assignments that help more than one individual learn?

Once you've had your team discussion and distilled responses to these questions, ask your team for ideas on goals. Use dots or checks to have everyone vote on the highest priority goals and come to agreement on the final goals together. If you have a large staff, have small groups of cross-functional teams come up with draft goals together, and then come together as a full staff to complete the voting process and to finalize goals.

FIGURE 8.2
Talent Development Platform: Small Grassroots Organization

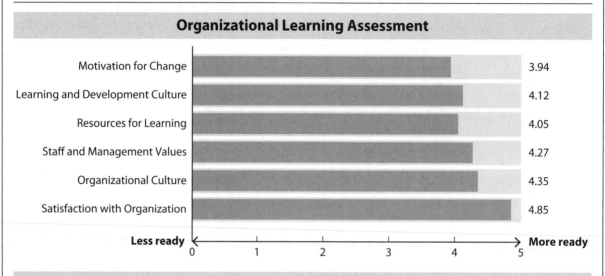

Organizational Learning Assessment

Motivation for Change	3.94
Learning and Development Culture	4.12
Resources for Learning	4.05
Staff and Management Values	4.27
Organizational Culture	4.35
Satisfaction with Organization	4.85

Less ready ← → More ready
0   1   2   3   4   5

Learning Styles Map

Participant	Avoidant
● ● ●	
Independent	**Dependent**
● ● ●	
Collaborative	**Competitive**
● ● ● ● ●	●

Goals and Objectives

Goal 1: Improve staff proficiency levels in Human Resources and Volunteerism in order to increase volunteer retention.	**01:** ALL staff responsible for one aspect of a volunteer recruitment plan.
	02: Community engagement supervisor mentors and as project lead; works one-on-one with each employee.
	03: Depending on the individual employees' learning preference they attend volunteer management seminar, webinar, or workshop.
Goal 2: Improve board proficiency levels in Financial Management to ensure strong internal controls and financial reporting.	**01:** One staff member each month assigned to review financial statements and report three findings.
	02: CPA and board treasurer mentor board members.
	03: Board members receive financial management book and links to video. CPA and board treasurer do two in-service trainings on financial statements during the board meeting.
Goal 3: Begin to introduce professional development in Advocacy and Public Policy so that the organization can become stronger advocates in the issue areas of the organization.	**01:** ALL staff brainstorms advocacy ideas for future years.
	02: Staff collaboratively identifies who they want to mentor them on nonprofit advocacy.
	03: Staff attends training provided by mentor.

01 = Learning on the Job; **02** = Mentoring and Peer-to-Peer Opportunities; **03** = Trainings

FIGURE 8.2
Talent Development Platform: Small Grassroots Organization, Cont'd

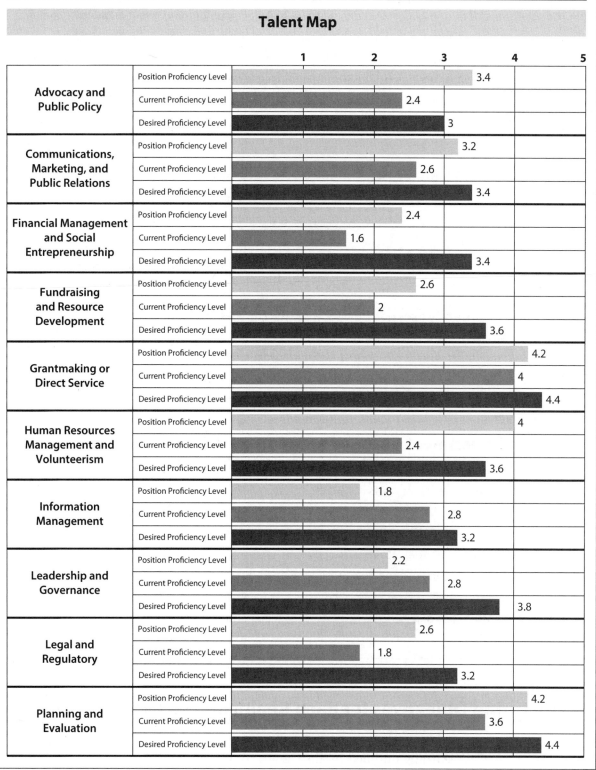

Talent Map

		1	2	3	4	5
Advocacy and Public Policy	Position Proficiency Level			3.4		
	Current Proficiency Level		2.4			
	Desired Proficiency Level			3		
Communications, Marketing, and Public Relations	Position Proficiency Level			3.2		
	Current Proficiency Level		2.6			
	Desired Proficiency Level			3.4		
Financial Management and Social Entrepreneurship	Position Proficiency Level		2.4			
	Current Proficiency Level	1.6				
	Desired Proficiency Level			3.4		
Fundraising and Resource Development	Position Proficiency Level		2.6			
	Current Proficiency Level		2			
	Desired Proficiency Level			3.6		
Grantmaking or Direct Service	Position Proficiency Level				4.2	
	Current Proficiency Level				4	
	Desired Proficiency Level				4.4	
Human Resources Management and Volunteerism	Position Proficiency Level				4	
	Current Proficiency Level		2.4			
	Desired Proficiency Level			3.6		
Information Management	Position Proficiency Level	1.8				
	Current Proficiency Level		2.8			
	Desired Proficiency Level			3.2		
Leadership and Governance	Position Proficiency Level		2.2			
	Current Proficiency Level		2.8			
	Desired Proficiency Level			3.8		
Legal and Regulatory	Position Proficiency Level		2.6			
	Current Proficiency Level	1.8				
	Desired Proficiency Level			3.2		
Planning and Evaluation	Position Proficiency Level				4.2	
	Current Proficiency Level			3.6		
	Desired Proficiency Level				4.4	

EXHIBIT 8.1
Goal Setting: Small Grassroots Organization

The small grassroots organization that piloted the Talent Development Platform set their goals by gathering the board and staff to discuss the results from all the assessments. Together, led by the executive director, they came up with the following professional development goals. According to the results of the Individual Professional Development Assessments and talent mapping, the staff needed professional development in Advocacy and Public Policy, Financial Management, and Human Resources and Volunteerism. Those results, coupled with the organization's strategic vision, resulted in the following goals:

- Improve staff proficiency levels in Human Resources and Volunteerism in order to increase volunteer retention.

- Improve staff proficiency levels in Financial Management to ensure strong internal controls and financial reporting.

- Begin to introduce professional development in Advocacy and Public Policy so that the organization can become stronger advocates in the issue areas of the organization.

Although there were only three goals, they covered the strongest needs of staff, as well as the breadth of individuals working for the organization's mission.

EXHIBIT 8.2
Setting Department Goals in Large Organizations

If your organization has departments (for example, fundraising or direct service), it may be beneficial for each department to set its own learning goals, mirroring the organizational goals. After setting the organizational goals together, each department head should lead a similar goal-setting process and set goals related to its specific departmental function within the organization. It is extremely important for each department head to keep the goals in alignment with the strategic intent of the organization and the organization's overall strategic goals. It is also a good practice for each department head to come together to ensure each department's goals don't overlap or misalign with other departments across the organization.

Structuring Objectives for Each Realm of Learning

As we stated in chapter 1, we strongly believe in the 70–20–10 model of learning outlined by the Center for Creative Leadership (Rabin, 2014) and tying *all* professional development activities to on-the-job experiences.

Once you've identified your professional development goals, create professional development objectives that fit into each realm of learning (exhibit 8.3). You will identify learning opportunities that focus on on-the-job experiences and will create mentoring and professional development workshops and trainings tied to on-the-job experiences.

While setting objectives in each of these realms, keep efficiencies in mind. Some employees or volunteers may be interested in learning a similar skill and could work on a new team as a stretch assignment together. Or perhaps employees and volunteers could act as mentors or connect well in peer teams. You may also be able to bring in a trainer or buy a training package for more than one employee to participate at a cheaper cost, if several employees are in need of increasing their proficiency in the same competency.

Learning on the Job

The notion that 70 percent of learning occurs on the job means that you must be willing to create on-the-job learning assignments and experiences for your staff and volunteers. On-the-job learning experiences need to stretch employees or volunteers beyond their current routine. To meet your organizational goals we recommend setting objectives that give one or two staff members or a work team a stretch assignment to help meet your goal. Discuss employee and volunteer needs when setting goals so that you can identify the proper individuals to help you meet each goal.

The most common on-the-job learning experiences involve stretch assignments where an individual develops and executes an organizational or department initiative or is involved with an event she or he has never participated in before. In the stretch assignment, the employee or volunteer has the opportunity to take on leadership and demonstrate new ways of thinking and acting within the organization, while learning a new skill through the work. Types of stretch assignments vary based on the position, competency area, and proficiency level where individuals need learning. Some examples of stretch assignments are leading an advocacy event, managing a direct mail campaign, overhauling social media efforts, creating financial statements, conducting a board training, or implementing a volunteer recruitment strategy.

Outside of on-the-job learning, staff can learn through sabbatical opportunities. Sabbaticals are often seen as time off but are meant for the staff member to immerse himself or herself into a specific skill or learning. Often a sabbatical also includes retreat to allow the staff member to renew his or her spirit and to grow specific necessary skills to work more effectively. In most cases, the executive director gets time away to reflect on his or her experiences and engage in a project that is meaningful to him or her outside of the organizational setting. Sabbaticals, however, can be used for staff members at any level to give them the opportunity to rejuvenate and gain meaningful experiences to help them work more effectively.

On-the-job learning experiences need to fit with the professional development goals created by the organization and follow alongside mentoring and training. Strong supervision or mentoring will help the employee or volunteer have a beneficial on-the-job experience and provide the employer with successful results. An important part of identifying on-the-job learning experiences is matching these experiences to learning styles. The matrix shown in table 8.1 identifies which types of professional development work well with each different learning style.

Depending on their learning style, employees or volunteers will require more or less support during the on-the-job learning assignment. For example, on the one hand, an employee with independent or competitive learning styles will be more equipped to do on-the-job learning assignments with little monitoring. On the other hand, an employee or volunteer with a dependent or collaborative learning style prefers to learn with others and would learn more effectively if a peer or supervisor was supporting their assignment. This is where mentoring comes in. Employees and volunteers who learn better with others will be more successful if they are mentored during their stretch assignments.

Learning through Mentoring

Many research studies show that having a mentor provides increased job and career satisfaction (Aryee, Chay, & Chew, 1996; Aryee, Wyatt, & Stone, 1996; Chao, Walz, & Gardner, 1992). When thinking of mentoring, most people think of an older experienced person mentoring a younger up-and-comer. But mentoring can happen in a variety of ways. You will need to use the information gathered in the Individual Professional Development Assessment to identify experts who can mentor other staff or volunteers within the organization. If you have only one staff member, we recommend identifying a volunteer or a board member as a mentor, or giving your staff member the opportunity to participate in a peer coaching group. Executive directors of small nonprofits need connection with their peers, since they are unable to get it from fellow employees. Most executive directors perform better having external coaches and mentors due to their position in the organization.

TABLE 8.1
Learning Styles and Professional Development Preferences

Participant	Avoidant
Likes to be active in the learning experience.	Does not like learning opportunities.

Participant — Likes to be active in the learning experience.

- **Conferences:** Attending off-site, targeted trainings based on proficiencies needed.
- **Weeklong trainings:** On-site or off-site workshops that provide participants with an immersive experience that takes them out of their daily workflow.
- **Service learning:** Learning through experiences of giving to others and reflecting on that experience.
- **Increased community involvement:** Participating in volunteer experiences in the community or area of passion.

Avoidant — Does not like learning opportunities.

- **Mentoring:** An individual with higher proficiency levels supports learning in an individual with a lower proficiency level.
- **Coaching:** External, professional coaches work directly with an individual to increase proficiency levels.
- **Online videos/tutorials:** Short video-based lessons that individuals can watch on their own time.
- **Self-learning:** Individuals structure their own learning based on their goals.

Independent — Likes to learn on his or her own.

- **Self-learning:** Individuals structure their own learning based on their goals.
- **Computer directed:** Structured curriculum individuals can participate in on their own time. This type of learning involves software that guides participants through each step.
- **Coaching:** External, professional coaches work directly with an individual to increase proficiency levels.
- **Stretch assignment:** On-the-job assignments that give individuals a role outside their current position.
- **Training manual:** A book or guided curriculum individuals can do off-line.

Dependent — Needs assistance and guidance in learning.

- **Webinars:** Short online video sessions, often live and done with large groups.
- **Workshops:** Short in-person trainings done on specific topics.
- **Retreats:** Extended periods of time that allow individuals to step outside their regular environment and reflect on their work and growth.
- **Increased supervision:** An individual's regular supervisor schedules extra time with them to check in on tasks and discuss challenges and improvement areas.
- **Job shadowing:** An individual with a lower proficiency level works closely with and learns from someone with a higher proficiency level during their regular work day.

TABLE 8.1	
Learning Styles and Professional Development Preferences, Cont'd	
Collaborative	**Competitive**
Likes to cocreate knowledge.	Likes to compete when learning.
• **On-site trainings:** Bringing in external trainers or high proficiency individuals internally to provide a session on a specific topic.	• **On-site trainings:** Bringing in external trainers or high-proficiency individuals internally to provide a session on a specific topic.
• **Group learning:** Individuals with common needs and learning styles connect to learn a topic together, often through peer coaching and sharing reading materials.	• **Webinars:** Short online video sessions, often live and done with large groups.
• **Role playing or modeling:** A type of learning that puts the learner in the role of testing out new skills through practice in a controlled environment.	• **Computer testing:** Software that guides individuals through sessions that test their skills and proficiency levels.

Mentoring can occur in many different ways and generally refers to someone guiding or coaching another person through a process. Table 8.2 shows different types of mentor and mentee relationships. Use this table during this process to help you identify what would work best for your team.

We've benefited from mentoring throughout our careers. Tera has personally and professionally benefited from peer-to-peer mentoring. She has a close group of women friends of all different ages and professions where they have open, authentic conversations about challenges they are having in their careers and jobs. Together her group is a strong sounding board for developing personally and professionally. Heather professionally and personally benefited by having a formal executive coach while she served on the leadership team of several nonprofit organizations in the San Francisco Bay Area. Heather met with an executive coach on a monthly basis and discussed accomplishments and challenges in her job. The executive coach provided Heather with strategies and solutions to work through challenging leadership situations and interpersonal dilemmas.

EXHIBIT 8.3

On-the-Job Learning Objectives: Small Grassroots Organization

The following table shows how the small grassroots organization created professional objectives that fit their employees' learning styles.

As we saw in chapter 7, the majority of employees in the small grassroots organization scored participant, collaborative, and independent learning styles (see table 7.4); therefore, they identified group learning and stretch assignments as important on-the-job learning exercises. (They addressed their participant learning style when they identified their training objectives, which we will discuss in a later section of this chapter.) The table shows the on-the-job learning objectives the staff identified for each professional development goal.

On-the-Job Learning Objectives Tied to Professional Development Goals

Professional Development Goal	On-the-Job Learning Objective
Begin to introduce professional development in Advocacy and Public Policy so that the organization can become stronger advocates in the issue areas of the organization.	ALL staff brainstorms advocacy ideas for future years.
Improve staff proficiency levels in Financial Management to ensure strong internal controls and financial reporting.	One staff member each month assigned to review financial statements and report three findings.
Improve staff proficiency levels in Human Resources and Volunteerism in order to increase volunteer retention.	ALL staff responsible for one aspect of the volunteer recruitment plan.

Having all staff involved in brainstorming advocacy efforts relates to the employees' collaborative learning style, and having each staff member assigned to review the financial statements addresses the employees' independent learning style. The volunteer recruitment plan allows staff to collaborate on the job and gives them the freedom they need as independent learners.

Once you decide on the type of mentor and mentee relationship that will work best for each of professional development goals, you must determine the mentoring function or task. Mentors can perform two different functions: career functions and psychosocial functions (Ragins & Kram, 2007). Career function mentoring involves coaching, sponsoring advancement, increasing exposure and visibility, protection, and challenging assignments. Psychosocial mentors help mentees with "professional

TABLE 8.2 Types of Mentoring	
Types of Mentoring	**Definition**
Intergenerational mentoring	Mentoring that occurs across generations.
Peer mentoring	Mentoring that occurs from someone who is in a similar position or life stage.
Supervisor-employee mentoring	Someone who is a supervisor or a higher ranking staff mentors someone of lower status within the organization.
External mentor-internal mentee	Someone outside of an organization, such as a colleague or friend, mentors the person inside the organization.
Bottom up-top down	Someone with a lower ranking and responsibilities mentors someone higher within an organization.
Department to department	Someone from one department mentors a person from another department.

EXHIBIT 8.4

Identifying Mentors: Small Grassroots Organization

In the case of the small grassroots organization, during the process of setting professional development goals and objectives, the staff identified the community engagement supervisor to mentor fellow employees in the volunteer recruitment plan to meet their on-the-job learning objective. The community engagement supervisor was the only employee who had an advanced proficiency level in the Human Resources and Management competency. The team identified her to provide bottom-up mentoring to the executive director and peer mentoring to her fellow employees. Because no one on staff had advanced or expert Financial Management and Social Entrepreneurship proficiency, the staff decided that the certified public accountant (CPA) acting as their board treasurer would mentor the staff and executive director to increase their proficiency in the arena of Financial Management. Furthermore, the staff collaboratively decided on an outside consultant to mentor them on Advocacy.

---

and personal growth, identity, self-worth, and self-efficacy" (p. 5). Mentors may need to provide one or both functions for the mentee.

With the small grassroots nonprofit, all mentors would provide career function mentoring (exhibit 8.4). Once you have identified the mentoring function, there should be specific times for reflection. We outline specifics about how to reflect on the experience in chapter 10.

Successful mentoring is contingent upon the organizational culture, individual personalities, and the emotional intelligence of the mentor and mentee (a.k.a. protégé). Through the Organizational Learning Assessment, you got a sense of how employees and volunteers view the learning culture. Mentoring will thrive in places where employees and volunteers feel that learning is valued and they can express emotions. To promote successful mentoring relationships, you can formally designate times where employees can meet with their mentors or mentees. If your organization scored lower on the Learning and Development Domain in the Organizational Learning Assessment, then you will need to create formal structures to support mentoring; otherwise mentoring will not be successful.

Additionally, successful mentoring involves certain personality characteristics (Turban & Lee, 2007). During the initiation stage, the mentor and mentee get to know each other better. The mentee and mentor need to feel there is agreeableness, which is, they establish trust with one another (Graziano & Eisenberg, 1997, as cited by Turban & Lee 2007). The protégé specifically needs to feel that the mentor is supportive and open to the mentoring relationship. Depending on the type of on-the-job assignment, the mentee may need specific proficiency support or psychosocial support. Then during the cultivation process the mentor and mentee further develop their relationship. The mentor needs to create a safe climate for the mentee. At the end of the mentoring relationship, they both need to agree upon whether the mentoring relationship dissolves or evolves.

In order to nurture the relationship, the personalities of the individuals involved need to shift throughout the mentor-mentee relationship, as they both need to learn at the most optimal level. Table 8.3 shows the personality characteristics of the mentor and mentee that often occur through each level of their relationship.

In addition to personality characteristics, research also shows that emotional intelligence influences the mentoring relationship (Cherniss, 2007). Emotional intelligence is "the ability to monitor one's own and others' feelings and emotions, to discriminate among them and to use this information to guide one's thinking and actions" (Salovey & Mayer, 1990, p. 199). As discussed in chapter 3, Goleman (2005) lists five components of emotional intelligence:

- Self-Awareness
- Self-Regulation
- Motivation
- Empathy
- Social Skills

TABLE 8.3

Examples of Potentially Important Personality Variables at Different Phases of the Mentoring Relationship

Phase	Protégé Personality Characteristics	Mentor Personality Characteristics
Initiation	Agreeableness	Agreeableness
	Reciprocity Wariness	Reciprocation Wariness
	Conscientiousness	Emotional Stability
	Emotional Stability	Extraversion
	Extraversion	
	Self-Monitoring	
Cultivation	Agreeableness	Agreeableness
	Perspective-Taking	Perspective-Taking
	Conscientiousness	Empathetic Concern
	Emotional Stability	Conscientiousness
	Extraversion	Emotional Stability
	Openness to Experience	Extraversion
	Learning Goal Orientation	Openness to Experience
		Learning Goal Orientation
Dissolution/ Redefinition	Agreeableness	Agreeableness
	Emotional Stability	Emotional Stability

Source: Table 2.3, Turban & Lee, 2007, p. 44.

Each of these five components is important for mentoring success. Emotional intelligence allows both the mentor and mentee to learn from their relationship more effectively and equips them with the tools they need to avoid burnout in the relationship.

The best mentors we've had have stretched our ways of knowing and thinking. They were available and gave us constructive feedback on an ongoing basis. But they also gave us independence to learn and seek out solutions on our own. They were not threatened by our accomplishments, and they wanted us to succeed. They often set aside their personal agendas for the organizational agenda.

The mentor and mentee will need to create meetings to discuss the stretch assignment and the progress of their skill building. During those meetings the mentor needs to practice active listening and hear the mentee's challenges and frustrations. A good mentor is someone who can listen and see things from different perspectives. "The mentor becomes an emotional model for the mentee" (Cherniss, 2007, p. 436).

Professional Development and Training

Once you've identified on-the-job objectives and determined mentor or peer-to-peer opportunities, the next step is to identify professional development training. Training should complement your on-the-job and mentoring objectives. We've provided a Third-Party Professional Development Options Guide in the appendix to assist you in identifying specific training opportunities and resources. Training resources should be based on your type of organization, learning style, competency area, and geographic location. The training can also be specific for a department or position. You will choose training objectives based on your type of organization, your employees' and volunteers' learning styles, and the competency areas in which you need to improve.

By Type of Organization

In the directory we've provided several websites that offer resources and training based on type of organization. Due to the diverse types of organizations in the sector, third-party organizations often focus on specific types of organizations. For example, the National Council of Nonprofits provides links to a variety of training and professional development resources for nonprofit organizations. There are also training opportunities and resources specific to each subsector. The National Center for Charitable Statistics provides a list of subsectors, which includes Arts, Culture, and Humanities; Education; Environment and Animals; Health; Human Services; International, Foreign Affairs; Public, Societal Benefit; Religion Related; and Mutual/Membership Benefit. For example, the National Human Services Assembly provides training and resources for those involved in human service nonprofit organizations.

By Learning Style

As we discussed in chapter 7, it is important to create learning opportunities specific to your team's learning styles. We already discussed the importance of identifying learning activities that match learning styles. It is also important to pay attention to learning preferences among staff and volunteers, which includes identifying preferences regarding training locations, training formats, training time of day, training duration, and travel to training. We recognize that training availability varies by location, but paying attention to employees' and volunteers' preferences about training time, location, and travel increases the likelihood they will be satisfied with the training experience. For example, if the majority of your employees are willing to drive one hundred miles to training, you can plan a staff-training day in a large city nearby. Going into the training with specific preferences in mind provides a more beneficial learning experience for employees and volunteers.

By Competency Area

During the Talent Development Platform process, you identified competency deficiencies regarding the ten social change competencies. Now is the time to identify specific training that will support the on-the-job objectives you've identified. There are many resources and organizations that provide training in each specific competency area. For example, in the Leadership and Governance competency there are amazing training resources available through Boardsource and the Bridgespan Group. A variety of nonprofit leadership executive programs are also available through local universities and management support organizations. Another example, for the Financial Management and Social Entrepreneurship competency, is the Nonprofit Finance Fund and Nonprofit Assistance Group, which provides many trainings and resources to enhance financial management capabilities.

EXHIBIT 8.5

Training Options: Small Grassroots Organization

In the small grassroots organization, the CPA, board treasurer, and executive director provided two in-service trainings about financial management. Additionally, because employees differed in their learning styles preferences, as well as in their location and time of day preferences, they were given the option of attending an off-site volunteer management training at the local management support organization or participating in an online volunteer management webinar.

EXHIBIT 8.6

Proficiency Gaps: Small Grassroots Organizations

The small grassroots organization's proficiency gaps were in Advocacy and Public Policy, Financial Management and Social Entrepreneurship, and Human Resources Management and Volunteerism. The employees' on-the-job objectives were to review the financial statements each month. In order to review the financial statements in the correct manner, they needed to enhance their financial management capabilities. They decided their training would be to view some videos on the Nonprofit Assistance Fund's website. To address the Advocacy and Public Policy proficiency gap, the staff identified and selected an independent consultant who came in and provided a customized daylong training about advocacy.

Departmental Professional Development Objectives

In large organizations you should develop objectives for each department that are connected to the organization's overall goals and objectives. Each department should then set objectives for on-the-job learning, learning through mentoring, and learning in trainings as necessary to meet the strategic goals for their department. Remember to align your organization's strategic goals to your departmental professional development objectives.

Here's an example of how a fundraising department can set objectives related to its overall organizational goals of increasing advocacy proficiencies among all staff:

- Learning on the job. Employees take on some advocacy responsibilities. Each staff member is responsible for running a community education training or writing letters to congressional representative regarding your cause.

- Learning through mentoring or peer-to-peer opportunities. The staff member who scored the highest in advocacy proficiency or a board member who has some expertise in this arena works with the fundraising staff to add language to their fundraising pitches and annual giving campaign directly related to raising the importance of your mission and the people/animal/environment impacted by your cause.

- Professional development and training. Send staff to a third-party training on storytelling in fundraising, specifically focused on adding language and components to your fundraising work that support educating the community about your cause.

Just like in the organization objectives, be sure that departmental professional development objectives are displayed prominently for all staff in your department to focus on their learning. Include the learning objectives in the language of your regular department staff meetings as well. It's easy to start on your daily work and forget about the learning you are meant to do together for the betterment of the organization. As you set the individual professional development objectives of each of your staff members, you will look at both the organizational and departmental objectives and how each individual can align her or his objectives with those.

Finalizing Your Talent Development Platform

After you create goals and objectives for the organization, you will finalize your Talent Development Platform. You began filling in the Talent

Development Platform with the Organizational Learning Assessment, then you filled in the results from the Individual Professional Development Assessments, and the Learning Styles Assessments. In the following section you can see the completed Talent Development Platforms for each of the various organizations.

Once you add the organizational professional development goals and objectives, display the Platform prominently in your office (or take a photo to put online for your virtual office). Provide individual employees and volunteers the full Platform, so they can finalize their individual learning goals and objectives. You will also revisit the Platform during the evaluation stage and throughout implementation.

Goals and Objectives in Practice

Each of the organizations that piloted the Talent Development Platform completed the goal-setting process. Here, we walk you through each of their goal-setting processes and their finalized Talent Development Platforms, which include their organizational professional development goals and objectives.

Volunteer-Run Organization

Using their Talent Development Platform (figure 8.3), the volunteer-run organization had a full board discussion regarding the assessment results and created three goals and concurrent objectives for the organization. Figure 8.4 includes a full list of the volunteer-run organization's professional development goals and objectives organized in the three learning realms.

Small Grassroots Organization

For ease of reference, we have reproduced the Talent Development Platform of the small grassroots organization again in figure 8.5.

In the small grassroots organization, the professional development goals and objectives were set as a team with the executive director as the lead. The organization developed three objectives that fit with the three different domains of learning for each goal. See figure 8.6 for their full list of goals and objectives.

Midsized Organization

Due to their larger size staff the midsized organization had each supervisor sit down and go through assessments with both their staff and the

FIGURE 8.3
Talent Development Platform: Volunteer-Run Organization

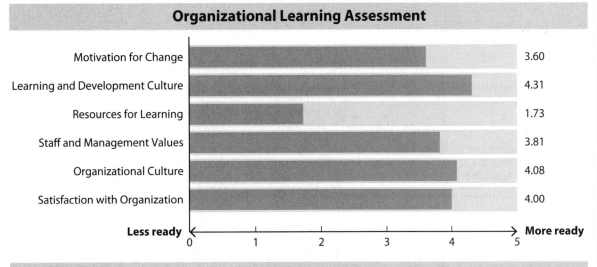

Organizational Learning Assessment

Motivation for Change	3.60
Learning and Development Culture	4.31
Resources for Learning	1.73
Staff and Management Values	3.81
Organizational Culture	4.08
Satisfaction with Organization	4.00

Less ready ← 0   1   2   3   4   5 → **More ready**

Learning Styles Map

Participant ●	Avoidant
Independent ● ● ● ●	Dependent
Collaborative ● ● ● ●	Competitive

Goals and Objectives

Goal 1: Improve recordkeeping so that technology aids in the organizational sustainability.	**01:** Implement a new technological recordkeeping system.
	02: Work with a nonprofit technology consulant or professional pro bono consultant to develop a list of needs.
	03: Attend a recordkeeping training.
Goal 2: Make legal and regulatory aspects part of everyday work.	**01:** Develop and implement event risk management policy. Develop and implement conflict of interest policy. Develop and implement recordkeeping policy.
	02: Board president to work closely with assigned board members to learn all necessary legal requirements and implement.
	03: Select board members to attend a policies and procedures workshop for small nonprofits.
Goal 3: Use the recordkeeping system to track program outcomes and evaluate results.	**01:** Create logic model for the organization and track results from the logic model.
	02: Bring in evaluation consultant to guide the development of an organizational evaluation.
	03: Board members to attend training on developing program evaluation.

01 = Learning on the Job; **02** = Mentoring and Peer-to-Peer Opportunities; **03** = Trainings

FIGURE 8.3
Talent Development Platform: Voluteer-Run Organization, Cont'd

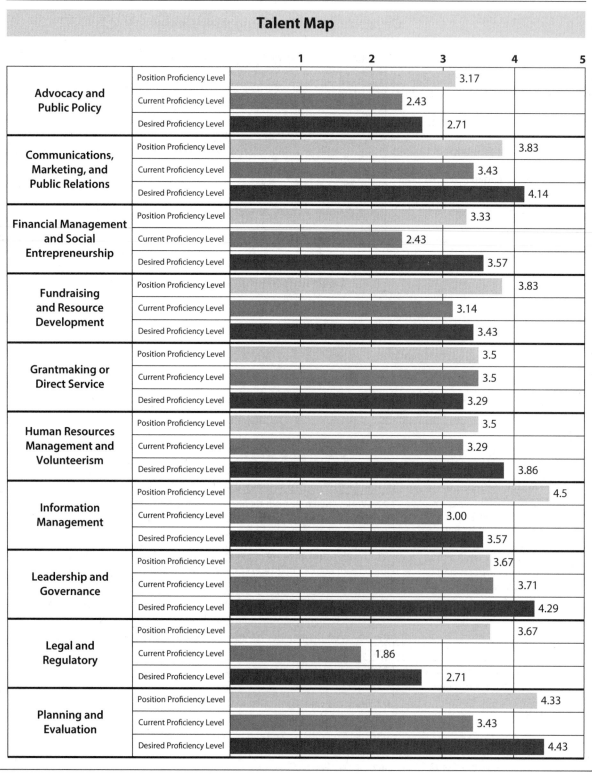

		1	2	3	4	5
Advocacy and Public Policy	Position Proficiency Level			3.17		
	Current Proficiency Level		2.43			
	Desired Proficiency Level		2.71			
Communications, Marketing, and Public Relations	Position Proficiency Level			3.83		
	Current Proficiency Level			3.43		
	Desired Proficiency Level				4.14	
Financial Management and Social Entrepreneurship	Position Proficiency Level			3.33		
	Current Proficiency Level		2.43			
	Desired Proficiency Level			3.57		
Fundraising and Resource Development	Position Proficiency Level			3.83		
	Current Proficiency Level			3.14		
	Desired Proficiency Level			3.43		
Grantmaking or Direct Service	Position Proficiency Level			3.5		
	Current Proficiency Level			3.5		
	Desired Proficiency Level			3.29		
Human Resources Management and Volunteerism	Position Proficiency Level			3.5		
	Current Proficiency Level			3.29		
	Desired Proficiency Level			3.86		
Information Management	Position Proficiency Level				4.5	
	Current Proficiency Level			3.00		
	Desired Proficiency Level			3.57		
Leadership and Governance	Position Proficiency Level			3.67		
	Current Proficiency Level			3.71		
	Desired Proficiency Level				4.29	
Legal and Regulatory	Position Proficiency Level			3.67		
	Current Proficiency Level	1.86				
	Desired Proficiency Level		2.71			
Planning and Evaluation	Position Proficiency Level				4.33	
	Current Proficiency Level			3.43		
	Desired Proficiency Level				4.43	

FIGURE 8.4
Goals and Objectives: Volunteer-Run Organization

Goal 1: Improve recordkeeping so that technology aids in the organizational sustainability.	01: Implement a new technological recordkeeping system.
	02: Work with a nonprofit technology consulant or professional pro bono consultant to develop a list of needs.
	03: Attend a recordkeeping training.
Goal 2: Make legal and regulatory aspects part of everyday work.	01: Develop and implement event risk management policy. Develop and implement conflict of interest policy. Develop and implement recordkeeping policy.
	02: Board president to work closely with assigned board members to learn all necessary legal requirements and implement.
	03: Select board members to attend a policies and procedures workshop for small nonprofits.
Goal 3: Use the recordkeeping system to track program outcomes and evaluate results.	01: Create logic model for the organization and track results from the logic model.
	02: Bring in evaluation consultant to guide the development of an organizational evaluation.
	03: Board members to attend training on developing program evaluation.

01 = Learning on the Job; 02 = Mentoring and Peer-to-Peer Opportunities; 03 = Trainings

full organization and develop suggestions for potential goals and objectives (figure 8.7). The full staff then came together to assess all the potential options and determine final goals and objectives for the organization. The operations manager led this process and gave them to the executive director to share with the board for some education on the process. The midsize organization finalized their Talent Development Platform, shown in figure 8.8.

Grantmaking Organization

Due to the small number of staff in the grantmaking organization, the staff worked as full team to go through all of the assessments and develop goals and objectives based on learning needs and their gap analysis. The Talent Development Platform in figure 8.9 shows the results for their small staff. Once the staff completed their goals and Platform together the president then presented the goals and objectives to the board for their approval (figure 8.10).

FIGURE 8.5
Talent Development Platform: Small Grassroots Organization

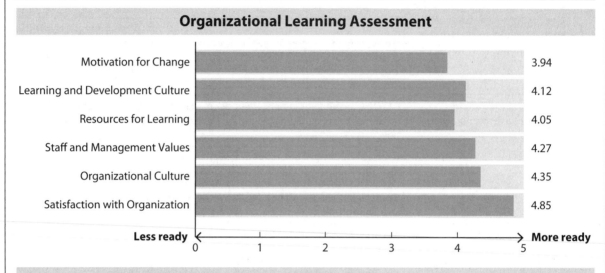

Organizational Learning Assessment

Motivation for Change	3.94
Learning and Development Culture	4.12
Resources for Learning	4.05
Staff and Management Values	4.27
Organizational Culture	4.35
Satisfaction with Organization	4.85

Less ready ← 0 1 2 3 4 5 → More ready

Learning Styles Map

Participant	Avoidant
● ● ●	
Independent	**Dependent**
● ● ●	
Collaborative	**Competitive**
● ● ● ● ●	●

Goals and Objectives

Goal 1: Improve staff proficiency levels in Human Resources and Volunteerism in order to increase volunteer retention.	**01:** ALL staff responsible for one aspect of a volunteer recruitment plan.
	02: Community engagement supervisor mentors and as project lead; works one-on-one with each employee.
	03: Depending on the individual employees' learning preference they attend volunteer management seminar, webinar, or workshop.
Goal 2: Improve board proficiency levels in Financial Management to ensure strong internal controls and financial reporting.	**01:** One staff member each month assigned to review financial statements and report three findings.
	02: CPA and board treasurer mentor board members.
	03: Board members receive financial management book and links to video. CPA and board treasurer do two in-service trainings on financial statements during the board meeting.
Goal 3: Begin to introduce professional development in Advocacy and Public Policy so that the organization can become stronger advocates in the issue areas of the organization.	**01:** ALL staff brainstorms advocacy ideas for future years.
	02: Staff collaboratively identifies who they want to mentor them on nonprofit advocacy.
	03: Staff attends training provided by mentor.

01 = Learning on the Job; **02** = Mentoring and Peer-to-Peer Opportunities; **03** = Trainings

FIGURE 8.5
Talent Development Platform: Small Grassroots Organization, Cont'd

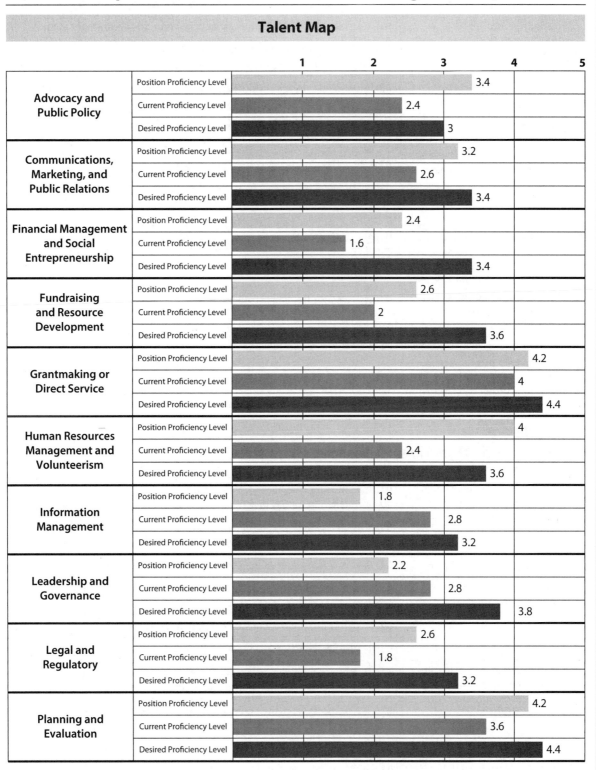

		Talent Map

		1	2	3	4	5
Advocacy and Public Policy	Position Proficiency Level			3.4		
	Current Proficiency Level		2.4			
	Desired Proficiency Level			3		
Communications, Marketing, and Public Relations	Position Proficiency Level			3.2		
	Current Proficiency Level		2.6			
	Desired Proficiency Level			3.4		
Financial Management and Social Entrepreneurship	Position Proficiency Level		2.4			
	Current Proficiency Level	1.6				
	Desired Proficiency Level			3.4		
Fundraising and Resource Development	Position Proficiency Level		2.6			
	Current Proficiency Level	2				
	Desired Proficiency Level			3.6		
Grantmaking or Direct Service	Position Proficiency Level				4.2	
	Current Proficiency Level				4	
	Desired Proficiency Level				4.4	
Human Resources Management and Volunteerism	Position Proficiency Level				4	
	Current Proficiency Level		2.4			
	Desired Proficiency Level			3.6		
Information Management	Position Proficiency Level	1.8				
	Current Proficiency Level		2.8			
	Desired Proficiency Level			3.2		
Leadership and Governance	Position Proficiency Level		2.2			
	Current Proficiency Level		2.8			
	Desired Proficiency Level				3.8	
Legal and Regulatory	Position Proficiency Level		2.6			
	Current Proficiency Level	1.8				
	Desired Proficiency Level			3.2		
Planning and Evaluation	Position Proficiency Level				4.2	
	Current Proficiency Level			3.6		
	Desired Proficiency Level				4.4	

FIGURE 8.6
Goals and Objectives: Small Grassroots Organization

Goal 1: Improve staff proficiency levels in Human Resources and Volunteerism in order to increase volunteer retention.	**01:** ALL staff responsible for one aspect of a volunteer recruitment plan.
	02: Community engagement supervisor mentors and as project lead works one-on-one with each employee.
	03: Depending on the individual employees' learning preference they attend volunteer management seminar, webinar, or workshop.
Goal 2: Improve board proficiency levels in Financial Management to ensure strong internal controls and financial reporting.	**01:** One staff member each month assigned to review financial statements and report three findings.
	02: CPA and board treasurer mentor board members.
	03: Board members receive financial management book and links to video. CPA and board treasurer do two in service training on financial statements during the board meeting.
Goal 3: Begin to introduce professional development in Advocacy and Public Policy so that the organization can become stronger advocates in the issue areas of the organization.	**01:** ALL staff brainstorms advocacy ideas for future years.
	02: Staff collaboratively identifies who they want to mentor them on nonprofit advocacy.
	03: Staff attends training provided by mentor.

01 = Learning on the Job; **02** = Mentoring and Peer-to-Peer Opportunities; **03** = Trainings

FIGURE 8.7
Goals and Objectives: Midsized Organization

Goal 1: Plan and implement advocacy event to raise awareness of hunger issues within the community	**01:** Specific responsibility in organizing the day of action: funding for day of action, marketing for day of action, and volunteer recruitment for day of action.
	02: Bring in an advocacy consultant to advise the planning of the advocacy event and help staff learn the intricacies of the work.
	03: Have advocacy consultant lead a training during a regular staff meeting.
Goal 2: Improve volunteer and donor recordkeeping system.	**01:** Identify and implement volunteer management and fundraising tracking database.
	02: Bring in a pro bono IT consultant to advise the process.
	03: Read articles and watch videos from Idealware on best practices.
Goal 3: Reduce legal liability and improve risk management practices throughout the warehouse.	**01:** Create and implement risk management policy and procedures—specifically focusing on warehouse volunteers.
	02: Have attorney from the board work with staff to identify best practices and ensure the correct policies and procedures are being implemented.
	03: Attend a risk management planning or management workshop.

01 = Learning on the Job; **02** = Mentoring and Peer-to-Peer Opportunities; **03** = Trainings

FIGURE 8.8
Talent Development Platform: Midsized Organization

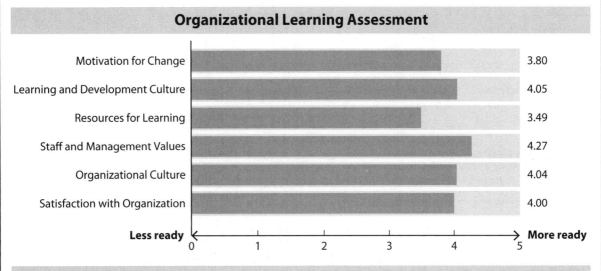

Organizational Learning Assessment

Motivation for Change	3.80
Learning and Development Culture	4.05
Resources for Learning	3.49
Staff and Management Values	4.27
Organizational Culture	4.04
Satisfaction with Organization	4.00

Less ready ← 0   1   2   3   4   5 → More ready

Learning Styles Map

Participant	Avoidant
● ● ● ● ● ● ● ● ●	
Independent	**Dependent**
● ● ● ● ● ● ● ● ● ● ● ●	
● ● Collaborative ● ●	Competitive
● ● ● ● ● ● ● ● ● ● ●	

Goals and Objectives

Goal 1: Plan and implement advocacy event to raise awareness of hunger issues within the community.	01: Specific responsibility in organizing the day of action: funding for day of action, marketing for day of action, and volunteer recruitment for day of action.
	02: Bring in an advocacy consultant to advise the planning of the advocacy event and help staff learn the intricacies of the work.
	03: Have advocacy consultant lead a training during a regular staff meeting.
Goal 2: Improve volunteer and donor recordkeeping system.	01: Identify and implement volunteer management and fundraising tracking database.
	02: Bring in a pro bono IT consultant to advise the process.
	03: Read articles and watch videos from Idealware on best practices.
Goal 3: Reduce legal liability and improve risk management practices throughout the warehouse.	01: Create and implement risk management policy and procedures—specifically focusing on warehouse volunteers.
	02: Have attorney from the board work with staff to identify best practices and ensure the correct policies and procedures are being implemented.
	03: Attend a risk management planning or management workshop.

01 = Learning on the Job; **02** = Mentoring and Peer-to-Peer Opportunities; **03** = Trainings

FIGURE 8.8
Talent Development Platform: Midsized Organization, Cont'd

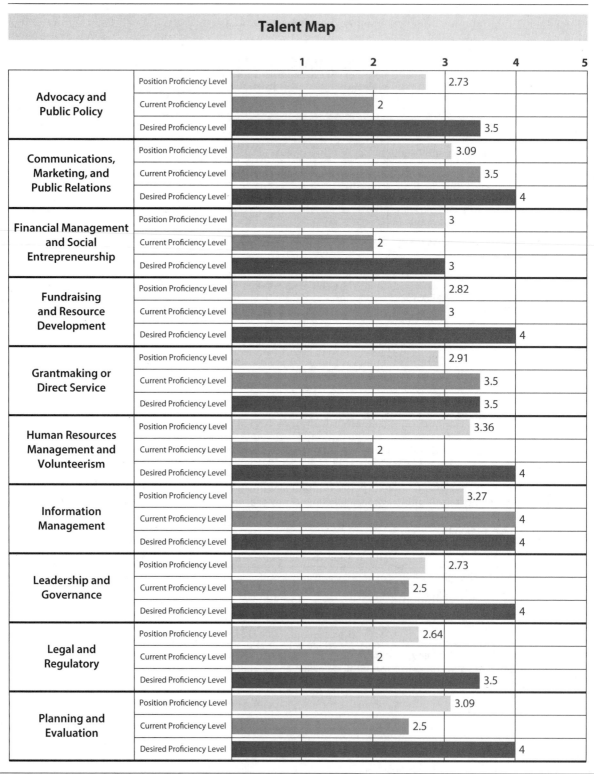

Talent Map

		1	2	3	4	5
Advocacy and Public Policy	Position Proficiency Level			2.73		
	Current Proficiency Level		2			
	Desired Proficiency Level			3.5		
Communications, Marketing, and Public Relations	Position Proficiency Level			3.09		
	Current Proficiency Level			3.5		
	Desired Proficiency Level				4	
Financial Management and Social Entrepreneurship	Position Proficiency Level			3		
	Current Proficiency Level		2			
	Desired Proficiency Level			3		
Fundraising and Resource Development	Position Proficiency Level			2.82		
	Current Proficiency Level			3		
	Desired Proficiency Level				4	
Grantmaking or Direct Service	Position Proficiency Level			2.91		
	Current Proficiency Level			3.5		
	Desired Proficiency Level			3.5		
Human Resources Management and Volunteerism	Position Proficiency Level			3.36		
	Current Proficiency Level		2			
	Desired Proficiency Level				4	
Information Management	Position Proficiency Level			3.27		
	Current Proficiency Level				4	
	Desired Proficiency Level				4	
Leadership and Governance	Position Proficiency Level			2.73		
	Current Proficiency Level		2.5			
	Desired Proficiency Level				4	
Legal and Regulatory	Position Proficiency Level			2.64		
	Current Proficiency Level		2			
	Desired Proficiency Level			3.5		
Planning and Evaluation	Position Proficiency Level			3.09		
	Current Proficiency Level		2.5			
	Desired Proficiency Level				4	

FIGURE 8.9
Talent Development Platform: Grantmaking Organization

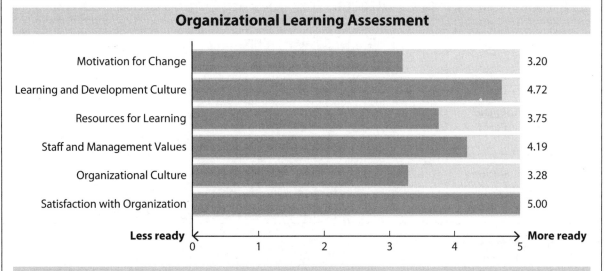

Organizational Learning Assessment

Motivation for Change	3.20
Learning and Development Culture	4.72
Resources for Learning	3.75
Staff and Management Values	4.19
Organizational Culture	3.28
Satisfaction with Organization	5.00

Less ready ← → More ready
0   1   2   3   4   5

Learning Styles Map

Participant ●	Avoidant
Independent ● ●	Dependent
Collaborative ● ●	Competitive

Goals and Objectives

Goal 1: Raise awareness of foundation issue areas.	01: Present issue areas to policy makers.
	02: Work with an advocacy consultant or local volunteer.
	03: Participate in a nonprofit lobbying and advocacy day.
Goal 2: Increase financial acumen of staff, board, and grantees.	01: Create financial management trainings for board and grantees.
	02: Work with board treasurer to plan trainings.
	03: Hold an in-service workshop for board members and grantees.
Goal 3: Incorporate planning and evaluation into daily work.	01: Implement program plan and evaluation for financial trainings.
	02: Work with local evaluation consultant.
	03: Have staff members attend a strategic planning workshop.

01 = Learning on the Job; 02 = Mentoring and Peer-to-Peer Opportunities; 03 = Trainings

FIGURE 8.9

Talent Development Platform: Grantmaking Organization, Cont'd

	Talent Map	1	2	3	4	5
Advocacy and Public Policy	Position Proficiency Level			3.25		
	Current Proficiency Level		2.25			
	Desired Proficiency Level			3.5		
Communications, Marketing, and Public Relations	Position Proficiency Level				3.75	
	Current Proficiency Level			3.25		
	Desired Proficiency Level				3.75	
Financial Management and Social Entrepreneurship	Position Proficiency Level				3.75	
	Current Proficiency Level			3		
	Desired Proficiency Level				3.75	
Fundraising and Resource Development	Position Proficiency Level		2.5			
	Current Proficiency Level			3		
	Desired Proficiency Level			3.25		
Grantmaking or Direct Service	Position Proficiency Level					4.5
	Current Proficiency Level				3.75	
	Desired Proficiency Level				4.25	
Human Resources Management and Volunteerism	Position Proficiency Level			2.75		
	Current Proficiency Level		2.5			
	Desired Proficiency Level			3.25		
Information Management	Position Proficiency Level			3.5		
	Current Proficiency Level			3.5		
	Desired Proficiency Level				3.75	
Leadership and Governance	Position Proficiency Level				3.75	
	Current Proficiency Level			3		
	Desired Proficiency Level				4	
Legal and Regulatory	Position Proficiency Level				3.75	
	Current Proficiency Level			2.75		
	Desired Proficiency Level				4	
Planning and Evaluation	Position Proficiency Level				4	
	Current Proficiency Level			3		
	Desired Proficiency Level				4	

FIGURE 8.10
Goals and Objectives: Grantmaking Organization

Goal 1: Raise awareness of foundation issue areas.	01: Present issue areas to policy makers.
	02: Work with an advocacy consultant or local volunteer.
	03: Participate in a nonprofit lobbying and advocacy day.
Goal 2: Increase financial acumen of staff, board, and grantees.	01: Create financial management trainings for board and grantees.
	02: Work with board treasurer to plan trainings.
	03: Hold an in-service workshop for board members and grantees.
Goal 3: Incorporate planning and evaluation into daily work.	01: Implement program plan and evaluation for financial trainings.
	02: Work with local evaluation consultant.
	03: Have staff members attend a strategic planning workshop.

01 = Learning on the Job; 02 = Mentoring and Peer-to-Peer Opportunities; 03 = Trainings

Conclusion

In this chapter we discussed setting goals and objectives for your organization and departments, if you have them. We described the importance of including full staff in discussions, allowing time for reflection, and connecting goals and objectives to your organization's strategic goals and business plan. Remember, employees and volunteers who help develop goals and objectives will be more apt to own and complete those goals. You will use the organizational goals and objectives to help individuals set their own goals and objectives, which we discuss in the next chapter.

Chapter 9
Setting Individual Goals and Objectives

Now that you have set your organization's professional development goals and objectives, we'll show you how to help employees and volunteers intentionally develop individual professional development goals and objectives. You have already established some of their goals and objectives during the organizational goal-setting process. Some employees and volunteers may be paired as mentors and mentees or assigned a stretch assignment. However, individual goal setting allows individuals to take the organizational goals to the next level, building their skills to do their work more effectively and develop their careers. In this chapter we discuss the process for setting individual professional development goals and objectives. Figure 9.1 provides you with an individual goals and objectives checklist.

Preparing for Individual Goal Setting

Before the individual goal-setting process begins, all staff and volunteers need to

- have an updated job description with proficiency mapping, and a thorough understanding of their job description;

- have a discussion with their supervisor regarding their IPDA and ILSA results;

- understand the organization's professional development goals and objectives; and

- understand their department's professional development objectives, if any were set.

FIGURE 9.1
Individual Goals and Objectives Checklist

INDIVIDUAL GOALS AND OBJECTIVES ·····▶

- Have individuals draft learning goals and objectives based on organizational and departmental goals and their own learning needs.
- Meet with each employee and volunteer to review results of his or her Individual Professional Development Assessment, Individual Learning Styles Assessment, and draft goals.
- Finalize individual goals and objectives.

You will want to have your professional budget in mind for employees and volunteers prior to the individual goal-setting process. We talk more extensively about budgets in chapter 10, and implementing learning in the Platform will require time, resources, and intentionality to be successful. Be sure employees and volunteers understand the organization's professional development funding as they set their objectives. Some professional development objectives may require a shift in employee or volunteer time rather than money.

It is also essential that employees and volunteers know the most important parts of their job while setting their goals and objectives. This is done through role clarification exercises, improved job descriptions, performance review sessions, and other behaviorally anchored rating procedures (Campbell & Lee, 1988). We discussed the job realignment process during the job description and proficiency mapping chapters. It is quite possible, however that an employee or volunteer may still have questions about their role after finishing that process. During the proficiency mapping step be sure to clarify any remaining questions employees and volunteers may have about their roles.

If employees or volunteers took on new roles during the talent mapping process (in chapters 4, 5, and 6), take extra time with them during this step as well. Don't let those individuals implement their professional development goals and objectives without having a strong understanding of their new roles.

Setting Individual Goals and Objectives

Just like in the process of setting organizational goals and objectives, the individual goal-setting process should fit your organization's culture. Be sure to include the individual professional development goal-setting process within a regular performance review system if you have one in place. If you do not have a performance system, use the individual goal-setting process to establish one, but be sure to keep in mind your organizational calendar. For example, you may not want individuals to participate in this process during the annual giving campaign or at the beginning of the school year if you run an afterschool program. Find the time that fits best for your staff and volunteers.

In the organizational goal-setting stage we recommended leadership lead employees and volunteers through the goal-setting process. In the individual professional development goal-setting process, adult learning is enhanced when individuals have control over the way they learn (Rabin, 2014). Therefore, allow for employees and volunteers to set their own professional development goals and objectives tied to their proficiency gaps and the professional development goals of the organization. Individuals should draft their goals and learning objectives, and then meet with their supervisors to confirm and finalize the list. If you have teams, you should plan for the team members to review each other's goals and find synergies in learning opportunities. In the following sections we explain how to set objectives or activities for each individual professional development goal.

Analyzing the IPDA and ILSA Prior to Goal Setting

As we mentioned in chapter 6, each employee should have the opportunity to review his or her Individual Professional Development Assessment and Individual Learning Styles Assessment prior to goal setting.

The review meeting should include the following areas:

Individual proficiency strengths. Identify and applaud expert and advanced proficiency levels. Employees and volunteers can use their skills in these competency areas to act as mentors or peer leaders in the organization.

Individual proficiency deficiencies. Identify and discuss areas in which the individual identified their proficiency levels as fundamental awareness and novice. These are competency areas the employee or volunteer has learning needs in.

Individual position proficiency gaps and examples. Discuss proficiency areas where the position requires higher proficiency levels but the employee's current proficiency level is lower. Then provide examples of why the position requires specific proficiency levels.

Individual desired proficiency gaps and examples. Identify and discuss where employees' desired proficiency level is higher than the position's required proficiency level. Then provide examples to justify position proficiency levels.

Individual professional development goals. Identify future expectations for proficiency level increases and individual professional development goals of the employee or volunteer.

EXHIBIT 9.1

Individual Goal Setting: Executive Director, Small Grassroots Organization

When the executive director of the small grassroots organization sat down with her board chair to set goals, they discussed her individual strengths, deficiencies, and gaps as identified in the Individual Professional Development Assessment. Together they realized she had proficiency strengths in Direct Service and in Planning and Evaluation, as well gaps within all competencies except for Direct Service. After further discussion they determined that the executive director should prioritize five of the competencies for her learning: Advocacy and Public Policy; Marketing, Communications, and Public Relations; Financial Management and Social Entrepreneurship; Fundraising and Resource Development; and Legal and Regulatory. The executive director then came up with three specific professional development goals to achieve during the year to address her proficiency gaps:

- Increase organizational brand awareness.
- Enhance financial leadership.
- Improve Legal and Regulatory proficiency level.

Once professional development goals are established, individuals should identify three objectives, one for each learning realm, connected to each professional development goal.

Connecting Learning Activities to Goals and Objectives

In chapter 8, we discussed how to set organizational professional development objectives in each of the three realms of learning: on the job, mentoring or peer relationships, and training. The process is similar when setting individual professional development goals and objectives. Employees and volunteers will set their goals and objectives (and learning activities) that directly enhance their proficiency levels and their career aspirations.

Individuals should identify professional development objectives in each learning realm and bring the objectives to their team or supervisor to determine synergy during implementation. Table 9.1 shows potential objectives for individuals, related to each of the three learning realms. You might also consider providing employees and volunteers with table 8.1, "Learning Styles and Professional Development Preferences" from the previous chapter.

EXHIBIT 9.2

Goals and Objectives Tied to Mission versus Career Building

It is important that employees and volunteers set professional development goals and objectives that reflect and tie back to the goals and mission of the organization as well as set goals related to career aspirations. Individuals can do this in two ways:

- **Mentoring Others.** If an employee or volunteer is looking to enhance her leadership skills or to be viewed more as a leader, suggest that she act as a mentor. In a mentoring relationship the mentor gets the opportunity to express a learning need as well as enhance her leadership skills. Mentors take on the responsibility of a leader in their mentoring relationship and express skills they might not be able to express otherwise. Skills used as a mentor include troubleshooting, coaching, and strategy development, all skills leaders need.

- **Stretch Assignment in Different Role.** If an employee is interested in becoming a fundraiser, but he works in your marketing and communications department, give him a stretch assignment in the fundraising department. Be sure to give him an assignment of real purpose and not a fluffy add-on. The employee acting in the new role needs to get a real, challenging experience to learn most effectively. Stretch assignments may be just that—a stretch—but will give employees the satisfaction of working toward their long-term career goals while also filling an organizational need.

Meeting with Supervisees

Once employees have drafted their goals and objectives, it is important for supervisors to sit down with each of their supervisees to finalize their goals and objectives. It is very likely that the Individual Professional Development Assessment and individual professional development goal-setting discussions could happen together; however, the individual goal-setting meeting should not be the first time staff members have seen their IPDA and ILSA results.

You may have your meetings during the annual review process or at another time, whichever works for your organization. In chapter 11, we'll discuss more about the annual performance review process. As supervisors enter these meetings, they should be aware of any potential biases they may be entering with and focus their discussion on learning objectives instead of personal issues or opinions they may have of their supervisees. Any type of feedback meeting is uncomfortable, so being intentional about the focus of the meetings will help to diffuse any issues. We are all passionate people working in social change organizations.

TABLE 9.1
Individual Objectives by Learning Realm

Learning Realm	Potential Objectives
On-the-Job Learning	<ul><li>Stretch assignments: An opportunity to try out an assignment outside of your typical role that may be at a higher proficiency level or in a different competency area.</li><li>Team projects: Individuals who are interested in learning a similar skill work on a project together.</li><li>Joining a new team: This objective is similar to a stretch assignment; however, instead of taking on an individual task the employee or volunteer would join a group already doing an activity the individual would like to learn.</li></ul>
Mentoring or Peer Relationships	<ul><li>External mentor: Mentor-mentee relationship with a volunteer or employee from a similar organization that has skills the employee or volunteer needs to enhance.</li><li>External coach: Certified career coach that gives the employee or volunteer the opportunity to troubleshoot and enhance his or her self-efficacy.</li><li>Peer/colleague mentor: Mentor-mentee relationship between two employees or volunteers within your organization. This relationship will have to be managed a bit more carefully than an external mentor relationship to keep trust among employees.</li><li>Peer learning or coaching groups: Peers building similar competencies connect regularly to discuss challenges and learn from each other.</li></ul>
Trainings	<ul><li>In-house: Trainers come into the office to work with staff on a competency.</li><li>Third-party trainings: Employees or volunteers attend trainings led by third-party learning providers.</li><li>Online trainings: Webinars or self-directed learning opportunities individuals can participate in online.</li></ul>

EXHIBIT 9.3
Objectives for Leadership

To enhance talent development and learning within your organization, consider creating learning objectives for enhancing leaders' and supervisors' proficiencies in providing feedback, giving staff assessments, and adding other learning culture elements to your work. A good leadership goal, for example, could be "Develop skills in assessing staff and providing feedback." This could also be a space where you set goals to improve areas of the Organizational Learning Assessment.

Supervisors should start with a discussion of proficiency strengths, which sets a good tone for the meeting and allows both the supervisor and supervisee to get comfortable with the conversation. Once you've discussed strengths, move to opportunities and constructive feedback of proficiency deficiencies and the gap analysis. Make sure to give the employee or volunteer plenty of time and space to express their frustrations and don't take it personally. In many cases employees and volunteers just want to be heard and may not always get one-on-one time with their supervisor.

End the meeting by confirming the professional development goals and objectives the employee or volunteer created. If you are planning on moving an employee into a new role, be sure to have that conversation with them prior to this goal-setting meeting so that their goals and objectives won't shift dramatically during the meeting.

Finalizing Individual Talent Development Platforms

Once individuals have finalized their goals and objectives, they will complete their own Individual Talent Development Platforms. The Individual Talent Development Platform gives employees and volunteers a snapshot of their proficiency levels, their learning needs and styles, and the organization's and their own individual professional development goals and objectives. In the next section you can see the finalized Individual Talent Development Platforms for the individuals we have been tracking in each of the four organization types.

Individual Goals and Objectives in Practice
Volunteer-Run Organization

All of the board members from the volunteer-run organization created individual professional development goals and objectives based on the organizational goals and objectives. Figure 9.2 includes the board chair's

FIGURE 9.2
Individual Talent Development Platform: Board Chair, Volunteer-Run Organization

Individual Professional Development Assessment						
		1	2	3	4	5
Advocacy and Public Policy	Position Proficiency Level					
	Current Proficiency Level					
	Desired Proficiency Level					
Communications, Marketing, and Public Relations	Position Proficiency Level					
	Current Proficiency Level					
	Desired Proficiency Level					
Financial Management and Social Entrepreneurship	Position Proficiency Level					
	Current Proficiency Level					
	Desired Proficiency Level					
Fundraising and Resource Development	Position Proficiency Level					
	Current Proficiency Level					
	Desired Proficiency Level					
Grantmaking or Direct Service	Position Proficiency Level					
	Current Proficiency Level					
	Desired Proficiency Level					
Human Resources Management and Volunteerism	Position Proficiency Level					
	Current Proficiency Level					
	Desired Proficiency Level					
Information Management	Position Proficiency Level					
	Current Proficiency Level					
	Desired Proficiency Level					
Leadership and Governance	Position Proficiency Level					
	Current Proficiency Level					
	Desired Proficiency Level					
Legal and Regulatory	Position Proficiency Level					
	Current Proficiency Level					
	Desired Proficiency Level					
Planning and Evaluation	Position Proficiency Level					
	Current Proficiency Level					
	Desired Proficiency Level					

Top Three Learning Styles

1. Collaborative

2. Independent

3. Participant

FIGURE 9.2

Individual Talent Development Platform: Board Chair, Volunteer-Run Organization, Cont'd

Organizational Goals and Objectives

Goal 1: Improve recordkeeping so that technology aids in the organizational sustainability.	**01:** Implement a new technological recordkeeping system.
	02: Work with a nonprofit technology consultant or professional pro bono consultant to develop a list of needs.
	03: Attend a recordkeeping training.
Goal 2: Make legal and regulatory aspects part of everyday work.	**01:** Develop and implement event risk management policy. Develop and implement conflict of interest policy. Develop and implement recordkeeping policy.
	02: Board president to work closely with assigned board members to learn all necessary legal requirements and implement.
	03: Select board members to attend a policies and procedures workshop for small nonprofits.
Goal 3: Use the recordkeeping system to track program outcomes and evaluate results.	**01:** Create logic model for the organization and track results from the logic model.
	02: Bring in evaluation consultant to guide the development of an organizational evaluation.
	03: Board members to attend training on developing program evaluation.

01 = Learning on the Job; **02** = Mentoring and Peer-to-Peer Opportunities; **03** = Trainings

Individual Professional Development Goals and Objectives

	Learning on the Job	Mentoring and Peer-to-Peer	Trainings
Goal 1: Lead implementation of legal and regulatory requirements for the organization.	Mentor the board to develop and implement conflict of interest/event risk management policy, and data recordkeeping policy.	Work closely with a pro bono nonprofit attorney to ensure all the correct legal and regulatory policies are in place for the organization.	Attend a nonprofit risk management training.
Goal 2: Demonstrate financial leadership.	Determine the financial sustainability of the organization and work with full board to implement any necessary changes or enhance areas that are working well.	Work with a pro bono nonprofit accountant or CPA to get guidance on any necessary procedures that should be in place.	Attend a financial sustainability workshop.
Goal 3: None Identified			

individual professional development goals and objectives. The board chair focused on one organizational professional development goal and one goal that would improve his individual proficiency levels.

Small Grassroots Organization

The board and executive director worked together to personalize objectives for the executive director connected to the organization's goals and objectives. During the IPDA discussion, the executive director created goals with her board chair. Figure 9.3 shows her Platform, including her professional development goals and objectives.

Midsized Nonprofit

During the IPDA process the executive director identified that the development coordinator exhibited advanced proficiency levels and was overqualified for her position. The executive director promoted her to development manager. The development coordinator drafted her professional development goals based on her new position. Figure 9.4 shows her Platform, including her finalized goals and objectives.

Grantmaking Organization

The president of the grantmaking organization worked with the program associate to personalize objectives connected to the organization's goals and objectives, and her own learning needs. During the IPDA, the program associate created her goals and finalized them soon after with the president. Figure 9.5 shows her Platform, including her goals and objectives.

Conclusion

In this chapter we discussed how to set individual professional development goals and objectives. As in the process of setting organizational goals and objectives, it is important to include everyone in conversations and to connect individual professional development goals and objectives to organizational strategy. We discussed strategies for successful individual goal-setting meetings, including creating safe, unbiased conversations and allowing individuals to lead their own goal-setting process. Keep these strategies in mind when heading into the next step in the process, implementing goals and objectives.

FIGURE 9.3

Individual Talent Development Platform: Executive Director, Small Grassroots Organization

Individual Professional Development Assessment

Competency	Measure	1	2	3	4	5
Advocacy and Public Policy	Position Proficiency Level					
	Current Proficiency Level					
	Desired Proficiency Level					
Communications, Marketing, and Public Relations	Position Proficiency Level					
	Current Proficiency Level					
	Desired Proficiency Level					
Financial Management and Social Entrepreneurship	Position Proficiency Level					
	Current Proficiency Level					
	Desired Proficiency Level					
Fundraising and Resource Development	Position Proficiency Level					
	Current Proficiency Level					
	Desired Proficiency Level					
Grantmaking or Direct Service	Position Proficiency Level					
	Current Proficiency Level					
	Desired Proficiency Level					
Human Resources Management and Volunteerism	Position Proficiency Level					
	Current Proficiency Level					
	Desired Proficiency Level					
Information Management	Position Proficiency Level					
	Current Proficiency Level					
	Desired Proficiency Level					
Leadership and Governance	Position Proficiency Level					
	Current Proficiency Level					
	Desired Proficiency Level					
Legal and Regulatory	Position Proficiency Level					
	Current Proficiency Level					
	Desired Proficiency Level					
Planning and Evaluation	Position Proficiency Level					
	Current Proficiency Level					
	Desired Proficiency Level					

Top Three Learning Styles

1. Collaborative

2. Independent

3.

FIGURE 9.3

Individual Talent Development Platform: Executive Director, Small Grassroots Organization, Cont'd

Goals and Objectives

Goal 1: Improve staff proficiency levels in Human Resources and Volunteerism in order to increase volunteer retention.	**01:** ALL staff responsible for one aspect of a volunteer recruitment plan.
	02: Community engagement supervisor mentors and as project lead; works one-on-one with each employee.
	03: Depending on the individual employees' learning preference they attend volunteer management seminar, webinar, or workshop.
Goal 2: Improve board proficiency levels in Financial Management to ensure strong internal controls and financial reporting.	**01:** One board member each month assigned to review financial statements and report three findings.
	02: CPA and board treasurer mentor board members.
	03: Board members receive financial management book and links to video. CPA and board treasurer do two in-service trainings on financial statements during the board meeting.
Goal 3: Begin to introduce professional development in Advocacy and Public Policy so that the organization can become stronger advocates in the issue areas of the organization.	**01:** ALL staff brainstorms advocacy ideas for future years.
	02: Staff collaboratively identifies who they want to mentor them on nonprofit advocacy.
	03: Staff attends training provided by mentor.

01 = Learning on the Job; **02** = Mentoring and Peer-to-Peer Opportunities; **03** = Trainings

Individual Professional Development Goals and Objectives

	Learning on-the-Job	Mentoring and Peer-to-Peer	Trainings
Goal 1: Increase organizational brand awareness.	Implement a brand strategy specifically with the website.	Work with a local pro bono assist from a PR firm.	Read Kivi Miller's book, *Content Marketing for Nonprofits*.
Goal 2: Enhance financial leadership.	Lead financial management trainings to the board.	Get mentored by board treasurer or CPA.	Watch Nonprofit Assistance Fund's videos.
Goal 3: Improve Legal and Regulatory proficiency level.	Prepare for Charity Navigator.	Partner with local executive director who has gone through Charity Navigator rating process.	Watch Charity Navigator's webinar.

FIGURE 9.4
Individual Talent Development Platform: Development Coordinator, Midsized Organization

Individual Professional Development Assessment

Competency	Measure	1	2	3	4	5
Advocacy and Public Policy	Position Proficiency Level	■	■			
	Current Proficiency Level	■	■	■		
	Desired Proficiency Level	■	■	■	■	■
Communications, Marketing, and Public Relations	Position Proficiency Level	■	■			
	Current Proficiency Level	■	■	■	■	
	Desired Proficiency Level	■	■	■	■	■
Financial Management and Social Entrepreneurship	Position Proficiency Level	■	■	■		
	Current Proficiency Level	■	■	■	■	
	Desired Proficiency Level	■	■	■	■	
Fundraising and Resource Development	Position Proficiency Level	■	■	■		
	Current Proficiency Level	■	■	■	■	
	Desired Proficiency Level	■	■	■	■	■
Grantmaking or Direct Service	Position Proficiency Level	■				
	Current Proficiency Level	■	■	■	■	
	Desired Proficiency Level	■	■	■	■	■
Human Resources Management and Volunteerism	Position Proficiency Level	■	■			
	Current Proficiency Level	■	■			
	Desired Proficiency Level	■	■	■	■	■
Information Management	Position Proficiency Level	■	■	■	■	
	Current Proficiency Level	■	■	■		
	Desired Proficiency Level	■	■	■	■	
Leadership and Governance	Position Proficiency Level	■	■			
	Current Proficiency Level	■	■	■		
	Desired Proficiency Level	■	■	■	■	■
Legal and Regulatory	Position Proficiency Level	■	■			
	Current Proficiency Level	■	■	■		
	Desired Proficiency Level	■	■	■	■	
Planning and Evaluation	Position Proficiency Level	■	■	■		
	Current Proficiency Level	■	■	■	■	
	Desired Proficiency Level	■	■	■	■	■

Top Three Learning Styles

1. Collaborative

2. Independent

3. Participant

FIGURE 9.4

Individual Talent Development Platform: Development Coordinator, Midsized Organization, Cont'd

Organizational Goals and Objectives

Goal 1: Plan and implement advocacy event to raise awareness of hunger issues within the community.	**01:** Specific responsibility in organizing the day of action: funding for day of action, marketing for day of action, and volunteer recruitment for day of action.
	02: Bring in an advocacy consultant to advise the planning of the advocacy event and help staff learn the intricacies of the work.
	03: Have advocacy consultant lead a training during a regular staff meeting.
Goal 2: Improve volunteer and donor recordkeeping system.	**01:** Identify and implement volunteer management and fundraising tracking database.
	02: Bring in a pro bono IT consultant to advise the process.
	03: Read articles and watch videos from Idealware on best practices.
Goal 3: Reduce legal liability and improve risk management practices throughout the warehouse.	**01:** Create and implement risk management policy and procedures—specifically focusing on warehouse volunteers.
	02: Have attorney from the board work with staff to identify best practices and ensure the correct policies and procedures are being implemented.
	03: Attend a risk management planning or management workshop.

01 = Learning on the Job; **02** = Mentoring and Peer-to-Peer Opportunities; **03** = Trainings

Individual Professional Development Goals and Objectives

	Learning on the Job	Mentoring and Peer-to-Peer	Trainings
Goal 1: Improve information technology proficiency to increase development tracking.	Implement new donor database.	Connect with the executive director and other senior staff, including an IT consultant.	Attend a training at the Fundraising School at Indiana University.
Goal 2: Develop leadership in new role as development manager.	Develop orientation manual for new development employees and volunteers.	Connect with a nonprofit faculty member or pro bono trainer to discuss leadership and development.	Attend a course or certificate program in nonprofit management class where one of the applied projects in an orientation manual.
Goal 3: None Identified.			

FIGURE 9.5
Individual Talent Development Platform: Program Associate, Grantmaking Organization

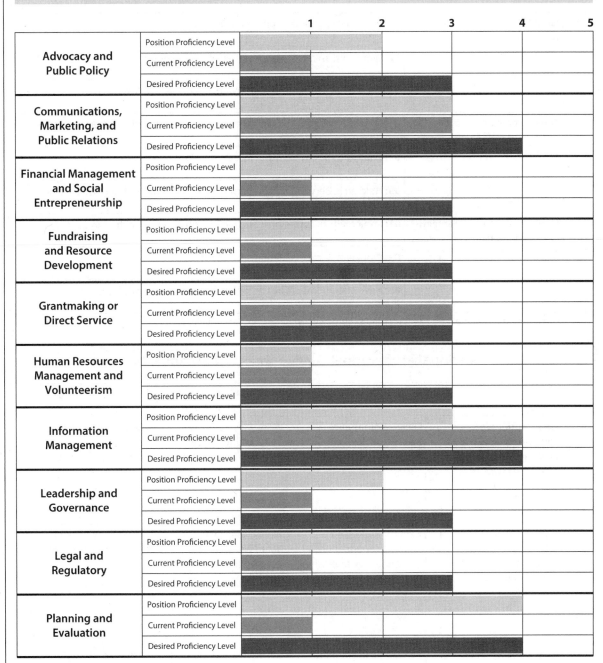

Individual Professional Development Assessment

		1	2	3	4	5
Advocacy and Public Policy	Position Proficiency Level					
	Current Proficiency Level					
	Desired Proficiency Level					
Communications, Marketing, and Public Relations	Position Proficiency Level					
	Current Proficiency Level					
	Desired Proficiency Level					
Financial Management and Social Entrepreneurship	Position Proficiency Level					
	Current Proficiency Level					
	Desired Proficiency Level					
Fundraising and Resource Development	Position Proficiency Level					
	Current Proficiency Level					
	Desired Proficiency Level					
Grantmaking or Direct Service	Position Proficiency Level					
	Current Proficiency Level					
	Desired Proficiency Level					
Human Resources Management and Volunteerism	Position Proficiency Level					
	Current Proficiency Level					
	Desired Proficiency Level					
Information Management	Position Proficiency Level					
	Current Proficiency Level					
	Desired Proficiency Level					
Leadership and Governance	Position Proficiency Level					
	Current Proficiency Level					
	Desired Proficiency Level					
Legal and Regulatory	Position Proficiency Level					
	Current Proficiency Level					
	Desired Proficiency Level					
Planning and Evaluation	Position Proficiency Level					
	Current Proficiency Level					
	Desired Proficiency Level					

Top Three Learning Styles

1. Collaborative

2. Independent

3.

FIGURE 9.5

Individual Talent Development Platform: Program Associate, Grantmaking Organization, Cont'd

Organizational Goals and Objectives

Goal 1: Raise awareness of foundation issue areas.	**01:** Present issue areas to policy makers.
	02: Work with an advocacy consultant or local volunteer.
	03: Participate in a nonprofit lobbying and advocacy day.
Goal 2: Increase financial acumen of staff, board, and grantees.	**01:** Staff create financial management trainings for staff, boad, and grantees.
	02: Work with board treasurer to plan trainings.
	03: Hold an in-service workshop for staff and potentially board members.
Goal 3: Incorporate planning and evaluation into daily work.	**01:** Implement program plan and evaluation for financial trainings.
	02: Work with local evaluation consultant.
	03: Have staff members attend a strategic planning workshop.

01 = Learning on the Job; **02** = Mentoring and Peer-to-Peer Opportunities; **03** = Trainings

Individual Professional Development Goals and Objectives

	Learning on the Job	Mentoring and Peer-to-Peer	Trainings
Goal 1: Improve community awareness of foundation's issue areas.	Deliver community awareness day.	Work with a trustee of the board to increase community awareness.	Read a book on nonprofit and/or community advocacy.
Goal 2: Increase financial acumen in order to mentor and improve financial acumen of grantees.	Monitor budget and financial reports for the community awareness day.	Work closely with the board treasurer to develop the trainings.	Attend the financial management in-service.
Goal 3: Incorporate planning and evaluation into daily work.	Participate in planning and evaluation of financial management trainings.	Get advice and mentoring from the organization's president.	Attend a strategic planning workshop.

Chapter 10
Implementing the Plan

Now that you have created your goals and objectives, it is time to begin implementation. In this chapter we'll discuss the budget, time, and resources your organization needs to implement the professional development objectives you have set for your organization, employees, and volunteers. We'll also provide you with specific resources for implementation success and ideas for how to deal with common barriers to implementation. Figure 10.1 gives you an overview of the implementation of professional development.

Implementation Best Practices

It is important to take into consideration the time, budget, and resources you need to carry out professional development activities. Our research shows that organizations typically devote 2 percent of their budgets to professional development activities (Carpenter, Clarke, & Gregg, 2013). In most cases, the 2 percent consists of a set amount of money that employees use to attend trainings or conferences. As we've discussed throughout this book, a strong talent development system requires an investment beyond an allocation of funds. We believe professional development should be a strategic part of your organization's budgeting process. Although we have an appendix devoted to the topic of funding and revenue development for professional development, don't wait around for the funding to come in to implement your professional development. As we discussed at the very beginning of the book, an important part of this process is showing your board and the general public how much money will be saved if you invest in your talent now!

The organizations we work with make professional development part of everyone's responsibility; therefore professional development isn't an additional expense. Professional development is a part of everyday operations. Even though you can make professional development part of your day-to-day operations, you will still need to create a budget for employee time devoted to professional development.

FIGURE 10.1
Implementation Overview

IMPLEMENTATION OF PROFESSIONAL DEVELOPMENT	·····▶	• Organizational goals and objectives determine the timeline and steps during the implementation stage. Timelines will be set for organizational benchmarks, as well as for individual objectives. • This process will also include reflection and potential adaptation points as necessary.

The costs of implementing the Talent Development Platform can be broken in to three categories: (1) salary adjustments, (2) time and money for creating the Talent Development Platform, and (3) time and costs for implementing professional development goals and objectives. These costs should be aligned with your strategic plan and organizational budget. Do not create a separate budget for these processes now; simply add room in your already existing budget for each of these items.

Salary Adjustments

You had the opportunity in chapters 3, 4, and 5 to go through each position in your organization to realign job descriptions, adjust titles, and create new roles. With each of these staffing changes, salary adjustments may have been needed in your budget, whether these adjustments were for title increases or for the addition of new staff.

If you do increase someone's responsibilities or title, the adjustment should be met with a salary increase. Due to your renewed focus on your people you should also ensure that all positions in your organization have salaries comparable to those of their peers.

Remember back to chapter 1 when we discussed the return on investment for developing a strong talent development system? In that section, we explained that turnover costs your organization 75 to 150 percent of the salary of each departing employee. Due to your work implementing the Talent Development Platform and your renewed investment in employees, you are more likely to retain employees for longer periods. An increase of staff salaries, such as those completed by the small grassroots organization (exhibit 10.1). will save you money in the long run. For example, if the program coordinator (who is paid $25,000) decides to leave the organization, it will cost between $18,750 and $37,500 to replace that position. This amount is dependent on the time it takes to hire, interview, and orientate new staff and on the loss of productivity while trying to replace the position. A $5,000 yearly salary increase is a good investment considering the actual costs of turnover.

EXHIBIT 10.1

Salary Adjustments: Small Grassroots Organization

In the small grassroots organization, the executive director realized her employees' salaries were lower than those in organizations of comparable type and size. She put together a proposal to her board, which included a recommendation for staff salary increases, shown in the table. The information gleaned from the talent mapping process gave her the data to make this request to her board. She provided accurate job responsibilities and proficiency levels for each role and used the state's compensation and benefits report for nonprofit organizations to determine the salary each position deserved.

Staff Salaries Budget: Small Grassroots Organization

Title	Current Salary	Proposed Salary
Executive Director (FT)	$31,000 ($15hr)	$45,000 ($21hr)
Community Engagement Supervisor (PT)	$13,000 ($12.50hr)	$17,280 ($16.60hr)
Program Coordinator (FT)	$25,000 ($12hr)	$30,000 ($15hr)
Community Worker (PT)	$10,000 ($9.60hr)	$13,000 ($12.50hr)
Education Supervisor (PT)	$13,000 ($12.50hr)	$17,280 ($16.60hr)
Total	$92,000	$122,560

Time and Budget Estimates: Creating the Talent Development Platform

We've discussed throughout the book that it takes time to create and fill in your organizational Talent Development Platform. Although the additional work is minimal for each employee—with the exception of the individual leading the effort—employees and volunteers should not feel like this is extra work. When calculating your budget for developing the Talent Development Platform, instead of adding extra responsibilities to just one person's plate, consider giving extra responsibilities to all employees and volunteers. For example, if you have a big program launch coming, move the Talent Development Platform planning out a few weeks so that employees and volunteers do not become overwhelmed. As we've discussed in previous chapters, if your employees and volunteers are running on a regular workload and your organizational culture encourages learning and development, your employees and volunteers should be able to fit in the time to complete the planning steps.

When you calculate the actual costs of creating the Talent Development Platform, consider employee hourly rates or the estimated hourly rate for volunteers. Independent Sector provides a value of volunteer time annually (see https://www.independentsector.org/volunteer_time). Table 10.1 provides a time estimate for an organization to go through the Talent Development Platform process (before implementation), using the small grassroots organization as an example. To figure out what to budget for your organization, use your employee's hourly rates and the most current hourly rate for a volunteer. We'll discuss the implementation budget in the next section.

As you can see from these calculations, the Talent Development Platform does take an investment. Well, you already knew that since you've come this far in the book. Our critics told us to avoid creating a comprehensive and strategic tool for professional development because of the time investment. However, we ignored them because the organizational benefits of putting people first and investing in talent are too great to ignore. We've seen a lot of people leave organizations and the sector due to burnout, the feeling of little support, and lack of professional development. We've also seen organizations that put their people first—they keep their employees and volunteers and get more out of them. The second group of organizations is leaps and bounds ahead of others. Organizations with strong talent development practices are more effective and competitive for top talent.

Time and Budget Estimates: Implementing the Talent Development Platform

The goal-setting portion of the Talent Development Platform determines the hours, time frame, and costs you need to budget for implementing the Talent Development Platform. For the timeline part of the work, be more specific on time frames for implementing the on-the-job, mentoring, and training activities. All time frames for professional development activities should occur within ten months to one year, depending on the time frame you specify when setting goals and objectives. Your timeline should bring together the practices you've developed during the Talent Development Platform process and integrate best practices in adult learning, staff time, supervision, and time for reflection. Estimate time for each of the three realms of learning and add in reflection time as well as points for feedback and discussion among employees and volunteers. We have provided sample timelines from each of the four organization types as examples of how all these components can be integrated into a ten- to twelve-month timeline (exhibits 10.9 to 10.12). Depending on the size of your organization you may want timelines for separate departments as well.

Your employees and volunteers will also have timelines. Their timelines will integrate activities they have within the organization's timeline as well as their own individual activities, and are shown side by side with

TABLE 10.1

Time and Cost Estimates: Creating the Talent Development Platform, Small Grassroots Organization

Activity	Time Frame	Time Spent	Calculation*	Cost
Organizational Learning Assessment	2 Months	Executive director = 10 hours	$21 × 10 hours	$210.00
		Employees = 30 minutes for assessment	($16.60 + $15 + $12.50 + $16.60) = $60.70 × .5 hours	$30.35
		Employees = 2 hours for reviewing results	($16.60 + $15 + $12.50 + $16.60) = $60.70 × 2 hours	$121.40
Total:				**$361.75**
Talent Map, Job Descriptions, and Sub-competencies	4 Months	Executive director = 40 hours	$21 × 40 hours	$840.00
		Employees = 2 hours for reviewing assessments	($16.60 + $15 + $12.50 + $16.60) = $60.70 × 2 hours	$121.40
		Employees = 2 hours for Talent Map discussion	($16.60 + $15 + $12.50 + $16.60) = $60.70 × 2 hours	$121.40
Total:				**$1,082.80**
Individual Professional Development Assessment and Individual Learning Styles Assessment	2 Months	Executive director = 12 hours	$21 × 12 hours	$252.00
		Employees = 45 minutes for assessments	($16.60 + $15 + $12.50 + $16.60) = $60.70 × .75 hours	$45.53
		Employees = 2 hours for calculating results and meeting with executive director	($16.60 + $15 + $12.50 + $16.60) = $60.70 × 2 hours	$121.40
Total:				**$418.93**

TABLE 10.1

Time and Cost Estimates: Creating the Talent Development Platform, Small Grassroots Organization, Cont'd

Activity	Time Frame	Time Spent	Calculation*	Cost
Goals and Objectives	2 Months	Executive director = 15 hours	$21 × 15 hours	$315.00
		Employees = 2 hours for goal setting and meeting with executive director	($16.60 + $15 + $12.50 + $16.60) = $60.70 × 2 hours	$121.40
		Employees = 2 hours for full staff goal meeting	($16.60 + $15 + $12.50 + $16.60) = $60.70 × 2 hours	$121.40
Total:				**$557.80**
Evaluation	2 Months	Executive director = 10 hours	$21 × 10 hours	$210.00
		Employees = 2 hours for retaking all assessments	($16.60 + $15 + $12.50 + $16.60) = $60.70 × 2 hours	$121.40
		Employees = 2 hours for discussion meeting	($16.60 + $15 + $12.50 + $16.60) = $60.70 × 2 hours	$121.40
Total:				**$452.80**
Grand Total:				**$2,874.08**

Note: *The dollar amounts used in this column are the hourly rates for each of the organization's employees.

the organization's timeline. When developing timelines keep a few things in mind:

- Space activities out throughout the year to avoid overload.

- Keep individual activities in mind as much as you can; for example, keep periods of time at the organization level open or focused on a particular topic. You may want to start the year out focused on a specific objective or spread them all throughout the year. Be conscious of how you are managing your employees' time in either case.

- Honor the timeline as much as you can, but be flexible. There may be some points throughout the year that get overloaded unexpectedly. Go with the flow, as we're sure you already do in your everyday work, and move things around as necessary.

- When glitches happen in the timeline, discuss why and then set new timelines together. Do the same if an activity didn't occur at all within your year of implementation. Discuss why any issues may have occurred and adjust or plan as necessary.

Now that you have determined employee and volunteer hours and created a timeline of professional development activities, you can budget for these activities. This budgeting process includes determining a portion of each employee's and volunteer's time, along with their corresponding hourly rate.

Table 10.2 shows a sample of what the small grassroots organization budgeted for professional development goals and objectives and implementing the Talent Development Platform.

The small grassroots organization included employee time, training time, and coaching costs. When you determine your budget, do the same. Also as a cost savings, look for ways to use pro bono support, and your staff and volunteers who scored at the advanced or expert proficiency levels to support mentoring and coaching.

Resources and Tools for Implementation

The three realms of learning in which you set your goals and objectives and on which you have built your timelines require varying degrees of resources and tools. We touched on this when looking at the timeline and budget, but we'll now share specific resources and tools you will need for each realm of learning.

On-the-Job Resources

On-the-job goals and objectives range from employees taking on entirely new roles to teams working together on learning a new task, to an employee taking on a new task for a few weeks to a few months. In each of these potential on-the-job learning experiences, employees and volunteers need time to reflect on their learning and growth. Reflection time also allows adjustments to be made to the on-the-job experience as they become necessary. Employees and volunteers taking on these on-the-job learning experiences need to be able share their other work with other employees or volunteers, or freeze work on nonpriority projects for the duration of the on-the-job learning experience.

Successful on-the-job learning experiences have the following five components:

- Employees or volunteers must have been employed with the organization or have volunteered for at least three months, which allows them

TABLE 10.2

Time and Budgeted Costs: Implementing the Talent Development Platform, Small Grassroots Organization

Activity	Estimated Staff Costs*	Estimated Activity Costs
Goal 1		
On-the-Job Learning	Executive director = 10 hours × $21 = $210.00 Employees = ($16.60 + $15 + $12.50 + $16.60) × 6 hours = $364.20	
Mentoring	-	Pro bono mentor = $22.65 (in-kind rate) × 8 hours = $181.20
Trainings	Employees & executive director = ($21 + $16.60 + $15 + $12.50 + $16.60) × 2 hours = $163.40	5 Employee Trainings = $625
Goal 2		
On-the-Job Learning	Executive director = 25 hours × $21 = $525.00	-
Mentoring	Executive director = 8 hours × $21 = $168.00 Employee = 8 hours × $16.60 = $132.80	Pro bono mentor = $22.65 (in-kind rate) × 8 hours = $181.20
Trainings	Employees & executive director = ($21 + $16.60 + $15 + $12.50 + $16.60) × 2 hours = $163.40	5 Employee trainings = $625
Goal 3		
On-the-Job Learning	Executive director = 5 hours × $21 = $105.00	-
Mentoring	-	Pro bono mentor = $22.65 (in-kind rate) × 8 hours = $181.20
Trainings	Employees & executive director = ($21 + $16.60 + $15 + $12.50 + $16.60) × 2 hours = $163.40	5 Employee trainings = $625
Total:	**$1,995.20**	**$2,418.60**
Grand Total:	**$4,413.80**	

Note: *The dollar amounts used in this column are the hourly rates for each of the organization's employees.

to get past the probationary period before beginning and on-the-job learning assignment.

- Properly trained mentors must support the on-the-job learning experience.

- Agreed-upon operating procedures should be stated before the on-the-job learning experience begins.

- A structured but flexible schedule should be applied to keep the mentor and employee or volunteer on track and allow for follow-up if needed.

- An evaluation should occur at the end of the on-the-job learning experience to determine whether the employee or volunteer has acquired the skills necessary, and a plan to reinforce skills not obtained during the on-the-job learning period should be implemented (adapted from Molnar & Watts, 2002, p. 5).

Employees and volunteers can fill out a worksheet to plan their on-the-job learning experience worksheet (shown in Exhibit 10.2).

EXHIBIT 10.2

Plan for On-the-Job Learning

Name of Assignment:

Task Plan/Deliverables:

(That is, what you will do in the assignment)

Competency Categories:

Learning Goals:

(Examples: Learn strategies for handling resistance to change; Gain skill and experience in giving difficult feedback)

1.

2.

3.

Resources Needed:

(expertise; time)

Who will give you feedback?

(peers, mentor, managers, direct reports)

Time frame:

Source: Adapted from Scontrino, M. P., & Powell, J. K. (2013). Developmental plan for on-the-job learning. Retrieved www.scontrino-powell.com/wp-content/uploads/2013/06/Developmental-Plan-Template-for-On-the-Job-Learning.pdf

Request for Proposals

You may need to create a request for proposal (RFP) for your on-the-job learning experience. The request gives employees the opportunity to recruit a consultant or mentor or to select a tool or piece of software. You can access a template RFP created by one of Heather's previous employers, Aspiration. Although the template has a technology focus, it has all the necessary components that should be included in an RFP and will help you during the RFP creation process. https://aspirationtech.org/training/workflow/templates/rfp

Reflection

The Foundation for Critical Thinking (2014) developed a set of questions you can use to reflect on any type of activity or experience. We've adapted these questions to apply to the on-the-job learning experience (exhibit 10.3). The questions help the employee and volunteer review all aspects of their on-the-job experience and think of the assignment in different ways. We recommend having the employee or volunteer reflect on the on-the-job learning experience halfway through and at the completion of the assignment. Employees and volunteers should discuss the reflection results with their mentor to receive new insights and perspectives on the assignment.

EXHIBIT 10.3

On-the-Job Assignment Reflection Questions

Purpose: What is the assignment I am trying to accomplish? What is my purpose for completing this assignment? How does this assignment aid in overall mission accomplishment?

Questions: What questions do I have about the assignment? What questions, challenges, or problems am I addressing through this assignment? What questions do I need answered before I can move forward with this assignment?

Information: What information do I have to complete this assignment? What experiences have I had thus far that have prepared me for this assignment? What information do I need to complete this assignment?

Inferences/Conclusions: How will I know that I have completed the assignment? How did I reach this conclusion?

Concepts: What is the main idea/concept/competency I am covering during my assignment? Can I explain this idea/concept/competency to staff, volunteers, external constituents, etc.?

Assumptions: What assumptions do I have about this assignment? What have I taken for granted about the circumstances? Can I reframe my assumptions?

Implications/Consequences: If someone else was completing this assignment, what would be the implications? How might they complete the assignment?

Points of View: From what point of view am I looking at this assignment? Is there another point of view I should consider?

Source: Adapted from Paul, R., & Elder, L. (2014). *The miniature guide to critical thinking concepts and tools* (7th ed.). Tomales, CA: Foundation for Critical Thinking.

Mentoring Resources

Many factors influence the success or failure of the mentoring relationship, which we discussed in chapter 8. To ensure your employee and volunteer mentor relationships are a success, here are some resources and tips for both the mentor and mentee (exhibit 10.4).

EXHIBIT 10.4

Tips for Mentors and Mentees

Tips for Mentors

- Listen carefully; everyone has a wealth of wisdom and unique gifts to share. As the mentor you may learn something from your mentee, and with better listening you can better help your mentee find solutions to his learning challenges.

- Ask good questions rather than give advice. After the mentee has done her best thinking, you can ask if she wants any additional information or suggestions. Asking questions allows the mentee to find the solution on her own, with guidance. This type of learning is more effective.

- Use open-ended questions that begin with *what, when,* or *who,* which often lead to more creative ideas and concrete actions than those that begin with *why*.

- Use the conversation as an opportunity to learn and discover. If an obstacle is encountered, try to identify the real barriers and ways to get through them. Let go of judging, advising, and thinking you know all the answers. Learn together and discover new possibilities.

- Keep the conversation focused, fun, and moving forward. When your mentee gets stuck, refocus on the results and reasons they are desirable.

- Affirm your mentee's progress and potential to succeed. Remember the power of validation, acknowledgment, and encouragement.

- Lift the energy level to generate creativity, deep insights, new possibilities, and renewed commitment, so your mentee feels empowered, energized, and eager to move forward.

Source: Adapted from Fellner, K., Keleher, T., & Oritz, E. (2008). *Work with me: Intergenerational conversations for nonprofit leadership*. National Council of Nonprofit Associations.

Tips for Mentees

- Be ready to work at the relationship. Good relationships don't just happen; they take work. It takes time and effort to get to know each other and build trust. Establishing and maintaining trust is essential to a good mentoring relationship.

- Be open-minded and willing to learn. No matter who your mentor is, he or she has experience and expertise to share with you. You and your mentor may have a lot in common or very little.

EXHIBIT 10.4
Tips for Mentors and Mentees, Cont'd

Regardless, if you remain open-minded and want to learn, you will learn and become a better professional as a result.

- Be honest and real. Your mentor will be better able to help you if you are open and honest about who you are and what you want out of the on-the-job learning experience.

- Be proactive and take initiative. Mentoring should be an active and engaging experience for both parties. You should not rely on your mentor to do everything. Make sure that you are in frequent contact with your mentor. Let your mentor know when you need help. Ask questions. Follow through on items the two of you discuss.

- Be prepared for your meetings with your mentor: Think about the topics you would like to discuss with your mentor ahead of time, write them down, and possibly even e-mail them to your mentor in advance of your meeting. The more you prepare, the more you will get out of your meetings with your mentor.

- Be a good listener. It is your mentor's job to give you honest feedback and advice, some of which will be positive and some of which will be constructive. Rather than ignoring your mentor's criticism or constructive feedback, or letting it make you feel bad, listen to what your mentor has to say and consider how you can use that information to improve yourself. Regardless of whether you choose to take your mentor's advice, listening to what your mentor has to share with you is important.

- Be forward-thinking. Talk to your mentor about where you are presently, but focus your energy on building for the future. Define your goals for the semester, year, graduation, or early-career. In conversation with your mentor, determine the skills sets, knowledge, and abilities you need to acquire in order to achieve these goals.

Source: Adapted from Executive Mentor Program, College of Business Administration, Kansas State Univeristy. (n.d.). 7 tips for being a good mentee. Retrieved from
https://cba.k-state.edu/current-students/documents/executive-mentor/Tips%20for%20being%20a%20good%20mentee.pdf

Mentoring Plans

To get the most out of the mentoring experience both parties should reflect on their experiences and adapt their relationship or topics of conversation as necessary. This sample mentoring timeline will help the mentors and mentees plan their mentoring relationship and plan which topics they will cover during each mentoring meeting (exhibit 10.5).

EXHIBIT 10.5

Sample Mentoring Timeline

8 hours over 10 months	Meeting 1	in-person 1 hour	• Get to know each other • Share expectations of each other • Mentee outlines learning goals for the mentoring relationship • Sign mentor-mentee agreement
	Meeting 2	in-person 1 hour	• Mentor and mentee review professional development learning goals and objectives • Review timeline for achieving learning goals and objectives • Trust exercise
	Meeting 3	in-person 1 hour	• Review on-the-job assignment reflection • Review mentee's learning progress and on-the-job learning experience
	Meeting 4	online or phone 1/2 hour	• Review mentee's learning progress and on-the-job learning experience
	Meeting 5	in-person 1 hour	• Assess mentoring relationship — what's working what's not — re-review expectations • Make adjustments to the mentoring agreement
	Meeting 6	in-person 1 hour	• Review mentee's learning progress and on-the-job learning experience • Adjust on-the-job learning experience timeline
	Meeting 7	online or phone 1/2 hour	• Review mentee's learning progress and on-the-job learning experience
	Meeting 8	online or phone 1/2 hour	• Review mentee's learning progress and on-the-job learning experience
	Meeting 9	in-person 1 hour	• Review mentee's learning progress and on-the-job learning experience • Evaluate the mentoring relationship
	Meeting 10	in-person 1/2 hour	• Debrief and end mentoring relationship

Source: Adapted from McFarlane, H. (2007). *Board mentoring handbook.* Retrieved from maytree.com/PDF_Files/BoardMentoring Handbook.pdf

Mentoring Agreement

Another key aspect of a successful mentoring relationship is a mentoring agreement. The agreement provides the mentor and mentee with a common understanding of the expectations of their relationship as well as a safe space for conversation and learning together. Both the mentor and mentee should sign the agreement before beginning their relationship. Exhibit 10.6 shows a sample mentor-mentee agreement.

EXHIBIT 10.6

Sample Mentor-Mentee Agreement

A mentor-mentee agreement is signed once a mentor and mentee have been matched. This agreement forms the basis of the mentor-mentee relationship.

Mentor-Mentee Agreement

A successful mentee-mentor relationship requires a commitment on the part of both partners. The following agreement is intended to provide a starting framework for the partnership. Either party should understand that they may withdraw from the relationship at any time. Each party should keep a copy of this agreement and make every effort to fulfill the terms of the agreement.

Mentor _____

Contact Number/E-mail_____

Mentee _____

Contact Number/E-mail_____

Employed by _____

Job Title _____

Mentor and mentee are encouraged to share additional contact information as needed.

Mentee Goals

The mentee should establish with the mentor at least three professional development or personal growth goals. *Goals should be specific, measurable, attainable, relevant and have a time frame.*

GOAL #1 _____

_____

GOAL #2 _____

_____

GOAL #3 _____

_____

Contact Agreement

The duration of the mentoring agreement is _____. Mentor or mentee may exit this agreement at any time by notifying either party. Contacts with mentee may be in person or by telephone to be agreed upon by both mentor and mentee. Mentor and mentee should allow enough time during a meeting for discussion of goals, as well as questions from the mentee concerning professional and/or personal development.

EXHIBIT 10.6
Sample Mentor-Mentee Agreement, Cont'd

Mentee and Mentor agree to meet (list frequency) _____.

Mentee and Mentor agree to evaluate the mentoring relationship at the end of the formal program.

_____   _____

Mentee Signature and Date   Mentor Signature and Date

_____

Source: Adapted from South Delta Mentor Mentee Form. jfs.ohio.gov/owd/WorkforceProf/Docs/South-Delta-Mentor-Mentee-Agreement-Forms.doc

Peer Group Resources

Putting together peer groups is another way to provide employees and volunteers with an experience similar to a mentor-mentee relationship. In the peer group, individuals are able to learn from a bit larger group—usually three to ten people—through troubleshooting. Groups of this kind can be made up of a group of employees or volunteers from the same organization, or a group of employees from similar organizations working through similar challenges.

Peer groups allow the individuals participating to develop their proficiency levels in a specific competency area while also learning how to support their colleagues and have healthy conversations. According to Cathy Davidson (2013), peer learning "creates an atmosphere of mutual learning, contribution, and collaboration that not only enhances our engagement in the quality and content of the learning experience but provides a life-skill for future interactions." The twofold nature of peer learning situations makes on-the-job learning even more effective for participants.

Peer Group Timeline

Peer groups should have structures similar to the mentor-mentee relationship. A timeline should be put in place when the group meets. The timeline can include meeting anywhere from once a week to once a month to once a quarter. The frequency will really depend on how the groups change and the pace at which they need to learn. If on the one hand the goal of the group is to learn more about annual campaigns and they are starting their work in the spring, they may want to meet semimonthly to increase their proficiency before there campaign starts in the fall. On the other hand if the group is trying to increase their leadership skills and is working independently throughout the year to do this, they may only want to meet every other month to touch base and check up on each other.

Group Member Agreement

As with the mentor-mentee relationship, each member of the group should sign a member agreement. The agreement can be based on the agreement letter in exhibit 10.6. During the first meeting each member of the group should state their purpose for attending and everyone should sign the agreement together. We also recommend having the group develop ground rules during the first meeting. The statements in the agreement are a first start, but others may be developed if the group believes they are necessary. Here are some more resources to ensure your peer groups are successful.

Peer Group Agenda

Each peer group session will consist of an opening, a coaching slot for each participant, and a closing. This agenda structure allows each participant time to be coached by peers in the group. Exhibit 10.7 shows a sample agenda.

EXHIBIT 10.7
Sample Peer Group Agenda

Opening (as a group): 5–10 minutes

- Create values and ground rules
- Select a coaching goal
- Review guidelines for Getting Coached and Coaching Your Peers

Coaching Time Slots (one-on-one): 10–15 minute time slots

- Each member gets an equal time slot to be coached and to be the presenter
- Each member coaches others during the others' time slots

Closing: 15 minutes

- Share action items and learning
- Share learnings out loud
- Evaluate the session

1. All quietly rate the Circle session from 1 (low) to 5 (high)
2. Then each member shares

   a. The rating
   b. Why he or she selected it
   c. What he or she could have done in that meeting to make it a 5

Getting Coached

One of the keys to a successful peer group is learning how to get coached. Here are some tips for how to learn through coaching:

- Present your coaching goal: what you want to get coached on.
- Use no more than 20 percent of your time slot to explain your coaching goal.
- Explain your coaching goal in terms of the here and now.
- Use "I" statements as much as possible in your explanations.
- Only share what's comfortable—this is your time slot.
- Don't repeat yourself. Explain your goal once.

EXHIBIT 10.7
Sample Peer Group Agenda, Cont'd

Coaching Your Peers

If you are accepting coaching in a peer group, you must also be able to coach your peers. Here are some tips for how to coach your peers:

- Completely listen to the presenter. Let your brain be quiet, and maintain eye contact with presenter.
- Quickly ask useful questions about the presenter's current perspectives, assumptions, actions, etc.
- Limit advice. Do not jump in and "save" the presenter by doing most of the talking yourself.
- Limit general discussion. Focus on helping the presenter address his or her coaching goal.
- Avoid lecturing the presenter. For example, don't say "you should" or "you have to."
- Help the presenter come up with specific actions during his or her time slot.
- Intervene if the Circle gets off track.

Source: Adapted from CompassPoint Nonprofit Services, Authenticity Circles Peer Learning Groups. www.compasspoint.org/sites/default/files/documents/SVForum/Peer%20Coaching%20Quick%20Reference%20Tool%20and%20Member .pdf

---

Training Resources

As we've emphasized throughout the book, making professional development that is strategic and tied to the organizational goals is important for employee success. In order to ensure that training becomes useful to on-the-job experiences, one must assess the training experience. We'll go into more detail about evaluating the entire Talent Development Platform process in the next chapter, but one way to ensure that training experiences are successful is by implementing Kirkpatrick's four-level training model:

1. **Reaction to the Training:** What was the employee's or volunteer's experience in the training?

2. **Learning from the Training:** What did the employee or volunteer learn during the training? Did the training match his or her learning style and learning format preferences?

3. **Behavior Change as a Result of the Training:** What will the employee or volunteer do differently with on-the-job experience as a result of the training? This should be documented and discussed with the mentor as well.

4. **Outcomes and Results of the Training:** How did the employee or volunteer perceive the overall training experience? Was the training well done? What could have been done differently to improve the training experience? (This part is especially important if the training was in-house. [Kirkpatrick & Kirkpatrick, 2006; MindTools, n.d.]).

We've provided a Sample Training Evaluation Form that staff and volunteers can fill out after each training (exhibit 10.8). The Sample Training Evaluation Form uses the aspects from Kirkpatrick's model and asks the training participant to reflect on each aspect of the training.

To enhance learning from the training, it might be useful for individuals who participated in the training to discuss what they learned and their answers to the questions in this form with their team. Team members may help the individual integrate learning into his or her everyday work and potentially adapt their own work as a result. If employees and volunteers do share in this way, ensure that the experience is successful by leaving time for conversation instead of simply asking the participant to present to his or her team.

EXHIBIT 10.8

Sample Training Evaluation Form

Identify three experiences from the training.

1. _____

2. _____

3. _____

Identify three things learned from the training.

1. _____

2. _____

3. _____

Identify three ways you will apply the training to your on-the-job learning experience.

1. _____

2. _____

3. _____

Evaluate the entire training experience. What could have been done differently to improve the training experience?

Overcoming Barriers to Implementation

When we started the process of piloting the Talent Development Platform, we offered a free one-hour brown bag lunch-and-learn, and forty social change organizations signed up and attended the free workshop. Then we offered a paid workshop series, which included three four-hour sessions (which cost only $100), and six organizations signed up. This is one small sign of the barriers organizations have in front of them for professional development. Even small costs, with a small time commitment, seem like too much for organizations to handle when they're already running thin on time and money. Other barriers come with crisis events, and then staff turnover occurs. This happened to some organizations testing our tools; we didn't hear from some organizations again after they started the assessments. We even had an organization that volunteered to send out the assessment to their staff and when we followed up, they said they had completely forgotten.

We get it—we've worked in these crazy busy environments—but now is the time to stop and do things differently. Despite the barriers, creating and implementing a talent development system is worth it. This process is a proactive solution, something we don't always have the luxury of in social change organizations, but if you take the time to step back and make the effort now, you won't regret it. To ensure your organization is ready, take the time for the Organizational Learning Assessment presented in chapter 2. Get your team in the right mind-set before getting started.

Throughout this book we've discussed the importance of readiness and how the preparation with each of the tools targets adult learners. Both of these require providing the time and space for developing talent within an organization. You've taken a lot of steps to ensure that professional development can and will happen in a strategic way in your organization. But as with any new thing, there will be challenges to creating and implementing the Talent Development Platform. Here is some further information (adapted from Tough, 1979, p. 106) on barriers and challenges you may encounter with your staff and volunteers as you implement these tools.

Unaware of Needing Help

As we piloted the Individual Professional Development Assessment, we noticed that some staff and volunteers with little experience rate themselves as advanced or experts in all areas. It is helpful to realize at the outset that certain people lack humility and are unaware they need professional development. We also noticed that individuals who scored low in the Motivation for Change domain in the Organizational Learning Assessment did not believe they needed learning.

We know there are many overachievers involved in social change organizations, many of whom don't go into the work for the money but do it for their passion. We can speak from personal experience that passion is a strength and a weakness. In order for the professional development exercises to be effective, employees and volunteers must accept the talent development process, self-exploration, and the fact that their passion can only get them so far.

Part of the problem of being unaware of needing help is that employees and volunteers may be at a lower developmental stage than what they believe they are at. Adult development is complex, and scholars refer to the developmental stages as having variations of action logic (Rooke & Torbert, 2005). Some staff and volunteers may be at a lower action logic than what they believe. If they are, they may be making decisions outside of their ability, which can cause them stress or anxiety without the proper mentoring and reflection on the process. Rooke and Torbert developed seven action logics, shown in table 10.3.

Understanding your employees' and volunteers' action logic will help you to reconsider some points:

- Are they in the right role?

- What professional development exercises can I implement to help them transition to another action logic stage?

- Is the mentor-mentee relationship the "right one"—do the developmental stages match up?

TABLE 10.3
Developmental Stages (Action Logics) and Their Characteristics

Action Logic	Characteristics
Opportunist	Wins any way possible. Self-oriented; manipulative; "might makes right."
Diplomat	Avoids overt conflict. Wants to belong; obeys group norms; rarely rocks the boat.
Expert	Rules by logic and expertise. Seeks rational efficiency.
Achiever	Meets strategic goals. Effectively achieves goals through teams; juggles managerial duties and market demands.
Individualist	Interweaves competing personal and company action logics. Creates unique structures to resolve gaps between strategy and performance.
Strategist	Generates organizational and personal transformations. Exercises the power of mutual inquiry, vigilance, and vulnerability for both the short and long term.
Alchemist	Generates social transformations. Integrates material, spiritual, and societal transformation.

Source: Reprinted with permission from "Seven Transformations of Leadership" by David Rooke and William R. Torbert. *Harvard Business Review,* April 2005. Copyright 2005 by Harvard Business Publishing; all rights reserved.

Some researchers—ourselves included—argue that organizations should not strive to have all the people within the organization at the same developmental level, but instead they consider that all people, even if emotionally irrational, bring skills and experiences that are important for organizational success.

It is helpful if you understand your employees' and volunteers' emotional intelligence throughout the process as well. In this way, you can help employees know where they are in action logic and rate themselves in more accurate domains. As a recap, emotional intelligence is "the ability to monitor one's own and others' feelings and emotions, to discriminate among them and use this information to guide one's thinking and actions" (Salovey & Mayer as cited by Tan, 2012, p. 10). This means you, as an organization leader, must continually communicate the importance of self-awareness and of everyone learning. You may even consider having all the staff participate in an emotional intelligence workshop so that staff and volunteers can complete self-awareness exercises.

Uncertain How or Where to Help

Once you get staff and volunteers to agree to take the assessments, you will move on to the challenges of determining what professional development each individual needs in each realm of learning (on-the-job experience, mentoring, and training). The assessments, discussions, and reflection time will help you with these determinations, but every individual is different. All professional development should be individualized as much as possible. You may even set someone's development activities and then realize he or she needs to adapt to a different type of learning in the middle of their work. This is okay. We've provided you some examples and suggestions throughout the book on how to manage individual needs, but the most important thing is coming together as a team. Brainstorm on-the-job learning experiences based on competency area, potential mentors, and training experiences that will advance proficiency levels for all members of the team.

No Action

Some employees may have personal experiences they bring into the learning process that can cause hesitancy or challenges with learning on the job, connecting with a mentor, or attending training. To support individuals who may have challenges with taking action in any of the three learning realms, we've built time into the planning timelines for reflection on each of these experiences. It is important, specifically in mentoring or peer relationships, that the mentor be proactive with the employee in activating the relationship. Connecting for the first time can often be the biggest barrier for individuals who have trouble with initiating action. It is also important that there be follow-up with the employee to see how their on-the-job experience is progressing to ensure they are taking action on their own. If you have people who are struggling with inaction, that doesn't mean they don't want to learn; sometimes they just don't know how and may just need a bit more support through the learning process.

Unable to Reach or Connect with the Resource

A big event or funding loss may cause the employee or organization to shift priorities. These shifts may cause necessary adjustments in all learning activities. There may also be a roadblock when someone who agrees to be a mentor becomes unavailable. Sometimes an employee or volunteer will select the wrong mentor or training. In each of these cases, the organization as a whole or the individual who is unable to connect with his or her resource or has a bad experience, should take some time for reflection and adaptation. Maybe learning needs to be put on hold so that everyone can focus on a crisis or shift in resources. You may also need to get someone a new mentor or to pause his or her experience for a bit. No matter the cause or solution, give yourself a break and begin again when you can. Don't let learning go completely by the wayside during these times, though. Use team meetings and reflection to keep your learning culture alive.

In conclusion, everyone's past experiences and learning styles are different, so responses to the Talent Development Platform planning and implementation will be different for everyone. There will be emotional triggers based on experiences and things said and done that you may not expect. As a leader you must figure out how to handle these challenges in the most professional way and to keep the process moving. This requires time and intention to overcome all barriers and to enhance your learning culture.

Implementation in Practice

To help you with implementing the Talent Development Platform, here are timelines and budgets from each of the four organizations.

Volunteer-Run Organization

The budget for the volunteer-run organization is based on the number of hours needed from each board member. The volunteer-run organization has seven board members. Tables 10.4 and 10.5 show the organization's estimated hours and budget for Talent Development Platform planning and implementation. Exhibit 10.9 shows the implementation timeline.

TABLE 10.4

Time and Cost Estimates: Creating the Talent Development Platform, Volunteer-Run Organization

Activity	Time Frame	Estimated Time Needed
Organizational Learning Assessment	2 Months	Board president = 8 hours
		Board members = 30 minutes for assessment × 6 = 3 hours
		Board members = 2 hours for reviewing results as an entire board
Talent Map, Job Descriptions, and Sub-competencies	4 Months	Board president = 10 hours
		Board members = 2 hours × 6 = 12 hours
Individual Professional Development Assessment and Individual Learning Styles Assessment	2 Months	Board president = 20 hours
		Board members = 45 minutes for assessments × 11 = 8.25 hours
		Board members = 2 hours for calculating results and meeting with the board president × 11 = 22 hours
Goals and Objectives	2 Months	Board president = 15 hours
		Employees = 2 hours for full board meeting × 11 = 22 hours
Evaluation	2 Months	Board president = 10 hours
		Board members = 1 hour for retaking all assessments × 11 = 11 hours
		Board members = 2 hours for full board meeting × 11 = 22 hours
Total:	**12 Months**	**165.25 Hours**

TABLE 10.5 **Time and Budgeted Costs: Implementing the Talent Development Platform, Volunteer-Run Organization**		
Activity	**Estimated Time Needed**	**Estimated Activity Costs**
Goal 1		
On-the-Job Learning	1 Board member = 10 hours	Technology record system = approx. $2,000
Mentoring	1 Board member = 3 hours	Technology consultant = approx. $1,000
Trainings	1 Board member = 2 hours	Recordkeeping training = $50
Goal 2		
On-the-Job Learning	3 Board members = 50 hours	-
Mentoring	2 Board members = 20 hours	-
Trainings	3 Board members = 9 hours	Policy workshop for 3 board members = $150
Goal 3		
On-the-Job Learning	Full board = 50 hours	-
Mentoring	2 Board members = 10 hours	Evaluation consultant = $3,000
Trainings	Full board = 25 hours	In-house training = $1,500
Total:	**327 hours**	**$7,700**

Small Grassroots Organization

The small grassroots organization adjusted its staff salaries to be more in line with salary ranges in the region and to support development of its employees. Total salaries before beginning the process were $92,000, and they are now $122,560, a difference of $30,560.

The organization budgeted $7,287.88 for implementing the Talent Development Platform and its learning goals. The budget was shown in detail in tables 10.1 and 10.2.

EXHIBIT 10.9

Implementation Timeline: Volunteer-Run Organization

	Organizational Goal	Organizational Goal	Organizational Goal	Individual Goal	Individual Goal	Individual Goal
Month 1	(O, M) Board (with board chair support) creates request for proposal for technology consultant.	(M) Board chair gathers board members to discuss policy-making process.	(These will happen in Year 2, after the database has been implemented). (O, M) Board (with board chair support) creates a request for proposal for an evaluation consultant.	(O) Board chair gathers board members to discuss policy-making process. (M) Board chair connects with nonprofit attorney.	(T) Board chair attends financial sustainability workshop.	
Month 2	(O) Board reviews technology consultant proposals, interview, checks references, and selects consultant.	(T) Board members attend policies and procedures workshop.	(O) Board reviews evaluation consultant proposals, interviews, checks references, and selects consultant.	(T) Board chair attends nonprofit risk management training. (M) Board chair meets with nonprofit attorney.	(M) Board chair meets with CPA. (O) Board chair creates an action plan for financial sustainability practices.	

Key: (O) = On-the-Job Activity; (M) = Mentoring Activity; (T) = Training Activity; (R) = Reflection Activity

EXHIBIT 10.9
Implementation Timeline: Volunteer-Run Organization, Cont'd

	Organizational Goal	Organizational Goal	Organizational Goal	Individual Goal	Individual Goal	Individual Goal
Month 3	(M) Consultant meets with board members. (O) Board brainstorms recordkeeping systems and needs of the new system.	(O) Board members (with guidance from board chair) pull examples of sample policies and bring back and discuss at board meeting. (M) Board chair assigns board members pieces of each policy. (R) Board members complete reflection exercise.	(M) Consultant meets with board members. (T) Board attends evaluation training.	(O) Board chair assigns board members pieces of each policy.	(O) Board chair presents action plan to CPA. (M) CPA reviews action plan and discusses revisions.	
Month 4	(T) Board attends technology record-keeping/database training.	(O) Board members draft the policies and bring back to the board chair for review. (M) Board members check in with board chair.	(M) Consultant meets with board members. (O) Board creates an evaluation logic model and discusses evaluation process.	(O, M) Board chair reviews draft policies with assistance from nonprofit attorney. (O) Board chair checks in with board members.	(O) Board chair meets with the board to discuss and vote on financial sustainability practices and changes. (M) Board chair meets with CPA.	

Key: (O) = On-the-Job Activity; (M) = Mentoring Activity; (T) = Training Activity; (R) = Reflection Activity

EXHIBIT 10.9
Implementation Timeline: Volunteer-Run Organization, Cont'd

	Organizational Goal	Organizational Goal	Organizational Goal	Individual Goal	Individual Goal	Individual Goal
Month 5	(O/M) Board and technology consultant create RFP for database/recordkeeping system.	(O) Board chair and board members review polices and make necessary changes, then vote.	(M) Board members meet with evaluation consultant. (O) Board begins evaluation process.	(O) Board chair and board members review polices and make necessary changes, then vote. (M) Board checks in with nonprofit attorney. (O) Board chair determines best practices for policy implementation.	(O) Board chair guides board through financial sustainability practices. (M) Board chair meets with CPA.	
Month 6	(R) Board completes reflection exercise. (O, M) Board, along with technology consultant reviews recordkeeping proposals, checks, references, and selects database.	(O) Board implements new policies.	(R) Board completes reflection exercise. (O) Board ensures that necessary data is collected during festival. (M) Board meets with evaluation consultant.	(O) Board implements new policies. (M) Board chair checks in with nonprofit attorney.	(R) Board chair completes reflection exercise. (M) Board chair and CPA debrief.	

Key: (O) = On-the-Job Activity; (M) = Mentoring Activity; (T) = Training Activity; (R) = Reflection Activity

EXHIBIT 10.9
Implementation Timeline: Volunteer-Run Organization, Cont'd

	Organizational Goal	Organizational Goal	Organizational Goal	Individual Goal	Individual Goal	Individual Goal
Month 7	(T) Technology consultant provides training on new database.	(M) Board checks in with board chair.	(O) Board conducts more evaluation. (M) Board meets with evaluation consultant.	(R) Board chair completes reflection exercise.		
Month 8	(O) Database is implemented. (T) More training occurs.			(M) Board chair debriefs with nonprofit attorney.		
Month 9	(T) More training occurs.					
Month 10	Board completes IPDA, evaluates professional development experiences and effectiveness of new database/ recordkeeping system.	Board completes IPDA, evaluates professional development experiences and effectiveness of new policies.	Board completes IPDA, evaluates professional development experiences and effectiveness of evaluation process.			

Key: (O) = On-the-Job Activity; (M) = Mentoring Activity; (T) = Training Activity; (R) = Reflection Activity

EXHIBIT 10.9

Implementation Timeline: Volunteer-Run Organization, Cont'd

	Organizational Goal	Organizational Goal	Organizational Goal	Individual Goal	Individual Goal	Individual Goal
Month 11	(R) Board completes reflection exercise. (M) Board debriefs with technology consultant.	(R) Board completes reflection exercise. (M) Board debriefs with board chair.	(R) Board completes reflection exercise. (M) Board debriefs with board chair.			
Month 12	Board plans next year's professional development activities.	Board plans next year's professional development activities.	Board plans next year's professional development activities.			

Key: (O) = On-the-Job Activity; (M) = Mentoring Activity; (T) = Training Activity; (R) = Reflection Activity

EXHIBIT 10.10

Implementation Timeline: Small Grassroots Organization

	Organizational Goal 1	Organizational Goal 2	Organizational Goal 3	Individual Goal 1	Individual Goal 2	Individual Goal 3
Month 1	(M) Community engagement supervisor meets with staff. (O) Staff select volunteer recruitment plan component.	(M) CPA and board treasurer meet with ED.	(O) Staff meets and develops a request for proposal for an advocacy consultant.	(O) ED develops a request for proposal for pro bono communications consulting.	(M) CPA and board treasurer meet with ED.	(O) ED identifies another ED who has gone through charity navigation rating. (M) ED meets with colleague.

Key: (O) = On-the-Job Activity; (M) = Mentoring Activity; (T) = Training Activity; (R) = Reflection Activity

EXHIBIT 10.10

Implementation Timeline: Small Grassroots Organization, Cont'd

	Organizational Goal 1	Organizational Goal 2	Organizational Goal 3	Individual Goal 1	Individual Goal 2	Individual Goal 3
Month 2	(T) All employees attend volunteer recruitment training. (M) Staff checks in with community engagement supervisor.	(M) CPA, board treasurer, and executive director meet with staff. (O) Staff assigned a specific month to review financial statements. (T) Executive Director watches Nonprofit Assistance Fund's financial management videos.	(O) Staff reviews advocacy consultants and selects one.	(O) ED reviews proposal results and selects a communications consultant. (M) ED meets with consultant to discuss project goals. (T) ED reads Kivi Miller's book, *Content Marketing for Nonprofit Organizations*.	(O) CPA, board treasurer, and executive director meet with staff. (T) Executive director watches Nonprofit Assistance Fund's financial management videos.	(T) ED watches Charity Navigator webinar. (M) ED meets with colleague.
Month 3	(O) Staff works on aspects of volunteer recruitment plan. (M) Staff checks in with community engagement supervisor.	(T) CPA and board treasurer provide first financial management training to staff.	(M) Staff meets with advocacy consultant and discusses what aspects of advocacy they want to learn about.	(M) ED and consultant discuss some possible brand awareness strategies, especially having to do with the website.	(M) ED meets with board treasurer and CPA (T) ED attends CPA and board treasurer financial management training. (O) ED prepares for staff in-service financial management training.	(O) ED gathers all information needed for Charity Navigator.

Key: (O) = On-the-Job Activity; (M) = Mentoring Activity; (T) = Training Activity; (R) = Reflection Activity

EXHIBIT 10.10

Implementation Timeline: Small Grassroots Organization, Cont'd

	Organizational Goal 1	Organizational Goal 2	Organizational Goal 3	Individual Goal 1	Individual Goal 2	Individual Goal 3
Month 4	(O) Staff submits volunteer recruitment components to community engagement supervisor.	(O) ED provides first review of financial statements and reports three findings to staff as an example. (M) Staff checks in with executive director regarding outstanding questions.	(T) Advocacy consultant provides training to all staff. (M) Staff brainstorms advocacy ideas for the organization to implement in future years.	(O) ED drafts brand strategy.	(O) ED provides first review of financial statements and reports three findings to staff as an example. (O) Staff checks in with executive director regarding outstanding questions.	(O) ED reviews accountability practices of the organization. (M) ED checks in with colleague.
Month 5	(M) Community engagement supervisor provides feedback on volunteer recruitment plan components.	(T) ED provides in-service financial management training to staff.	(M) Staff meets with advocacy consultant and discusses how to plan for future advocacy activities.	(M) Communications consultant reviews brand strategy and gives feedback to ED.	(O) ED provides in-service financial management training to staff. (M) ED debriefs with CPA and board treasurer about staff training.	(O) ED reviews transparency practices of the organization. (M) ED checks in with colleague.

Key: (O) = On-the-Job Activity; (M) = Mentoring Activity; (T) = Training Activity; (R) = Reflection Activity

EXHIBIT 10.10
Implementation Timeline: Small Grassroots Organization, Cont'd

	Organizational Goal 1	Organizational Goal 2	Organizational Goal 3	Individual Goal 1	Individual Goal 2	Individual Goal 3
Month 6	(O) Staff provides revisions to volunteer recruit-ment plan. (R) Staff completes reflection exercise.	(O) Another staff member reviews financial statements and reports three findings. (M) Executive director checks in with staff. (R) Staff completes reflection activity.	(R) Staff completes reflection activity. (M) Staff debriefs with advocacy consultant.	(R) ED completes reflection exercise.	(R) ED completes reflection exercise. (O) Executive director checks in with staff regarding preparing for their financial manage-ment presenta-tion.	(R) ED completes reflection exercise. (M) ED debriefs with colleague.
Month 7	(O) Volunteer recruitment plan is implemented.	(O) Another staff member reviews financial statements and reports three findings. (M) Executive director checks in with staff.		(O) ED implements new brand strategy.	(M) ED checks in with board chair and treasurer.	
Month 8	(M) Mentor meets with staff and provides feedback on volunteer recruitment plan imple-mentation.	(O) Another staff member reviews financial statements and reports three findings. (T) Executive director provides last financial management training to staff.		(M) ED checks in with communi-cations consultant (O) ED tweaks brand awareness activities based on feedback from communi-cations consultant.	(O) Executive director provides last financial manage-ment training to staff.	

Key: (O) = On-the-Job Activity; (M) = Mentoring Activity; (T) = Training Activity; (R) = Reflection Activity

EXHIBIT 10.10
Implementation Timeline: Small Grassroots Organization, Cont'd

	Organizational Goal 1	Organizational Goal 2	Organizational Goal 3	Individual Goal 1	Individual Goal 2	Individual Goal 3
Month 9	(O) Staff is involved in volunteer recruitment. (M) Staff checks in with mentor about volunteer recruitment plan implementation.	(R) Staff completes reflection activity. (M) Staff checks in with executive director to debrief.		(M) ED checks in with communications consultant.	(O) Staff checks in with executive director to debrief.	
Month 10	Staff completes IPDA, evaluates professional development experiences and effectiveness of volunteer recruitment plan.	Staff completes IPDA, evaluates professional development experiences and understanding of financial management.	Staff completes IPDA, evaluates professional development experiences and understanding of advocacy.	(R) ED completes reflection exercise. (M) ED and mentor debrief.	(R) ED completes reflection exercise. (M) ED and mentor debrief.	(R) ED completes reflection exercise. (M) ED and mentor debrief.
Month 11	(R) Staff completes self-reflection. (M) Staff debriefs with mentor.	Staff plans next year's professional development activities.	Staff plans next year's professional development activities.			
Month 12	Staff plans next year's professional development activities.					

Key: (O) = On-the-Job Activity; (M) = Mentoring Activity; (T) = Training Activity; (R) = Reflection Activity

The small grassroots organization was able to estimate its full budget because of the extensive timeline they developed. Exhibit 10.10 shows the full timeline for implementing the organization's goals and objectives in a twelve-month time frame.

Midsized Organization

The executive director from the midsized organization determined that employees would be eligible for a 5 percent increase in their salaries. All of the organization's employees were able to achieve their goals in order to receive that increase. The organization's salary investment was $789,648 in the previous year. With the 5 percent increase, the organization is now investing $829,130.40 (an increase of $39,442.40).

The midsized organization has eleven employees, making its budget a bit higher monetarily, but the executive director and her leadership team were able to share the work. The budget in table 10.6 shows how they divided the work; the leadership team has a separate category of hours represented. Table 10.7 shows the time and budgeted costs of implementing the talent development platform in a midsized organization.

Exhibit 10.11 shows the full implementation timeline attached to this budget for the midsized organization.

Grantmaking Organization

The grantmaking organization, which has four employees, determined during the talent mapping process that its employees were making sufficient salaries based on regional norms. The president determined that the employees would receive only their cost of living increase in the implementation year, an amount we are not attributing to the Talent Development Platform work.

The grantmaking organization did budget for time spent both on planning and implementing the Talent Development Platform. The organization's budget was structured similarly to that of the small grassroots organization, despite the difference in salaries. Tables 10.8 and 10.9 show the organization's budgets.

Exhibit 10.12 shows the full implementation timeline attached to this budget for the grantmaking organization.

TABLE 10.6
Time and Cost Estimates: Creating the Talent Development Platform, Midsized Organization

Activity	Time Frame	Time Spent	Calculation*	Cost
Organizational Learning Assessment	2 Months	Executive director = 5 hours	$35.40 × 5 hours	$177.00
		Leadership team = 2 hours each	($31.70 × 3) = $95.10 × 2 hours	$190.20
		Employees = 30 minutes for assessment	($21.95 × 5) + ($16.70 × 2) = $143.15 × .5 hours	$71.58
		Employees = 2 hours for reviewing results	($21.95 × 5) + ($16.70 × 2) = $143.15 × 2 hours	$286.30
			Total:	**$725.08**
Talent Map, Job Descriptions, and Sub-competencies	4 Months	Executive director = 10 hours	$35.40 × 10 hours	$354.00
		Leadership team = 30 hours total	$31.70 × 30 hours	$951.00
		Employees = 2 hours for reviewing assessments	($21.95 × 5) + ($16.70 × 2) = $143.15 × 2 hours	$286.30
		Employees = 2 hours for Talent Map discussion	($21.95 × 5) + ($16.70 × 2) = $143.15 × 2 hours	$286.30
			Total:	**$1,877.60**
Individual Professional Development Assessment and Individual Learning Styles Assessment	2 Months	Executive director = 8 hours	$35.40 × 8 hours	$283.20
		Leadership team = 5 hours each	($31.70 × 3) = $95.10 × 5 hours	$475.50
		Employees = 45 minutes for assessments	($21.95 × 5) + ($16.70 × 2) = $143.15 × .75 hours	$107.36

TABLE 10.6
Time and Cost Estimates: Creating the Talent Development Platform, Midsized Organization, Cont'd

Activity	Time Frame	Time Spent	Calculation*	Cost
		Employees = 2 hours for calculating results and meeting with executive director	($21.95 × 5) + ($16.70 × 2) = $143.15 × 2 hours	$286.30
			Total:	**$1,152.36**
Goals and Objectives	2 Months	Executive director = 5 hours	$35.40 × 5 hours	$177.00
		Leadership team = 10 hours each	($31.70 × 3) = $95.10 × 10 hours	$951.00
		Employees = 2 hours for goal setting and meeting with supervisor	($21.95 × 5) + ($16.70 × 2) = $143.15 × 2 hours	$286.30
		Employees = 2 hours for full staff goal meeting	($21.95 × 5) + ($16.70 × 2) = $143.15 × 2 hours	$286.30
			Total:	**$1,700.60**
Evaluation	2 Months	Executive director = 5 hours	$35.40 × 5 hours	$177.00
		Leadership team = 5 hours each	($31.70 × 3) = $95.10 × 5 hours	$475.50
		Employees = 2 hours for retaking all assessments	($21.95 × 5) + ($16.70 × 2) = $143.15 × 2 hours	$286.30
		Employees = 2 hours for discussion meeting	($21.95 × 5) + ($16.70 × 2) = $143.15 × 2 hours	$286.30
Total:				**$1,225.10**
Grand Total:				**$6,680.74**

Note: *The dollar amounts used in this column are the hourly rates for each of the organization's employees.

TABLE 10.7
Time and Budgeted Costs: Implementing the Talent Development Platform, Midsized Organization

Activity	Estimated Staff Costs	Estimated Activity Costs
Goal 1		
On-the-Job Learning	3 Employees = 200 hours × $21.95 + 100 hours × $31.71 = $7,561.00	
Mentoring	3 Employees = 10 hours × $21.95 + 5 hours × $31.71 = $378.05	Advocacy consultant = $1,500
Trainings	11 Employees = 3 hours × ($31.95 + (3 × $31.71) + (5 × $21.95) + (2 × $16.70)) = $810.69	In-house training = $2,500
Goal 2		
On-the-Job Learning	2 Employees = 25 hours × $21.95 + 25 hours × $16.70 = $966.25	Database software = $3,000
Mentoring	2 Employees = 3 hours × $21.95 + 3 hours × $16.70 = $115.95	Database consultant = $1,500
Trainings	2 Employees = 3 hours × $21.95 + 3 hours × $16.70 = $115.95	Nonprofit technology training = $100
Goal 3		
On-the-Job Learning	1 Employee = 20 hours × $21.95 = $439.00	-
Mentoring	1 Employee = 5 hours × $21.95 = $109.75	Board attorney (pro bono) = 5 hours × $22.65 (in-kind rate) = ($113.25)
Trainings	1 Employee = 3 hours × $21.95 = $65.85	Risk management workshop = $60
Total:	$10,562.49	$8,773.25
Grand Total:	$19,335.74	

EXHIBIT 10.11

Implementation Timeline: Midsized Organization

	Organizational Goal	Organizational Goal	Organizational Goal	Individual Goal	Individual Goal	Individual Goal
Month 1	(O) Staff creates request for proposal for advocacy consultants.	(O) Staff creates request for proposal for technology consultant.	(M) Staff meets with attorney from the board. (O) Staff and attorney do walk through of warehouse and discuss risk and liability issues.	(M) Development coordinator meets with development director to plan participation in implementing new database.	(M) Development coordinator connects with nonprofit faculty member at local university and discusses leadership development. (T) Development coordinator enrolls in course on nonprofit management at local university.	
Month 2	(O) Staff reviews advocacy consultant proposals, interviews, checks references, and selects consultant. (M) Staff meets with advocacy consultant.	(O) Staff reviews technology consultant proposals, interview, checks references, and selects consultant.	(T) Staff attends risk management workshop offered by Nonprofit Risk Management Center. (M) Staff checks in with attorney from board. (O) Staff starts drafting risk management policies and procedures.	(T) Development coordinator attends fundraising training at the Fundraising School, specifically around donor tracking. (M) Development coordinator meets with development director.	(M) Development coordinator meets with faculty member. (O) Development coordinator creates proposal for orientation manual for her organization. (T) Development coordinator attends class (specifically, class session on human resources management).	

Key: (O) = On-the-Job Activity; (M) = Mentoring Activity; (T) = Training Activity; (R) = Reflection Activity

EXHIBIT 10.11

Implementation Timeline: Midsized Organization, Cont'd

	Organizational Goal	Organizational Goal	Organizational Goal	Individual Goal	Individual Goal	Individual Goal
Month 3	(O, M) Staff works with advocacy consultant and discuss community awareness day. (T) Advocacy consultant provides training during staff meeting.	(M) Consultant meets with staff. (O) Staff brainstorms volunteer management and fundraising tracking needs and requirements of the new system. (T) Staff reviews articles, videos, and best practices on volunteer management and fundraising database systems.	(O) Staff continues to draft risk management policies and procedures. (M) Staff checks in with attorney from the board and receives feedback on policies and procedures.	(M) Development coordinator meets with IT consultant.	(O) Development coordinator interviews current development employees to get information for orientation manual. (M) Development coordinator checks in with faculty member.	
Month 4	(O, M) With guidance from the advocacy consultant, staff discusses and delegates responsibilities for day of action.	(O/M) Staff and technology consultant create request for proposal for database/recordkeeping system.	(O) Staff makes revisions to risk management policies and procedures. (M) Staff checks in with attorney from the board.	(O/M) Development coordinator works with staff and technology consultant to create request for proposal for database/recordkeeping system.	(O) Development coordinator finishes manual. Manual includes information about how use of the manual will be implemented. (M) Nonprofit faculty member reviews manual and gives feedback.	

Key: (O) = On-the-Job Activity; (M) = Mentoring Activity; (T) = Training Activity; (R) = Reflection Activity

EXHIBIT 10.11

Implementation Timeline: Midsized Organization, Cont'd

	Organizational Goal	Organizational Goal	Organizational Goal	Individual Goal	Individual Goal	Individual Goal
Month 5	(O) Staff prepares for community awareness day. (M) Staff checks in with advocacy consultant.	(O, M) Staff, along with technology consultant, reviews recordkeeping proposals, checks references, and selects database.	(O) Staff presents risk management policies and procedures to board of directors for a vote.	(O, M) Development coordinator works with staff and technology consultant to review recordkeeping proposals, checks references, and selects database.	(O) Development coordinator makes revisions to the manual.	
Month 6	(O) Staff prepare for community awareness day. (R) Staff completes reflection exercise. (M) Staff checks in with advocacy consultant.	(T) Technology consultant provides training on new database.	(R) Staff completes reflection exercise. (M) Staff checks in with attorney from board. (O) Staff implements risk management policies and procedures.	(M) Development coordinator meets with technology consultant to plan database implementation.	(O) Development coordinator implements the manual with new development volunteers. (R) Development coordinator completes reflection exercise. (M) Development coordinator meets with nonprofit faculty member.	
Month 7	(O) Community awareness day occurs. (M) Staff checks in with advocacy consultant.	(R) Staff completes reflection exercise. (O) Database is implemented. (T) More training occurs.		(R) Development coordinator completes reflection exercise. (O) Development coordinator coordinates database implementation.	(M) Development coordinator debriefs with nonprofit faculty member.	

EXHIBIT 10.11

Implementation Timeline: Midsized Organization, Cont'd

	Organizational Goal	Organizational Goal	Organizational Goal	Individual Goal	Individual Goal	Individual Goal
Month 8	(O) Staff reviews evaluation results from community awareness day. (M) Staff checks in with advocacy consultant.	(T) More training occurs.		(O) Development coordinator checks in with staff regarding database implementation. (M) Development coordinator meets with both development director and technology consultant.		
Month 9				(R) Development coordinator completes reflection exercise. (M) Development coordinator debriefs with development director.		
Month 10	Staff completes IPDA, evaluates professional development experiences, and effectiveness of community awareness day.	Staff completes IPDA, evaluates professional development experiences, and effectiveness of new database.	Staff completes IPDA, evaluates professional development experiences, and effectiveness of risk management policies and procedures.			

Key: (O) = On-the-Job Activity; (M) = Mentoring Activity; (T) = Training Activity; (R) = Reflection Activity

EXHIBIT 10.11
Implementation Timeline: Midsized Organization, Cont'd

	Organizational Goal	Organizational Goal	Organizational Goal	Individual Goal	Individual Goal	Individual Goal
Month 11	(R) Staff completes reflection exercise. (M) Staff debriefs with advocacy consultant.	(R) Staff completes reflection exercise. (M) Staff debriefs with technology consultant.	(R) Staff completes reflection exercise. (M) Staff debriefs with attorney from the board.			
Month 12	Staff plans next year's professional development activities.	Staff plans next year's professional development activities.	Staff plans next year's professional development activities.			

Key: (O) = On-the-Job Activity; (M) = Mentoring Activity; (T) = Training Activity; (R) = Reflection Activity

TABLE 10.8
Time and Cost Estimates: Creating the Talent Development Platform, Grantmaking Organization

Activity	Time Frame	Time Spent	Calculation*	Cost
Organizational Learning Assessment	2 Months	President = 10 hours	$60 × 10 hours	$600
		Employees = 30 minutes for assessment	($26.83 + $39 + $43.90) = $109.73 × .5 hours	$54.87
		Employees = 2 hours for reviewing results	($26.83 + $39 + $43.90) = $109.73 × 2 hours	$219.46
Total:				**$874.33**

TABLE 10.8

Time and Cost Estimates: Creating the Talent Development Platform, Grantmaking Organization, Cont'd

Activity	Time Frame	Time Spent	Calculation*	Cost
Talent Map, Job Descriptions, and Sub-competencies	4 Months	President = 40 hours	$60 × 40 hours	$2,400
		Employees = 2 hours for reviewing assessments	($26.83 + $39 + $43.90) = $109.73 × 2 hours	$219.46
		Employees = 2 hours for Talent Map discussion	($26.83 + $39 + $43.90) = $109.73 × 2 hours	$219.46
Total:				**$ 2,838.92**
Individual Professional Development Assessment and Individual Learning Styles Assessment	2 Months	President = 12 hours	$60 × 12 hours	$720
		Employees = 45 minutes for assessments	($26.83 + $39 + $43.90) = $109.73 × .75 hours	$82.30
		Employees = 2 hours for calculating results and meeting with president	($26.83 + $39 + $43.90) = $109.73 × 2 hours	$219.46
Total:				**$1,021.76**
Goals and Objectives	2 Months	President = 15 hours	$60 × 15 hours	$900.00
		Employees = 2 hours for goal setting and meeting with president	($26.83 + $39 + $43.90) = $109.73 × 2 hours	$219.46
		Employees = 2 hours for full staff goal meeting	($26.83 + $39 + $43.90) = $109.73 × 2 hours	$219.46
Total:				**$1,338.92**

TABLE 10.8

Time and Cost Estimates: Creating the Talent Development Platform, Grantmaking Organization, Cont'd

Activity	Time Frame	Time Spent	Calculation*	Cost
Evaluation	2 Months	President = 10 hours	$60 × 10 hours	$600.00
		Employees = 2 hours for retaking all assessments	($26.83 + $39 + $43.90) = $109.73 × 2 hours	$219.46
		Employees = 2 hours for discussion meeting	($26.83 + $39 + $43.90) = $109.73 × 2 hours	$219.46
Total:				**$1,038.92**
Grand Total:				**$7,112.84**

Note: *The dollar amounts used in this column are the hourly rates for each of the organization' employees.

TABLE 10.9

Time and Budgeted Costs: Implementing the Talent Development Platform, Grantmaking Organization

Activity	Estimated Staff Costs	Estimated Activity Costs
Goal 1		
On-the-Job Learning	1 Employees = 20 hours × $39 = $780.00	-
Mentoring	1 Employee = 5 hours × $39 = $195.00	Advocacy consultant = $2,000
Trainings	1 Employee = 10 hours × $39 = $390.00	Lobbying Day = $200 (includes travel)
Goal 2		
On-the-Job Learning	2 Employees = 50 hours × $43.90 + 50 hours × $26.83 = $3,536.50	-
Mentoring	2 Employees = 8 hours × $43.90 + 8 hours × $26.83 = $565.84	Board treasurer = 20 hours × $22.65 (in-kind rate) = ($453.00)
Trainings	4 Employees = 4 hours × ($60 + $26.83 + $39 + $43.90) = $678.92	In-service workshop = $5,000
Goal 3		
On-the-Job Learning	1 Employee = 20 hours × $39 = $780.00	-
Mentoring	1 Employee = 10 hours × $39 = $390.00	Evaluation consultant = $2,500
Trainings	1 Employee = 3 hours × $39 = $117.00	Strategic planning workshop = $75
Total:	**$7,433.26**	**$9,322.00**
Grand Total:	**$16,755.26**	

EXHIBIT 10.12

Implementation Timeline: Grantmaking Organization

	Organizational Goal	Organizational Goal	Organizational Goal	Individual Goal	Individual Goal	Individual Goal
Month 1	(O) Staff creates request for proposal for advocacy consultants.	(M) Staff meets with board treasurer to discuss financial training needs.	(O) Staff creates request for proposal for evaluation consultant.	(This is to happen after Organizational Goals 1 and 2 are fulfilled.) (M) Program associate meets with trustee. (O) Program associate discusses components of low-income communities' earned income tax issue.	Same as organizational goal 2.	(O) Works with staff to create request for proposal for evaluation consultant.
Month 2	(O) Staff reviews advocacy consultant proposals, interview, checks references, and selects consultant. (M) Staff meets with advocacy consultant.	(O, M) Staff, with assistance from board treasurer, creates plan for conducting financial management trainings to board, staff, and grantees.	(O) Staff reviews evaluation consultant proposals, interview, checks references and selects consultant. (M) Staff meets with evaluation consultant.	(T) Program associate reads book on nonprofit advocacy. (M) Program associate checks in with trustee.		(O) Program associate works with staff to review evaluation consultant proposals, interviews, checks references, and selects consultant. (M) Program associate meets with president.

Key: (O) = On-the-Job Activity; (M) = Mentoring Activity; (T) = Training Activity; (R) = Reflection Activity

EXHIBIT 10.12
Implementation Timeline: Grantmaking Organization, Cont'd

	Organizational Goal	Organizational Goal	Organizational Goal	Individual Goal	Individual Goal	Individual Goal
Month 3	(O, M) Staff work with advocacy consultant and identify key issue areas, then potential policy makers associated with each issue area.		(T) Staff attend strategic planning workshop.

(O, M) Staff, with assistance from evaluation consultant creates program plan and evaluation of financial management trainings. | (O, M) With assistance from trustee, program associate plans community aware-ness day.

(O) Program associate works with board treasurer to include a budget for the community awareness day (Goal 2). | | (T) Program associate attends strategic planning workshop.

(O) Program associate, with other staff, create program plan and evaluation of financial manage-ment trainings. |
| Month 4 | (T) Staff attends lobby day (through Council on Foundations). (M) Staff checks in with advocacy consultant. | (O, M) Staff drafts training materials with assistance from board treasurer. | (O) Staff follows program plan when creating training materials.

(M) Staff checks in with evaluation consultant. | (O, M) With assistance from trustee, program associate plans community awareness day. | | (O) Program associate creates evaluation plan for her own program.

(M) Program associate checks in with president. |
| Month 5 | (O) Staff prepares for and sets meetings with legislators around issue areas. (M) Staff checks in with advocacy consultant. | (O) Staff pilots training materials with board treasurer.

(M) Staff checks in with board treasurer. | (O, M) Staff evaluates training materials with guidance from evaluation consultant. | (O, M) With assistance from trustee, program associate plans community awareness day. | | (O) Program associate works with other staff to evaluate training materials. |

Key: (O) = On-the-Job Activity; (M) = Mentoring Activity; (T) = Training Activity; (R) = Reflection Activity

EXHIBIT 10.12

Implementation Timeline: Grantmaking Organization, Cont'd

	Organizational Goal	Organizational Goal	Organizational Goal	Individual Goal	Individual Goal	Individual Goal
Month 6	(O) Staff meets with legislators. (R) Staff completes reflection exercise. (M) Staff checks in with advocacy consultant.	(O) Staff holds in-service workshop for board members and grantees. (M) Staff checks in with board treasurer.	(O) Staff evaluates in-service workshop. (M) Staff checks in with evaluation consultant.	(O, M) With assistance from trustee, program associate plans community awareness day. (R) Program associate completes reflection exercise.		(O) Program associate completes reflection exercise. (M) Program associate debriefs with president.
Month 7	(O) Staff meets with legislators. (M) Staff checks in with advocacy consultant.	(R) Staff completes reflection exercise. (M) Staff checks in with board treasurer. (O) Staff discusses in-service workshop evaluation results and makes changes to financial management training materials.	(R) Staff completes reflection exercise. (O) Staff discusses in-service workshop evaluation results and makes changes to financial management training materials. (M) Staff checks in with evaluation consultant.	(O) Community awareness day occurs. (M) Program associate checks in with trustee.		

Key: (O) = On-the-Job Activity; (M) = Mentoring Activity; (T) = Training Activity; (R) = Reflection Activity

EXHIBIT 10.12

Implementation Timeline: Grantmaking Organization, Cont'd

	Organizational Goal	Organizational Goal	Organizational Goal	Individual Goal	Individual Goal	Individual Goal
Month 8				(O) Program associate reviews community awareness day evaluations and financial reports. (M) Program associate checks in with trustee. (M) Program associate checks in with board treasurer.		
Month 9				(R) Program associate completes reflection exercise. (M) Program associate debriefs with trustee.		
Month 10	Staff completes IPDA, evaluates professional development experiences and effectiveness of advocacy/issue areas work.	Staff completes IPDA, evaluates professional development experiences and effectiveness of financial management in-service training.	Staff completes IPDA, evaluates professional development experiences and effectiveness of evaluation process.			

Key: (O) = On-the-Job Activity; (M) = Mentoring Activity; (T) = Training Activity; (R) = Reflection Activity

EXHIBIT 10.12
Implementation Timeline: Grantmaking Organization, Cont'd

	Organizational Goal	Organizational Goal	Organizational Goal	Individual Goal	Individual Goal	Individual Goal
Month 11	(R) Staff completes reflection exercise. (M) Staff debriefs with advocacy consultant.	(R) Staff completes reflection exercise. (M) Staff debriefs with board treasurer.	(R) Staff completes reflection exercise. (M) Staff debriefs with evaluation consultant.			
Month 12	Staff plans next year's professional development activities.	Staff plans next year's professional development activities.	Staff plans next year's professional development activities.			

Key: (O) = On-the-Job Activity; (M) = Mentoring Activity; (T) = Training Activity; (R) = Reflection Activity

Conclusion

In this chapter we provided you with resources as well as budget and implementation timeline templates to help you implement the Talent Development Platform effectively. We also provided suggestions and strategies to overcome barriers during implementation. The next chapter shows you how to evaluate the shifts in staff members' and employees' proficiency levels after implementation and how to evaluate the entire Talent Development Platform implementation.

Chapter 11
Organizational Evaluation and Performance Assessment

Now that you've implemented your Talent Development Platform, it's time to evaluate it! Evaluation of the Talent Development Platform process is essential to solidify a strong return on your talent investment and the shift in your learning culture. In this chapter we discuss strategies for successful evaluations, a process for how to assess staff and organizational progress toward professional development goals, and how to calculate the return on your talent investment. Figure 11.1 provides you with the steps for organizational evaluation and individual performance assessment.

In chapter 9, when we discussed implementing the Platform, we recommended reflection time, evaluation, and action planning following all learning activities. The evaluation process we discuss in this chapter allows you to assess staff progress and the effectiveness of the talent development system as a whole.

The Evaluation Process

The evaluation process duplicates the Talent Development Platform process itself and adds year-to-year comparisons and qualitative data on how the learning process is going for staff and volunteers. During the evaluation process

- have employees and volunteers retake the Organizational Learning Assessment;

- have employees and volunteers retake the Individual Professional Development Assessment, with additional questions about their experience;

- reassess your organizational Talent Map: review job descriptions and employee and volunteer position placement; and

- reset your professional development goals and objectives for the next year.

FIGURE 11.1
Evaluation and Performance Assessment Steps

ORGANIZATIONAL
EVALUATION
AND INDIVIDUAL
PERFORMANCE
ASSESSMENT

······▶

- Retake Organizational Learning Assessment.
- Update Talent Development Platform.
- Discuss results, challenges, and progress made this year.
- Set new goals and objectives.
- Retake Individual Professional Development Assessment, including additional questions about progress toward goals and objectives, and the professional development process.
- Meet with employees and volunteers to discuss results of the Individual Professional Development Assessment alongside results from the previous year.
- Use employee and volunteer results to develop Talent Map to determine necessary staff changes and salary increases for the year.

For the evaluation process to go smoothly, you will need a copy of your employees' and volunteers' assessments. You will also need to understand how organizational leadership interacts with staff and volunteers, make a plan for how to include your board in the evaluation process, provide time for everyone to discuss results, and allow participation in planning for next year's work.

During the evaluation process you will reassess the culture of your organization to ensure that the process goes smoothly and is in line with the positive side of all the domains in the Organizational Learning Assessment. For some of you, beginning the Talent Development Platform meant taking some time to improve your organization's learning culture. Keep that work in mind as you go through the evaluation. A good performance assessment process is one of the pillars of a strong learning culture.

There are specific components that must be included in the evaluation process. You can use these components alone or include them in your already established evaluation process. Each component is outlined in the following sections. The evaluation process will take approximately one to two months, which can overlap with the first year of implementation, if necessary.

Retake the Organizational Learning Assessment

The components of the Talent Development Platform are meant to strengthen or help you maintain your already strong learning culture. Retaking the Organizational Learning Assessment at this time will help you to establish any progress that has been made in your organization's culture and identify any challenges you may have had in keeping that culture strong. When you re-administer the assessment, keep the ground rules and the safe, anonymous environment intact. A thorough explanation of how to administer the assessment can be found in chapter 2.

Use the results from this second round of the assessment to compare progress or dips in your learning culture in each of the five domains. When comparing the results, use table 11.1 to identify potential reasons and solutions for each level of change in your results.

Retake the Individual Professional Development Assessment

The Looking Glass Institute states, "Critical feedback is a must in stimulating people toward self-improvement … we have to get feedback on strengths and weaknesses; on the things that really matter now and in the future; to motivate people, on a timely basis for anything meaningful to happen" (Bonner & Obergas, n.d., p. 16). Feedback and assessment are critical to an enhanced learning experience for staff and volunteers. Back in chapter 1, we stated that adults need recognition of accomplishments and opportunities to compare personal performance favorably with that of others (Rabin, 2014). Retaking the Individual Professional Development Assessment allows staff and volunteers to see how their proficiency levels have changed as a result of the professional development and to get recognition of their improvements. These types of assessments "increase employee commitment and satisfaction, due to improvements in organizational communication," according to Wiese and Buckley (1998, p. 240). A good performance assessment process is one of the pillars of a strong learning culture.

EXHIBIT 11.1
Assessing the Performance of Board Members

If you included your board in the Platform process, whether they assessed the executive director or took the assessments themselves, board members should be included in this process as well. At the very least the board will assess the executive director again during this stage. However, if you have a working board, each board member should retake the assessments and perform assessments of one another. Although the board chair is the leader of the board, we recommend having more than one individual on the board assess each of the other board members. A best practice is to have three board members assess each one board member, acting in the same manner as the supervisor in the staff assessment process.

TABLE 11.1
Organizational Learning Assessment Results Comparison

Score Change	Potential Reasons for Change	Solution
Negative change in scores	1. Your organization's culture was not strong enough for the change.	• Before going any further, spend some time discussing results and implementing interventions to improve your organization's learning culture.
	2. Your leadership was not committed to the process.	• Use an external facilitator to lead conversations and work with you on solutions and the process moving forward.
	3. The Talent Development Platform was not integrated into your work and was considered an additional work from daily activities.	• Take a look at the workloads of each of your staff members and volunteers. Eliminate waste and give them space to learn.
No change in scores	1. Your score was already indicating a sufficient learning culture.	• If your score was already sufficient and it did not change, you are on the right track. Keeping a good organizational culture good is tough work.
	2. Your team did not take on a sufficient number of objectives to improve your learning culture, or your objectives were not the right ones.	• If your score was low and stayed low, you have some more work to do. Try some new activities, take some time talking and innovating with staff, and do more check-ins throughout the next year.
	3. Your team experienced a significant barrier during the year so that professional development efforts stopped midstream.	• If you experienced a significant barrier, assess the barrier; discuss potential solutions, and reset goals and objectives as necessary.
Positive change in scores	1. You did everything right, either setting objectives for learning or implementing changes brought about by staff. Either way, nice work!	• Keep doing whatever you have been doing. Don't let things go, though. Keep learning at the forefront and fresh in the minds of leadership, staff, and volunteers.

Remember the Goals of Performance Assessment

We've discussed this a little already, but it's important to note the goals you should have in mind while conducting the performance assessment process. Be clear with staff about the goals of the process, about why they are participating in the process, and about what you hope to get out of the process.

The goals of the assessment process may be a bit different for each organization. For example, you might not use the process for salary increase, because you have another process for that portion of talent management. However, the items below should be included in your performance assessment process. "Instead of just assisting an organization make decisions concerning an individual, performance appraisals should be used to help an individual make personal decisions regarding his/her current performance and provide strategies for future development" (Wiese & Buckley, 1988). According to McConnell (1986) your process should

- increase performance by providing healthy feedback;
- provide employees with space for advancement; and
- collect the information needed for salary increase recommendations.

Overcome Bias and Set the Right Tone

During this process be sure to set the right tone for the evaluation. Your assessment should be targeted toward feedback and growth in competencies, rather than toward coaching. If a staff member needs support with emotional intelligence, risk assessment, or conflict resolution, suggest a coach. Trying to assess these skills as their supervisor is a tough and often biased position to be in during the assessment process. It is hard for a supervisor not to be subjective when providing this type of feedback. You can set objectives early on in the process for supervisors to learn the skills necessary to create the right environment when conducting performance assessments. The better the environment during the assessment, the better the results.

Wiese and Buckley state, "Effective managers recognize performance appraisal systems as a tool for managing, rather than a tool for measuring" (1998, p. 338). The assessment should focus on the proficiency levels of staff in their identified competencies. To have this discussion, supervisors should also make each individual feel comfortable with being open to voicing their challenges and troubleshooting if necessary. Nobody should feel like anything they say in these meetings could be used against them in any way. If a staff member or volunteer needs to be fired, for any particular reason, or has large areas of improvement, we suggest using these meetings to discuss a plan for improvement rather than to simply let the person go.

Give individuals who are struggling an opportunity to improve and then manage them more closely, letting them go later if no improvement has been made over a reasonable (agreed upon) amount of time.

During the evaluation process, the Individual Professional Development Assessment tool (IPDA) has some additional questions to use as discussion starters. Refer back to chapter 6 for a rundown of the full IPDA process. Keep in mind that during the evaluation stage all of the same rules apply for both the process of administering the IPDA and the environment in which it should be taken. Using the IPDA during this stage meets a best practice of incorporating competencies in evaluation. Gangani, McLean, and Braden state, "Incorporating competencies into the performance evaluation system ensures alignment of individual objectives with organizational goals" (2006, p. 136).

If you are interested in implementing a 360-degree approach for performance assessment, you can also assign teams of three people to retake the IPDA, one of whom should be the intended employee's supervisor. Each team takes the IPDA for the other staff members in their group, in addition to taking their own assessment. The supervisor then gathers the three assessments for each individual and compiles the results before meeting with the staff member to discuss goal setting and any interventions in their performance assessment meeting. This type of 360 degree feedback is a great way to enhance your learning culture and eliminate bias during this performance assessment process. Often during performance assessment both the individual being assessed and the supervisor add bias to the process unintentionally. We'll talk about this more in a bit.

Exhibit 11.2 shows the IPDA with the additional questions for use during the performance assessment. The additional questions are added for three reasons: an opportunity for individuals to reflect on their own learning; an opportunity for individuals to reflect on the learning activities they participated in; and an opportunity for all participants to reflect on the organization's new talent development system.

Review the Results of the IPDA for Performance Assessment

Once staff and volunteers retake the Individual Professional Development Assessment, the supervisor should review results with each of them individually. Target these meetings toward feedback and growth in competencies, rather than coaching. Recall that the goals of the individual performance assessment meeting are to provide healthy feedback and reassess the person's role and compensation. Refer to the sections titled "Remember the Goals of Performance Assessment" and "Overcome Bias and Set the Right Tone" earlier in this chapter as you prepare to meet with each individual.

EXHIBIT 11.2

The Individual Professional Development
Assessment — Evaluation Stage

Please identify the competencies that are essential behaviors and duties within your job or volunteer role. Then rate your proficiency level in each competency and what proficiency level you hope to obtain. The data will be used to determine common proficiency levels within core competencies across the organization.

Participation in this survey is entirely voluntary; you can choose to opt out at any time. The information collected in this survey will be shared with your organization and will be used for research purposes. There are no risks for you to participate in this survey that exceed the risks encountered in everyday life.

(* = Required)

I have read and understand this form, and consent to the process and research it describes to me.*

- ❏ Yes
- ❏ No

1. Name of Organization* _____

2. Job Title or Volunteer Role* _____

3. Please indicate your essential job function(s) or volunteer role(s)*

Check all that apply.

- ❏ Accounting and Finance
- ❏ Administration
- ❏ Advocacy/Lobbying
- ❏ Communications
- ❏ Community Organizing
- ❏ Counseling
- ❏ Direct Service
- ❏ Education
- ❏ Event Planning
- ❏ Facilities and Property Management
- ❏ Food Services and Housing
- ❏ Fundraising
- ❏ Grants Management
- ❏ Information Technology

EXHIBIT 11.2
The Individual Professional Development Assessment — Evaluation Stage, Cont'd

- ❏ Human Resources
- ❏ Legal — Law Services
- ❏ Medical and/or Health
- ❏ Program Management
- ❏ Public Relations
- ❏ Other:

Social Change Competencies and Descriptions

Read the descriptions below and use the information to answer question 4.

Advocacy and Public Policy: Uses community organizing, public education, policy research, and lobbying effectively to educate government officials, organize community support, garner social change, and influence public policy.

Communications, Marketing, and Public Relations: Demonstrates principles and techniques that provide transparency and accountability, while understanding and communicating specifically to various constituents — including internal stakeholders — using communications, general and social media marketing, and public relations that develop financial and nonfinancial support for your organization.

Financial Management and Social Entrepreneurship: Applies critical financial concepts and GAAP practices to establish and maintain realistic budgets, internal controls, financial statements, cash flow maintenance, audits and tax reporting. Creates and maintains sustainable business models, impact and/or social investment strategies, hybrid organizational forms, and innovative revenue structures.

Fundraising and Resource Development: Demonstrates ability to develop a diversified fund development strategy that is proactive and integrated into the organization's long-term strategic plan and budget projections. Is familiar with and able to execute several different fundraising strategies, including but not limited to stewardship and cultivation of donors, gift processing, developing new business, event planning, planned giving and major gifts campaigns, and grantwriting.

Grantmaking: Identifies and works with prospective and existing grantees, monitors grantee progress, and explore new grantmaking areas. Provides recommendation for funding and conducts grant reviews. Has in-depth knowledge of program area(s).

Direct Service: Effectively work with clients and/or constituents. Has expertise in specific field of service, client relations, and intercultural competency.

Human Resources Management and Volunteerism: Applies knowledge of employment laws and practices for nonprofit recruitment and selection, for managing employees and volunteers, and for monitoring performance, diversity and intercultural competency, compensation and benefits, training and development, labor relations, and health and safety.

EXHIBIT 11.2
The Individual Professional Development Assessment—Evaluation Stage, Cont'd

Information Management: Supports the development, maintenance, and application of information technology planning, budgeting, staffing and training, evaluation, selecting hardware and software, social media, and website capabilities and use.

Leadership and Governance: Appreciate the relationship between leadership and management in establishing and attaining mission and long- and short-term organizational goals. Is able to look within self and team members in order to understand how personal backgrounds and experience shape the leadership experience. Demonstrates ability to lead effectively and manage the governing board of the organization.

Legal and Regulatory: Understands influences of external and internal stakeholders in creating and maintaining legal compliance, ethical and risk management practices, and professional standards in the appropriate settings.

Planning and Evaluation: Understands external and internal influences of program and organizational development, as well as organizational life cycles. Creates logic models, data-based decision making, program feasibility, and continuous improvement plans for effective management. Is able to develop a theory of change and apply various methods of evaluation to comprehensively evaluate performance measurement and program and organizational effectiveness.

4. Using the descriptions provided, please select the frequency with which you perform the ESSENTIAL duties in your job or volunteer role*

Check only one box per row.

	Never	Occasionally (several times a year)	Frequently (at least once a month)
Advocacy and Public Policy			
Communications, Marketing, and Public Relations			
Financial Management and Social Entrepreneurship			
Fundraising and Resource Development			
Grantmaking or Direct Service			
Human Resources Management and Volunteerism			
Information Management			
Leadership and Governance			
Legal and Regulatory			
Planning and Evaluation			

EXHIBIT 11.2
The Individual Professional Development Assessment — Evaluation Stage, Cont'd

Proficiency Level Scores and Descriptions

Read the descriptions below and use the information to answer questions 5, 6, 8, and 9.

Fundamental Awareness (basic knowledge): You have a common knowledge or an understanding of basic techniques and concepts.

Novice (limited experience): You have the level of experience gained in a classroom, in experimental scenarios, or as a trainee on the job. You are expected to need help when performing this skill.

Intermediate (practical application): You are able to successfully complete tasks in this competency as requested. Help from an expert may be required from time to time, but you can usually perform the skill independently.

Advanced (applied theory): You can perform the actions associated with this skill without assistance. You are certainly recognized within your immediate organization as "a person to ask" when difficult questions arise regarding this skill.

Expert (recognized authority): You are known as an expert in this area. You can provide guidance, troubleshoot, and answer questions related to this area of expertise and the field where the skill is used.

5. Using the descriptions provided, rate your proficiency level in the essential duties of your job or volunteer role.*

Check only one box per row.

	Fundamental Awareness	Novice	Intermediate	Advanced	Expert
Advocacy and Public Policy					
Communications, Marketing, and Public Relations					
Financial Management and Social Entrepreneurship					
Fundraising and Resource Development					
Grantmaking or Direct Service					
Human Resources Management and Volunteerism					
Information Management					
Leadership and Governance					
Legal and Regulatory					
Planning and Evaluation					

EXHIBIT 11.2
The Individual Professional Development Assessment—Evaluation Stage, Cont'd

6. Using the descriptions provided, rate the proficiency level you would like to be at in one year in the essential duties of your job or volunteer role.

Check only one box per row.

	Fundamental Awareness	Novice	Intermediate	Advanced	Expert
Advocacy and Public Policy					
Communications, Marketing, and Public Relations					
Financial Management and Social Entrepreneurship					
Fundraising and Resource Development					
Grantmaking or Direct Service					
Human Resources Management and Volunteerism					
Information Management					
Leadership and Governance					
Legal and Regulatory					
Planning and Evaluation					

Organizational, Department, and Position Competencies

7. If your organization has created specific competencies for your organization, department, and position, please list them here, being as specific as possible. For example: Our first organizational competency is _____. Our first department competency is _____.

Organizational Sub-competencies _____

_____

_____

_____

EXHIBIT 11.2

The Individual Professional Development Assessment — Evaluation Stage, Cont'd

Department Sub-competencies _____

_____

_____

_____

Position Sub-competencies _____

_____

_____

_____

8. Please rate your proficiency level in the organizational, department, and/or position competencies you listed in question 7.

Check only one box per row.

	Fundamental Awareness	Novice	Intermediate	Advanced	Expert
Organizational Competency 1					
Organizational Competency 2					
Organizational Competency 3					
Organizational Competency 4					
Organizational Competency 5					
Department Competency 1					
Department Competency 2					
Department Competency 3					
Department Competency 4					
Department Competency 5					
Position Competency 1					
Position Competency 2					
Position Competency 3					
Position Competency 4					
Position Competency 5					

EXHIBIT 11.2
The Individual Professional Development Assessment — Evaluation Stage, Cont'd

9. Please rate the proficiency level you would like to be at in one year in the organizational, department, and/or position competencies you marked in question 8.

Check only one box per row.

	Fundamental Awareness	Novice	Intermediate	Advanced	Expert
Organizational Competency 1					
Organizational Competency 2					
Organizational Competency 3					
Organizational Competency 4					
Organizational Competency 5					
Department Competency 1					
Department Competency 2					
Department Competency 3					
Department Competency 4					
Department Competency 5					
Position Competency 1					
Positions Competency 2					
Position Competency 3					
Position Competency 4					
Position Competency 5					

Assessment Questions

Please list the learning activities you participated in during the last year.

Which activities did you find the most effective for your learning?

EXHIBIT 11.2
The Individual Professional Development Assessment — Evaluation Stage, Cont'd

Which activities were the least effective for your learning?

Were you able to meet your learning objectives this year? If not, please state the objectives you were not able to meet, and outline a potential plan for meeting those objectives in the next year.

Do you believe you were able to contribute to organizational goals and objectives throughout the past year? Please be specific about how you contributed and to which goals.

What parts of our professional development process worked well?

Are there any ways we could improve the professional development process?

Please identify specific objectives you believe you should have in mind for the next year.

Thank you for taking the time to fill out the evaluation version of the Individual Professional Development Assessment. Data collected in this survey will be used to understand common competency preferences across the organization.

Reassessing Your Talent Map

Leadership should use the IPDA results to determine if they need to revisit job descriptions, shift positions, or increase pay or benefits for any employee or volunteer. If someone is taking on a new position, he should use the already established job description for that position to determine his new role and seek information from others who have worked in that position previously to set goals and objectives for learning. All employees and volunteers should complete a job analysis form to ensure their job description is completely accurate. This form is the same one that employees and volunteers used to set their original descriptions, but it should be fully completed again to adjust job descriptions for shifting roles and environments. Remember, this process should be done yearly to keep job descriptions current and maintain a common understanding of roles between employees, volunteers, and leadership.

Once each individual completes a job analysis form, managers compare the job activities to job descriptions that were previously created or revised prior to implementing the Talent Development Platform. Using the job analysis form, the managers then make revisions to the job descriptions (exhibit 11.3). During this process you may identify new competencies for positions or departments. The new competency should be integrated into the individual employee's professional development goals and objectives for the upcoming year.

Resetting Professional Development Goals

Now that you have updated information from the Organizational Learning Assessments and Individual Professional Development Assessments and you've revised your Talent Map and reevaluated job descriptions, it is time to discuss progress toward organizational and individual professional goals and objectives.

Add the results of each of your assessments to an updated Talent Development Platform for the discussion. Don't worry if you have a different number of staff, or if employees have left and you've filled new positions. That is all part of growth and should be reflected in your proficiency levels in each competency. The most important questions for the goal-setting process is "Do you believe you were able to contribute to organizational goals and objectives throughout the past year? Please be specific about how you contributed and to which goals." Distribute your updated Talent Development Platform, along with the summary responses to questions in the evaluation version of the Individual Professional Development Assessment to all employees and volunteers.

EXHIBIT 11.3

Job Analysis Form

Name _____ Date _____

Position _____

Department _____

Daily Activities _____

_____

Weekly Activities _____

_____

Monthly activities _____

_____

Annual activities _____

_____

> **EXHIBIT 11.4**
> ## Employee Performance Interventions
>
> If you have an employee who does not improve throughout the year, now is the time to manage interventions for that employee. You should establish policies for handling underperforming employees and follow these policies during performance assessment. If necessary, add goals and objectives that focus on growth areas to the employee's plate. You may also consider giving the employee some shorter-term goals to achieve. This will allow her a time after three or six months to improve and then sit down with her supervisor to set further goals for the year.

In your discussion meeting, go through each objective and goal to discuss progress and completion. Allow all participants an opportunity to talk, and keep conversations about activities and progress, rather than personal opinions of people or competencies. If a goal or objective comes up that hasn't been met, have a discussion about why it went unmet and whether it's still relevant to your organization's needs. There are several reasons goals and objectives may remain unmet:

- The goal or objective became irrelevant throughout the year, and therefore should be dismissed.

- Staff or volunteers ran into one of the barriers to implementation outlined in chapter 10.

- The process was not implemented correctly.

- Leadership did not communicate or champion the efforts appropriately, and staff lost interest.

If there was a barrier, discuss which barrier presented itself, and come up with a solution for how to complete the goal or objective. The last two reasons are a bit tougher to tackle and involve heavy discussion and assessment. We recommend that if you have made a misstep in implementing the process, or if staff and volunteers have lost interest, you should focus the goals and objectives for the next year on rebuilding your organizational learning culture and working with staff and volunteers on their emotional intelligence and intercultural competence skills. This process takes due diligence and may require some intervention from time to time. It's also important for leadership to be the inspiration and demonstrate the importance of moving forward and overcoming any barriers you may have encountered along the way.

Assessing the Talent Development Process

To ensure that the process you use for implementation in the next year is the right process for your organization in its current state, you will need to take some time to reflect on how the process went for staff and volunteers. You may want to have this conversation at the same time as you reflect on your goals from the previous year, as we're sure that many of the barriers, challenges, and successes of the process will emerge during that discussion. If it's helpful for you in planning, note specific examples in each of those three categories as reminders when you begin planning. If no specifics come up during the goal reflection process, take the time to have intentional conversations about barriers, challenges, and successes.

To further reflect on the process, use responses from the following questions located in the evaluation IPDA:

- What parts of our professional development process worked well?

- Are there any ways we could improve the professional development process?

Bring the results from these questions and any previous reflections on the process along with the calculations from your return on investment (which we'll discuss in the next section) to your leadership team or all staff, depending on the size of your organization. You may want to give this information to your board also in order to get their buy-in for a new year of implementation.

Following this work it is time for you to finalize your implementation plans for the next year. Use the same timelines, tools, and resources from chapter 10 to help you structure implementation for the new year. Pay close attention to any shifts that may be needed, though. You discussed barriers, challenges, and successes throughout the process. Be sure all that feedback is reflected when you reach the moment of implementation.

Calculating Your Return on Investment

Now is the time for you to calculate your return on investment. As you recall from chapter 1, we discussed the intricacies of the tangible and intangible returns your organization will experience from the Talent Development Platform. Use these calculations to review the process for yourself, to provide ammunition to your board to allocate budget money for learning, and to make a case for funding. Be careful, though. The full return on your investment will take time. You may see small gains in these numbers in the first year, but they will grow more and more each year.

If your organization stays steady or declines in a specific year, don't stop the work. Great returns take time. Use regular evaluation and adaptation to achieve greater returns as you enter each new year of implementation. Give yourself at least three years to see where your organization is truly moving using these processes. To help you calculate your return on investment we will walk you through the calculations using the small grassroots organization as an example whenever possible.

Determine the Benefits of the Professional Development Investment

How will professional development improve employees' and volunteers' ability to do their work and achieve the mission of the organization? Intangible benefits have an important effect on the organization, even though they are not easily measured. Tangible benefits are objective and easily measurable. They are usually in monetary form (e.g., money and time saved on doing something, money saved on less turnover, increased clients served).

Intangible Benefits

Intangible benefits are subjective and not easily measured; they tend to be behavioral (e.g., increase in staff morale or staff collaboration, improved image in the community, indirect impact on clients). You can calculate the intangible benefits of the Talent Development Platform using responses from the Organizational Learning Assessment and IPDA results. The following three groups of responses should be pulled from those assessments:

- *Increased satisfaction among staff and volunteers.* Calculate the difference in the "Staff and Volunteer Satisfaction" domain from the beginning of the Platform implementation to now.

- *New skills learned and higher proficiency levels of staff and volunteers.* You will see efficiencies in employee and volunteer work and an improvement in staff and volunteer scores in the IPDA.

- *Stronger learning culture.* You may notice this most in the attitudes of staff and volunteers and through the number of complaints or praises you get about your work from external stakeholders. If you want a calculation, however, use the full score of the Organizational Learning Assessment to see if you increased scores in any of the domains.

Tangible Benefits

As we saw in chapter 1, there are three turnover ratios you can use to get a strong picture of turnover, which are presented again in exhibit 11.5. For

---

EXHIBIT 11.5

Turnover Ratios

Staff (or Volunteer) Turnover Rate

$$(\text{\# of terminations per year} \;/\; \text{avg. \# of active employees in the same year}) \times 100$$

This calculation determines your overall turnover rate without any other factors in mind.

New Hire Turnover Rate

$$(\text{\# of terminations within first year} \;/\; \text{\# of hires}) \times 100$$

This calculation gives you an idea of the number of employees you are losing within their first year in your organization. If new hire turnover is high, it is a sign that your learning culture is negative and new hires are seeing no room for growth.

Functional Turnover Rate

$$(\text{\# of poor performers who leave} - \text{\# of good performers who leave}) \;/\; \text{total \# who leave}$$

This ratio is a bit subjective; however, it provides a good view of whether or not you are losing top performers. If you are losing more good performers than poor performers, this is a sign of an unsatisfactory organizational culture. There are many possible reasons for this, however, so use the assessments and the time spent working on the Talent Development Platform to determine what might be the core reasons top performers are leaving your organization (O'Connell & Kung, 2007).

---

an even stronger picture, calculate the difference over a three-year range comparing each year's scores.

You can also use table 11.2 to find examples of categories in which you will benefit from the Talent Development Platform process. Remember, some of these calculations are only possible if employees and volunteers are aware of the time they spend on varying items. Be sure employees are aware that the time tracking is for planning and evaluation and not for micromanaging their work. Often when employees feel their supervisor is micromanaging their time, they will misrepresent time or avoid calculating it all together.

We have provided an estimate of what it costs for employee turnover in your organization. However, the actual numbers are going to vary based on the role of the individual and your process for hiring and firing. By tracking the costs here, you'll have a better idea of what turnover costs your organization.

TABLE 11.2
Tangible Benefit Calculations

Item	Unit of Analysis	Cost	Cost Savings/Benefit
Time spent on staff hiring and firing (including all hours on recruitment and time spent by all staff in the interview and orientation process)	Number of total hours spent by all staff and volunteers	hours × rate (staff or volunteer hourly rates) = cost	last year's cost minus this year's cost
Hiring of consultants to make up for lack of staff proficiency in a specific competency	Consultant contracts	Total contract costs	last year's cost minus this year's cost
Time spent redoing projects	Number of total hours spent by all staff and volunteers	hours × rate (staff or volunteer hourly rates) = cost	last year's cost minus this year's cost
Grant successes	Grant awards	Total amount of grant awards	this year's awards minus last year awards
Donations	Amount and number of donations	Total amount or number of donations	this year's donations minus last year's

Now let's take a look at the small grassroots organization to see a specific example of benefits, costs, and net benefits of the talent development process (exhibits 11.6 and 11.7).

Determine the Costs of the Talent Development Investment

After you determine benefits, then you'll need to calculate the cost of the talent development investment. This includes actual monetary cost, which we discussed in detail in chapter 10. As you'll recall, the monetary costs of implementing the Talent Development Platform are greatly related to the time you spend on the process. Monetary costs that are not related to time will also come into play during implementation. Costs accrued during implementation in the form of trainings and external providers are secondary to the costs of time spent during on-the-job learning, which is where

---

EXHIBIT 11.6

Tangible Benefits of Talent Development Platform: Small Grassroots Organization

The executive director of the small grassroots organization determined the benefits of lower employee turnover (because, as we saw previously, the average turnover rate in organizations is 17 percent, which for this organization equates to less than one employee). With a turnover of even only one employee, such as the community engagement supervisor (at the old salary rate), the cost of turnover for this position would be between $9,750 and $19,500. Another tangible benefit is the improvement in volunteer recruitment. The organization realizes it will now be able to recruit six more tutors at a volunteer hourly rate of $18. The tutors volunteer five hours a week (for fifty weeks), so the estimated value of new volunteers would be $27,000 for one year. A third tangible benefit stems from the staff's increasing financial acumen, particularly that of the executive director, which will allow the organization to on CPA costs in future years.

Benefits	$ Gained
Turnover Savings	$9,750 to $19,500 (for one employee)
Reduction in CPA cost	$3,000
Value of New Volunteers	$27,000
Total Benefits:	$39,750 to $49,500

The executive director also determines the intangible benefits of improved staff morale of being able to collaboratively work together on the volunteer recruitment plan. In addition, morale is increased because staff can utilize their strengths moving forward and identify activities that match up with their learning styles.

---

the most significant learning will occur. Consider the following elements of time in your calculation of costs:

- Time to complete the Talent Map and administer and take the assessments

- Time to review and develop goals and objectives

- Time to implement the training, which includes the cost of the actual on-the-job learning activities

- Staff time for the on-the-job experience, mentoring, and training experiences

- Time to evaluate the talent development process

EXHIBIT 11.7

Staff Costs: Talent Development Platform, Small Grassroots Organization

Creating and Implementing the Platform

As we saw in chapter 10, the small grassroots organization determined the cost of staff time to undertake the Organizational Learning Assessment, complete the job descriptions and Talent Map, administer and take the Professional Development and Learning Styles Assessments, review results, and develop goals and objectives. The total cost of staff time for planning and creating the Talent Development Platform was $2,874.08 (table 10.1). The organization also calculated the costs of implementing the on-the-job learning, mentoring, and training components of the Platform. These implementation costs totaled $2,418.60 (table 10.2).

Increased Salary

The small grassroots organization has five staff members and an annual budget of $200,000, of which $92,000 is devoted to staff wages. The executive director is in the process of showing the benefits of investing in talent by increasing staff salaries to a living wage. After doing a review of salaries of similar organizations and typical salary increases in the region, she realized she needed to increase her staff salary budget to $122,560, which is a 25 percent increase. The current and proposed increases for each position were detailed in exhibit 10.1. The total increase is $30,560.

The table summarizes the total staff costs of adopting and following through with the Talent Development Platform.

Total Costs: Talent Development Platform

Costs	$ spent
Planning Talent Development Platform (table 10.1)	$2,874
Implementing Talent Development Platform (table 10.2)	$4,414
Increase in Staff Salaries (exhibit 10.1)	$30,560
Total Costs	**$37,848**

Remember, when you are calculating the time spent by your employees in each of these sections, you should include time spent by any volunteers. To calculate volunteer time and cost, use Independent Sector's (2014) value of volunteer time. Be sure that this volunteer value calculation is for skilled volunteers.

The small grassroots organization previously had a professional development budget of $4,300, which is approximately $500 less than the amount spent on the planning and implementation of the Talent Development Platform. Not shown here are any additional costs, such as for externally provided training, that the organization undertook during the implementation of the Platform.

Determine Net Benefits of Talent Development Investment

This is the easy part. Take the total benefits minus total costs to determine the net benefits. Table 11.3 shows that the small grassroots organization has a net monetary benefit of talent development of between $1,902 to $11,652. These net benefits do not include future nonmonetary benefits, which will be many.

TABLE 11.3 **Net Benefits of Talent Development Investment, Small Grassroots Organization**	
Total Benefits	$39,750 to $49,500
Total Costs	$37,848
Net Benefits	$1,902 to $11,652

Share Your Results and Learn from Them

Now that your organization has a more prevalent learning culture, this step should be second nature, but we'd be remiss if we didn't include a reminder for you to talk about the results with your entire staff. Include them in the process of evaluation and have healthy conversations regarding how the process went. If the process didn't work, talk about that too. In failure comes the most learning. Use this time as an opportunity to reassess how the organization did and discuss what could have been done better and what could you do to make it work the next time.

Evaluation in Practice

In this section we show the return on investment calculations for the four organizations. We also discuss the shifting that occurred as a result of Talent Development Platform implementation and evaluation, resulting in new scores from both the Organizational Learning Assessment and the Individual Professional Development Assessment.

Volunteer-Run Organization
Organizational Learning Assessment

Overall the organization did not see much change in their learning culture, except for in the area of resources available for learning. That area increased simply due to the effort spent implementing the Talent Development Platform. The fact that the other domains stayed consistent is an achievement as well, considering that the organization saw an increase in the number of volunteers participating and that they took on more hours in planning the festival the year they implemented the Talent Development Platform. Figure 11.2 shows the organization's before and after scores on the Organizational Learning Assessment.

Individual Professional Development Assessment

Overall the Individual Professional Development Assessment scores did not shift much for the volunteer-run organization. They did see a slight increase in Information Management, Financial Management and Social Entrepreneurship, and Fundraising and Resource Development. In the next year the board is hoping to focus more on Fundraising and Resource Development, as well as on Communications, Marketing, and Public Relations. Figure 11.3 shows their before and after Talent Maps.

Return on Investment

The return on investment for the volunteer-run organization showed high program returns and an increase in volunteers. The volunteer-run organization is a festival. In the year they implemented the Platform, the organization sold fifty more tickets to the festival at $15 apiece, which amounts to $750 in additional revenue. The organization also recruited twenty new volunteers for the festival at a volunteer rate of $18 an hour, which was an additional benefit of $360. Further, the organization secured four additional $2,500 sponsors. The organization also saved $1,500 in its festival liability insurance due to the policies the board created and $2,880 in festival costs due to the financial sustainability practices implemented. Exhibit 11.8 shows the volunteer-run organization's calculated return on investment.

The organization did not incur any specific costs for the hours spent by their board members in planning the Talent Development Platform; however it is important to note that the board spent an extra **165.25 hours** total for planning. The board members also spent **327 hours** implementing their learning activities.

The organization saw a **$7,700** net monetary benefit of implementing the Platform. The board also estimates that they saved over 500 hours in tracking sales, volunteer hours, and having their record system in place

FIGURE 11.2
Before and After Comparison: Organizational Learning Assessment, Volunteer-Run Organization

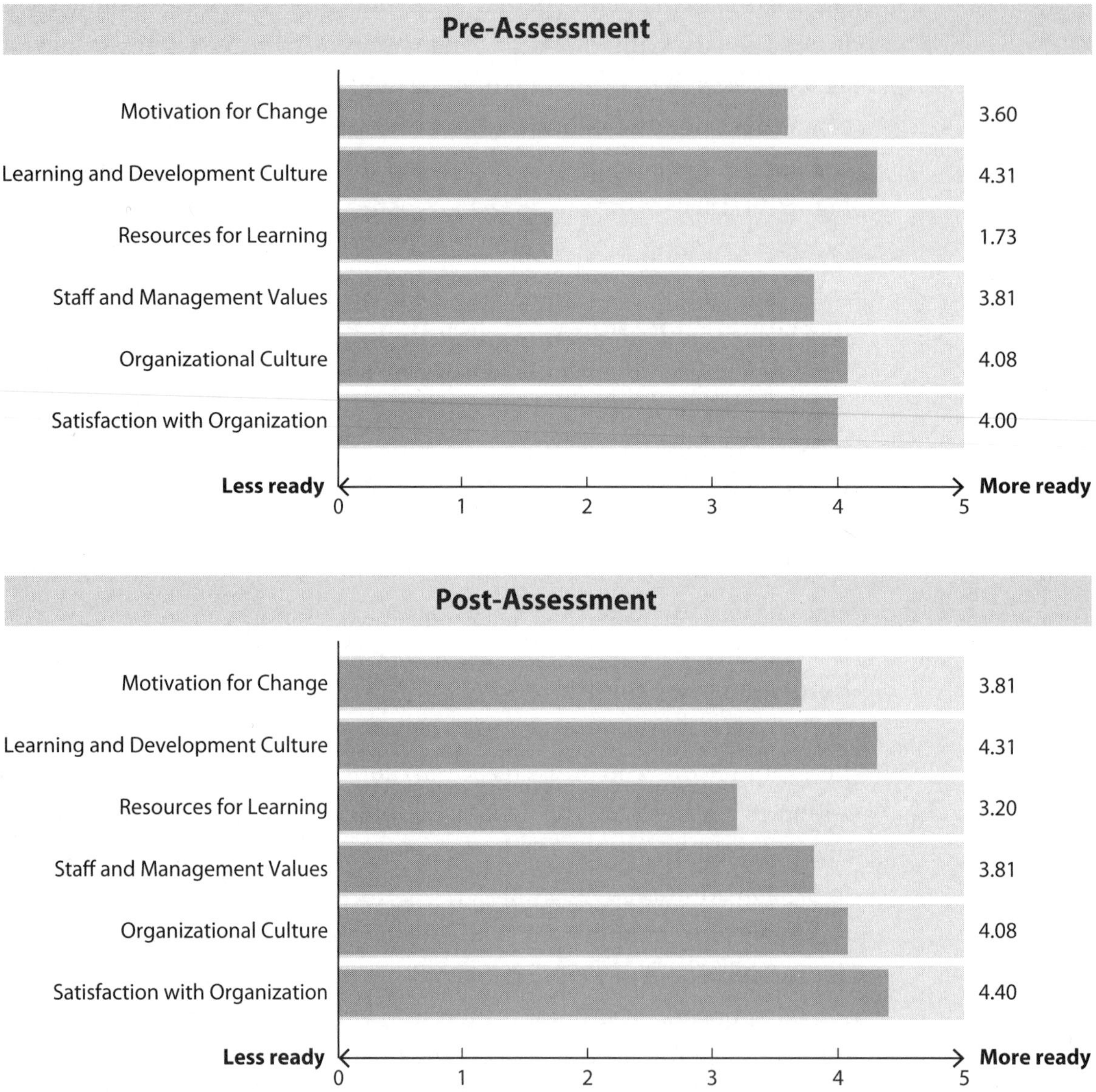

Pre-Assessment

Motivation for Change	3.60
Learning and Development Culture	4.31
Resources for Learning	1.73
Staff and Management Values	3.81
Organizational Culture	4.08
Satisfaction with Organization	4.00

Less ready ← 0 1 2 3 4 5 → More ready

Post-Assessment

Motivation for Change	3.81
Learning and Development Culture	4.31
Resources for Learning	3.20
Staff and Management Values	3.81
Organizational Culture	4.08
Satisfaction with Organization	4.40

Less ready ← 0 1 2 3 4 5 → More ready

for each festival due to new efficiencies. The organization anticipates that sponsorships, ticket sales, and volunteer hours will increase in future years as they focus more on learning related to community engagement and volunteer management.

FIGURE 11.3
Before and After Comparison: Talent Map, Volunteer-Run Organization

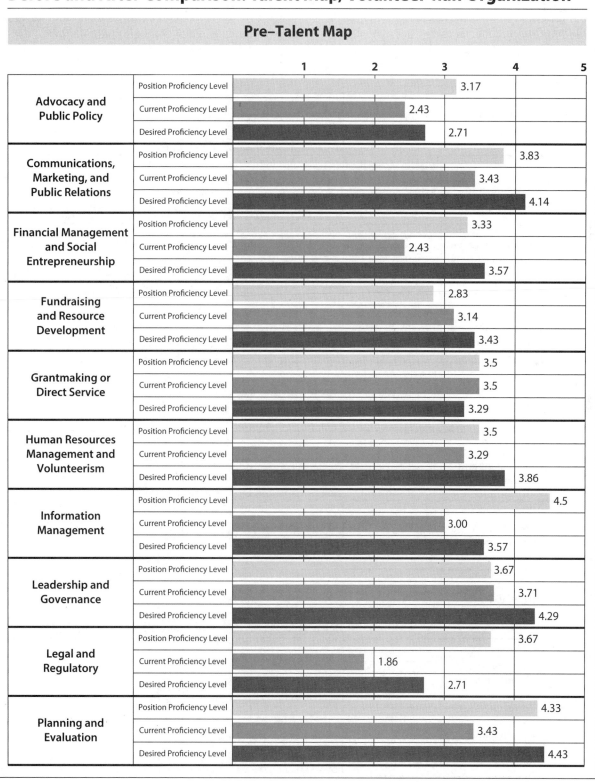

		1	2	3	4	5
Advocacy and Public Policy	Position Proficiency Level			3.17		
	Current Proficiency Level		2.43			
	Desired Proficiency Level		2.71			
Communications, Marketing, and Public Relations	Position Proficiency Level				3.83	
	Current Proficiency Level			3.43		
	Desired Proficiency Level				4.14	
Financial Management and Social Entrepreneurship	Position Proficiency Level			3.33		
	Current Proficiency Level		2.43			
	Desired Proficiency Level			3.57		
Fundraising and Resource Development	Position Proficiency Level			2.83		
	Current Proficiency Level			3.14		
	Desired Proficiency Level			3.43		
Grantmaking or Direct Service	Position Proficiency Level			3.5		
	Current Proficiency Level			3.5		
	Desired Proficiency Level			3.29		
Human Resources Management and Volunteerism	Position Proficiency Level			3.5		
	Current Proficiency Level			3.29		
	Desired Proficiency Level			3.86		
Information Management	Position Proficiency Level				4.5	
	Current Proficiency Level			3.00		
	Desired Proficiency Level			3.57		
Leadership and Governance	Position Proficiency Level			3.67		
	Current Proficiency Level			3.71		
	Desired Proficiency Level				4.29	
Legal and Regulatory	Position Proficiency Level			3.67		
	Current Proficiency Level	1.86				
	Desired Proficiency Level		2.71			
Planning and Evaluation	Position Proficiency Level				4.33	
	Current Proficiency Level			3.43		
	Desired Proficiency Level				4.43	

FIGURE 11.3

Before and After Comparison: Talent Map, Volunteer-Run Organization, Cont'd

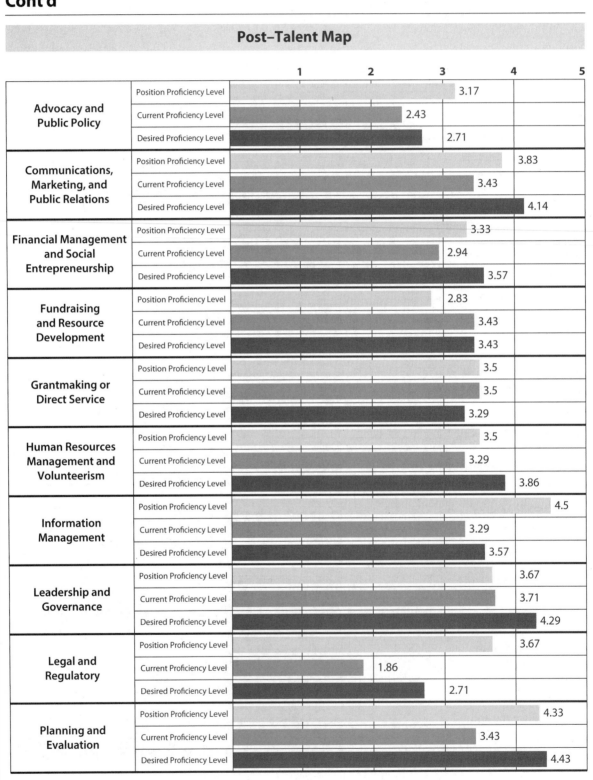

		1	2	3	4	5
Advocacy and Public Policy	Position Proficiency Level			3.17		
	Current Proficiency Level		2.43			
	Desired Proficiency Level		2.71			
Communications, Marketing, and Public Relations	Position Proficiency Level				3.83	
	Current Proficiency Level			3.43		
	Desired Proficiency Level				4.14	
Financial Management and Social Entrepreneurship	Position Proficiency Level			3.33		
	Current Proficiency Level			2.94		
	Desired Proficiency Level			3.57		
Fundraising and Resource Development	Position Proficiency Level		2.83			
	Current Proficiency Level			3.43		
	Desired Proficiency Level			3.43		
Grantmaking or Direct Service	Position Proficiency Level			3.5		
	Current Proficiency Level			3.5		
	Desired Proficiency Level			3.29		
Human Resources Management and Volunteerism	Position Proficiency Level			3.5		
	Current Proficiency Level			3.29		
	Desired Proficiency Level			3.86		
Information Management	Position Proficiency Level				4.5	
	Current Proficiency Level			3.29		
	Desired Proficiency Level			3.57		
Leadership and Governance	Position Proficiency Level			3.67		
	Current Proficiency Level			3.71		
	Desired Proficiency Level				4.29	
Legal and Regulatory	Position Proficiency Level			3.67		
	Current Proficiency Level	1.86				
	Desired Proficiency Level		2.71			
Planning and Evaluation	Position Proficiency Level				4.33	
	Current Proficiency Level			3.43		
	Desired Proficiency Level				4.43	

Post–Talent Map

EXHIBIT 11.8

Return on Investment: Volunteer-Run Organization

Benefits	$ Gained
Increased sponsorship, $2,500 × 4	$10,000
Increased ticket sales	$750
Value of new volunteers	$360
Reduction in insurance premium	$1,500
Reduction in festival costs	$2,880
Total Benefits:	$15,490

Costs	$ Spent
Implementing Talent Development Platform	$7,700
Total Costs:	$7,700

Net Benefits	
Total Benefits	$15,490
Total Costs	$7,700
Net Benefits:	$7,790

Small Grassroots Organization
Organizational Learning Assessment

Overall, the small grassroots organization saw a slight increase in each one of the six domains in the Organizational Learning Assessment. Figure 11.4 shows the before and after Organizational Learning Assessments for the small grassroots organization.

Individual Professional Development Assessment

The small grassroots organization saw an increase in their Communications, Marketing, and Public Relations and Financial Management and Social Entrepreneurship competencies. The organization focused on the Legal and Regulatory category as well but did not see an increase. Although the executive director was able to increase her proficiency levels, the organization wasn't able to make a huge change in its proficiency level in the Legal and Regulatory category. The executive director hopes to focus a bit more on the Legal and Regulatory competency in the next year,

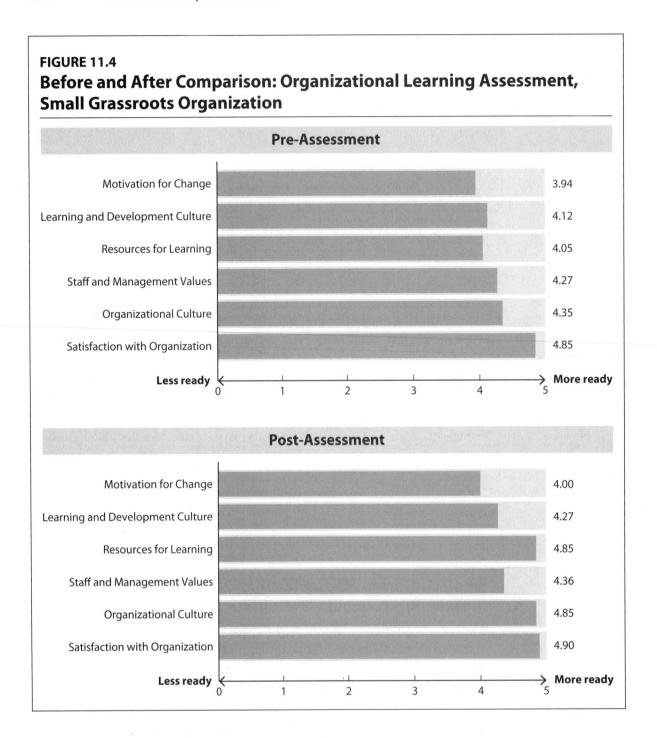

FIGURE 11.4
Before and After Comparison: Organizational Learning Assessment, Small Grassroots Organization

Pre-Assessment

Motivation for Change	3.94
Learning and Development Culture	4.12
Resources for Learning	4.05
Staff and Management Values	4.27
Organizational Culture	4.35
Satisfaction with Organization	4.85

Less ready ← 0 1 2 3 4 5 → More ready

Post-Assessment

Motivation for Change	4.00
Learning and Development Culture	4.27
Resources for Learning	4.85
Staff and Management Values	4.36
Organizational Culture	4.85
Satisfaction with Organization	4.90

Less ready ← 0 1 2 3 4 5 → More ready

as well as some development in their Human Resources Management and Volunteerism and Communications, Marketing, and Public Relations competencies. Figure 11.5 shows the before and after Talent Maps for the small grassroots organization.

Return on Investment

The small grassroots organization saw organizational benefits of decreased turnover and an increase in volunteer engagement. As we've already

FIGURE 11.5
Before and After Comparison: Talent Map, Small Grassroots Organization

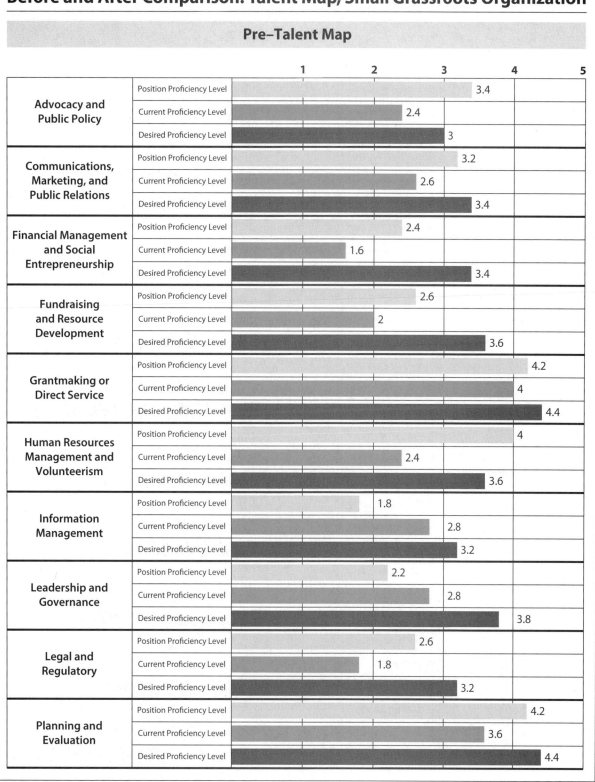

Pre–Talent Map

		1	2	3	4	5
Advocacy and Public Policy	Position Proficiency Level			3.4		
	Current Proficiency Level		2.4			
	Desired Proficiency Level			3		
Communications, Marketing, and Public Relations	Position Proficiency Level			3.2		
	Current Proficiency Level		2.6			
	Desired Proficiency Level			3.4		
Financial Management and Social Entrepreneurship	Position Proficiency Level		2.4			
	Current Proficiency Level	1.6				
	Desired Proficiency Level			3.4		
Fundraising and Resource Development	Position Proficiency Level		2.6			
	Current Proficiency Level	2				
	Desired Proficiency Level			3.6		
Grantmaking or Direct Service	Position Proficiency Level				4.2	
	Current Proficiency Level				4	
	Desired Proficiency Level				4.4	
Human Resources Management and Volunteerism	Position Proficiency Level				4	
	Current Proficiency Level		2.4			
	Desired Proficiency Level			3.6		
Information Management	Position Proficiency Level	1.8				
	Current Proficiency Level		2.8			
	Desired Proficiency Level			3.2		
Leadership and Governance	Position Proficiency Level		2.2			
	Current Proficiency Level		2.8			
	Desired Proficiency Level			3.8		
Legal and Regulatory	Position Proficiency Level		2.6			
	Current Proficiency Level	1.8				
	Desired Proficiency Level			3.2		
Planning and Evaluation	Position Proficiency Level				4.2	
	Current Proficiency Level			3.6		
	Desired Proficiency Level				4.4	

FIGURE 11.5
Before and After Comparison: Small Grassroots Organization, Cont'd

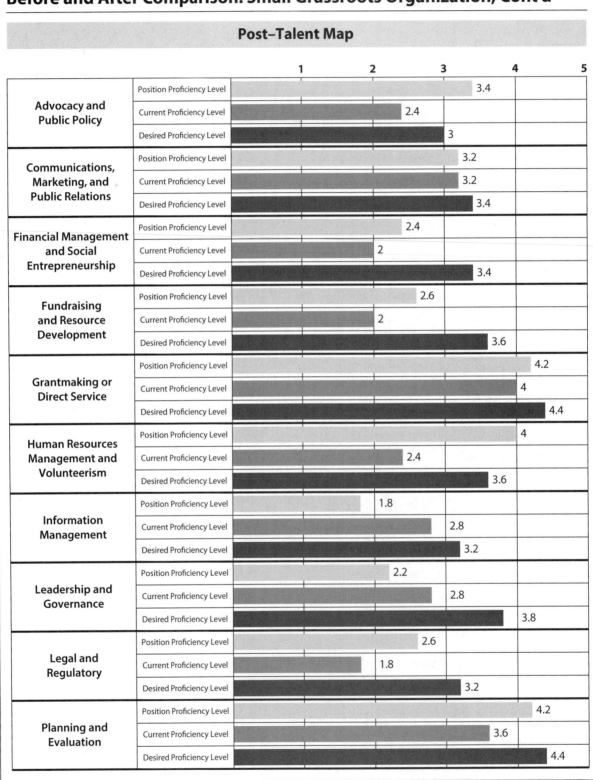

discussed, an organization's average turnover rate is 17 percent, which equates to less than one employee for the small grassroots organization. The organization saw a cost savings of **$9,750 and $19,500** (75 to 150 percent of the employee's salary) for the community engagement supervisor (at the old salary rate) position.

The organization also saw a return tied directly to their increased financial acumen. The organization also recruited six more tutors at a volunteer hourly rate of $18. The tutors volunteer five hours a week for fifty weeks. The value of new volunteers was **$27,000 for one year**. Exhibit 11.9 summarizes the calculations for these benefits along with the costs the organization incurred during the creation and implementation of the Talent Development Platform. In the end, the organization was able to see a monetary return on investment.

EXHIBIT 11.9

Return on Investment: Small Grassroots Organization

Benefits	$ Gained
Turnover Savings	$9,750–$19,500
Reduction in CPA cost	$3,000
Value of New Volunteers	$27,000
Total Benefits:	$39,750–$49,500
Costs	$ Spent
Planning Talent Development Platform	$2,874
Implementing Talent Development Platform	$4,414
Increase in Staff Salaries	$30,560
Total Costs:	$37,848

Net Benefits	
Total Benefits	$39,750–$49,500
Total Costs	$37,848
Net Benefits:	$1,902–$11,652

Midsized Organization
Organizational Learning Assessment

The midsized organization saw increases in the first five domains of the Organizational Learning Assessment. The "Staff and Volunteer Satisfaction" domain stayed consistent. Because the midsized organization already had high satisfaction levels among its employees, they considered the consistent score in this domain a positive. The organization was able to improve other areas of its organizational learning culture while maintaining satisfaction. Figure 11.6 shows the organization's before and after Organizational Learning Assessments.

Individual Professional Development Assessment

The midsized organization saw increases in their proficiency levels in both the Leadership and Governance and Information Management competency categories. The other proficiency levels did not change. The organization did not set goals and objectives for the next year immediately following the Talent Development Platform implementation, because they entered a strategic planning cycle. The organization set learning goals and objectives in their second year of implementation. Figure 11.7 shows the before and after Talent Maps for the midsized organization.

Return on Investment

With increased salaries and investment in professional development the organization also decreased their turnover rates. In the previous year, the midsized organization had lost five employees, whereas this year they lost only two. One of the employees was a mid-level staff member making $45,000, while the other was a low-level staff member making $33,000. In the past year, the organization lost three mid-level employees averaging $50,000 in salaries and two low-level employees average $30,000 in salaries. In the previous year, the organization spent approximately $189,000 (90 percent of the terminated employees' salaries) recruiting new employees and in loss of productivity. In the new year, the organization spent $70,200 on turnover. The difference in the two years was a **savings of $118,800** for the organization.

Due to their more efficient recordkeeping system of volunteers, the midsized organization turned volunteers into donors. During its year of implementation, the organization then began to focus on cultivating those volunteers to become donors. Their increased efforts in this area resulted in an 88 percent retention in their volunteers from the previous year (up from 60 percent in the year before) and a **4.5 percent increase** in their donations. Their organization's total donations were $1,983,047 in the previous year,

FIGURE 11.6
Before and After Comparison: Organizational Learning Assessment, Midsized Organization

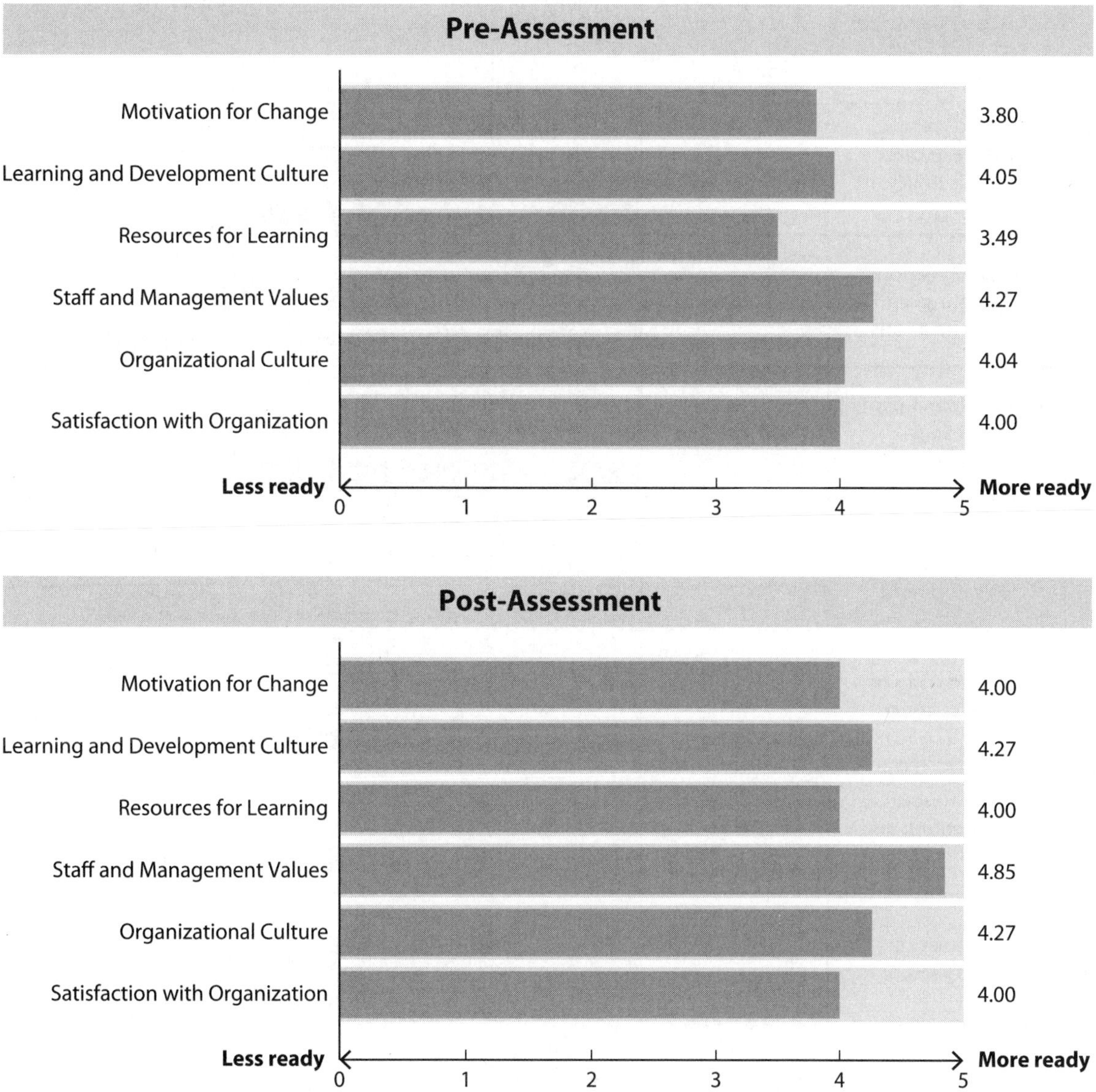

Pre-Assessment

Motivation for Change	3.80
Learning and Development Culture	4.05
Resources for Learning	3.49
Staff and Management Values	4.27
Organizational Culture	4.04
Satisfaction with Organization	4.00

Less ready ← 0 1 2 3 4 5 → More ready

Post-Assessment

Motivation for Change	4.00
Learning and Development Culture	4.27
Resources for Learning	4.00
Staff and Management Values	4.85
Organizational Culture	4.27
Satisfaction with Organization	4.00

Less ready ← 0 1 2 3 4 5 → More ready

and $2,072,284 in the implementation year, an increase of **$89,237** (exhibit 11.10).

Grantmaking Organization
Organizational Learning Assessment

The grantmaking organization did not see any changes in their organizational learning scores. They maintained the scores within the same areas in

FIGURE 11.7

Before and After Comparison: Talent Map, Midsized Organization

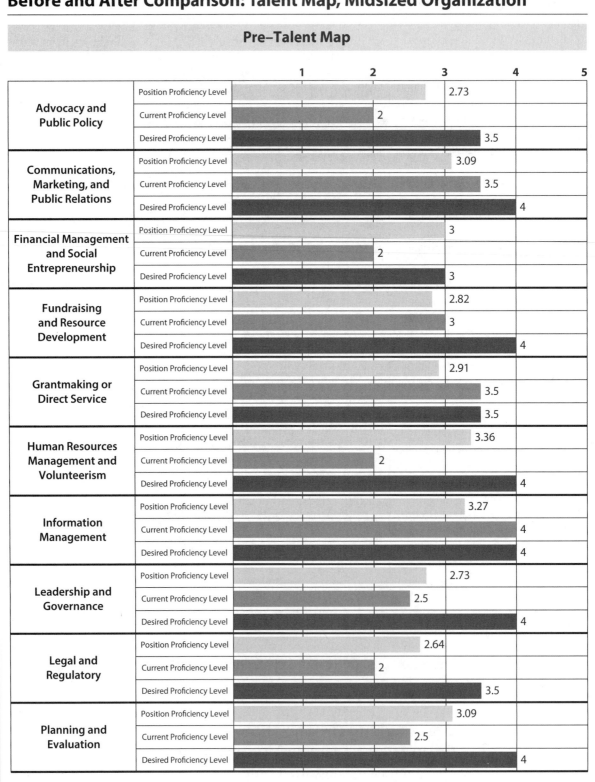

		1	2	3	4	5
Pre–Talent Map						
Advocacy and Public Policy	Position Proficiency Level			2.73		
	Current Proficiency Level		2			
	Desired Proficiency Level			3.5		
Communications, Marketing, and Public Relations	Position Proficiency Level			3.09		
	Current Proficiency Level			3.5		
	Desired Proficiency Level			4		
Financial Management and Social Entrepreneurship	Position Proficiency Level			3		
	Current Proficiency Level		2			
	Desired Proficiency Level			3		
Fundraising and Resource Development	Position Proficiency Level			2.82		
	Current Proficiency Level			3		
	Desired Proficiency Level			4		
Grantmaking or Direct Service	Position Proficiency Level			2.91		
	Current Proficiency Level			3.5		
	Desired Proficiency Level			3.5		
Human Resources Management and Volunteerism	Position Proficiency Level			3.36		
	Current Proficiency Level		2			
	Desired Proficiency Level			4		
Information Management	Position Proficiency Level			3.27		
	Current Proficiency Level			4		
	Desired Proficiency Level			4		
Leadership and Governance	Position Proficiency Level			2.73		
	Current Proficiency Level		2.5			
	Desired Proficiency Level			4		
Legal and Regulatory	Position Proficiency Level			2.64		
	Current Proficiency Level		2			
	Desired Proficiency Level			3.5		
Planning and Evaluation	Position Proficiency Level			3.09		
	Current Proficiency Level		2.5			
	Desired Proficiency Level			4		

FIGURE 11.7

Before and After Comparison: Talent Map, Midsized Organization, Cont'd

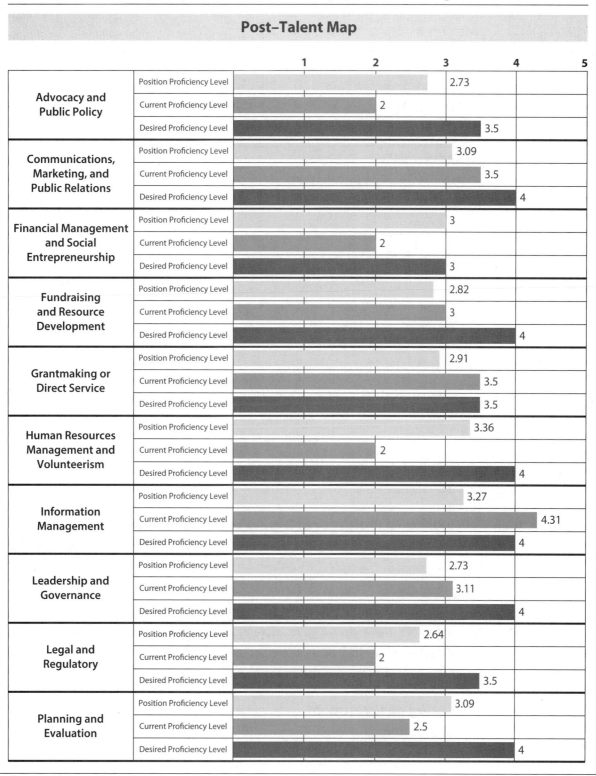

Post–Talent Map

		1	2	3	4	5
Advocacy and Public Policy	Position Proficiency Level			2.73		
	Current Proficiency Level		2			
	Desired Proficiency Level			3.5		
Communications, Marketing, and Public Relations	Position Proficiency Level			3.09		
	Current Proficiency Level			3.5		
	Desired Proficiency Level			4		
Financial Management and Social Entrepreneurship	Position Proficiency Level			3		
	Current Proficiency Level		2			
	Desired Proficiency Level			3		
Fundraising and Resource Development	Position Proficiency Level			2.82		
	Current Proficiency Level			3		
	Desired Proficiency Level			4		
Grantmaking or Direct Service	Position Proficiency Level			2.91		
	Current Proficiency Level			3.5		
	Desired Proficiency Level			3.5		
Human Resources Management and Volunteerism	Position Proficiency Level			3.36		
	Current Proficiency Level		2			
	Desired Proficiency Level			4		
Information Management	Position Proficiency Level			3.27		
	Current Proficiency Level				4.31	
	Desired Proficiency Level			4		
Leadership and Governance	Position Proficiency Level			2.73		
	Current Proficiency Level			3.11		
	Desired Proficiency Level			4		
Legal and Regulatory	Position Proficiency Level			2.64		
	Current Proficiency Level		2			
	Desired Proficiency Level			3.5		
Planning and Evaluation	Position Proficiency Level			3.09		
	Current Proficiency Level		2.5			
	Desired Proficiency Level			4		

EXHIBIT 11.10

Return on Investment: Midsized Organization

Benefits	$ Gained
Turnover Savings	$118,800
Donation Increase	$89,237
Total Benefits:	$208,037

Costs	$ Spent
Planning Talent Development Platform	$6,680
Implementing Talent Development Platform	$19,336
Increase in Staff Salaries	$39,442
Total Costs:	$65,458

Net Benefits	
Total Benefits	$208,037
Total Costs	$65,458
Net Benefits:	$142,579

each domain. Figure 11.8 shows the before and after Organizational Learning Assessment.

Individual Professional Development Assessment

The grantmaking organization also did not see much shift in their overall scores in the Individual Professional Development Assessments for the organization. They did, however, see some slight increases in the Advocacy and Public Policy and the Planning and Evaluation categories. The increases were due to the increased proficiency levels of the director of Grantmaking and Nonprofit Services. Figure 11.9 shows the before and after Talent Maps for the grantmaking organization.

Return on Investment

The grantmaking organization did not see any change in turnover rates, as it has not lost any employees in the last couple of years. The steady turnover

FIGURE 11.8

Before and After Comparison: Organizational Learning Assessment, Grantmaking Organization

Pre-Assessment

Motivation for Change	3.20
Learning and Development Culture	4.72
Resources for Learning	3.75
Staff and Management Values	4.19
Organizational Culture	3.28
Satisfaction with Organization	5.00

Less ready ← 0 1 2 3 4 5 → More ready

Post-Assessment

Motivation for Change	3.75
Learning and Development Culture	4.72
Resources for Learning	3.75
Staff and Management Values	4.19
Organizational Culture	3.28
Satisfaction with Organization	5.00

Less ready ← 0 1 2 3 4 5 → More ready

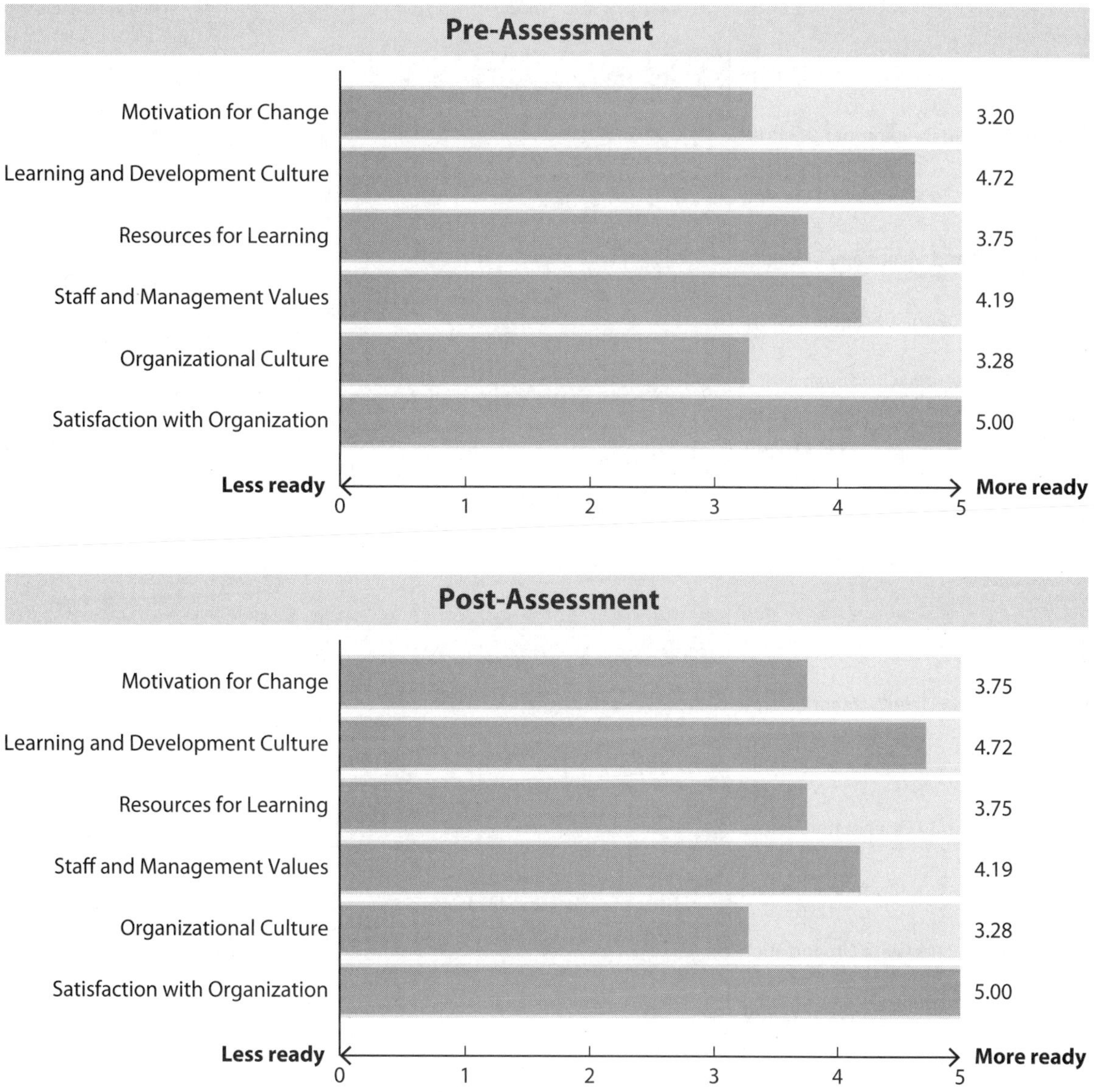

rate is a good sign that they are continuing to maintain a strong learning culture.

The grantmaking organization saw increase in grantee satisfaction, due to the focus on evaluation practices. Grantees reported time savings and better outcome information. The organization brought in three new scholarship funds, **totaling $150,000**, which they believe was linked to

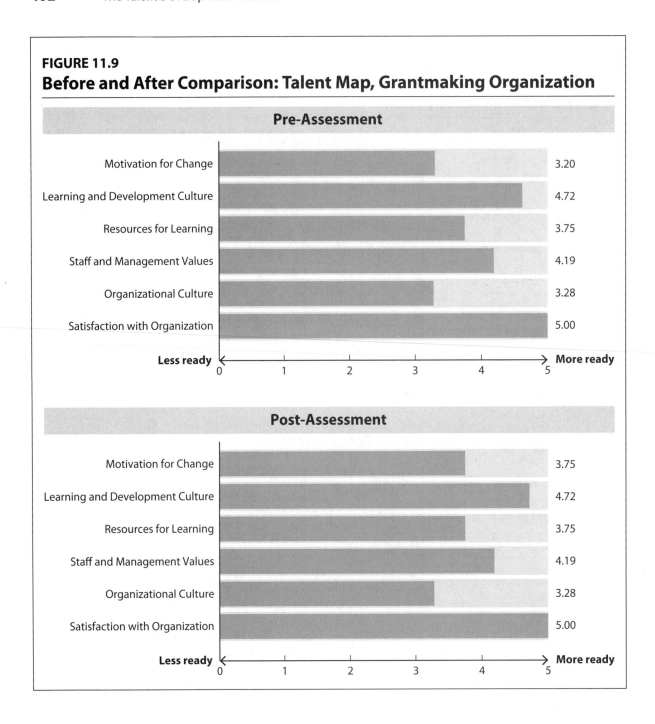

FIGURE 11.9
Before and After Comparison: Talent Map, Grantmaking Organization

Pre-Assessment

Motivation for Change	3.20
Learning and Development Culture	4.72
Resources for Learning	3.75
Staff and Management Values	4.19
Organizational Culture	3.28
Satisfaction with Organization	5.00

Less ready ← 0 1 2 3 4 5 → More ready

Post-Assessment

Motivation for Change	3.75
Learning and Development Culture	4.72
Resources for Learning	3.75
Staff and Management Values	4.19
Organizational Culture	3.28
Satisfaction with Organization	5.00

Less ready ← 0 1 2 3 4 5 → More ready

their advocacy (exhibit 11.11). Their employees also reported spending less time managing financials due to their increased financial acumen.

EXHIBIT 11.11

Return on Investment: Grantmaking Organization

Benefits	$ Gained
Turnover Savings	
Scholarship Increase	
Total Benefits:	

Costs	$ Spent
Planning Talent Development Platform	$7,113
Implementing Talent Development Platform	$16,755
Increase in Staff Salaries	-
Total Costs:	$23,868

Net Benefits	
Total Benefits	$150,000
Total Costs	$23,868
Net Benefits:	$126,132

Conclusion

As the journey ends each year when you complete the evaluation and performance assessment stage of the process, take some time to reflect on the true returns you had on your investment. Are you feeling better about where your organization is when it comes to learning and how you are impacting your mission? Are there further changes you need to make in order to enhance the support and investment you make in your employees and volunteers? Do you feel good about how the process went, or does it need improvements? No matter the answer to these questions, give yourself a pat on the back. You've taken huge strides in intentionally supporting your people! Keep the process moving, no matter the struggles you may find in your organization. Your people and your mission are worth it.

Guide 1
Third-Party Professional Development Options

This list of third-party professional development providers is not all encompassing but meant to cover those who provide support for professional development at the national and state level. This list is subject to change and will be updated annually online.

Washington, DC

Action without Borders (Idealist)

1519 Connecticut Avenue NW, Washington, DC 20036

www.idealist.org

Mission/Focus Area: Connect individuals with employment and volunteer opportunities

Competencies: Human Resources Management and Volunteerism

● ● ●

Africa Grantmakers' Affinity Group

1776 I Street NW, Suite 900, Washington, DC 20006

www.africagrantmakers.org

Mission/Focus Area: AGAG promotes robust, effective, and responsive philanthropy benefiting African communities.

Competencies: Advocacy and Public Policy; Grantmaking

● ● ●

Alliance for Justice

11 Dupont Circle NW, 2nd Floor, Washington, DC 20036

www.afj.org

Mission/Focus Area: Alliance for Justice is a national association of over 100 organizations, representing a broad array of groups committed to progressive values and the creation of an equitable, just, and free society.

Competencies: Advocacy and Public Policy

• • •

AmeriCorps VISTA

1201 New York Avenue NW, Washington, DC 20525

www.nationalservice.gov

Mission/Focus Area: Through AmeriCorps VISTA, you can make a tangible difference. And you'll find the fulfillment that comes from using your knowledge and skills to help those in disadvantaged circumstances turn their dreams into reality.

Competencies: Advocacy and Public Policy; Human Resources Management and Volunteerism; Leadership and Governance

• • •

America's Promise Alliance

1110 Vermont Avenue NW, Washington, DC 20005

www.americaspromise.org

Mission/Focus Area: We are the nation's largest partnership of our kind, bringing together hundreds of national nonprofits, businesses, communities, educators, and ordinary citizens behind the idea of making the promise of America accessible to all young people.

Competencies: Advocacy and Public Policy

• • •

Board Source

750 9th Street NW, Suite 650, Washington, DC 20001

www.boardsource.org

Mission/Focus Area: BoardSource has become the go-to resource for funders, partners, and nonprofit leaders who want to magnify their impact within their community through exceptional governance practices.

Competencies: Leadership and Governance; Fundraising and Resource Development; Human Resources Management and Volunteerism

• • •

Capital Research Center

1513 16th Street NW, Washington, DC 20036

http://capitalresearch.org

Mission/Focus Area: We support the principles of individual liberty, a free market economy, and limited constitutional government.

Competencies: Advocacy and Public Policy

• • •

Center for Lobbying in the Public Interest

1200 New York Avenue NW, Suite 700, Washington, DC 20005

www.clpi.org

Mission/Focus Area: Protection of advocacy and lobbying of 501(c)(3) nonprofits

Competencies: Advocacy and Public Policy; Grantmaking; Leadership and Governance

• • •

Corporation for National and Community Service

1201 New York Avenue NW, Washington, DC 20525

www.nationalservice.gov

Mission/Focus Area: We invest in thousands of nonprofit and faith-based groups that are making a difference across the country.

Competencies: Advocacy and Public Policy; Grantmaking; Leadership and Governance

• • •

Forum of Regional Association of Grantmakers

1111 19th Street NW, Suite 650, Washington, DC 20036

www.givingforum.org

Mission/Focus Area: Educating grantmakers on effective philanthropy.

Competencies: Advocacy and Public Policy; Communications, Marketing, and Public Relations; Grantmaking; Financial Management and

Social Entrepreneurship, Information Management; Legal and Regulatory; Planning and Evaluation

• • •

Foundation Center

1627 K Street NW, Washington, DC 20006

http://foundationcenter.org

Mission/Focus Area: Advance knowledge of philanthropy at every level; connect grantmakers and grantseekers

Competencies: Financial Management and Social Entrepreneurship; Grantmaking; Fundraising and Resource Development

• • •

Funders Concerned About AIDS

1100 Connecticut Avenue NW, Suite 1200, Washington, DC 20036

www.fcaaids.org

Mission/Focus Area: Funders Concerned About AIDS (FCAA) mobilizes the leadership, ideas, and resources of funders to eradicate the global HIV/AIDS pandemic and to address its social and economic dimensions.

Competencies: Advocacy and Public Policy; Grantmaking

• • •

Grants Managers Network

1666 K Street NW, Suite 440, Washington, DC 20006

www.gmnetwork.org

Mission/Focus Area: Grants Managers Network is a thriving national association with a mission to improve grantmaking by advancing the knowledge, skills, and abilities of grants management professionals and leading grantmakers to adopt and incorporate effective practices that benefit the philanthropic community.

Competencies: Fundraising and Resource Development; Grantmaking

• • •

Grantmakers for Effective Organizations

1725 DeSales Street NW, Suite 404, Washington, DC 20036

www.geofunders.org

Mission/Focus Area: Helping grantmakers improve practices in the following areas: Learning for Improvement, Collaborative Problem Solving, The Money, Stakeholder Engagement, and Scaling What Works

Competencies: Grantmaking; Leadership and Governance; Legal and Regulatory; Planning and Evaluation

• • •

Grantmakers in Health

1100 Connecticut Avenue NW, Washington, DC 20036

www.gih.org

Mission/Focus Area: Grantmakers in Health (GIH) is a nonprofit, educational organization dedicated to helping foundations and corporate giving programs improve the health of all people.

Competencies: Advocacy and Public Policy; Grantmaking

• • •

Hudson Institute

1015 15th Street NW, Suite 600, Washington, DC 20005

www.hudson.org

Mission/Focus Area: Hudson Institute challenges conventional thinking and helps manage strategic transitions to the future through interdisciplinary studies in defense, international relations, economics, health care, technology, culture, and law.

Competencies: Advocacy and Public Policy

• • •

Independent Sector

1602 L Street NW, Suite 900, Washington, DC 20036

www.independentsector.org

Mission/Focus Area: Independent Sector serves as the premier meeting ground for the leaders of America's charitable and philanthropic sector. www.independentsector.org/about

Competencies: Human Resources Management and Volunteerism; Leadership and Governance

• • •

Innovation Network

1625 K Street NW, Suite 1050, Washington, DC 20006

www.innonet.org

Mission/Focus Area: We provide program planning and evaluation consulting, training, and web-based tools to nonprofits and funders across geographic and programmatic boundaries.

Competencies: Planning and Evaluation

• • •

International Center for Not-for-Profit Law

1126 16th Street NW, Suite 400, Washington, DC 20036

www.icnl.org

Mission/Focus Area: We seek a legal environment that strengthens civil society, advances the freedoms of association and assembly, fosters philanthropy, and enables public participation around the world.

Competencies: Legal and Regulatory

• • •

Management Assistance Group

1155 F Street NW, Suite 1050, Washington, DC 20004

www.managementassistance.org

Mission/Focus Area: Organizational Growth and Change; Strategic Planning; Strengthening Management; Coaching and Training Leaders; Board Development; Leadership Transitions; Raising More Money; Creating Successful Coalitions and Collaborations; Strengthening Affiliate Networks; Working with Funders; Workshops and Speaking Engagements

Competencies: Advocacy and Public Policy; Fundraising and Resource Development; Leadership and Governance; Planning and Evaluation

• • •

National Center for Family Philanthropy

1101 Connecticut Avenue NW, Suite 220, Washington, DC 20036

www.ncfp.org

Mission/Focus Area: Family philanthropy—promoting philanthropic values, vision, and excellence across generations of philanthropists and their families

Competencies: Grantmaking

• • •

National Human Services Assembly

1101 14th Street, NW Suite 600, Washington, DC, 20005

http://nassembly.org

Mission/Focus Area: The National Assembly is a learning community where leaders with parallel responsibilities at different national non-profit human service organizations (e.g., CEOs, HR directors) share knowledge and expertise about their work in this sector.

Competencies: Advocacy and Public Policy; Leadership and Governance

• • •

National Committee for Responsive Philanthropy

1331 H Street NW, Suite 200, Washington, DC, 20005

www.ncrp.org

Mission/Focus Area: NCRP promotes philanthropy that serves the public good, is responsive to people and communities with the least wealth and opportunity, and is held accountable to the highest standards of integrity and openness.

Competencies: Advocacy and Public Policy; Grantmaking; Legal and Regulatory

• • •

National Council of Nonprofits (formerly, NCNA)

1200 New York Avenue NW, Suite 700, Washington, DC 20005

www.councilofnonprofits.org

Mission/Focus Area: To advance the vital role, capacity, and voice of charitable nonprofit organizations through our state and national networks—see more at: www.councilofnonprofits.org/who-we-are #ataglance

Competencies: Advocacy and Public Policy; Communications, Marketing, and Public Relations; Financial Management and Social

Entrepreneurship; Fundraising and Resource Development; Grantmaking; Human Resources Management and Volunteerism; Information Management; Leadership and Governance; Legal and Regulatory; Planning and Evaluation

• • •

National Council on Aging

1901 L Street NW, 4th Floor, Washington, DC 20036

www.ncoa.org

Mission/Focus Area: To improve the lives of millions of older adults, especially those who are vulnerable and disadvantaged—see more at: www.ncoa.org/about-ncoa

Competencies: Advocacy and Public Policy

• • •

New Voices Fellowship Program

1825 Connecticut Avenue NW, Washington, DC 20009

http://newvoices.aed.org

Mission/Focus Area: Offers development experts from Africa and other parts of the developing world a yearlong program of media support, training, research, and writing

Competencies: Advocacy and Public Policy; Communications, Marketing, and Public Relations; Fundraising and Resource Development

• • •

Nonprofit HR Solutions

1400 Eye Street NW, Suite 500, Washington, DC 20005

www.nonprofithr.com

Mission/Focus Area: To help nonprofits achieve their missions through people

Competencies: Human Resources Management and Volunteerism

• • •

The Nonprofit Roundtable of Greater Washington

1201 15th Street NW, Suite 420, Washington, DC 20005

http://nonprofitroundtable.org

Mission/Focus Area: The Nonprofit Roundtable is an alliance of over three hundred nonprofits and community partners building the strength, visibility, and influence of the nonprofit sector.

Competencies: Advocacy and Public Policy; Leadership and Governance

• • •

OMB Watch

2040 S Street NW, 2nd Floor, Washington, DC. 20009

www.foreffectivegov.org

Mission/Focus Area: To build an open, accountable government

Competencies: Advocacy and Public Policy

• • •

Peace Corps

1111 20th Street NW, Washington, DC 20526

www.peacecorps.gov

Mission/Focus Area: To promote world peace and friendship

Competencies: Advocacy and Public Policy

• • •

Philanthropic Initiative for Racial Equity

1720 N. Street NW, Washington, DC 20036

www.racialequity.org

Mission/Focus Area: Providing resources to combat racism

Competencies: Advocacy and Public Policy; Grantmaking

• • •

Philanthropy for Active Civic Engagement

1201 15th Street NW, Suite 420, Washington, DC 20005

www.pacefunders.org

Mission/Focus Area: Increasing the quality of civic engagement within the philanthropic sector

Competencies: Advocacy and Public Policy; Grantmaking

• • •

Senior Corps

1111 20th Street NW, Washington, DC 20526

www.peacecorps.gov

Mission/Focus Area: To promote world peace and friendship

Competencies: Advocacy and Public Policy

• • •

The Urban Institute

2100 M St NW, Washington, DC 20037

www.urban.org

Mission/Focus Area: Gathers data, conducts research, evaluates programs, offers technical assistance overseas, and educates Americans on social and economic issues

Competencies: Information Management; Planning and Evaluation

• • •

Venture Philanthropy Partners

1201 15th Street NW, Suite 510, Washington, DC 20005

www.vppartners.org

Mission/Focus Area: Helps great leaders build strong, high-performing nonprofit institutions and concentrates on money, expertise, and personal contacts to improve the lives and boost the opportunities of children and youth of low-income families

Competencies: Advocacy and Public Policy; Financial Management and Social Entrepreneurship; Human Resources Management and Volunteerism

• • •

Washington Regional Association of Grantmakers

1400 16th Street NW, Suite 740, Washington, DC 20036

www.washingtongrantmakers.org

Mission/Focus Area: We provide a variety of services to our members to facilitate more effective, strategic, and efficient grantmaking.

Competencies: Grantmaking; Leadership and Governance

Alabama

Alabama Association of Nonprofits

800 Lakeshore Drive, Brock School of Business, Suite 412, Birmingham, Alabama 35229

http://alabamanonprofits.org

Mission/Focus Area: The mission of the Alabama Association of Nonprofits (AAN) is to strengthen and support Alabama nonprofit organizations in serving their communities.

Competencies: Grantmaking

• • •

Alabama Giving

P.O. Box 530727 Birmingham, AL 35253

http://alabamagiving.infomedia.net/showandtell.asp?id=24415

Mission/Focus Area: Alabama Giving is a project to increase, promote, and encourage philanthropy statewide.

Competencies: Grantmaking

Alaska

Alaska Community Foundation

3201 C Street, Suite 110, Anchorage, AK 99503

http://alaskacf.org

Mission/Focus Area: The Alaska Community Foundation (ACF) cultivates, celebrates, and sustains all forms of philanthropy to strengthen Alaska's communities forever.

Competencies: Grantmaking

Arizona

Alliance of Arizona Nonprofits

5150 N 16th St., Suite C-152, Phoenix, AZ 85016

www.arizonanonprofits.org

Mission/Focus Area: Providing quality information, training, and networking opportunities

Competencies: Advocacy and Public Policy; Financial Management and Social Entrepreneurship; Fundraising and Resource Development; Human Resources Management and Volunteerism; Information Management; Leadership and Governance; Legal and Regulatory; Planning and Evaluation

• • •

Arizona Grantmakers Forum

2201 E. Camelback Road, Suite 405B, Phoenix, AZ 85016

arizonagrantmakersforum.org

Mission/Focus Area: To increase, enhance, and improve philanthropy in Arizona

Competencies: Grantmaking

• • •

Lodestar Center for Philanthropy and Nonprofit Innovation (Arizona State)

411 N. Central Avenue, Suite 500, Phoenix, AZ 85004-0691

http://lodestar.asu.edu

Mission/Focus Area: The ASU Lodestar Center exists to advance nonprofit leadership practice so that organizations can better achieve their mission.

Competencies: Communications Marketing and Public Relations; Financial Management and Social Entrepreneurship; Grantmaking; Human Resources Management and Volunteerism; Leadership and Governance

• • •

Wholonomy Consulting

PO Box 42035, Tucson, AZ 85733

www.wholonomyconsulting.com

Mission/Focus Area: Consultants and coaches who are passionate about increasing impact through the use of strengths-based approaches to change, evaluation, and sustainability

Competencies: Human Resources Management and Volunteerism; Planning and Evaluation

Arkansas

Arkansas Community Foundation

1400 W. Markham, Suite 206, Little Rock, AR 72201

www.arcf.org

Mission/Focus Area: Arkansas Community Foundation engages people, connects resources, and inspires solutions to build community.

Competencies: Grantmaking

• • •

Arkansas Nonprofit Alliance

200 River Market Avenue, Suite 100, Little Rock, AR 72201

www.arkansasnonprofits.org

Mission/Focus Area: To provide resources, advocacy, and networking opportunities to strengthen nonprofits.

Competencies: Advocacy and Public Policy; Financial Management and Social Entrepreneurship; Fundraising and Resource Development; Human Resources Management and Volunteerism; Information Management; Leadership and Governance; Legal and Regulatory; Planning and Evaluation

California

Alliance of Nonprofits for Insurance

333 Front Street, Suite 200, Santa Cruz, CA 95060

www.ani-rrg.org

Mission/Focus: The Alliance of Nonprofits for Insurance, Risk Retention Group (ANI) is a 501(c)(3) tax-exempt nonprofit insurance company whose mission is to be a stable source of reasonably priced liability insurance for the specialized needs of 501(c)(3) nonprofits and to assist these organizations to develop and implement effective loss control and risk management programs.

Competencies: Legal and Regulatory; Human Resources Management and Volunteerism.

• • •

Aspiration

PO Box 880264,San Francisco, CA 94188-0264

http://aspirationtech.org

Mission/Focus Area: Aspiration's mission is to connect nonprofit organizations, foundations, and activists with software solutions and technology skills that help them better carry out their missions.

Competencies: Information Management

• • •

Asian Americans/Pacific Islanders in Philanthropy

211 Sutter Street, Suite 600, San Francisco CA 94108

www.aapip.org

Mission/Focus Area: Philanthropic advocacy; advancing philanthropy and Asian American/Pacific Islander (AAPI) communities

Competencies: Grantmaking; Leadership and Governance

• • •

California Association of Nonprofits

400 Montgomery St., Suite 500, San Francisco, CA 94104

http://calnonprofits.org

Mission/Focus Area: Brings nonprofits together to advocate for the communities we serve

Competencies: Advocacy and Public Policy

• • •

Center for Social Innovation

655 Knight Way, Stanford, CA 94305-7298

www.gsb.stanford.edu

Mission/Focus Area: SSIR is written for and by social change leaders in the nonprofit, business, and government sectors who view collaboration as key to solving environmental, social, and economic justice issues.

Competencies: Advocacy and Public Policy; Financial Management and Social Entrepreneurship

• • •

Center on Philanthropy and Civil Society (Stanford PACS)

559 Nathan Abbott Way, Stanford, CA 94305

http://pacscenter.stanford.edu

Mission/Focus Area: The Stanford Center on Philanthropy and Civil Society develops and shares knowledge to improve philanthropy, strengthen civil society, and effect social change. Stanford PACS connects students, scholars, and practitioners and publishes the preeminent journal *Stanford Social Innovation Review (SSIR)*.

• • •

Center on Philanthropy and Public Policy (University of Southern California)

University of Southern California, Lewis Hall 210, Los Angeles, CA 90089-0626

http://cppp.usc.edu

Mission/Focus Area: To foster a better understanding of philanthropy and the nonprofit sector—current roles, emerging trends, and future possibilities— to help philanthropic organizations and individuals develop more strategic philanthropy with a particular focus on public problem solving across sectors, and to encourage philanthropic stewardship and public accountability

Competencies: Advocacy and Public Policy; Grantmaking

• • •

Civic Ventures

PO Box 29542, Presidio of San Francisco, San Francisco, CA 94129

www.encore.org

Mission/Focus Area: Transitioning to jobs in the nonprofit world and the public sector

Competencies: Human Resources Management and Volunteerism

• • •

CompassPoint Nonprofit Services

500 12th Street, Suite 320, Oakland, CA 94607

www.compasspoint.org

Mission/Focus Area: Supporting the people of community nonprofits and the movements for social change that they both lead and build

Competencies: Advocacy and Public Policy; Communications Marketing and Public Relations; Financial Management and Social

Entrepreneurship; Fundraising and Resource Development; Human Resources Management and Volunteerism; Information Management; Leadership and Governance; Legal and Regulatory; Planning and Evaluation

• • •

Drucker Institute

1021 N. Dartmouth Avenue, Claremont, CA 91711

www.druckerinstitute.com

Mission/Focus Area: Development of management skills

Competencies: Leadership and Governance

• • •

Grantmakers Concerned with Immigrants and Refugees

PO Box 1100, Sebastopol, CA 95473-1100

www.gcir.org/www.gcir.org/

Mission/Focus Area: GCIR works with a growing network of member foundations, as well as the greater philanthropic community, on a wide range of immigration and immigrant integration issues, including education, health, employment, civic participation, racial and economic justice, and other concerns affecting immigrant children, youth, and families.

Competencies: Advocacy and Public Policy; Grantmaking

• • •

Grassroots Institute for Fundraising Training

1904 Franklin Street, Suite 705, Oakland, CA 94612

www.grassrootsfundraising.org

Mission/Focus Area: Promoting the connection between fundraising, social justice, and movement building

Competencies: Fundraising and Resource Development; Leadership and Governance

• • •

Human Interaction Research Institute

5435 Balboa Boulevard, Suite 115, Encino, CA 91316

www.humaninteract.org

Mission/Focus Area: Nonprofit capacity building, community collaborations and philanthropy, dissemination and utilization of innovations, health communication, health and human services, arts and culture

Competencies: Grantmaking; Planning and Evaluation

• • •

Institute for Nonprofit Education and Research (University of San Diego)

5998 Alcala Park, San Diego, CA 92110-2492

www.sandiego.edu/soles/centers-and-research/nonprofit/

Mission/Focus Area: The Institute for Nonprofit Education and Research educates leaders and advances best practices in the nonprofit and philanthropic community through academic excellence, applied learning, and research that examines issues of strategic importance to the sector.

Competencies: Information Management

• • •

Master of Nonprofit Administration (University of San Francisco)

2130 Fulton Street, San Francisco, CA 94117-1080

www.usfca.edu/management/mna/

Mission/Focus Area: The MNA program includes a variety of course activities and discussions with contemporary scholars and current leaders in California's nonprofit sector so that you may broaden your leadership and critical thinking skills.

Competencies: Information Management

• • •

Northern California Grantmakers

160 Spear Street, Suite 360, San Francisco, CA 94105-1543

www.ncg.org/s_ncg/index.asp

Mission/Focus Area: Enhancing the effectiveness of philanthropy, and strengthening the ties between philanthropy and its many stakeholders in nonprofit organizations, government, business, media, academia, and the public at large

Competencies: Grantmaking; Planning and Evaluation

• • •

International Funders for Indigenous Peoples

PO Box 29184, San Francisco, CA 94129-0184

www.internationalfunders.org

Mission/Focus Area: We work to increase philanthropic investment in Indigenous communities around the world, promoting cross-cultural understanding, sharing of knowledge, and the cultivation of relationships among international donors and Indigenous grant-seekers.

Competencies: Grantmaking; Leadership and Governance

• • •

Leadership Learning Community

1203 Preservation Park Way, Oakland, CA 94612

www.leadershiplearning.org

Mission/Focus Area: We combine our expertise in identifying, evaluating and applying cutting-edge ideas and promising practices in the leadership development field, with access to our engaged national network of hundreds of experienced funders, consultants, and leadership development programs, to drive the innovation and collaboration needed to make leadership more effective.

Competencies: Leadership and Governance

• • •

MBA Nonprofit Connection (MNC)

PO Box 640, Palo Alto, CA 94302

www.mnconnection.org

Mission/Focus Area: Bringing MBA skills and energy to the nonprofit sector while bringing exciting new job opportunities to the business school student/alumni community

Competencies: Human Resources Management and Volunteerism; Leadership and Governance

• • •

Neighborhood Funders Group

436 14th Street, Suite 425, Oakland, CA 94612

www.nfg.org

Mission/Focus Area: To build the capacity of philanthropy to advance social justice and community change

Competencies: Advocacy and Public Policy; Grantmaking

• • •

Net Impact

150 Spear Street, Suite 500, San Francisco, CA 9410

https://netimpact.org

Mission/Focus Area: Empowering individuals to create social and environmental change

Competencies: Advocacy and Public Policy

• • •

Rockwood Leadership Program

426 17th Street, Fourth Floor, Oakland, CA 94612

www.rockwoodleadership.org

Mission/Focus Area: Provides individuals, organizations, and networks in the social benefit sector with powerful and effective training in leadership and collaboration

Competencies: Leadership and Governance

• • •

San Diego Grantmakers

5060 Shoreham Place, Suite 350, San Diego, CA 92122

www.sdgrantmakers.org

Mission/Focus Area: SDG is a leading convener and resource for organized philanthropy in the San Diego region.

Competencies: Grantmaking; Leadership and Governance

• • •

Southern California Grantmakers

1000 N. Alameda Street, Suite 230, Los Angeles, CA 90012

www.socalgrantmakers.org

Mission/Focus Area: We are a leadership hub for our members to connect with each other, improve their grantmaking, and amplify their independent efforts through collaborative work

Competencies: Grantmaking; Leadership and Governance

• • •

Spin Academy

354 Pine Street, Suite 700, San Francisco, CA 94104

http://spinacademy.org

Mission/Focus: The Spin Academy strengthens nonprofit organizations working for public policy by teaching them to communicate effectively for themselves.

Competencies: Communications, Marketing, and Public Relations

• • •

Tech Soup

435 Brannan Street, Suite 100, San Francisco, CA 94107

www.techsoup.org

Mission/Focus Area: TechSoup is a 501(c)(3) nonprofit with a clear focus: connecting your nonprofit, charity, or public library with tech products and services, plus learning resources to make informed decisions about technology.

Competencies: Information Management; Planning and Evaluation

• • •

Volunteer Match (Impact Online)

550 Montgomery Street, 8th Floor, San Francisco, CA 94111

www.impactonline.org

Mission/Focus Area: Connects volunteers to volunteer opportunities

Competencies: Human Resources Management and Volunteerism

• • •

Women's Funding Network

505 Sansome Street, 2nd Floor, San Francisco, CA 94111

www.womensfundingnetwork.org

Mission/Focus Area: Women's Funding Network is the largest philanthropic network in the world devoted to women and girls.

Competencies: Advocacy and Public Policy

Colorado

Colorado Association of Funders

600 S Cherry Street, Suite 1200, Denver, CO 80246

http://coloradofunders.org

Mission/Focus Area: The Colorado Association of Funders offers networking opportunities, educational programs, peer groups, and tools to ensure members stay informed about critical, timely issues and innovations in grantmaking.

Competencies: Grantmaking, Information Management

• • •

Colorado Nonprofit Association

789 Sherman Street, Suite 240, Denver, CO 80203

www.coloradononprofits.org

Mission/Focus Area: Colorado Nonprofit Association leads, serves, and strengthens Colorado's nonprofit community to improve the quality of life throughout our state.

Competencies: Advocacy and Public Policy; Financial Management and Social Entrepreneurship; Fundraising and Resource Development; Human Resources Management and Volunteerism; Information Management; Leadership and Governance; Legal and Regulatory; Planning and Evaluation

• • •

The Inclusiveness Project

55 Madison Street, 8th Floor, Denver, CO 80206

www.nonprofitinclusiveness.org

Mission/Focus Area: The mission of the Inclusiveness Project is to engage with Metro Denver nonprofit organizations, including funders, to become more inclusive of people of color.

Competencies: Advocacy and Public Policy; Human Resources Management and Volunteerism

Connecticut

Connecticut Association of Nonprofits

75 Charter Oak Avenue, Suite 1–100, Hartford, CT 06106-1903

www.ctnonprofits.org

Mission/Focus Area: By connecting organizations with information, education, advocacy, and collaboration, we help members focus their energy on the people and communities they serve.

Competencies: Advocacy and Public Policy; Financial Management and Social Entrepreneurship; Fundraising and Resource Development; Human Resources Management and Volunteerism; Information Management; Leadership and Governance; Legal and Regulatory; Planning and Evaluation

• • •

Connecticut Council for Philanthropy

221 Main Street, Hartford, CT 06106

www.ctphilanthropy.org

Mission/Focus Area: The Connecticut Council for Philanthropy is an association of grantmakers committed to promoting and supporting effective philanthropy for the public good.

Competencies: Grantmaking

• • •

Commonfund

15 Old Danbury Road, Wilton, CT 06897

www.commonfund.org

Mission/Focus Area: To deliver solutions for strategic investors within both the nonprofit and pension investment communities, to enhance the financial resources of clients, and to improve the investment management practices of clients

Competencies: Financial Management and Social Entrepreneurship

Delaware

Center for Community Research and Service (CCRS) (University of Delaware)

297 Graham Hall, Newark, DE 19716

www.ccrs.udel.edu

Mission/Focus Area: The mission of the Center for Community Research and Service is to provide usable knowledge, education, training, and services that increase the ability of government, nonprofit agencies, philanthropic organizations, and citizens to enhance the quality of their communities.

Competencies: Leadership and Governance

• • •

Delaware Alliance for Nonprofit Advancement

www.delawarenonprofit.org

Mission/Focus Area: The mission of the Delaware Alliance for Nonprofit Advancement, a leader of the nonprofit sector, is to strengthen, enhance, and advance nonprofits and the sector in Delaware through advocacy, training, capacity building, and research.

Competencies: Advocacy and Public Policy; Financial Management and Social Entrepreneurship; Fundraising and Resource Development; Human Resources Management and Volunteerism; Information Management; Leadership and Governance; Legal and Regulatory; Planning and Evaluation

• • •

Delaware Grantmakers Association

100 W. 10th Street, Wilmington, DE 19801

www.delawaregrantmakers.org

Mission/Focus Area: The Delaware Grantmakers Association exists to provide information, education, networking, and collaboration opportunities to individuals, corporations, and foundations who make significant charitable contributions in Delaware, and to strengthen philanthropy through public information and advocacy.

Competencies: Advocacy and Public Policy; Grantmaking

Florida

Florida Association of Nonprofit Organizations

7480 Fairway Drive, Suite 205, Miami Lakes, FL 33014

www.fano.org

Mission/Focus Area: FANO is a statewide center and professional network of 501 (c)(3) nonprofit organizations in Florida. It was founded by nonprofit leaders in 1989 to enhance the well-being of all people in the communities in Florida by building the capacity of the nonprofit sector. FANO assists 52,000 nonprofits to reach their mission by strengthening their leadership, management, financial, and public policy capacity.

Competencies: Advocacy and Public Policy; Financial Management and Social Entrepreneurship; Fundraising and Resource Development; Human Resources Management and Volunteerism; Information Management; Leadership and Governance; Legal and Regulatory; Planning and Evaluation

• • •

Florida Philanthropic Network

1211 N. Westshore Boulevard, Suite 314, Tampa, FL 33607

www.fpnetwork.org

Mission/Focus Area: The vision of Florida Philanthropic Network is for Florida to be successful in modeling and facilitating cooperation and collaboration among all sectors—business, government, and nonprofit—to promote the best interest of all Floridians.

Competencies: Advocacy and Public Policy; Grantmaking

• • •

Funders' Network for Smart Growth and Livable Communities

1500 San Remo Avenue, Suite 249, Coral Gables, FL 33146

www.fundersnetwork.org

Mission/Focus Area: Our mission is to inspire, strengthen, and expand funding and philanthropic leadership that yield environmentally sustainable, socially equitable, and economically prosperous regions and communities.

Competencies: Advocacy and Public Policy, Grantmaking

• • •

Nonprofit Leadership Center of Tampa Bay

1401 N. Westshore Boulevard, Tampa, FL 33607

www.nonprofitleadershipcenter.com

Mission/Focus Area: Educates and connects local nonprofits to strengthen their missions

Competencies: Advocacy and Public Policy; Financial Management and Social Entrepreneurship; Fundraising and Resource Development; Human Resources Management and Volunteerism; Information Management; Leadership and Governance; Legal and Regulatory; Planning and Evaluation

Georgia

Institute for Public and Nonprofit Studies

PO Box 8048, Statesboro, GA 30460-8048

http://class.georgiasouthern.edu/ipns/

Mission/Focus Area: The Institute for Public and Nonprofit Studies (IPNS) serves as the focal point for scholarship, teaching, and professional service in the fields of public administration and public policy at Georgia Southern University, throughout southeast Georgia, and beyond.

Competencies: Advocacy and Public Policy; Financial Management and Social Entrepreneurship; Fundraising and Resource Development; Human Resources Management and Volunteerism; Information Management; Leadership and Governance; Legal and Regulatory; Planning and Evaluation

• • •

Nonprofit and Civic Engagement Center

4225 University Avenue, Columbus, GA 31907

http://npace.columbusstate.edu

Mission/Focus Area: The Nonprofit and Civic Engagement (NPACE) Center is the Department of Communication's bridge to nonprofit organizations in Columbus and the Chattahoochee Valley. Through the center, we bring nonprofit organizations together with our experienced faculty to discuss the needs of each organization and what support and resources the Department of Communication can provide through its service-learning courses.

Competencies: Communications, Marketing, and Public Relations.

• • •

Opportunity Knocks (Georgia Center for Nonprofits)

100 Peachtree Street, Suite 1500, Atlanta, GA 30303

www.gcn.org

Mission/Focus Area: The mission of the Georgia Center for Nonprofits is to build thriving communities by helping nonprofits succeed.

Competencies: Human Resources Management and Volunteerism

• • •

Points of Light Institute (Hands on Network)

600 Means Street, Suite 210, Atlanta, GA 30318

www.pointsoflight.org

Mission/Focus Area: We inspire, equip, and mobilize people to take action that changes the world.

Competencies: Human Resources Management and Volunteerism

• • •

Southeastern Council on Foundations

50 Hurt Plaza, Suite 350, Atlanta, GA 30303

www.secf.org

Mission/Focus Area: Access to education, resources, and networking by serving as a convener and facilitator, offering a diverse range of voices and perspectives

Competencies: Grantmaking; Leadership and Governance

Hawaii

Hawaii Alliance of Nonprofit Organizations

1020 S. Beretania Street, Second Floor, Honolulu, Hawaii 96814

http://hano-hawaii.org/newhano/

Mission/Focus Area: The Hawaii Alliance of Nonprofit Organizations unites and strengthens the nonprofit sector as a collective force to improve the quality of life in Hawaii.

Competencies: Advocacy and Public Policy; Financial Management and Social Entrepreneurship; Fundraising and Resource Development; Human Resources Management and Volunteerism; Information Management; Leadership and Governance; Legal and Regulatory; Planning and Evaluation

Idaho

Idaho Community Foundation

210 W. State Street, Boise, ID 83702

www.idcomfdn.org

Mission/Focus Area: Since 1988, ICF has been in Idaho working with generous people who want to give to trusted, deserving organizations.

Competencies: Grantmaking

• • •

Idaho Nonprofit Center

5440 W. Franklin Road, Suite 202, Boise, ID 83705

www.idahononprofits.org

Mission/Focus Area: We act as a vehicle of information, a convener of leaders and allies, and a bridge between the nonprofit, public, and private sectors.

Competencies: Leadership and Governance

Illinois

American Institute of Philanthropy

3450 N. Lake Shore Drive, Chicago, IL 60657

www.charitywatch.org

Mission/Focus Area: Serves as a review and regulation service for nonprofit organizations

Competencies: Legal and Regulatory

• • •

Axelson Center for Nonprofit Management

3225 Foster Avenue, Chicago, IL 60625-4895

www.northpark.edu/axelson

Mission/Focus Area: The mission of the Axelson Center for Nonprofit Management at North Park University is to enhance performance and effectiveness of organizations and individuals in the nonprofit sector through education, service, and resources.

Competencies: Advocacy and Public Policy; Financial Management and Social Entrepreneurship; Fundraising and Resource Development; Human Resources Management and Volunteerism; Information Management; Leadership and Governance; Legal and Regulatory; Planning and Evaluation

• • •

Donors Forum

www.donorsforum.org

Mission/Focus Area: Networking and education, information and knowledge, and leadership and advocacy

Competencies: Advocacy and Public Policy; Grantmaking; Information Management; Leadership and Governance

• • •

IFF

One North LaSalle Street, Suite 700, Chicago, IL 60602

www.iff.org

Mission/Focus Area: One of America's leading nonprofit community development financial institutions, IFF strengthens nonprofits and their communities through lending and real estate consulting.

Competencies: Advocacy and Public Policy; Financial Management and Social Entrepreneurship

• • •

International Association of Advisors in Philanthropy

216 W. Jackson Blvd., Suite 625, Chicago, Illinois, 60606

www.advisorsinphilanthropy.org

Mission/Focus Area: AiP is a network of diverse professional advisors who are devoted to mastering and promoting the principles and practices of client-centered planning.

Competencies: Financial Management and Social Entrepreneurship

• • •

Lumity

55 W. Van Buren Street, Suite 420, Chicago, IL 60605

www.lumity.org

Mission/Focus Area: Lumity mobilizes the corporate and nonprofit community to make Chicagoland a better place to work and live by providing access to real-world readiness and connecting nonprofits to vital resources.

Competencies: Human Resources Management and Volunteerism

• • •

School of Public Service (DePaul University)

990 W. Fullerton Ave, Suite 4200, Chicago, IL 60614

las.depaul.edu/departments/school-of-public-service/pages/default.aspx

Mission/Focus Area: Effective leadership in all three sectors has never been more important. Our advanced professional degrees combine management training with practical skills to develop the next generation of leaders in nonprofit and government sectors.

Competencies: Advocacy and Public Policy; Financial Management and Social Entrepreneurship; Fundraising and Resource Development; Human Resources Management and Volunteerism; Information Management; Leadership and Governance; Legal and Regulatory; Planning and Evaluation

• • •

The Communications Network

1717 N. Naper Boulevard, Suite 102, Naperville, IL 60563

www.comnetwork.org

Mission/Focus Area: The Communications Network supports foundations and nonprofits to improve lives through the power of smart communications.

Competencies: Communications

Indiana

Association for Research on Nonprofit Organizations and Voluntary Action (ARNOVA)

www.arnova.org

Mission/Focus Area: National and international association that connects scholars, teachers, and practice leaders interested in research on nonprofit organizations, voluntary action, philanthropy, and civil society

Competencies: Information Management

• • •

Indiana Nonprofit Resource Network

3901 N. Meridian Street, Suite 306, Indianapolis, IN 46208-4026

www.inrn.org

Mission/Focus Area: The original vision endures, to take services anywhere in the state upon request. The commitment to serve organizations most in need is vital to INRN's role throughout the state.

Competencies: Advocacy and Public Policy

• • •

Indiana Philanthropy Alliance

32 E. Washington Street, Suite 1100, Indianapolis, IN 46204

www.inphilanthropy.org

Mission/Focus Area: Our mission is to champion, support, and connect our members as they transform Indiana through effective philanthropy.

Competencies: Advocacy and Public Policy

• • •

Lilly Family School of Philanthropy

550 W. North Street, Suite 301, Indianapolis, IN 46202

www.philanthropy.iupui.edu

Mission/Focus Area: The Indiana University Lilly Family School of Philanthropy is a leading academic institution dedicated to increasing the understanding of philanthropy and improving its practice worldwide through research, teaching, training, and civic engagement.

Competencies: Information Management

• • •

Master of Nonprofit Administration

University of Notre Dame, Notre Dame, Indiana 46556-5646

http://business.nd.edu/mna/

Mission/Focus Area: Mendoza College is the only top business school to offer a graduate business degree designed to advance business leadership and managerial skills while keeping nonprofit leaders in their jobs.

Competencies: Advocacy and Public Policy; Communications, Marketing, and Public Relations; Financial Management and Social Entrepreneurship; Fundraising and Resource Development; Grantmaking; Human Resources Management and Volunteerism; Information Management; Leadership and Governance; Legal and Regulatory; Planning and Evaluation

• • •

The Fundraising School (Indiana University-Purdue University Indianapolis)

550 W. North Street, Suite 301, Indianapolis, IN 46202

www.philanthropy.iupui.edu/the-fund-raising-school

Mission/Focus Area: The Fundraising School plays an integral part in the School of Philanthropy and its mission by helping thousands of fundraising professionals around the world every year to improve their fundraising.

Competencies: Fundraising and Resource Development

Iowa

Iowa Council of Foundations

PO Box 13229, Des Moines, IA 50310

www.iowacounciloffoundations.org/philanthropy.aspx

Mission/Focus Area: The Iowa Council of Foundations is the place where grantmakers come together to access information, build skills, and develop relationships to enhance philanthropy in Iowa.

Competencies: Grantmaking

• • •

Nonprofit Association of the Midlands

11205 Wright Circle, Suite 210, Omaha, NE 68144

www.nonprofitam.org

Mission/Focus Area: We strengthen the collective voice, leadership, and capacity of nonprofit organizations to enrich the quality of community life throughout Nebraska and western Iowa.

Competencies: Advocacy and Public Policy

Kansas

Kansas Association of Community Foundations

PO BOX 298, Hutchinson, KS 67504-0298

www.kansascfs.org

Mission/Focus Area: The mission of the Kansas Association of Community Foundations is to leverage the resources of community foundations in the state of Kansas so as to strengthen and promote community philanthropy and inspire action that will improve the quality of life in Kansas communities.

Competencies: Grantmaking

Kentucky

Southeastern Council of Foundations

50 Hurt Plaza, Suite 350, Atlanta, GA 30303

www.secf.org/statement-of-intent

Mission/Focus Area: The Southeastern Council of Foundations strives to support members and grantmakers with access to education, resources and networking by serving as a convener and facilitator, offering a diverse range of voices and perspectives.

Competencies: Advocacy and Public Policy; Grantmaking

Louisiana

Institute for Nonprofit Administration and Research (Louisiana State University Shreveport)

One University Place, Shreveport, LA 71115

www.lsus.edu/offices-and-services/community-outreach/institute-for-nonprofit-administration-and-research

Mission/Focus Area: The Institute for Nonprofit Administration and Research was established in 2001 to conduct research and disseminate knowledge about nonprofit organizations and social research.

Competencies: Information Management

• • •

Louisiana Association of Nonprofit Organizations

www.lano.org

447 Third Street, Suite 200, Baton Rouge, LA, 70802

Mission/Focus Area: Advocates for the nonprofit community and strengthens the effectiveness of those committed to improving Louisiana

Competencies: Advocacy and Public Policy; Leadership and Governance

Maine

Idealware

1 Pleasant Street, Suite 4E, Portland, ME 04101

www.idealware.org

Mission/Focus Area: Provides thoroughly researched, impartial, and accessible resources about software to help nonprofits make smart software decisions

Competencies: Information Management

• • •

Maine Association of Nonprofits

565 Congress Street, Suite 301, Portland, ME 04101

www.nonprofitmaine.org

Mission/Focus Area: Strengthen the leadership, voice, and organizational effectiveness of nonprofits

Competencies: Leadership and Governance

• • •

Maine Philanthropy Center

314 Forest Avenue, Portland, ME 04101

www.mainephilanthropy.org

Mission/Focus Area: Founded in 1995, the Maine Philanthropy Center is a regional association of grantmakers—small and large private foundations, community foundations, public foundations, corporate giving programs, family foundations, and philanthropic individuals—who share a commitment to increasing the vitality and visibility of Maine's philanthropy community.

Competencies: Advocacy and Public Policy; Grantmaking

Maryland

The Association of Baltimore Area Grantmakers

2 E. Read Street, 2nd Floor, Baltimore, MD 21202

www.abagrantmakers.org

Mission/Focus Area: ABAG's mission is to maximize the impact of philanthropic giving on community life through a growing network of diverse, informed, and effective grantmakers.

Competencies: Advocacy and Public Policy; Grantmaking

• • •

Grantmakers for Children, Youth, and Families

8757 Georgia Avenue, Suite 540, Silver Spring, MD 20910

www.gcyf.org

Mission/Focus Area: To promote effective grantmaking that integrates research, policy, and practice to bring about systemic change for children, youth, and families

Competencies: Advocacy and Public Policy; Grantmaking

• • •

International Leadership Association

1110 Bonifant Street, Suite 510, Silver Spring, MD 20910

www.ila-net.org

Mission/Focus Area: The ILA promotes a deeper understanding of leadership knowledge and practices for the greater good of individuals and communities worldwide.

Competencies: Leadership and Governance

• • •

International Society for Third-Sector Research (ISTR)

624 N. Broadway Hampton House # 356, Baltimore, MD 21205

www.istr.org

Mission/Focus Area: ISTRs mission is to increase, share, and apply knowledge about the Third Sector in all countries of the world.

Competencies: Advocacy and Public Policy; Financial Management and Social Entrepreneurship; Fundraising and Resource Development; Grantmaking; Human Resources Management and Volunteerism; Information Management; Leadership and Governance; Legal and Regulatory; Planning and Evaluation

• • •

Johns Hopkins Center for Civil Society Studies

Johns Hopkins University, 3400 N. Charles Street, Wyman Building, 5th Floor, Baltimore, MD 21218-2688

http://ccss.jhu.edu

Mission/Focus Area: The Center conducts research and educational programs that seek to improve current understanding, analyze emerging trends, and promote promising innovations in the ways that government, civil society, and business can collaborate to address social and environmental challenges.

Competencies: Advocacy and Public Policy; Financial Management and Social Entrepreneurship; Grantmaking; Human Resources Management and Volunteerism; Leadership and Governance; Legal and Regulatory; Planning and Evaluation

• • •

Johns Hopkins Listening Post Project

Johns Hopkins University, 3400 N. Charles Street, Wyman Building, 5th Floor, Baltimore, MD 21218-2688

Mission/Focus Area: Monitoring in a systematic and timely way what is happening to nonprofit organizations in the United States

Competencies: Legal and Regulatory

• • •

Maryland Association of Nonprofit Organizations (Maryland Nonprofits)

1500 Union Avenue, Suite 2500, Baltimore, MD 21211

www.marylandnonprofits.org

Mission/Focus Area: Strengthening, educating, and engaging nonprofits

Competencies: Advocacy and Public Policy; Leadership and Governance; Legal and Regulatory

• • •

School of Public Policy (University of Maryland)

2101 Van Munching Hall, College Park, MD 20742

www.publicpolicy.umd.edu

Mission/Focus Area: The School of Public Policy offers a diverse array of academic, executive, and research programs for the diverse needs of students, scholars, policy leaders, organizational staff, and citizens.

Competencies: Information Management

• • •

Standards for Excellence Institute (Maryland Association of Nonprofit Organizations)

1500 Union Avenue, Suite 2500, Baltimore, MD 21211

www.standardsforexcellenceinstitute.org

Mission/Focus Area: The Standards for Excellence Institute is a national initiative established to promote the highest standards of ethics, effectiveness, and accountability in nonprofit governance, management, and operations.

Competencies: Leadership and Governance

Massachusetts

Alliance for Nonprofit Management

PO Box 67061, Chestnut Hill, MA 02467

www.allianceonline.org

Mission/Focus Area: Alliance for Nonprofit Management is a catalyst to ignite and accelerate the impact of individuals and organizations, helping nonprofits achieve positive public policy.

Competencies: Financial Management and Social Entrepreneurship; Information Management; Leadership and Governance

Associated Grantmakers

133 Federal Street, Suite 802, Boston, MA 02110

www.agmconnect.org

Mission/Focus Area: AGM's mission is to promote the practice and expansion of effective and responsible philanthropy to improve the health and vitality of its region.

Competencies: Advocacy and Public Policy; Grantmaking

• • •

Center for Effective Philanthropy

675 Massachusetts Avenue, Cambridge, MA 02139

www.effectivephilanthropy.org

Mission/Focus Area: CEP's mission is to provide data and create insight so philanthropic funders can better define, assess, and improve their effectiveness, and, as a result, their intended impact.

Competencies: Advocacy and Public Policy; Grantmaking

• • •

Center on Wealth and Philanthropy

142 Beacon Street, Chestnut Hill, MA 02467

www.bc.edu/research/cwp/

Mission/Focus Area: Advance understanding of philanthropy and increase both the quality and quantity of individual charitable giving

Competencies: Grantmaking

• • •

Commongood Careers

38 Chauncy Street, Suite 1001, Boston, MA

www.commongoodcareers.org

Mission/Focus Area: To provide nonprofits with innovative recruitment solutions that result in faster and better hires

Competencies: Human Resources Management and Volunteerism

• • •

FSG Social Impact Advisors

500 Boylston Street, Suite 600, Boston, MA 02116

www.fsg.org

Mission/Focus Area: FSG is a nonprofit consulting firm specializing in strategy, evaluation, and research.

Competencies: Advocacy and Public Policy; Fundraising; Grantmaking; Planning and Evaluation

• • •

Funders Together to End Homelessness

89 South Street, Suite 803, Boston, MA 02111

www.funderstogether.org

Mission/Focus Area: Harness philanthropy's expanding potential for impact and change to help end homelessness in America.

Competencies: Advocacy and Public Policy

• • •

Massachusetts Council of Human Service Providers

88 Broad Street, Fifth Floor, Boston, MA 02110

http://providers.org

Mission/Focus Area: To promote a healthy, productive, and diverse human services industry

Competencies: Advocacy and Public Policy; Human Resources Management

• • •

Massachusetts Nonprofit Network

89 South Street, Suite 603, Boston, MA 02111

www.massnonprofitnet.org

Mission/Focus Area: The Massachusetts Nonprofit Network (MNN) is the voice of the nonprofit sector and the only statewide organization in the Commonwealth dedicated to uniting and strengthening the entire nonprofit sector through advocacy, public awareness, and capacity building.

Competencies: Advocacy and Public Policy; Financial Management and Social Entrepreneurship; Fundraising and Resource Development; Human Resources Management and Volunteerism; Information Management; Leadership and Governance; Legal and Regulatory; Planning and Evaluation

• • •

MS in Nonprofit Management, Philanthropy, and Strategic Fundraising Programs, School of Management and Social Justice (Bay Path)

588 Longmeadow Street, Longmeadow, MA 01106

http://graduate.baypath.edu/graduate-programs/programs-online/ms-programs/nonprofit-management-and-philanthropy

Mission/Focus Area: The MS in Nonprofit Management and Philanthropy is designed for nonprofit senior professionals or people who want to be the CEO of their organization.

Competencies: Advocacy and Public Policy; Financial Management and Social Entrepreneurship; Fundraising and Resource Development; Grantmaking; Human Resources Management and Volunteerism; Information Management; Leadership and Governance; Legal and Regulatory; Planning and Evaluation

• • •

New Profit

200 Clarendon Street, 9th Floor, Boston, MA 02116

http://newprofit.com

Mission/Focus Area: Improving the lives of children, families, and communities by empowering social innovators

Competencies: Advocacy and Public Policy; Financial Management and Social Entrepreneurship; Grantmaking; Leadership and Governance

• • •

Nonprofit Professionals Advisory Group

75 Summit Street, Newton, MA 02458

www.nonprofitprofessionals.com

Mission/Focus: We work worldwide with mission-driven client organizations in the nonprofit, academic, and public sectors, as well as with the job seekers who serve them. For organizations, we offer executive search and leadership transition services. For candidates, we provide leadership development, job search strategy creation, and resume/cover letter assistance. For both organizations and candidates, we supply professional and organizational development in person through our customized training programs and online with our "NPAG U" webinar series.

Competencies: Human Resources Management and Volunteerism

• • •

Nonprofit Voter Engagement Network

89 South Street, Suite 203, Boston, MA 02111

www.nonprofitvote.org/about/

Mission/Focus Area: Helps nonprofits integrate voter engagement into their practices

Competencies: Advocacy and Public Policy

• • •

The Philanthropic Initiative

420 Boylston Street, Boston, MA 02116

www.tpi.org

Mission/Focus Area: From strategy through implementation to management and evaluation, we provide high-impact philanthropic solutions at the local, national, and global level.

Competencies: Leadership and Governance; Planning and Evaluation

Michigan

Council of Michigan Foundations

One South Harbor Drive, Suite 3, Grand Haven, MI 49417

www.michiganfoundations.org

Mission/Focus Area: To grow the impact of Michigan philanthropy

Competencies: Advocacy and Public Policy

• • •

Johnson Center for Philanthropy and Nonprofit Leadership (Grand Valley State University)

201 Front Avenue SW, Suite 200, Grand Rapids, MI 49504

www.gvsu.edu/jcp/www.gvsu.edu/jcp/

Mission/Focus Area: Increasing the efficiency and effectiveness of the charitable sector; enhancing the impact of foundations nationally and nonprofit organizations regionally; improving the quality of community decision making with community members in West Michigan; and encouraging a habit of civic engagement among students, staff, and faculty at GVSU

Competencies: Financial Management and Social Entrepreneurship; Fundraising and Resource Development; Grantmaking; Human Resources Management and Volunteerism; Leadership and Governance; Planning and Evaluation

• • •

Michigan Nonprofit Association

330 Marshall Street, Suite 200, Lansing, MI 48912

www.mnaonline.org

Mission/Focus Area: Michigan Nonprofit Association serves nonprofits to advance their missions.

Competencies: Advocacy and Public Policy; Information Management; Planning and Evaluation

• • •

School of Public, Nonprofit, and Health Administration (Grand Valley State University)

2nd Floor, DeVos Center Building C, 401 W. Fulton Street, Grand Rapids, MI 49504

www.gvsu.edu/spnha/

Mission/Focus Area: The mission of the graduate programs in public and nonprofit administration is to develop both the general knowledge and specific abilities needed for leadership in a fast changing world. The curriculum is designed to prepare students to act ethically and effectively in public management, urban and regional policy and planning, nonprofit management and leadership, criminal justice, and health care administration, and to transcend traditional boundaries in the pursuit of prosperous, safe, and healthy communities.

Competencies: Advocacy and Public Policy; Communications, Marketing, and Public Relations; Financial Management and Social Entrepreneurship; Fundraising and Resource Development; Grantmaking; Human Resources Management and Volunteerism; Information Management; Leadership and Governance; Legal and Regulatory; Planning and Evaluation

• • •

SCORE

111 Pearl Street NW, Grand Rapids, MI 49503

www.score.org

Mission/Focus Area: SCORE grows successful small businesses across America.

Competencies: Communications, Marketing, and Public Relations; Financial Management and Social Entrepreneurship; Fundraising and Resource Development; Human Resources Management and Volunteerism; Information Management; Leadership and Governance; Legal and Regulatory; Planning and Evaluation

• • •

Society for Nonprofit Organizations

PO Box 510354, Livonia, MI 48151

www.snpo.org

Mission/Focus Area: Provides nonprofit executives, fundraisers, volunteers, board members, consultants, and other professionals with the resources and information needed to work effectively and efficiently toward accomplishing your mission

Competencies: Advocacy and Public Policy; Communications Marketing and Public Relations; Financial Management and Social Entrepreneurship; Fundraising and Resource Development; Grantmaking; Human Resources Management and Volunteerism; Leadership and Governance; Legal and Regulatory; Planning and Evaluation

• • •

The BEST Project

310 E. Third Street, Flint, MI 48502

www.bestprojectonline.org

Mission/Focus Area: To strengthen the nonprofit sector by providing capacity building support and technical assistance

Competencies: Advocacy and Public Policy; Financial Management and Social Entrepreneurship; Fundraising and Resource Development; Human Resources Management and Volunteerism; Information Management; Leadership and Governance; Legal and Regulatory; Planning and Evaluation

Minnesota

Center for Nonprofit Management (University of St. Thomas)

1000 LaSalle Avenue, Minneapolis, MN 55403

www.stthomas.edu/business/centers/nonprofit/

Mission/Focus Area: We are committed to educating students and practitioners to lead differently to meet the demands of today's rapidly changing nonprofit and social business environment.

Competencies: Advocacy and Public Policy; Financial Management and Social Entrepreneurship; Fundraising and Resource Development; Human Resources Management and Volunteerism; Information Management; Leadership and Governance; Legal and Regulatory; Planning and Evaluation

• • •

Minnesota Council on Foundations

100 Portland Avenue S, Suite 225, Minneapolis, MN 55401-2575

www.mcf.org

Mission/Focus Area: Minnesota Council on Foundations (MCF) works actively to expand and strengthen a vibrant community of diverse grantmakers who individually and collectively advance the common good.

Competencies: Advocacy and Public Policy; Grantmaking; Leadership and Governance

• • •

Minnesota Council of Nonprofits

2314 University Avenue W, Suite 20, St. Paul, MN 55114

www.minnesotanonprofits.org

Mission/Focus Area: To meet the increasing information needs of nonprofits and to convene nonprofits to address issues facing the sector

Competencies: Advocacy and Public Policy; Financial Management and Social Entrepreneurship; Fundraising and Resource Development;

Human Resources Management and Volunteerism; Information Management; Leadership and Governance; Legal and Regulatory; Planning and Evaluation

• • •

Native Americans in Philanthropy

2801 21st Street S, Suite 132D, Minneapolis, MN 55407

www.nativephilanthropy.org

Mission/Focus Area: Provides philanthropic opportunities for its members

Competencies: Advocacy and Public Policy; Grantmaking; Leadership and Governance

• • •

Nonprofits Assistance Fund

2801 21st Avenue S, Suite 210, Minneapolis, MN 55407

nonprofitsassistancefund.org

Mission/Focus: Nonprofits Assistance Fund invests capital and financial expertise in nonprofits through loans, training, practical guidance, and financial management resources.

Competencies: Financial Management and Social Entrepreneurship

• • •

Public and Nonprofit Leadership Center (University of Minnesota)

301 19th Avenue S, Minneapolis, MN 55455

www.hhh.umn.edu

Mission/Focus Area: Creates and nurtures excellence in public affairs management and leadership through research, teaching, and outreach.

Competencies: Advocacy and Public Policy; Financial Management and Social Entrepreneurship; Fundraising and Resource Development; Human Resources Management and Volunteerism; Information Management; Leadership and Governance; Legal and Regulatory; Planning and Evaluation

• • •

Social Enterprise Alliance

4737 County Road 101, Suite 311, Minnetonka, MN 55345

www.se-alliance.org/www.se-alliance.org/

Mission/Focus Area: Provides social enterprises with the tools and resources they need to succeed and work on building an optimal environment in which they can thrive

Competencies: Financial Management and Social Entrepreneurship; Leadership and Governance; Planning and Evaluation

Mississippi

Mississippi Center for Nonprofits

201 W. Capitol Street, Suite 700, Jackson, MS 39201

www.msnonprofits.org

Mission/Focus Area: Strengthen the capacity of nonprofits to serve the people and communities of Mississippi

Competencies: Advocacy and Public Policy; Financial Management and Social Entrepreneurship; Fundraising and Resource Development; Human Resources Management and Volunteerism; Information Management; Leadership and Governance; Legal and Regulatory; Planning and Evaluation

Missouri

CFLeads: Community Foundations Leading Change

1055 Broadway, Suite 130, Kansas City, MO, 64105

www.cfleads.org

Mission/Focus Area: CFLeads helps community foundations advance the practice of community leadership to build thriving communities.

Competencies: Grantmaking; Leadership and Governance

• • •

Midwest Center for Nonprofit Leadership (University of Missouri-Kansas City)

4747 Troost Avenue, Suite 207, Kansas City, MO 64110

http://bloch.umkc.edu

Mission/Focus Area: Our mission is to develop purposeful, entrepreneurial, and innovative leaders to meet changing global demands, and advance knowledge and practice through excellent teaching, scholarship, outreach, and service.

Competencies: Advocacy and Public Policy; Leadership and Governance; Financial Management and Social Entrepreneurship; Fundraising and Resource Development; Legal and Regulatory

• • •

Nonprofit Administration (Lindenwood University)

209 S Kingshighway, St. Charles, MO 63301

www.lindenwood.edu/humanServices/npa/index.html

Mission/Focus Area: The Nonprofit Administration Program (NPA) can lead to a meaningful career of helping others by leading and serving others. Students are educated to be nonprofit leaders and managers through service learning—learning by doing.

Competencies: Advocacy and Public Policy; Financial Management and Social Entrepreneurship; Fundraising and Resource Development; Human Resources Management and Volunteerism; Information Management; Leadership and Governance; Legal and Regulatory; Planning and Evaluation

• • •

Nonprofit Leadership Alliance

1100 Walnut, Suite 1900, Kansas City, MO 64106

www.nonprofitleadershipalliance.org

Mission/Focus Area: Strengthens the nonprofit sector by partnering with students to help qualified young people enter the nonprofit field

Competencies: Advocacy and Public Policy; Financial Management and Social Entrepreneurship; Fundraising and Resource Development; Human Resources Management and Volunteerism; Information Management; Leadership and Governance; Legal and Regulatory; Planning and Evaluation

• • •

Nonprofit Leadership Studies (Rockhurst University)

www.rockhurst.edu/academics/undergraduate/majors/nonprofit-leadership/overview/

1100 Rockhurst Road, Kansas City, MO 64110

Mission/Focus Area: Rockhurst University's Nonprofit Leadership Studies program prepares students for successful careers and leadership roles with nonprofit organizations.

Competencies: Advocacy and Public Policy; Financial Management and Social Entrepreneurship; Fundraising and Resource Development; Human Resources Management and Volunteerism; Information Management; Leadership and Governance; Legal and Regulatory; Planning and Evaluation

• • •

Nonprofit Management and Leadership Program (University of Missouri–St. Louis)

406 Tower One, University Boulevard, St. Louis, MO 63121-4400

www.umsl.edu/divisions/graduate/ppa/npml/index.html

Mission/Focus Area: NPML's mission is to foster the growth and effectiveness of nonprofit professionals and of those aspiring to such work.

Competencies: Advocacy and Public Policy; Financial Management and Social Entrepreneurship; Fundraising and Resource Development; Human Resources Management and Volunteerism; Information Management; Leadership and Governance; Legal and Regulatory; Planning and Evaluation

• • •

Nonprofit Missouri

PO Box 704, Jefferson City, MO 65102

www.nonprofitmissouri.org

Mission/Focus Area: Nonprofit Missouri (NPMO) is the collective voice to unite, strengthen, and advance the nonprofit sector in Missouri. Created by and for nonprofits, it is Missouri's first organization to promote the common interests of the state's more than 15,000 nonprofits.

Competencies: Advocacy and Public Policy; Financial Management and Social Entrepreneurship; Fundraising and Resource Development; Human Resources Management and Volunteerism; Information Management; Leadership and Governance; Legal and Regulatory; Planning and Evaluation

Montana

Montana Nonprofit Association

7 W. 6th Avenue, Suite G West, PO Box 1744, Helena, MT 59624

www.mtnonprofit.org

Mission/Focus Area: Strengthen the capacity of nonprofits to serve the people and communities of Montana

Competencies: Advocacy and Public Policy; Financial Management and Social Entrepreneurship; Fundraising and Resource Development; Human Resources Management and Volunteerism; Information Management; Leadership and Governance; Legal and Regulatory; Planning and Evaluation

• • •

The Montana Community Foundation

1 N. Last Chance Gulch, Suite 1 Helena, MT 59601

www.mtcf.org/index.html

Mission/Focus Area: The Montana Community Foundation is all about Montana's future. Our mission is to cultivate a culture of giving so Montana communities can flourish.

Competencies: Advocacy and Public Policy; Grantmaking

Nebraska

Nebraska Community Foundation

3833 S 14th Street, Lincoln, NE 68501

www.nebcommfound.org

Mission/Focus Area: The Nebraska Community Foundation uses the tools of philanthropy, community development, and economic development to help communities help themselves.

Competencies: Advocacy and Public Policy; Grantmaking

• • •

Nonprofit Association of the Midlands

11205 Wright Circle, Suite 210, Omaha, NE 68144

www.nonprofitam.org

Mission/Focus Area: We strengthen the collective voice, leadership, and capacity of nonprofit organizations to enrich the quality of community life throughout Nebraska and western Iowa.

Competencies: Advocacy and Public Policy; Financial Management and Social Entrepreneurship; Fundraising and Resource Development; Human Resources Management and Volunteerism; Information Management; Leadership and Governance; Legal and Regulatory; Planning and Evaluation

Nevada

Alliance for Nevada Nonprofits

639 Isbell Court, Suite 460, Reno, NV 89509

http://alliancefornevadanonprofits.com

Mission/Focus Area: Strengthening communities by increasing influence and capacity of Nevada's nonprofit sector

Competencies: Advocacy and Public Policy; Financial Management and Social Entrepreneurship; Fundraising and Resource Development; Human Resources Management and Volunteerism; Information Management; Leadership and Governance; Legal and Regulatory; Planning and Evaluation

• • •

Nevada Community Foundation

1635 Village Center Circle, Suite 160, Las Vegas, NV 89134

www.nevadacf.org

Mission/Focus Area: The Nevada Community Foundation was incorporated in 1988 with its first endowment, established through a significant contribution from Moe Dalitz to support human service needs. Since that time, NCF has helped hundreds of donors find their charitable passion, fulfill their philanthropic dreams, and make a lasting impact in our community.

Competencies: Advocacy and Public Policy; Grantmaking

New Hampshire

New Hampshire Center for Nonprofits

84 Silk Farm Road, Suite 1, Concord, NH 03301

www.nhnonprofits.org

Mission/Focus Area: The New Hampshire Center for Nonprofits strengthens and gives voice to the state's nonprofit sector through leadership, collaboration, and learning opportunities.

Competencies: Advocacy and Public Policy; Financial Management and Social Entrepreneurship; Fundraising and Resource Development; Human Resources Management and Volunteerism; Information Management; Leadership and Governance; Legal and Regulatory; Planning and Evaluation

• • •

New Hampshire Charitable Foundation

37 Pleasant Street, Concord, NH 03301

www.nhcf.org/page.aspx?pid=387

Mission/Focus Area: We reach deep into every community through a network of regional advisory boards and staff who live and work locally. Both the breadth of vision and deep local knowledge can help you focus your giving where it will have the greatest impact.

Competencies: Advocacy and Public Policy; Grantmaking

• • •

Planned Giving Council of NH and VT

PO Box 974, Hanover, NH 03755

www.leavealegacynhvt.org

Mission/Focus Area: Promotes the personal and community benefits of charitable giving by supporting planned giving professionals

Competencies: Fundraising and Resource Development

New Jersey

Center for Nonprofit Corporations

3575 Quakerbridge Road, Suite 102, Mercerville, NJ 08619

www.njnonprofits.org

Mission/Focus Area: Provides advocacy, resources, training and information to strengthen nonprofits and help them thrive.

Competencies: Advocacy and Public Policy; Financial Management and Social Entrepreneurship; Fundraising and Resource Development;

Human Resources Management and Volunteerism; Information Management; Leadership and Governance; Legal and Regulatory; Planning and Evaluation

• • •

Center for Public Service

400 South Orange Avenue, South Orange, NJ 07079

www.shu.edu/academics/artsci/public-service/

Mission/Focus Area: Since its founding almost 20 years ago the Center for Public Service has brought over $5 million to Seton Hall University in grants, contracts, and scholarships for students in the Department of Political Science and Public Affairs. The center has also been a focus for community outreach for the university by offering pro bono technical assistance to many community-based organizations in our area.

Competencies: Advocacy and Public Policy; Financial Management and Social Entrepreneurship; Fundraising and Resource Development; Human Resources Management and Volunteerism; Information Management; Leadership and Governance; Legal and Regulatory; Planning and Evaluation

• • •

Charity Navigator

139 Harristown Road, Suite 101, Glen Rock, NJ 07452

www.charitynavigator.org

Mission/Focus Area: Charity Navigator works to guide intelligent giving. By guiding intelligent giving, we aim to advance a more efficient and responsive philanthropic marketplace, in which givers and the charities they support work in tandem to overcome our nation's and the world's most persistent challenges.

Competencies: Legal and Regulatory

• • •

Council of New Jersey Grantmakers

221 W. Hanover Street, Trenton, NJ 08608

http://cnjg.org

Mission/Focus Area: The Council of New Jersey Grantmakers exists to strengthen and promote effective philanthropy throughout New Jersey.

Competencies: Advocacy and Public Policy; Grantmaking

New Mexico

Center for Nonprofit Excellence

2340 Alamo Avenue SE, 2nd Floor, Albuquerque, NM 87106

www.centerfornonprofitexcellence.org

Mission/Focus Area: We help nonprofits build partnerships to transform communities.

Competencies: Advocacy and Public Policy; Financial Management and Social Entrepreneurship; Fundraising and Resource Development; Human Resources Management and Volunteerism; Information Management; Leadership and Governance; Legal and Regulatory; Planning and Evaluation

• • •

New Mexico Association of Grantmakers

PO Box 9280, Santa Fe, NM 87504-9280

www.nmag.org

Mission/Focus Area: Increase the effectiveness and impact of organized philanthropy in New Mexico

Competencies: Grantmaking; Leadership and Governance

New York

Association of Black Foundation Executives

333 Seventh Avenue, 14th Floor, New York, NY 10001

www.abfe.org/contact-us/

Mission/Focus Area: ABFE is a membership-based philanthropic organization that advocates for responsive and transformative investments in Black communities.

Competencies: Advocacy and Public Policy; Grantmaking; Leadership and Governance

• • •

Center for Nonprofit Strategy and Management

One Bernard Baruch Way (55 Lexington at 24th Street), New York, NY 10010

www.baruch.cuny.edu/spa/researchcenters/nonprofitstrategy/

Mission/Focus Area: The Center for Nonprofit Strategy and Management (CNSM) is a globally recognized leader in analyzing the evolving role of nonprofit organizations within the context of society, politics, and the economy.

Competencies: Advocacy and Public Policy; Financial Management and Social Entrepreneurship; Fundraising and Resource Development; Human Resources Management and Volunteerism; Information Management; Leadership and Governance; Legal and Regulatory; Planning and Evaluation

• • •

Center on Philanthropy and Civil Society

535 E. 80th Street, New York, NY 10028

www.cuny.edu

Mission/Focus Area: Highlights the philanthropic activities of different institutions and groups, with a particular emphasis on multiculturalism—the patterns of giving and voluntarism by different religious, ethnic, racial, gender, and economic groups; linking academic approaches with practitioner needs

Competencies: Advocacy and Public Policy; Financial Management and Social Entrepreneurship; Fundraising and Resource Development; Human Resources Management and Volunteerism; Information Management; Leadership and Governance; Legal and Regulatory; Planning and Evaluation

• • •

Committee Encouraging Corporate Philanthropy

5 Hanover Square, Suite 2102, New York, NY 10004

www.cecp.co

Mission/Focus Area: To draw together and empower senior executives of the world's leading companies to achieve unprecedented progress on societal challenges while driving business performance

Competencies: Grantmaking

• • •

Emerging Practitioners in Philanthropy

10 E. 34th Street, Suite 10, New York, NY 10016

www.epip.org

Mission/Focus Area: Nonprofit leadership, networking, and advocacy for younger generation of nonprofit managers and philanthropists.

Competencies: Grantmaking; Leadership and Governance

• • •

Environmental Grantmakers Association

475 Riverside Drive, Suite 960, New York, NY 10115

http://ega.org

Mission/Focus Area: EGA works with members and partners to promote effective environmental philanthropy by sharing knowledge, fostering debate, cultivating leadership, facilitating collaboration, and catalyzing action.

Competencies: Advocacy and Public Policy; Grantmaking

• • •

Funders for Lesbian-Gay Issues

116 E. 16th Street, Suite 7, New York, NY 10003

www.lgbtfunders.org

Mission/Focus Area: Funders for LGBTQ Issues seeks to mobilize philanthropic resources that enhance the well-being of lesbian, gay, bisexual, transgender, and queer communities, promote equity, and advance racial, economic, and gender justice.

Competencies: Advocacy and Public Policy; Grantmaking; Leadership and Governance

• • •

Heyman Center for Philanthropy and Fundraising

7 E. 12th Street, New York, NY 10003

www.scps.nyu.edu

Mission/Focus Area: Professional certificate programs examine timely subjects ranging from global philanthropy to ethics and governance in the nonprofit sector.

Competencies: Financial Management and Social Entrepreneurship; Grantmaking; Leadership and Governance, Fundraising; Legal and Regulatory

• • •

Hispanics in Philanthropy

55 Exchange Place, New York, NY 10005

www.hiponline.org

Mission/Focus Area: HIP's mission is to strengthen Latino communities by increasing resources for the Latino and Latin American civil sector; increasing Latino participation and leadership throughout the field of philanthropy, and fostering policy change to enhance equity and inclusiveness.

Competencies: Advocacy and Public Policy; Grantmaking; Leadership and Governance

• • •

International Human Rights Funders Group

498 Seventh Avenue, 15th Floor, New York, New York 10018

www.ihrfg.org

Mission/Focus Area: The International Human Rights Funders Group is a global network of donors and grantmakers committed to advancing human rights around the world through effective philanthropy.

Competencies: Advocacy and Public Policy; Grantmaking

• • •

Jewish Funders Network

150 W. 30th Street, Suite 900, New York, NY 10001

www.jfunders.org

Mission/Focus Area: Education and networking on effective giving for Jewish funders.

Competencies: Advocacy and Public Policy; Grantmaking

• • •

Milano School of International Affairs, Management, and Urban Policy (The New School)

66 W. 12th Street, New York, NY 10011

www.newschool.edu/public-engagement/milano-school/

Mission/Focus Area: The Milano School is widely recognized for its innovative approach to educating leaders who make a measurable difference. Its activities focus on addressing complex real-world problems in cities, organizations, and communities.

Competencies: Advocacy and Public Policy; Financial Management and Social Entrepreneurship; Fundraising and Resource Development; Human Resources Management and Volunteerism; Information Management; Leadership and Governance; Legal and Regulatory; Planning and Evaluation

• • •

National Center on Philanthropy and the Law (NCPL) (New York University)

139 MacDougal Street, 1st Floor, New York, NY 10012

www1.law.nyu.edu/ncpl/

Mission/Focus Area: The National Center on Philanthropy and the Law (NCPL) was established in 1988 at New York University School of Law (NYU School of Law) to explore a broad range of legal issues affecting the nation's nonprofit sector and to provide an integrated examination of the legal doctrines related to the activities of charitable organizations.

Competencies: Information Management; Legal and Regulatory

• • •

NPower

3 Metrotech Center, Mezzanine, Brooklyn, NY 11201

www.npower.org

Mission/Focus Area: Provides individuals, nonprofits, and schools access and opportunity to build tech skills and achieve their potential

Competencies: Advocacy and Public Policy; Information Management

• • •

New York Council of Nonprofits

272 Broadway, Albany, NY 12204

www.nycon.org

Mission/Focus Area: The New York Council of Nonprofits (NYCON) works together with our members, other nonprofits, communities, funders, and stakeholders to build the capacity of nonprofits and communities to enhance the quality of life through responsive, cost-effective service and by forming a long-term, multilayered service relationship with our member nonprofits.

Competencies: Advocacy and Public Policy; Financial Management and Social Entrepreneurship; Fundraising and Resource Development; Human Resources Management and Volunteerism; Information Management; Leadership and Governance; Legal and Regulatory; Planning and Evaluation

• • •

NYU Wagner, Research Center for Leadership in Action

295 Lafayette Street, New York, NY 10012-9604

www.wagner.nyu.edu

Mission/Focus Area: Advancing leadership in the nonprofit sector

Competencies: Advocacy and Public Policy; Financial Management and Social Entrepreneurship; Fundraising and Resource Development; Human Resources Management and Volunteerism; Information Management; Leadership and Governance; Legal and Regulatory; Planning and Evaluation

• • •

Philanthropy New York

79 Fifth Avenue, Fourth Floor, New York, NY 10003-3076

https://philanthropynewyork
.org/what-we-dophilanthropynewyork.org/what-we-do

Mission/Focus Area: Philanthropy New York promotes effective, strategic philanthropy and supports meaningful collaboration and knowledge sharing for funders and their grantees.

Competencies: Grantmaking; Leadership and Governance

• • •

Public and Nonprofit Management and Policy Program, Robert F. Wagner Graduate School of Public Service (New York University)

295 Lafayette Street, New York, NY 10012-9604

http://wagner.nyu.edu

Mission/Focus Area: Students arrive at NYU Wagner with the desire to serve the public. They leave with the skills and experience to bring about change. Combining coursework in management, finance, and policy with cutting-edge research and work experience in urban communities, the NYU Wagner education will enable you to transform your personal commitment into public leadership.

Competencies: Advocacy and Public Policy; Financial Management and Social Entrepreneurship; Fundraising and Resource Development; Human Resources Management and Volunteerism; Information Management; Leadership and Governance; Legal and Regulatory; Planning and Evaluation

• • •

Rensselaerville Institute

Two Oakwood Place, Delmar, New York 12054

www.rinstitute.org

Mission/Focus Area: Improve people's lives by helping the innovators who spark change using a results framework

Competencies: Advocacy and Public Policy

• • •

Resource Generation

18 W. 27th Street, 2nd Floor, New York, NY 10001

www.resourcegeneration.org

Mission/Focus Area: Organizes and connects wealthy young people to become leaders in creating wealth equality

Competencies: Advocacy and Public Policy; Grantmaking; Leadership and Governance

• • •

Rockefeller Archive Center

15 Dayton Avenue, Sleepy Hollow, New York 10591

www.rockarch.org

Mission/Focus Area: Collection of research on the nonprofit and philanthropic sector

Competencies: Advocacy and Public Policy; Financial Management and Social Entrepreneurship; Fundraising and Resource Development; Human Resources Management and Volunteerism; Information Management; Leadership and Governance; Legal and Regulatory; Planning and Evaluation

• • •

Rockefeller Philanthropy Advisors

6 W. 48th Street, 10th Floor, New York, NY 10036

www.rockpa.org

Mission/Focus Area: Provides research and counsel on charitable giving, develops philanthropic programs, and offers complete program, administrative, and management services for foundations and trusts

Competencies: Communications, Marketing, and Public Relations; Financial Management and Social Entrepreneurship; Fundraising and Resource Development; Grantmaking; Human Resources Management and Volunteerism; Information Management; Leadership and Governance; Legal and Regulatory; Planning and Evaluation

• • •

Western New York Grantmakers Association

PO Box 1333, Buffalo, NY 14205

www.wnygrantmakers.org

Mission/Focus Area: Through WNYGA, philanthropic organizations serving the western New York area advance their missions by working collaboratively with each other and being exposed to important information, people, emerging trends, and issues.

Competencies: Advocacy and Public Policy; Grantmaking

• • •

Young Nonprofit Professionals Network

244 Fifth Avenue, Suite T282, New York, NY 10001

http://ynpn.org

Mission/Focus Area: The Young Nonprofit Professionals Network (YNPN) is a movement activating emerging leaders to advance a diverse and powerful social sector.

Competencies: Advocacy and Public Policy; Leadership and Governance

North Carolina

Center for Creative Leadership

1 Leadership Place, Greensboro, NC 27438

www.ccl.org

Mission/Focus Area: CCL helps clients around the world cultivate creative leadership.

Competencies: Leadership and Governance

• • •

Center for Strategic Philanthropy and Civil Society (CSPCS)

Room 240, Sanford Building, Box 90524, Durham, NC 27708

http://cspcs.sanford.duke.edu

Mission/Focus Area: The mission of the Center for Strategic Philanthropy and Civil Society is to help philanthropy achieve broader and deeper impact in solving problems facing the social sector and the wider civic community.

Competencies: Advocacy and Public Policy; Grantmaking; Information Management

• • •

Center for Study of Philanthropy and Voluntarism

Box 90239, Durham, NC 27708-0239

http://philvol.sanford.duke.edu

Mission/Focus Area: Education and research in the area of philanthropy and voluntarism

Competencies: Grantmaking; Human Resources Management and Volunteerism; Leadership and Governance

• • •

Institute for Nonprofit Research, Education and Engagement (North Carolina State University)

James B. Hunt Junior Library, Campus Box 7011, Raleigh, NC 27695-7011

http://nonprofit.chass.ncsu.edu

Mission/Focus Area: The Institute for Nonprofit Research, Education and Engagement is a multidisciplinary center devoted to strengthening the capacity of nonprofit organizations and nonprofit leadership through research, education, and engagement.

Competencies: Advocacy and Public Policy; Information Management

• • •

NC Center for Nonprofits

1110 Navaho Drive, Suite 200, Raleigh, NC 27609

www.ncnonprofits.org

Mission/Focus Area: Our mission is to enrich North Carolina's communities and economy through a strong nonprofit sector and nonprofit voice.

Competencies: Advocacy and Public Policy; Financial Management and Social Entrepreneurship; Fundraising and Resource Development; Human Resources Management and Volunteerism; Information Management; Leadership and Governance; Legal and Regulatory; Planning and Evaluation

• • •

North Carolina Network of Grantmakers

3739 National Drive, Suite 100, Raleigh, NC 27612

www.ncgrantmakers.org

Mission/Focus Area: The North Carolina Network of Grantmakers (NCNG) connects more than one hundred North Carolina foundations and corporate giving programs to a network of knowledge, resources, and sector colleagues that help them meet their mission, serve the community, and operate more efficiently and effectively.

Competencies: Advocacy and Public Policy; Grantmaking

• • •

Philanthropy Journal (Fletcher Foundation)

1070 Partners Way, Raleigh, NC 27606

www.philanthropyjournal.org

Mission/Focus Area: Helping local people and organizations recognize and solve social and community problems.

Competencies: Advocacy and Public Policy; Financial Management and Social Entrepreneurship; Fundraising and Resource Development; Human Resources Management and Volunteerism; Information Management; Leadership and Governance; Legal and Regulatory; Planning and Evaluation

North Dakota

North Dakota Association of Nonprofit Organizations

1605 E. Capitol Avenue, PO Box 1091, Bismarck, ND 58502

www.ndano.org

Mission/Focus Area: NDANO is the statewide membership association advancing North Dakota nonprofits through advocacy and public policy, education and training, resources and research, cost-saving programs, and leadership and networking.

Competencies: Advocacy and Public Policy; Financial Management and Social Entrepreneurship; Fundraising and Resource Development; Human Resources Management and Volunteerism; Information Management; Leadership and Governance; Legal and Regulatory; Planning and Evaluation

• • •

North Dakota Community Foundation

309 N. Mandan Street, Suite 2, PO Box 387, Bismarck, ND 58502-0387

www.ndcf.net

Mission/Focus Area: The mission of the North Dakota Community Foundation is to improve the quality of life for North Dakota's citizens through charitable giving and promoting philanthropy.

Competencies: Advocacy and Public Policy; Grantmaking

Ohio

Center for Nonprofit Policy and Practice

2121 Euclid Avenue, Cleveland, OH 44115-2214

http://urban.csuohio.edu/nonprofit/

Mission/Focus Area: Nurture civil society by strengthening community and faith-based nonprofit organizations.

Competencies: Advocacy and Public Policy; Financial Management and Social Entrepreneurship; Fundraising and Resource Development; Human Resources Management and Volunteerism; Information Management; Leadership and Governance; Legal and Regulatory; Planning and Evaluation

• • •

Mandel Center for Nonprofit Organization

10900 Euclid Ave., Cleveland, Ohio 44106

http://mandelcenter.case.edu

Mission/Focus Area: The Mandel Foundation and Case Western Reserve University established a program for nonprofit leaders that set the standard for excellence in an emerging discipline.

Competencies: Advocacy and Public Policy; Financial Management and Social Entrepreneurship; Fundraising and Resource Development; Human Resources Management and Volunteerism; Information Management; Leadership and Governance; Legal and Regulatory; Planning and Evaluation

• • •

National Network of Consultants to Grantmakers

PO Box 40272, Cleveland, OH 44140

www.nncg.org

Mission/Focus Area: NNCG's mission is to increase the quality, effectiveness, and capacity of grantmakers by mobilizing and strengthening the work of knowledgeable, ethical, and experienced consultants.

Competencies: Grantmaking; Leadership and Governance

• • •

Nonprofit Academic Centers Council

2121 Euclid Avenue, Cleveland, OH 44115-2214

www.urban.csuohio.edu

Mission/Focus Area: Conducts research on the nonprofit and philanthropic sector and ways to improve the sector's civic engagement

Competencies: Advocacy and Public Policy; Financial Management and Social Entrepreneurship; Fundraising and Resource Development; Human Resources Management and Volunteerism; Information Management; Leadership and Governance; Legal and Regulatory; Planning and Evaluation

• • •

Ohio Association of Nonprofit Organizations

100 E. Broad Street, Suite 2440, Columbus, OH 43215-3119

www.oano.org

Mission/Focus Area: OANO's mission is to provide leadership, education, and advocacy to enhance the ability of Ohio's nonprofit organizations to serve their communities.

Competencies: Advocacy and Public Policy; Financial Management and Social Entrepreneurship; Fundraising and Resource Development; Human Resources Management and Volunteerism; Information Management; Leadership and Governance; Legal and Regulatory; Planning and Evaluation

• • •

Philanthropy Ohio

37 W. Broad Street, Suite 800, Columbus, OH 43215

www.philanthropyohio.org

Mission/Focus Area: The recognized advocate and convener trusted to represent the interests of Ohio philanthropy in the state and the nation

Competencies: Advocacy and Public Policy; Grantmaking; Leadership and Governance

Oklahoma

Oklahoma Center for Nonprofits

720 W. Wilshire Boulevard, Suite 115, Oklahoma City, OK 73116

www.oklahomacenterfornonprofits.org

Mission/Focus Area: The Oklahoma Center for Nonprofits is a nonprofit organization equipping and strengthening the Oklahoma nonprofit sector through training, consulting, advocacy, membership, networking, and awards.

Competencies: Advocacy and Public Policy; Financial Management and Social Entrepreneurship; Fundraising and Resource Development; Human Resources Management and Volunteerism; Information Management; Leadership and Governance; Legal and Regulatory; Planning and Evaluation

Oregon

Funders' Committee for Civic Participation

221 NW Second Avenue, Suite 207, Portland, OR 97209

http://funderscommittee.org

Mission/Focus Area: The Funders' Committee for Civic Participation (FCCP) exists to promote civic participation as a key to making our democracy work. We serve leaders in the philanthropic community working to further this vision with heightened attention to issues of equity and historically disenfranchised and underrepresented communities.

Competencies: Advocacy and Public Policy; Grantmaking

• • •

Grantmakers for Education

720 SW Washington Street, Suite 605, Portland, OR 97205

www.edfunders.org

Mission/Focus Area: Grantmakers for Education is a membership organization of hundreds of education grantmakers working to improve outcomes and expand opportunities for all learners across the education spectrum, from early learning through postsecondary and workforce development.

Competencies: Advocacy and Public Policy; Grantmaking

• • •

Grantmakers of Oregon and Southwest Washington

425 NW 10th Avenue, Suite 305, Portland, OR 97209

http://gosw.org

Mission/Focus Area: Grantmakers allows funders to engage at the local level by providing space—both literally and figuratively—for funders to come together to address community issues, explore solutions, celebrate successes and share best practices.

Competencies: Advocacy and Public Policy; Grantmaking

• • •

Master of Nonprofit Management (University of Oregon)

1209 University of Oregon, 119 Hendricks Hall, Eugene, OR 97403

http://pppm.uoregon.edu/grad/nonprofit-master/

Mission/Focus Area: The Master of Nonprofit Management is a professional degree providing training for students in administration of nonprofit organizations. Due to the astonishing growth of the nonprofit sector over the past three decades in the United States and the equally rapid growth of nongovernmental organizations internationally, the sector has professionalized.

Competencies: Advocacy and Public Policy; Financial Management and Social Entrepreneurship; Fundraising and Resource Development; Human Resources Management and Volunteerism; Information Management; Leadership and Governance; Legal and Regulatory; Planning and Evaluation

• • •

Nonprofit Association of Oregon

5100 SW Macadam Avenue, Suite 360, Portland, OR 97239

www.nonprofitoregon.org

Mission/Focus Area: The mission of the Nonprofit Association of Oregon is to strengthen the collective voice, leadership, and capacity of nonprofits to enrich the lives of all Oregonians.

Competencies: Advocacy and Public Policy; Financial Management and Social Entrepreneurship; Fundraising and Resource Development; Human Resources Management and Volunteerism; Information Management; Leadership and Governance; Legal and Regulatory; Planning and Evaluation

• • •

Nonprofit Technology Enterprise Network (NTEN)

1020 SW Taylor, Suite 800, Portland, OR 97205

www.nten.org

Mission/Focus Area: Helping nonprofits use technology effectively

Competencies: Information Management

Pennsylvania

Nonprofit Finance Fund

1528 Walnut Street, Suite 310, Philadelphia, PA 19102

http://nonprofitfinancefund.org

Mission/Focus Area: Helps organizations with financial management and supports innovations that will revitalize the nonprofit sector

Competencies: Financial Management and Social Entrepreneurship; Fundraising and Resource Development; Grantmaking

• • •

Pennsylvania Association of Nonprofit Organizations

2040 Linglestown Rodd, Suite 302, Harrisburg, PA 17110

www.pano.org

Mission/Focus Area: PANO is the statewide membership organization serving and advancing the nonprofit sector through advocacy, collaboration, education, and other services in order to improve the overall quality of life in Pennsylvania. PANO exists to support the incredible work of the nonprofit sector and highlight the critical role nonprofits serve.

Competencies: Advocacy and Public Policy; Financial Management and Social Entrepreneurship; Fundraising and Resource Development;

Human Resources Management and Volunteerism; Information Management; Leadership and Governance; Legal and Regulatory; Planning and Evaluation

• • •

Philanthropy Network

230 S. Broad Street, Suite 402, Philadelphia, PA 19102

www.philanthropynetwork.org

Mission/Focus Area: Our goal is to give funders the tools to keep their philanthropy vital and help strengthen communities.

Competencies: Advocacy and Public Policy; Grantmaking

Rhode Island

Grantmakers' Council of Rhode Island

5600 Post Road, Suite 114, PMB 166, East Greenwich, RI 02818

www.gc-ri.org

Mission/Focus Area: The Grantmakers Council of Rhode Island (GCRI), a membership organization of private, community, and corporate foundations, corporation giving programs, and individuals with organized grantmaking programs or charitable endowments, works to educate and inform individuals engaged in organized philanthropy in Rhode Island.

Competencies: Grantmaking

• • •

Rhode Island Foundation

One Union Station, Providence, RI 02903

www.rifoundation.org/Home.aspx

Mission/Focus Area: The Rhode Island Foundation is a proactive community and philanthropic leader dedicated to meeting the needs of the people of Rhode Island.

Competencies: Grantmaking; Leadership and Governance

South Dakota

South Dakota Community Foundation

1714 North Lincoln Ave, Box 296, Pierre, SD 57501

http://sdcommunityfoundation.org

Mission/Focus Area: To promote philanthropy, receive and administer charitable gifts, and invest in a wide range of programs promoting the social and economic well-being of the people of South Dakota.

Competencies: Grantmaking

Texas

American Leadership Forum

3101 Richmond Avenue, Suite 140, Houston, TX 77098

www.alfnational.org

Mission/Focus Area: The American Leadership Forum is a nonprofit organization whose mission is to join and strengthen diverse leaders to better serve the public good.

Competencies: Leadership and Governance

• • •

Grassroots Grantmakers

PO Box G, Hallettsville, TX 77964

www.grassrootsgrantmakers.org

Mission/Focus Area: Supporting a field of citizen-sector investing

Competencies: Advocacy and Public Policy; Grantmaking

• • •

Philanthropy Southwest

624 N. Good-Latimer Expressway, Suite 100, Dallas, TX 75204

www.philanthropysouthwest.org

Mission/Focus Area: Philanthropy Southwest actively promotes opportunities to exchange ideas, build relationships, and advance philanthropic excellence.

Competencies: Advocacy and Public Policy

• • •

Public Service Leadership Program (Texas A&M University)

4220 TAMU College Station, TX 77843-4220

http://bush.tamu.edu/pslp/

Mission/Focus Area: The Public Service Leadership Program (PSLP) integrates the development of student leadership knowledge, skills, attributes, and values throughout the two-year Bush School experience.

Competencies: Information Management

• • •

RGK Center for Philanthropy and Community Service (University of Texas)

2315 Red River Street, Austin, Texas 78712-1536

www.rgkcenter.org

Mission/Focus Area: To build knowledge about nonprofit organizations, philanthropy, and volunteerism, and to prepare students and practitioners to make effective contributions to their communities

Competencies: Advocacy and Public Policy; Financial Management and Social Entrepreneurship; Fundraising and Resource Development; Grantmaking; Human Resources Management and Volunteerism; Information Management; Leadership and Governance; Legal and Regulatory; Planning and Evaluation

• • •

Texas Association of Nonprofit Organizations

8001 Centre Park Drive, Austin, TX 78754-5118

http://tano.org/?

Mission/Focus Area: TANO advocates for issues that affect all nonprofits. We track state and federal legislation, educating nonprofits about policy developments, and mobilizing members and other nonprofits around critical policy issues.

Competencies: Advocacy and Public Policy; Financial Management and Social Entrepreneurship; Fundraising and Resource Development; Human Resources Management and Volunteerism; Information Management; Leadership and Governance; Legal and Regulatory; Planning and Evaluation

Utah

Utah Nonprofits Association

231 E. 400 South, Suite 345, Salt Lake City, Utah 84111

https://utahnonprofits.org

Mission/Focus Area: The Utah Nonprofits Association works to strengthen the Utah nonprofit community so that we may all work together to create a dynamic group of organizations that serve the various needs of our local and global community.

Competencies: Advocacy and Public Policy

Vermont

Common Good Vermont

294 N. Winooski Avenue, Burlington, VT 05401

http://share.commongoodvt.org

Mission/Focus Area: Common Good Vermont is a people and web-based network that enables community and nonprofit leaders to access their collective knowledge, build partnerships, solve problems, and achieve long-term social benefit for the people of Vermont.

Competencies: Advocacy and Public Policy

• • •

Institute for Sustainable Communities (Advocacy Institute)

535 Stone Cutters Way, Montpelier, VT 05602

www.iscvt.org

Mission/Focus Area: To help communities around the world address environmental, economic, and social challenges to build a better future shaped and shared by all

Competencies: Advocacy and Public Policy; Leadership and Governance

• • •

Planned Giving Council of NH and VT

PO Box 974, Hanover, NH 03755

www.leavealegacynhvt.org

Mission/Focus Area: Promotes the personal and community benefits of charitable giving by supporting planned giving professionals

Competencies: Fundraising and Resource Development

Virginia

Association of Fundraising Professionals

4300 Wilson Boulevard, Suite 300, Arlington, VA 22203

www.afpnet.org

Mission/Focus Area: AFP, an association of professionals throughout the world, advances philanthropy by enabling people and organizations to practice ethical and effective fundraising. The core activities through which AFP fulfills this mission include education, training, mentoring, research, credentialing, and advocacy.

Competencies: Advocacy and Public Policy; Fundraising and Resource Development

• • •

Better Business Bureau serving Central Virginia

720 Moorefield Park Drive, Suite 300, Richmond, VA 23236

www.richmond.bbb.org

Mission/Focus Area: Charity evaluation, informed decision making by donors

Competencies: Legal and Regulatory

• • •

Consortium of Foundation Libraries

2121 Crystal Drive, Suite 700, Arlington, VA 22202

www.foundationlibraries.info

Mission/Focus Area: The Consortium of Foundation Libraries provides its members a vehicle for enhancing learning, sharing resources, and coordinating information services among foundation libraries and archives.

Competencies: Information Management

• • •

Council on Foundations

2121 Crystal Drive, Arlington, VA 22202

www.cof.org

Mission/Focus Area: The Council's mission is to provide the opportunity, leadership, and tools needed by philanthropic organizations to expand, enhance, and sustain their ability to advance the common good. See more at: www.cof.org/about

Competencies: Communications, Marketing, and Public Relations; Grantmaking; Financial Management and Social Entrepreneurship;

Leadership and Governance; Legal and Regulatory; Planning and Evaluation

• • •

Disability Funders Network

14241 Midlothian Turnpike., Suite 151, Midlothian, VA 23113-6500

www.disabilityfunders.org

Mission/Focus Area: Disability Funders Network (DFN) is a national membership and philanthropic advocacy organization that seeks equality and rights for disabled individuals and communities by bridging philanthropic resources, disability, and community. DFN envisions an empowered and functioning democracy with full equality under the law, equal access to services, unconditional respect for difference, and the meaningful participation of all communities at tables where decisions are made.

Competencies: Advocacy and Public Policy; Grantmaking

• • •

Grant Makers in Aging

2001 Jefferson Davis Highway, Arlington, VA 22202

www.giaging.org

Mission/Focus Area: Strengthening grantmaking for an aging society

Competencies: Advocacy and Public Policy; Grantmaking

• • •

GuideStar

4801 Courthouse Street, Suite 220, Williamsburg, VA 23188

www.guidestar.org

Mission/Focus Area: To revolutionize philanthropy by providing information that advances transparency, enables users to make better decisions, and encourages charitable giving

Competencies: Legal and Regulatory

• • •

Institute for Policy and Governance (Virginia Tech University)

205 W. Roanoke Street, Blacksburg, VA 24061

www.ipg.vt.edu

Mission/Focus Area: We engage in research, capacity building, technical outreach, and community-based participatory inquiry with and on behalf of those we serve, principally disadvantaged and vulnerable populations.

Competencies: Information Management

• • •

National Center on Nonprofit Enterprise

205 S. Patrick Street, Alexandria, VA 22314

www.nationalcne.org

Mission/Focus Area: Economics of nonprofits, planning by nonprofits, measuring performance and impact, managing risk, financial management and investment strategies, financing nonprofits, earned income and social enterprise, understanding and managing costs, financing and leveraging capital

Competencies: Financial Management and Social Entrepreneurship

• • •

Nonprofit Risk Management Center

15 N. King Street, Suite 203, Leesburg, VA 20176

www.nonprofitrisk.org

Mission/Focus Area: Provides tools to help nonprofits "prepare for uncertainty"

Competencies: Legal and Regulatory

• • •

School of Policy, Government, and International Affairs

3351 Fairfax Drive, Arlington, VA 22201

http://spgia.gmu.edu

Mission/Focus Area: The School of Policy, Government, and International Affairs (SPGIA) prepares undergraduate and graduate students to be leaders in the private, public, and nonprofit sectors, and in all levels of government—local, state, regional, federal, and international.

Competencies: Advocacy and Public Policy; Financial Management and Social Entrepreneurship; Fundraising and Resource Development; Human Resources Management and Volunteerism; Information Management; Leadership and Governance; Legal and Regulatory; Planning and Evaluation

• • •

United Way of America

701 N. Fairfax Street, Alexandria, VA 22314

www.unitedway.org

Mission/Focus Area: Ignite a worldwide social movement, and thereby mobilize millions to action—to give, advocate, and volunteer to improve the conditions in which they live

Competencies: Advocacy and Public Policy; Financial Management and Social Entrepreneurship; Fundraising and Resource Development; Leadership and Governance

Washington

Daniel J. Evans School of Public Affairs (University of Washington)

Parrington Hall 4100, 15th Avenue NE, Seattle, WA 98195-3055

http://evans.uw.edu

Mission/Focus Area: Our programs prepare students for public service careers. Our graduates and faculty provide expertise and produce research that guides local, national, and global nonprofit organizations and government agencies.

Competencies: Advocacy and Public Policy; Financial Management and Social Entrepreneurship; Fundraising and Resource Development; Human Resources Management and Volunteerism; Information Management; Leadership and Governance; Legal and Regulatory; Planning and Evaluation

• • •

Grantmakers in the Arts

4055 21st Avenue W., Suite 100, Seattle, WA 98199-1247

www.giarts.org

Mission/Focus Area: The mission of Grantmakers in the Arts (GIA) is to provide leadership and service to advance the use of philanthropic resources on behalf of arts and culture.

Competencies: Advocacy and Public Policy; Grantmaking

• • •

Grantmakers of Oregon and Southwest Washington

425 NW 10th Avenue, Suite 305, Portland, OR 97209

http://gosw.org

Mission/Focus Area: Grantmakers allows funders to engage at the local level by providing space—both literally and figuratively—for funders to come together to address community issues, explore solutions, celebrate successes, and share best practices.

Competencies: Advocacy and Public Policy; Grantmaking

· · ·

Master of Nonprofit Leadership (Seattle University)

901 12th Avenue, Seattle, WA 98122

www.seattleu.edu/artsci/mnpl/

Mission/Focus Area: The Master of Nonprofit Leadership program teaches you how to lead so that you can change the world.

Competencies: Advocacy and Public Policy; Financial Management and Social Entrepreneurship; Fundraising and Resource Development; Human Resources Management and Volunteerism; Information Management; Leadership and Governance; Legal and Regulatory; Planning and Evaluation

· · ·

Philanthropy Northwest

2101 Fourth Avenue, Suite 650, Seattle, WA 98121

philanthropynw.org

Mission/Focus Area: Promotes, facilitates, and drives collaborative action by philanthropic organizations to strengthen communities in our region

Competencies: Grantmaking; Leadership and Governance

· · ·

Social Venture Partners

220 Second Avenue S., Suite 300, Seattle, WA 98104

www.socialventurepartners.org

Mission/Focus Area: SVP builds powerful relationships among people and organizations that are out to make the world a better place.

Competencies: Grantmaking

· · ·

Washington Nonprofits

120 State Avenue, Suite 303 Olympia, WA 98501

www.washingtonnonprofits.org

Mission/Focus Area: To build a strong, collaborative network of non-profits serving Washington communities through advocacy, education, and capacity building.

Competencies: Advocacy and Public Policy; Financial Management and Social Entrepreneurship; Fundraising and Resource Development; Human Resources Management and Volunteerism; Information Management; Leadership and Governance; Legal and Regulatory; Planning and Evaluation

West Virginia

Philanthropy West Virginia

PO Box 1584, Morgantown, WV 26505

www.wvgrantmakers.org

Mission/Focus Area: Philanthropy West Virginia is committed to helping its members fulfill their charitable goals. It does so by providing opportunities for trustees and staff to network, build skills, enhance knowledge, and demonstrate leadership. Philanthropy WV is the forum for funders to exchange information, discuss common interests, learn about relevant issues, hone their grantmaking skills, and establish networks of important relationships across the state.

Competencies: Advocacy and Public Policy; Grantmaking

• • •

West Virginia Nonprofit Association

PO Box 1452, Lewisburg, WV 24901

http://wvnpa.org

Mission/Focus Area: The WVNPA seeks to strengthen nonprofit organizations individually and the sector as a whole, catalyzing innovation, fostering a collective voice of its members, and increasing the reputation and influence of the nonprofit sector in West Virginia.

Competencies: Advocacy and Public Policy; Financial Management and Social Entrepreneurship; Fundraising and Resource Development; Human Resources Management and Volunteerism; Information

Management; Leadership and Governance; Legal and Regulatory; Planning and Evaluation

Wisconsin

Donors Forum of Wisconsin

759 N. Milwaukee Street, Suite 512, Milwaukee, WI 53202

www.dfwonline.org

Mission/Focus Area: To support and promote effective philanthropy

Competencies: Advocacy and Public Policy; Grantmaking

• • •

Helen Bader Institute for Nonprofit Management (University of Wisconsin–Milwaukee)

Rooms 381, 388, and 390, 3230 E. Kenwood Boulevard, Milwaukee, WI 53211

www4.uwm.edu/milwaukeeidea/hbi/

Mission/Focus Area: Through pioneering educational programs, applied research, and active engagement with nonprofit organizations of all types and sizes, the Helen Bader Institute for Nonprofit Management (HBI) develops nonprofit leaders who change lives.

Competencies: Advocacy and Public Policy; Financial Management and Social Entrepreneurship; Fundraising and Resource Development; Human Resources Management and Volunteerism; Information Management; Leadership and Governance; Legal and Regulatory; Planning and Evaluation

• • •

Public Allies

735 N. Water Street, Suite. 550, Milwaukee, WI 53202

www.publicallies.org

Mission/Focus Area: Advancing new leadership to strengthen communities, nonprofits, and civic participation

Competencies: Leadership and Governance

• • •

Wisconsin Nonprofits

2830 Agriculture Drive, Madison, WI 53727

www.wisconsinnonprofits.org

Mission/Focus Area: The Wisconsin Nonprofits Association grows through implementation of a strong business plan that focuses on building membership and partnerships that sustain the organization for the long term.

Competencies: Advocacy and Public Policy; Financial Management and Social Entrepreneurship; Fundraising and Resource Development; Human Resources Management and Volunteerism; Information Management; Leadership and Governance; Legal and Regulatory; Planning and Evaluation

Wyoming

Wyoming Nonprofit Network

1401 Airport Parkway, Suite 300, Cheyenne, WY 82001

www.wynonprofit.org

Mission/Focus Area: The purpose of the Wyoming Nonprofit Network is to strengthen the leadership, skills, effectiveness, and efficiency of Wyoming nonprofits, enabling them to further enrich the quality of community and personal life in Wyoming. The network will promote a stronger nonprofit sector and supportive public climate by providing member services, public awareness, and advocacy.

Competencies: Advocacy and Public Policy; Financial Management and Social Entrepreneurship; Fundraising and Resource Development; Human Resources Management and Volunteerism; Information Management; Leadership and Governance; Legal and Regulatory; Planning and Evaluation

Online Community

4good

http://4good.org

Mission/Focus: 4Good is the community for social impact. 4Good exists to empower nonprofits, social enterprises, and community groups by connecting like-minded professionals and community members, and by empowering the sharing of a wealth of resources from which they may benefit.

Competencies: Advocacy and Public Policy; Financial Management and Social Entrepreneurship; Fundraising and Resource Development; Human Resources Management and Volunteerism; Information Management; Leadership and Governance; Legal and Regulatory; Planning and Evaluation

• • •

Authenticity Consulting and Free Management Library

4008 Lake Drive Avenue N, Minneapolis, MN 55422-1508

www.authenticityconsulting.com

Mission/Purpose: The library provides free, easy-to-access, online articles to develop yourself, other individuals, groups, and organizations (whether the organization is for-profit or nonprofit). Since 1995, the library has grown to be one of the world's largest well-organized collections of these types of articles and resources.

Competencies: Advocacy and Public Policy; Financial Management and Social Entrepreneurship; Fundraising and Resource Development; Grantmaking; Human Resources Management and Volunteerism; Information Management; Leadership and Governance; Legal and Regulatory; Planning and Evaluation

• • •

Nonprofit Quarterly

112 Water Street, Suite 400, Boston, MA 02109

http://nonprofitquarterly.org

Mission/Focus Area: Provides information and research relating to the nonprofit sector

Competencies: Advocacy and Public Policy; Financial Management and Social Entrepreneurship; Fundraising and Resource Development; Human Resources Management and Volunteerism; Information Management; Leadership and Governance; Legal and Regulatory; Planning and Evaluation

• • •

Nonprofit World Magazine

www.snpo.org/publications/nonprofitworld.php

Mission/Focus Area: Nonprofit World is published quarterly, and offers nonprofits what few other magazines can. Sound advice, case studies, and easy-to-read format—all work together to create a publication of lasting value for board members, paid staff, and volunteers.

Competencies: Advocacy and Public Policy; Financial Management and Social Entrepreneurship; Fundraising and Resource Development;

Grantmaking; Human Resources Management and Volunteerism; Information Management; Leadership and Governance; Legal and Regulatory; Planning and Evaluation

• • •

Philanthropy Journal

www.philanthropyjournal.org

Mission/Focus Area: PJ delivers news, information, resources and opinion about charitable giving, fundraising, management, leadership, marketing and communications, focusing in particular on building organizational capacity. PJ is a publication of the Institute for Nonprofits at NC State University.

Competencies: Advocacy and Public Policy; Financial Management and Social Entrepreneurship; Fundraising and Resource Development; Grantmaking; Human Resources Management and Volunteerism; Information Management; Leadership and Governance; Legal and Regulatory; Planning and Evaluation

• • •

Society for Nonprofits

www.snpo.org/index.php

Mission/Focus Area: The Society for Nonprofits is a 501(c)(3) organization that has been serving the nonprofit sector for over 30 years. We provide nonprofit executives, fundraisers, volunteers, board members, consultants, and other professionals with the resources and information needed to work effectively and efficiently toward accomplishing your mission.

Competencies: Advocacy and Public Policy; Financial Management and Social Entrepreneurship; Fundraising and Resource Development; Grantmaking; Human Resources Management and Volunteerism; Information Management; Leadership and Governance; Legal and Regulatory; Planning and Evaluation

• • •

The Chronicle of Philanthropy

http://philanthropy.com/section/Home/172

Mission/Focus Area: *The Chronicle* provides news and information for executives of tax-exempt organizations in health, education, religion, the arts, social services, and other fields, as well as fundraisers, professional employees of foundations, institutional investors, corporate grantmakers, and charity donors. Along with news, it offers such service features as lists of grants, fundraising ideas and techniques, statistics, reports on tax and court rulings, summaries of books, and a calendar of events.

Competencies: Advocacy and Public Policy; Financial Management and Social Entrepreneurship; Fundraising and Resource Development; Grantmaking; Human Resources Management and Volunteerism; Information Management; Leadership and Governance; Legal and Regulatory; Planning and Evaluation

• • •

The Guardian Social Enterprise Network

www.theguardian.com/social-enterprise-network/2014/feb/11/how-to-get-involved-the-guardian-social-enterprise

Mission/Focus Area: The Guardian social enterprise network is a unique online community for social enterprise professionals to find, meet, and share expertise with others within the sector.

Competencies: Advocacy and Public Policy; Financial Management and Social Entrepreneurship; Fundraising and Resource Development; Grantmaking; Human Resources Management and Volunteerism; Information Management; Leadership and Governance; Legal and Regulatory; Planning and Evaluation

• • •

The NonProfit Times

www.thenonprofittimes.com

Mission/Focus Area: The NonProfit Times delivers news, business information, and original research on the daily operations of tax-exempt organizations.

Competencies: Advocacy and Public Policy; Financial Management and Social Entrepreneurship; Fundraising and Resource Development; Grantmaking; Human Resources Management and Volunteerism; Information Management; Leadership and Governance; Legal and Regulatory; Planning and Evaluation

Guide 2
Talent Investing
Raising and Granting Funds to Develop Social Change Leadership
Rusty Stahl

Putting people first in organizations takes time. And we all know that time is money. To carve out the space for developing staff and volunteers, leaders need operational support and the ability to focus their creativity and energy on their colleagues—while their other work still gets done. So even if you are crafting low-cost, in-house professional development, there are costs involved at a bedrock level. Many social change organizations are just beginning to make talent development an intentional part of their work, so new ways must be explored for funding this work. We asked Rusty Stahl, President and CEO of the Talent Philanthropy Project (www.talentphilanthropy.org), a new initiative housed at Community Partners (www.communitypartners.org), to provide some ideas to help organizations fundraise for their talent development work, and for foundations to underwrite such efforts in the organizations they support as well as internally within their own walls.

This guide focuses on the financial capital needed to develop talent. It is organized in three parts. It starts with a discussion of the nature of the social change sector's talent challenge and offers the idea of "talent philanthropy" as a response by fundraisers and funders. Second, it offers guidance to social change leaders on how to raise funds to develop talent in their organizations. In the last section, the guide discusses talent development from a funder's perspective, suggests opportunities for grantmakers to invest in grantee talent development systems, and address the unique professional development needs of their own employees.

The push to adapt business practices in philanthropy primarily focuses on the end result of social change work, but it too often ignores the ingredients needed on the front end to make impact possible. Many businesses understand that their employees, and a great workplace culture, are the main ingredients of productivity and profit. The best companies are achieving and earning more by plowing more resources back into their people (O'Leonard, 2014).

It is ironic that philanthropy, which literally means the love of humankind, overlooks the needs of human beings who make social change impact and sustainability possible. It's time to show love to those who serve as social change professionals. Not only is it the right thing to do, it's also good for the bottom line: changemakers *are* the change we want to see in the world, and there are no services without those who serve.

Talent Philanthropy

For nearly a decade, most conversations about the social change workforce have started with the premise that there is a looming leadership deficit. The idea, which grew out of an article by Thomas Tierney (2006), was that Baby Boomer executive directors would retire en masse, and there would not statistically be enough members of Generation X to fill their newly vacated seats. It turns out, there is not really a deficit of people working in the sector, nor is there a lack of people interested in joining the social change ranks or stepping into leadership. Indeed, the social change leadership highway is not vacant but packed with vehicles. A different kind of crisis is evolving, and it is fueled not by a deficit of leaders, but by a deficit of *investment in* those leaders.

One major difference between the for-profit and nonprofit contexts seems to be that many businesses have liquid capital from profits and investors, which can be easily directed by management into talent development, R&D, and other long-range investments. Social change leaders, on the other hand, rely on externally controlled, frozen capital: organizational budgets are often cobbled together from various restricted funding by an array of funders. And, many philanthropic funders are not interested in paying their share of grantees' talent development, so the resources for such functions are slim to nonexistent. In fact, my research with The Foundation Center shows that only 1 percent of foundation grant dollars on average per year went to grantee talent development over the last twenty years (Stahl, 2013). This dearth of investment creates many problems, including lack of training, dampened morale, and burnout. These conditions, in turn, increase the need for talent investments. It's a vicious cycle perpetuated by all the players involved. So when social change organizations and funders decide to break the cycle and steer adequate funds toward grantees' talent needs, new possibilities emerge for social change organizations, their staff, funders, and the communities or missions they mutually serve!

Turning this investment deficit into a surplus is within our reach. But it will take a major shift in the attitude and behavior of funders and social change leaders alike. With the right mix of intention and investment, our field can begin to meet the recruitment, retention, and transition needs of emerging, established, and deeply experienced leaders. "Talent philanthropy" is a new framework meant to enable that shift in thinking and practice amongst those engaged in funding and fundraising for social change organizations (Stahl, 2013).

Imagine for a moment that your organization is a fruit tree in a forest of other social change organization saplings. Funders are focused on making sure the tree is yielding sweet, crisp fruit—the ultimate outcomes of your productivity. Social change organization boards, executives, and staffers focus on the health of the tree's branches—the programs that reach out into the community and make an impact. The trunk is the core capacity that holds the programs and the entire enterprise up in the air. A small number of funders will support this trunk, and social change organization executives are constantly struggling to keep it strong. This is generally where the picture ends. But there is more going on out of sight below ground. The tree's network of roots acts as its talent system, pulling in thirst-quenching nutrients from the soil and water table. This is the talent pool, moving like a fast-running underground stream. Without strong systems to recruit, retain, and utilize talent, social change organization capacity is starved, and programs produce meager outcomes. Want to pick fruit? Nurture the roots. Want outcomes? Invest in talent.

Once you have accepted this truism, it is only reasonable to invest in social change organization human capital from whatever perch you occupy in the ecosystem. The process of creating such human capital opportunities is a two-way street. Leaders who need these funds must actively pursue them; the funders who control them must intentionally allocate them. Luckily, foundations and social change organizations are some of the most flexible institutions in society, and there is a significant amount of philanthropic capital available. It is a simple (although not necessarily easy) matter of board members, executives, and direct service staff at social change organizations and their funders cultivating the political will to redefine how we structure the resources at hand. To regain the deep connections between people, outcomes, and sustainability, this guide offers practical ideas for mobilizing financial resources to fuel social change talent development.

Fundraising for Talent

This section offers conceptual and practical ideas to help social change leaders increase the impact and sustainability of their organizations and colleagues through talent investments. You can serve as a champion for such investment from many different perches—as a board member, executive, program staffer, or fundraiser. Indeed, to build a culture of talent development that is needed within institutions, it is beneficial to have support from the top down and the bottom up.

Three dimensions of *talent philanthropy* will help you to succeed:

- **Attitude:** Use a "talent lens" as you manage/govern the organization (including you).

- **Aptitude:** Develop the knowledge and skills you need to invest in your talent.

- **Askitude:** Your ability to cultivate the support you need for talent investments.

Each of these ideas is explored in some depth in the following sections.

Attitude

Place a "talent lens" on your beliefs and assumptions about organizational life.

The organizational culture into which we are indoctrinated and acclimated shapes our attitudes of learning and development. Of course, norms vary widely across the diverse universe of the social change sector. Yet certain themes run across many, particularly small and midsized social change organizations that do not benefit from the endowments or vast earned income enjoyed by many universities and hospitals.

Culture of Martyrdom

Paul Light of New York University writes that the social change organization sector "survives because it has a self-exploiting workforce: Wind it up and it will do more with less until it just runs out. But at some point, the spring must break" (Light, 2004). Religious and civic ideas of charity, placing others before self, voluntarism, and service shape the field. Social change organizations gain unique strength and moral purpose from these traditions. But, taken to extremes, these values can debilitate organizations, disabling them from achieving their full potential. Social change professionals do not help others when they burn out. Similarly, when organizations burn out, they cannot achieve their missions. Organizations must replace unproductive martyrdom with cultures that emphasize a healthy and productive workforce, mission advancement, and sustainability for the long haul.

The Cost and Harm Argument

Heather and Tera wrote extensively about the cost of not investing in your people. It is important when fundraising to highlight the importance of investing in your people. For example, if a grant only enables your organization to pay sub-par wages, it can result in a burned-out program team and sub-par program services results. This in turn lowers effectiveness, increases turnover, or both. As noted earlier in the book, it costs between 75 and 150 percent of a person's annual salary to replace an employee. This cost does not simply represent wages and materials but also includes recruitment costs, loss of productivity, impacts on team morale, new training costs, and other more subtle expenses (Sage HRMS, 2013).

Beyond the high cost of turnover for each position, the impact on team morale and productivity means that the negative impacts can spread across employees and shape organizational culture with ever multiplying costs well into the future. Then, broken trust, pessimism, and mediocre performance become an accepted norm, which reduces mission commitment. The vicious cycle of turnover creates conditions in which mission impact and organizational sustainability are deeply wounded. As staff and volunteer morale and performance dwindle, people within the organization stop going the extra mile. Organizations need more external (expensive) incentives, which can never replace internal motivation. This results in weakened services for the community, with correspondingly meager outcomes and social impact.

As the value proposition of a social change organization weakens, it becomes increasingly difficult to fundraise for the organization. Individual donors, foundations, and government tend to avoid investing in any group perceived to be "a sinking ship." People want to get involved as champions for high-performing organizations. As morale and performance sink together, they drag down financial resources with them. It is possible that loyal board members or hard-working staff may underwrite costs or overwork to keep things afloat. But it is difficult to escape the whirlpool of declining morale, impact, and resources. The sustainability of organizations and their personnel is intrinsically linked.

The Moral Argument

One of the important reasons that not investing in talent can be so damaging to social change organizations is the moral contradiction it creates:

we work to increase the quality of life for people in the community outside our walls, while we are knowingly complicit in creating a decreased quality of life for those doing this work. A blog post by executive coach Natasha Golensky (2014) entitled "Nonprofit Leaders Need to Focus on Protecting Themselves as Much as They Protect Others," discussed this damage and stated, "Your unconditional availability to your organization is not a sign of dedication, it is a sign of your inability to set and maintain personal boundaries" (par 4). Social change leaders need to be guided and supported to create healthy personal and professional boundaries.

As a recent national study of compensation within social justice organizations stated, "Social justice groups make a big difference in issues as far-reaching as living wage, marriage equality and climate justice." Yet, "economic constraints and the difficult nature of social justice work will continue to place a heavy burden on staff and may contribute to turnover and instability in these organizations" (RoadMap et al., 2012, p. 3). Because of these strains, the internal working conditions of social justice organizations often do not mirror the vision these groups hold for the external world. Indeed, the study found that:

- "Fewer than half [of survey respondents] feel their compensation is 'competitive' and only 23 percent feel salaries are 'generous'. Twenty four percent want to increase salary levels—a relatively low desire to strengthen wages despite the finding that the groups do not see their scales as competitive or generous. This may simply be a reflection that funding limitations make it unrealistic to approach more competitive levels of compensation, or may reflect a priority on offering comprehensive benefits" (p. 22).

- "Only half of respondents offer pension plans to employees such as a 403(b) plan or IRA contributions" (p. 33).

- "20 percent of groups offer severance pay for long time employees, which is often seen as a reward for long tenure, to make transitions easier and to make up for relatively low salaries in the sector" (p. 34).

- "33 percent of groups offer some kind of paid sabbatical time" (p. 34).

Of course, it may be assumed that many of these groups would prefer to align their internal personnel practices with their guiding external values. However, they lack values symmetry due to their financial and time resources. If talent development was prioritized as being as important and urgent as the community work, then more time, financial, and policy resources would be mobilized to address these internal issues. In chapter

8, Heather and Tera discuss further how to align organizational mission and talent development goals and objectives.

The Business Argument

There is an alternative way of managing our organizations and movements. Just like economic justice organizers lobby for "high road economics" instead of the lowest common denominator in the global economy, there is the possibility of a high road for social change organization finances. Instead of the vicious cycle I've described, organizations can create a virtuous cycle in which investments in talent shape a self-perpetuating cultural of high performance and expanding sustainability.

An understanding of talent as central to impact has taken root in the business community. But the social change field has yet to catch up. The philanthropist and thinker Mario Marino in his book *Leap of Reason: Managing to Outcomes in an Era of Scarcity* (2011) illustrates the linkage between business thinking and a people-centered culture:

> Nurturing a performance culture begins with recruiting, developing and retaining the talented professionals you need to fulfill your mission. Failure to do is, to me, literally a dereliction of duty of board and management.... Best practices are wonderful, but they are most effective in the hands of highly talented people. I'd take the best talent over best practices and great plans any day of the week. Too many of us think that organizations and systems solve our challenges. They play a vital role, but the key lies in the people who execute those plans. (p. 24)

> What I wish is that all leaders would take the time to establish real clarity on the ends they want to achieve, have the courage to line up the right team to fulfill the mission, make clear what they expect of their teams, be disciplined in their execution, and model the behaviors they want the organization to exhibit. When you combine all these things with a good heart, respect, and genuine caring, you almost inevitably shape an organizational culture in which people take pride in what they do and are eager to excel and play a role in fulfilling the organization's mission. And that's a great formula for creating a real difference in the lives of those you serve. (p. 34)

Whether you approach the issue from the point of view of performance and impact, sustainability, moral alignment, or business values, the reasons to champion investing in social change organizational talent are numerous. Yet many foundations, despite yearning for grantees that are financially healthy, effective, and growing, remain skeptical when it comes to investing in talent. How can we begin to shift these attitudes?

When addressing an audience that believes business practices will improve the nonprofit sector, it is valuable to point out the central role that talent investment plays in building great companies. In conversation with those who are primarily concerned with social justice, it is worthwhile to remind them that the success of social justice organizations depends on building leaders externally in the community—and that the same principal applies internally. Lifting up the numerous arguments for talent investment is an important way to begin using the talent lens in your organization and your own professional practices.

Aptitude

To maximize the impact and sustainability of your organization, invest in your people—including yourself.

You've got a new attitude! Now what? How can you make concrete changes within your organization? This section provides a series of pointers to help you integrate talent development into your organization's goals, budget, behavior, and culture.

Budgeting for Talent Investments

The biggest cost for many social change organizations is personnel. However, it is often the case that few resources are allocated to develop the staff. In other words, organizations are not protecting their largest investment. Indeed, 90 percent of social change organizations do not have retention plans and very few have transition plans (Nonprofit HR Solutions, 2013). With some intentionality, attention, and added funding, you can make the dollars already spent on personnel go much further. Exhibit G2.1 offers a self-assessment meant to help you consider how your organization's budget may or may not reflect a priority on talent development. You likely won't be able to tackle these issues all at once in your budget, but this tool helps you consider the urgency of various issues. If you don't have enough information to answer a question, take your best guess. You should use this with staff and board members to get a sense of the collective perspective and knowledge.

At minimum, ensure that a professional development line item is included in your board-approved budget. Even if there are no dollars available this year and it is simply a placeholder, it can serve as an important discussion item and symbol of the values toward which the board and staff aspire. Grow the line item over time. Perhaps it will grow into a larger talent development line item that encompasses programmatic, managerial, and structural development.

EXHIBIT G2.1

Self-Assessment of Organizational Talent Development

Circle the response on a scale from (1) Never to (5) Always based on how often you believe your organization performs the activity in each statement.

A. Awareness and Recruitment

Outreach:

1. We make sure that young people and other potential future employees or volunteers are aware of our issue area, type of work, and/or organization.
   (1) Never (2) Rarely (3) Sometimes (4) Often (5) Always

2. We intentionally recruit potential staff from campuses, the community we serve, and other strategic venues.
   (1) Never (2) Rarely (3) Sometimes (4) Often (5) Always

3. Recruitment efforts consider issues of access and attraction for diversity, encompassing issues such as race, ethnicity, gender, sexuality, age/generation, nation of origin, physical ability, class, educational attainment, work styles, perspective and skills.
   (1) Never (2) Rarely (3) Sometimes (4) Often (5) Always

Apprenticeships:

4. We provide stipend-based or salaried internships or other forms of apprenticeship.
   (1) Never (2) Rarely (3) Sometimes (4) Often (5) Always

Salaries:

5. Our wages are at-market rate (or equal to the value of our staff members).
   (1) Never (2) Rarely (3) Sometimes (4) Often (5) Always

B. Development and Retention

Benefits:

6. We offer tuition reimbursement to encourage staff to advance their knowledge.
   (1) Never (2) Rarely (3) Sometimes (4) Often (5) Always

7. Our staff can earn the opportunity to take a sabbatical for personal and professional renewal and learning.
   (1) Never (2) Rarely (3) Sometimes (4) Often (5) Always

8. We offer flexible work schedules and work-from-home opportunities.
   (1) Never (2) Rarely (3) Sometimes (4) Often (5) Always

EXHIBIT G2.1
Self-Assessment of Organizational Talent Development, Cont'd

Annual Incentives:

9. We provide annual cost of living increases.
   (1) Never (2) Rarely (3) Sometimes (4) Often (5) Always

10. We offer performance bonuses, raises, and/or promotions to incentivize growth.
    (1) Never (2) Rarely (3) Sometimes (4) Often (5) Always

Staff Learning:

12. Our budget includes a line item for adequate staff professional development or integrates costs for professional development elsewhere in the budget (for example, in the Salary and Benefits line item).
    (1) Never (2) Rarely (3) Sometimes (4) Often (5) Always

13. We provide guidance, planning, and incentives to encourage effective use of professional development budgets.
    (1) Never (2) Rarely (3) Sometimes (4) Often (5) Always

14. Employees are encouraged to establish annual professional learning goals, and there is a system to encourage follow-through and support throughout the year.
    (1) Never (2) Rarely (3) Sometimes (4) Often (5) Always

Board and Volunteer Development:

14. We make funds and time for board learning on issues relevant to governance and mission.
    (1) Never (2) Rarely (3) Sometimes (4) Often (5) Always

15. We offer orientation, training, and recognition to nonboard volunteers.
    (1) Never (2) Rarely (3) Sometimes (4) Often (5) Always

Time for Development:

16. We pay managers with unrestricted funds, and they have unlimited time to manage their staff.
    (1) Never (2) Rarely (3) Sometimes (4) Often (5) Always

17. Job descriptions of managers include providing performance feedback and career support to their direct reports.
    (1) Never (2) Rarely (3) Sometimes (4) Often (5) Always

EXHIBIT G2.1
Self-Assessment of Organizational Talent Development, Cont'd

C. Transition and Retirement

18. We offer a retirement savings plan.

    (1) Never (2) Rarely (3) Sometimes (4) Often (5) Always

19. We provide matching funds as an incentive for staff to contribute to retirement savings.

    (1) Never (2) Rarely (3) Sometimes (4) Often (5) Always

20. Our board has approved an emergency plan in case our primary executives are unexpectedly sick or unavailable for an extended period of time.

    (1) Never (2) Rarely (3) Sometimes (4) Often (5) Always

21. There have been discussions on the board or staff about long-range executive transition plans.

    (1) Never (2) Rarely (3) Sometimes (4) Often (5) Always

22. There is an unspoken fear about how major leadership transitions will affect the organization.

    (1) Never (2) Rarely (3) Sometimes (4) Often (5) Always

Policy and Systems

Human Resources:

23. We have one (or more) employee(s) whose job(s) is/are *primarily* to provide a human resources or talent development function.

    (1) Never (2) Rarely (3) Sometimes (4) Often (5) Always

24. Our board and executive leadership review personnel policies and benefits packages to make sure they serve the current and future needs of the team.

    (1) Never (2) Rarely (3) Sometimes (4) Often (5) Always

25. Conflicts that arise amongst staff and/or volunteers are addressed in a timely and professional manner.

    (1) Never (2) Rarely (3) Sometimes (4) Often (5) Always

26. Our executive leaders intentionally create and/or maintain an organizational culture that values people and encourages high morale.

    (1) Never (2) Rarely (3) Sometimes (4) Often (5) Always

27. The physical surroundings of our workplace promote high morale and productivity.

    (1) Never (2) Rarely (3) Sometimes (4) Often (5) Always

EXHIBIT G2.1
Self-Assessment of Organizational Talent Development, Cont'd

Count up your score. Below write in the total number of 1s, 2s, 3s, 4s and 5s you have.

Number of 1s: _____ 2s: _____ 3s: _____ 4s: _____ 5s: _____

17 or more 1s or 2s = Low Talent Development Quotient

17 or more 3s = Mid-level Talent Development Quotient

17 or more 4s or 5s = High Talent Development Quotient

Now find the subtotals of your score by issue clusters, and circle the range in which your sub-totals fall.

1. Awareness and Recruitment (Ques. 1–5): 5–10 (Low) 11–15 (Medium) 16–20 (Good) 20–25 (Great)

2. Development and Retention (Ques. 6–17): 12–24 (Low) 25–35 (Medium) 36–54 (Good) 55–60 (Great)

3. Retirement and Transition (Ques. 18–22): 5–10 (Low) 11–15 (Medium) 16–20 (Good) 20–25 (Great)

4. Policy and Systems (Ques. 23–27): 5–10 (Low) 11–15 (Medium) 16–20 (Good) 20–25 (Great)

Based on previous rankings, circle the level of urgent attention each cluster needs in your organization.

1. Awareness and Recruitment: Not Urgent Somewhat Urgent Modestly Urgent Very Urgent

2. Development and Retention: Not Urgent Somewhat Urgent Modestly Urgent Very Urgent

3. Retirement and Transition: Not Urgent Somewhat Urgent Modestly Urgent Very Urgent

4. Policy and Systems: Not Urgent Somewhat Urgent Modestly Urgent Very Urgent

"Askitude"

Ask, invite, and encourage your funders to co-invest in your organization's team and talent systems.

Most foundation staff and donors will not ask about your talent development needs or strengths. It is simply not one of the issues generally on funder radar screens. Those that do invest heavily in leadership and professional development in their grantees generally do so in response to listening to the needs of their grantees! If you don't tell your funders that your organization needs and desires talent development resources, your funders most likely will not raise the issue with you. They may feel it is too invasive a line of questioning, or they may simply not be in the habit of addressing the issue with their resources.

If you were successful in including talent development in your organizational goals and annual budget, you now have the strongest mandate possible to speak directly to your donors and funders about why they ought to support your organization's efforts to build the strongest human capital possible. And you can talk about how strengthening your people will strengthen the goods and services you provide in the community, and make the organization more resilient for the long haul. Consider sharing the completed Talent Development Platform with your funders and show them the direction you are headed.

As I began planning my executive transition out of Emerging Practitioners in Philanthropy (EPIP), the first funder I approached about my transition plan was the Annie E. Casey Foundation. I had received executive coaching through them in the past, and had a trusting relationship with Rafael Lopez, our program contact there at the time. Most of all, I knew that Casey was proactive about supporting executive transitions for grantee organizations. When I told Rafael that I was leaving, he was extremely supportive of our plan and offered to help. Casey enabled EPIP to access consulting from TransitionGuides, a firm initiated by Kellogg Foundation and Annie E. Casey that helps social change organizations manage founder and executive transitions.

Your instinct and training may tell you to hide all your organizational and personal leadership weaknesses from your funders, and only tout your successes and strengths. Sharing your challenges and proficiency deficiencies with those who have funded your organization is certainly a risk. However, sharing challenges offers existing funders the opportunity to become even stronger allies and champions of your mission achievement. No leader knows everything they need to know to manage the complex roles and *all* competencies within their organizations. It is actually a sign of strong character to acknowledge an area of weakness in order to better yourself and those around you.

Rather than punishing you or repealing your grant, funders are likely to be appreciative of your forthrightness and take seriously the trust you have placed in them. In fact, most will start brainstorming with you to problem-solve together. Many funders have begun thinking about leadership issues in the context of what they call "capacity building," and some have mini-grants or other supplemental resources to build the capacity of their grantees. Other funders may not be institutionally equipped to fully fund your talent development plans, but they may be able to reallocate existing funds in your current grant, consider future support in a renewal, or simply start to consider how much of a challenge this is for all their grantees—which could spur even more action on a larger scale.

Funding Talent Development for Grantees

No matter the issue or geographic-based community they support, grantmakers often see the type of support they provide belonging to one of three general kinds of grants: programmatic, capacity building, and general operating support. When the issue of leadership or personnel development arises, it can feel like it doesn't belong anywhere. This is because it cuts across all three types of grants, and programs are impossible without people. Capacity does not exist without people. General operating support enables social change organizations to simply spend on their largest expense and greatest asset: people. The problem is that talent development needs more intentional focus and resource allocation. Talent philanthropy seeks to address this issue by offering a lens through which funders and fundraisers can see this issue that undergirds all the others.

Often, in responding to talent challenges raised by grantees, funders will lean toward "feel good" programmatic responses, such as hosting skills-based trainings, crafting a cohort-based fellowship, or supporting executive coaching. These programmatic responses are rare and critical resources themselves. They can also be viewed as a first step toward funders offering more intensive, systematic interventions to help their grantees and other social change organizations to address complex talent challenges.

One good example is the **Community Memorial Foundation** (CMF), a private foundation dedicated to improving the health of those who live and work in twenty-seven communities in the western suburbs of Chicago. One of its three primary grantmaking strategies focuses on building organizational effectiveness by providing grantees with resources to create great leaders, effective management, and sound governance. The first iteration of the program began in 2001, when the Foundation began hosting occasional workshops for grantees to learn about fund development and other management and governance issues. The effort has evolved, so that today CMF provides a more comprehensive portfolio of services to grantees:

- Small technical assistance grants

- Professional coaching to executive directors

- Educational workshops on board leadership

- An in-depth leadership development experience for middle-managers

- Organizational memberships in the Management Association of Illinois, a professional society focused on human resources issues

As they continue to enhance the program, they seek to "connect the dots" between these components and add new layers of value to serve many different stakeholders within their grantee organizations. Additionally, the foundation has leveraged its resources to bring the best professional development providers it can find from across the country to train the sixty or so social change organizations it funds. As program officer Tom Fuechtmann put it, "Why not? Why shouldn't our grantees and their leaders get the best that is available?" According to Fuechtmann, the CMF board has supported programs focused on grantee talent development because it is a great return on our investment (Stahl, 2013).

Another example is the **Evelyn and Walter Haas, Jr. Fund,** a national funder of gay and lesbian rights, immigrant rights, and educational equity. Haas Jr. launched their Flexible Leadership Awards in 2005. This effort enabled select grantees to work with a planning consultant to identify their own staff development goals that will help them reach their program and fundraising goals. The foundation provides multiyear funding to implement this talent development and convenes grantees to share their work across organizations. A five-year evaluation of the program, which used multiple data sources and three outside assessments, found that participating organizations were strikingly successful on all fronts: thirteen of fourteen groups met or surpassed their program goals; and twelve of fourteen met or surpassed their leadership development goals. On average, the fourteen organizations grew their budgets by 64 percent during the award period of 2005–2010, despite the economic hardships of the Great Recession.

Moreover, the evaluation found compelling examples of how the leadership work directly supported organizational impact. As one highlighted grantee executive director put it: "I feel like more funders need to understand that the work flows from the leadership, and so investing in leadership is investing in the work" (Ryan, 2013).

The Durfee Foundation makes this idea of leadership central to its grantmaking. Shelving the usual program areas, Durfee funds leadership development in Los Angeles social change organizations, without concern for specific issue areas. Their founding donor believed society was the ultimate beneficiary of the private sector's investments in creative and entrepreneurial leaders. The Durfee Foundation applies the same thinking to social change organizations and takes it one step further. Its goal is to build networks of talented leaders working in different social change organizations across Los Angeles.

Durfee's executive director, Claire Peeps, and president, Carrie Avery, recognized that talented social change leaders "have helped to transform the lives of individuals and communities in Los Angeles County, but often at a high personal cost. Many are overworked and underpaid, and almost all are stressed out.... Without time to replenish themselves, they may lose their creative edge or leave the field all together. Either would be a terrible blow to the individuals and communities they serve." The resulting Sabbatical Program provides grantee executives an unrestricted grant of $35,000 for a three-month leave of absence. In addition, Durfee gives a seed grant of $5,000 to the leaders' organizations to start a professional development fund to strengthen the skills of staff members. Funding these individuals is "part of a larger plan to build connections among grantees that benefit their organizations and, ultimately, their communities" (Durfee Foundation, 2011, p. 49).

An evaluation study of five foundation sabbatical-funding programs (including Durfee's) shows that funding sabbaticals as a talent investment tactic can yield significant positive outcomes. The report finds that these awards

- increase organizational capacity, as second-tier leadership steps up to the plate;

- are important tools for succession planning, as executives and interims clarify their interests;

- strengthen governance, with 60 percent of groups saying their boards are more effective as a result of planning and learning that surrounded the sabbatical; and

- benefit the funders themselves through increased grantee trust and community knowledge (Linnell & Wolfred, 2009).

The Community Memorial Foundation, Haas Jr. Fund, and Durfee Foundation fund in very different communities, at vastly different scales with different models and methods. But each of these foundations sees the results of investing in the impact and sustainability of individual leaders who compose those organizations.

The funders that I briefly profiled all say they came to talent investing by listening deeply and responding to the needs of their grantees. They also have board members who understand the pivotal role people play in creating great organizations, return on investment for talent development, as well as the cost of *not* investing in social change leaders. Recruiting board members who understand talent development, educating your current board members about talent issues in the social change sector, and starting conversations about talent development with your grantees are all tangible steps grantmakers can take to build the case from the top down and bottom up for investing in grantee talent development. Exhibit G2.2 offers a self-assessment meant to help you consider how your foundation prioritizes grantee talent development. This tool helps you brainstorm and consider how you might make grantee Talent Development a funding priority in the future.

Practicing What We Fund: Professional Development for Grantmakers

If you are going to invest in grantee talent, it seems wise to consider doing the same within the walls of your foundation. The Durfee Foundation provides sabbatical funding to their grantees. They also provide sabbatical funding to their own staff.

Since the onset of Durfee's Sabbatical Program, Claire Peeps had helped Fellows prepare for their leaves, yet it wasn't until the Durfee board insisted that she take a leave in 2003 that she fully understood the mixed emotions many Fellows experience at the beginning and end of the sabbatical. "I didn't know how hard it would be to get out the door," she says, "and I have a small staff and an organization with secure funding. Imagine what it's like for Fellows running bigger organizations that aren't financially stable."

Claire got the first inkling of what it meant to disconnect completely from her job on the first day of her sabbatical. At 8 p.m. she tried to log on to her office computer and discovered that her password had already been changed, a practice Durfee recommends to discourage recipients from checking their e-mail while on sabbatical. "That's when it hit me that my life was about to change," she says.

EXHIBIT G2.2

Self-Assessment for Funders: Preparedness for Investing in Grantee Talent

Intellectual Preparedness

1. I believe the primary *cultural or intellectual* barriers to advancing the idea of "talent investing" at my foundation would be:

    _____

    _____

    _____

    _____

2. On a priority list produced by the most influential person/people in our foundation, the importance of grantee leadership or talent development would appear

    __ High on the list __ Middle of the list __ Buried at bottom of list __ Not even on the list

3. The terminology that would be best received at my foundation would be:

    ___ Leadership Development

    ___ Human Capital

    ___ Talent Development

    ___ Human Resources

4. The type of intervention that would speak most directly to our culture would be:

    ___ Personal Leadership Development

    ___ Improving Managerial Skills

    ___ Personal Sustainability and Renewal

    ___ Executive Coaching

    ___ Investing in Emerging Leaders

Grantmaking Preparedness

5. My foundation only funds programs and services, and does not get involved in strengthening the organizations we fund.

    ___ Yes ___ No ___ Not Sure

EXHIBIT G2.2

Self-Assessment for Funders: Preparedness for Investing in Grantee Talent, Cont'd

6. My foundation currently includes "capacity building" in its toolbox of grantmaking or other activities.

    ___ Yes ___ No ___ Not Sure

7. If we had to choose between "buying" grantee programs or "building" grantee organizations, our foundation would choose:

    ___ Buying grantee programs ___ Building Grantee Programs ___ Not Sure

8. Efforts to invest in grantee talent have been made in the past. Here's a list.

    _____

    _____

    _____

    _____

9. In the examples listed in response to question 8, what happened? Were these efforts viewed as successes or failures? What challenges did they face? What can be learned from these experiences?

    _____

    _____

    _____

    _____

Leadership Preparedness

10. The most influential people on my board are business people who understand the importance of talent development in the context of their business lives, but not in the social change organization context.

    ___ Yes ___ No ___ Not Sure

11. Our board would not easily approve significant spending on grantee talent development.

    ___ Yes ___ No ___ Not Sure

12. The foundation has a commitment to offering professional development to *our own* staff. This could translate into investing in grantee talent development.

    ___ Yes ___ No ___ Not Sure

EXHIBIT G2.2
Self-Assessment for Funders: Preparedness for Investing in Grantee Talent, Cont'd

13. I believe the primary people who would be barriers to advancing a "talent investing" agenda at my foundation would be:

_____

_____

_____

_____

Logistical Preparedness

14. I believe the primary *logistical* barriers to advancing a "talent investing" agenda at my foundation would be:

_____

_____

_____

_____

15. How would the grants management department respond to the idea of grantee talent investing?

_____

_____

_____

_____

Making it Happen

16. The following individuals would be key allies needed to make talent investing possible at my foundation:

_____

_____

EXHIBIT G2.2
Self-Assessment for Funders: Preparedness for Investing in Grantee Talent, Cont'd

17. In my own words, the most compelling arguments or case statements would likely be:

_____
_____
_____
_____

18. The best place(s) inside the foundation to start this effort would likely be:

_____
_____
_____
_____

19. Examples I could cite from well-known grantees would be:

_____
_____
_____
_____

20. The following well-known grantees would be the right initial groups to provide talent investments:

_____
_____
_____
_____

21. I commit to taking the following actions to explore the opportunity to begin investing in grantee talent:

_____
_____
_____
_____

By the following date: _____

As a working mom, Claire's family life was tightly scheduled. "My usual conversation with my kids is, 'Hurry, hurry, hurry,' so it was wonderful to have relaxed, unbroken time with them. My daughter was ten years old at the time, and the leave gave me the chance to cement my relationship with her when she was at a critical age. Taking family vacations to London and Wyoming was also wonderful."

Like other Fellows, Claire discovered that the hardest parts of the sabbatical were learning to slow down at the start and getting back up to speed at the end. "I thought I knew all about sabbaticals, but going on leave made me more sensitive to the nuances of the experience" (Durfee, 2011, p. 51)

If foundations understand the benefits of investing in the professional development of their own staff, then they may be more interested and skilled at investing in their grantees' professional development. However, grantmaking has not traditionally been structured as a profession or career. Many foundation executives do not think it should be. Foundations tend to hire from outside their institutions *and* outside of philanthropy (Council on Foundations, 2009). Careers in grantmaking tend to zigzag across organizations and between fundraising and grantmaking institutions (which is the same for grantee organization staff as well). Many funders have multiple types of professional and content expertise (for example, a grantmaker who was trained as a lawyer and focused on human rights had little training specific to philanthropy and grantmaking, or how social change organizations operate). On top of this, there is no uniformity in style and process across foundations, making generic training less appealing.

For all these reasons and more, professionals working in foundations, which are some of the wealthiest organizations in the social change sector, actually get very little professional development. This can be problematic, because funders wield outsized power over the life and death of social change organizations that provide crucial services in our communities. It also means funders don't see a central role for talent investing in the wider social change community, including their grantees. Yet people are central to the effectiveness and impact of foundations. Alan Pifer, longtime president of the Carnegie Corporation of New York, said back in 1973:

> Above all other aspects of foundation work, I would put the human factor. I mean by this the attitudes and behavior of foundation staff members. If they are arrogant, self-important, dogmatic,

conscious of power and status, or filled with a sense of their own omniscience—traits which the stewardship of money tends to bring out in some people—the foundation they serve cannot be a good one. If, on the other hand, they have genuine humility, are conscious of their own limitations, are aware that money does not confer wisdom, are humane, intellectually alive and curious people—men and women who above all else are eager to learn from others—the foundation they serve will probably be a good one. In short, the human qualities of its staff may in the end be far more important to what a foundation accomplishes than any other considerations. (Pifer, 1982, p. 9)

In light of this still-relevant perspective from forty years ago, the particular dynamics of foundation staff recruitment, development, and retention ought to be considered of central import, rather than something to be left on the margins. A change of attitude and behavior amongst foundation boards and executives would be a major positive shift in the right direction.

Things are starting to change for the better. Just in the last decade alone, grantmaking has become more attractive to younger people, professionalism has become more important to foundations, and professional development has become more widely available. Efforts like the foundations profiled in this guide have helped to move this process forward. Additionally, the expanding academic study of philanthropy and social change organization management has meant that many younger grantmakers enter the foundation world with master's degrees focused on the field. Adequate professional development for foundation staff in grantmaking roles ought to cover the following terrain:

- Ethics and power dynamics

- Working with social change organizations as a funder

- History of philanthropy and foundations in America

- Cycle of grantmaking

- Mission and culture at your foundation

- Ecosystem of the funder community (associations, research centers, etc.)

- The literature, research, and trade press on philanthropy

Recent years have seen the development of excellent professional education for foundation professionals using a variety of formats and covering at least some of the topics I've outlined. The following list offers a few key resources:

- Academy for Grantmaking and Funder Education (a program of the George H. Heyman, Jr. Center for Philanthropy and Fundraising at New York University)

- LearnPhilanthropy.org (housed at the Johnson Center at Grand Valley State University)

- The Grantmaking School (a program of the Johnson Center at Grand Valley State University)

- *The Insider's Guide to Grantmaking* (a book by Joel Orosz)

- GrantCraft.org (part of Foundation Center and European Foundation Centre)

- Hull Fellowship, Advanced Leadership Institute, and CEO Forum (all programs of the Southeastern Council on Foundations)

- Essential Skills and Strategies for Grantmakers (cohosted by the Council on Foundations and various regional associations of grantmakers)

- Emerging Practitioners in Philanthropy

- Center for Effective Philanthropy

- Grantmakers for Effective Organizations [1]

Additionally, many funder affinity groups offer issue-specific funder education, and regional associations of grantmakers offer localized orientations for new foundation staffers, some of which are listed in the Third Party Professional Development Guide in this book.

Exhibit G2.3 provides a self-assessment to determine your foundation's views of internal talent investment. You can use this self-assessment as a starting off point for staff support.

---

[1] Full disclosure: I was a founding staff member of Emerging Practitioners in Philanthropy and played a consulting role in the creation of SECF's Advanced Leadership Institute

EXHIBIT G2.3

Self-Assessment for Funders: Practicing Talent Investment Internally

1. My foundation offers a robust orientation for new staff.

   ___ Yes ___No ___ Not sure

2. At my foundation, we learn our culture and practice but gain no context for how we fit into the wider foundation field.

   ___ Yes ___No ___ Not sure

3. Professional development funds and activities are widely available to staff.

   ___ Yes ___No ___ Not sure

4. Staff are encouraged to participate in our local regional association of Grantmakers.

   ___ Yes ___No ___ Not sure

5. Staff are encouraged to participate in one or more affinity groups or funder networks that they find relevant to their own needs, identity, or funding area.

   ___ Yes ___No ___ Not sure

6. Employees are encouraged to establish annual professional learning goals, and there is a system to encourage follow-through and support throughout the year.

   ___ Yes ___No ___ Not sure

7. I believe the following would increase morale and productivity amongst our staff:

   _____

   _____

   _____

   _____

8. I would help to translate internal talent investment within the foundation into external talent investing in our grantees by taking the following steps:

   _____

   _____

   _____

   _____

Conclusion

This guide encouraged you to change your attitude to include a talent lens, assess talent needs in your sphere of influence, plan and budget for responsive interventions, and use this mandate and your "confident vulnerability" to actively invite the financial investment needed for meaningful talent development. Such resources, in turn, can have a multiplicity of benefits for social change organizations, their employees, funders, and communities. Indeed, no matter where you sit in the social change ecosystem, the same mantra applies: If you want to succeed, *invest in people!*

Guide 3
A Practical Guide on Intercultural Competence for Nonprofit Managers

Alexis S. Terry

Each workday, professionals of various backgrounds and values who are looking to offer their best to their organizations are inadvertently challenged by assumptions and differing expectations about their colleagues, resulting in misunderstandings and miscommunication that impact their satisfaction and the success of their organizations. That's why we believe intercultural competency is extremely important, not only as an organizational value and practice, but as a competency each staff member and volunteer should possess or have intentional goals to better.

To further help your organization become interculturally competent we asked Alexis S. Terry, a leading expert in this arena for social change organizations, to produce a guide for you. We hope this guide provides the tools you need to become the type of workplace your employees and mission deserve. A large part of being a learning organization is ensuring you engrain these practices into the fabric of your work in leading teams, making organizational decisions, solving problems, and facilitating meetings that maximize others' contributions.

Do any of these situations sound familiar to you?

- A large group of people from various parts of the country and world attend your signature event. During lunch breaks and networking receptions, you cannot help but notice that many young people and people of color cling to their own identity groups. By the second day of the event, you notice on the golf course that the "old boys' network" prevails, too.

- You're the only person with your skin color, gender, or background around the decision-making table. Inside jokes or references go over your head, and it's an effort to fully participate in group dynamics and discussions. You've had the thought that people will respond to you *because* you're different, but often, nobody around the decision-making table is aware of what it is like to be the "only" in organizational settings.

- You released the annual call for volunteers to apply for a seat on your governing board. The call includes a statement encouraging candidates to apply if they can demonstrate diversity of thought or affinity with demographic identity groups (e.g., women, young professionals, racial and ethnic groups, people with disabilities, people of various sexual orientations). Few, if any, candidates apply that can demonstrate affinity with an identity group. No one can figure out why that happened. Furthermore, board members say they don't know "where to find them." And yet again, the roster and photos of board members do not reflect the organizations' commitment to diversity.

If you're like most managers of social change organizations, one, if not each, of these will resonate with you. In fact, the social change organizations that I work with—either as a consultant or coach—tend to vacillate between being too open and too closed off with respect to cultural considerations. For example, managers who get feedback that they have been too open by asking questions about identity will often start suppressing their natural curiosity. Conversely, managers who receive feedback that they are too closed off, may be misunderstood by others or miss opportunities to develop effective relationships on behalf of the organization. At either end of the spectrum, it can be tempting to throw up your hands in exasperation and feel you're damned if you do and damned if you don't.

This guide cuts to the heart of practicing intercultural competence— what it is exactly, and how to leverage it to become a more effective manager of a social change organization. It shows everyone—introverts, extroverts, new nonprofit professionals, and senior executives—how to overcome the struggle of connecting and communicating with people not like you, even amidst tangled nerves and confusion about how you might be perceived along the way.

If you're looking to be a more effective leader and social change organization yet it feels like a burden for you or others you work with to transcend differences and maximize the contributions of others, there's most likely a clear reason: intercultural competence. Intercultural competence is a set of views, attitudes, and behaviors that facilitate effective and appropriate interaction across cultural contexts (Bennett, 2011).

As the manager of a social change organization, practicing intercultural competence is directly connected to your ability to get noticed, forge trusting relationships, and get others on board with your vision. Think of the overextended supervisor who doesn't seem to know what's really going on with staff or how to motivate them, or the otherwise competent executive who makes a joke about someone's background and is met with uncomfortable laughter or awkward silence. Imagine not having to walk on eggshells with people, or be at the mercy of your own insecurities about what to say or not say to avoid coming across as insensitive, or worse, like a complete idiot.

This guide offers surefire strategies for

- recognizing when culture helps you and holds you back;

- staying open and confident through cultural conversations;

- engaging diverse groups that support your organizations' mission; and

- working skillfully with culturally different professionals and organizational stakeholders.

With sisterly insight and refreshing candor, I'll point out the things that might be in your blind spot: unhelpful attitudes and behaviors that are easy to see in other social change colleagues, but much more difficult to see in yourself. Then I'll show you how to adjust them to get the results that you and your organization deserve. Ultimately, this guide will help you assess and adjust behaviors that are limiting you and your organization from getting even better results through people who are different from you.

Here you will see tools, quizzes, and strategies for developing intercultural competence, starting with the Intercultural Competence Self-Assessment (exhibit G3.1). Along the way, you will learn how to surface opportunities to facilitate learning and conversations at any stage. Go for it! Really dig in and put your career experiences and views through cultural scrutiny to see an authentic reflection in the glass—the real you, with all your many facets, talents, and positive qualities to offer to the social change sector. It's all about you! Here we go!

Part A: Framing Intercultural Competence in Your Work

EXHIBIT G3.1

Intercultural Competence Self-Assessment

(Twenty reasons you might need this chapter)

Instructions: Read each statement and indicate if it is true or false for you. If you're unsure, skip to the next statement. If you feel that two seemingly opposite statements are both true or both false, mark them that way.

True or false

1. I like to be on time and expect the same of others.
2. What happens is more important than the time something starts and ends.
3. When rules are presented, I prefer that details are spelled out clearly.
4. Some rules are understood by everyone, so it's not necessary to spell everything out.
5. I prefer to work independently and be recognized individually.
6. I prefer to work as part of a group and think it's better when individuals are not singled out.
7. All people should be treated the same, no matter what their title or position is in the organization.
8. People should be treated differently depending on their title, position, or rank in the organization.
9. When working on a project, I'd rather focus and get the job done, and I become impatient with socializing.
10. When working on a project, I'd rather build relationships, and I work better with people when I get to know them.
11. I'd rather address issues when they arise, so they can be solved quickly.
12. I'd rather address issues indirectly, behind the scenes, to avoid causing distress.
13. It's better to keep emotions to myself.
14. It's better to express emotions openly.
15. I get more of my identity from who I am and who my family is.
16. I get more of my identity from what I do (title, volunteer activities, education, etc.).
17. I believe we're living in a post-racial society.
18. I believe we're not living in a post-racial society.
19. I don't care if someone is young, old, green, or purple because I don't see color or difference.
20. I can't help but feel different or wonder if I will be the only _____ person when I walk into a room.

EXHIBIT G3.1
Intercultural Competence Self-Assessment, Cont'd

Consider this

- For statements that are true for you, how do they contribute to your professional success?
- For statements that are true for you, how do they hold you back?
- For statements that are false for you, which are difficult for you to deal with in other people?
- How are your responses similar or different from those of your colleagues?

Add up your score

One point for each "True" statement. Don't cheat!

1–8 Points: You sort of need this chapter.

A lot of the content will be familiar to you, so read it as a refresher and then do your colleague, friend, supervisor, or "frenemy" a favor and buy another copy to pass on its contents. Take the opportunity yourself to reflect on where you are and start over in areas where you may be struggling. It's never too late to make a change or encourage one.

9+ Points: You absolutely, positively need this chapter.

You probably had a sense that your beliefs or behaviors are limiting you from connecting and getting organizational results through people who are different than you. What you didn't know until now is that nothing in your organizational life is working to connect and communicate with people different than you. Don't fret. This guide is going to make it a lot easier and more enjoyable than what you're doing now, which is trying to stay in denial about cultural differences and their impact on individual and institutional success.

Source: Based on research by Edward Hall, Geert Hofstede, and Aperian Global. Compiled by Alexis Terry.

Stages and Strategies for Developing Intercultural Competence

Bennett's Developmental Model of Intercultural Sensitivity frames the continuum of increasing sophistication in the experience and navigation of differences.

The first three stages indicate that the individual applies a dominant cultural view in some way. For example, have you ever heard someone say "We're all the same," as if to squelch the idea that differences are organizational assets? Do you ever sense there is an organizational preference for "sameness"? One of my favorite books is called *Work with Me,* by Barbara Annis and John Gray. In the book they note that a preference for "sameness" is one of the greatest barriers to "gender intelligence" and is a source of the most misunderstandings between men and women in almost every industry. Irrespective of gender, have you ever proposed an idea and received the following response: "That's just (not) the way we do things around here." Or, ever participate in a hiring interview as a group and heard someone offer the following rationale for rejecting a candidate: "This candidate doesn't fit in." Responses like these indicate that the dominant culture that influences organizational decision making may be too insular.

The latter three stages indicate that the individual adjusts ways of working and the organization avoids a "majority rules" way of operating in order to maximize diversity and the contributions of others who may not hold the dominant view. Decisions are made in the context of other cultural considerations. For example, the organization may offer domestic partner benefits even if a majority of the staff identify as heterosexual. An organization may decide to adjust the dress code to allow for religious attire or offer flexible arrangements on the holy days of various religions. In other words, there is no one-size-fits-all mentality or way of operating that is "reality" or "just the way we do things around here." Instead, social change organizations, particularly those seeking to be leaders who work skillfully with culturally different professionals and organizational stakeholders, focus on the latter three stages of the continuum by practicing intercultural competency behaviors.

I offer to you that the latter stages in the continuum are possible! The rest of this guide offers practical opportunities for you to improve your intercultural competence, show others how to do the same, and thus build toward becoming a social change organization where acceptance, adaptation, and integration of cultures becomes an indication of organizational satisfaction and success.

Spend a few moments on Tool 1 to help you reflect on the connections between culture and your role as a leader of a social change organization (exhibit G3.2).

EXHIBIT G3.2
Tool 1: Holding Up the Mirror

Imagine yourself in a house of mirrors, a place where you can change the view of yourself at will. All you've got is you and a bunch of metal, reflective glass, and your imagination. One mirror may reflect an image of you as thin as a pencil, while another may show you as tall as eight feet. What you see depends on the mirror and on how you position yourself. Each mirror tells a different story about you, but no one mirror can capture your true essence.

As a manager, you may never see yourself in any mirror the way others see you, but I invite you to know yourself so well that no reflection will fool you into believing you're something you're not. The "real" you—your preferences, talents, interests—helps inform your choices about a rewarding career and life. The knowledge you have of yourself and others is important and reflected in the ways in which you communicate and interact. The following self-assessment questions will assist you in reflecting on your level of intercultural competence. You'll discover where your cultural lenses help you and hinder you.

Read each statement below and rate yourself from 1 (never) to 5 (always). Be as candid as you can.

I reflect on my own cultural background as it relates to disability, ethnicity, gender, generations, race, religion, sexual orientation, and other areas of identity that may influence my behavior at work.	1 2 3 4 5
I reflect on my own attitudes and behaviors to determine how I am processing information and leading staff and other organizational stakeholders.	1 2 3 4 5
I educate myself about the culture and experience of others (e.g., professionals with disabilities, and other ethnicities, genders, generations, races, religions, sexual orientation) by attending programs, events, reading, interacting, etc.	1 2 3 4 5
I get involved, in a proper way, when I observe others behaving in ways that appear culturally insensitive or reflect prejudice.	1 2 3 4 5
I avoid generalizing about a person based on demographic identity (e.g., professionals with disabilities, and other ethnicities, genders, generations, races, religions, sexual orientation).	1 2 3 4 5
I act in ways consistent with my belief that all organizational stakeholders are capable of succeeding.	1 2 3 4 5
I am open to changing my behavior/work style from ways that are comfortable to me to ways that may be more helpful and better serve staff and organizational stakeholders not like me.	1 2 3 4 5
I am willing to initiate organizational changes that will better serve staff and organizational stakeholders from diverse backgrounds.	1 2 3 4 5
I utilize methods of communication (e.g., written, verbal, pictures, diagrams, examples, humor) appropriate for the populations my organization serves.	1 2 3 4 5

EXHIBIT G3.2
Tool 1: Holding Up the Mirror, Cont'd

For organizational stakeholders and constituents who have hearing impairments or speak languages other than English, I attempt to learn and use key words in their language, so I am better able to communicate with them on behalf of the organization.	1 2 3 4 5
I accept that religion or other beliefs may influence how organizational stakeholders and constituents make decisions.	1 2 3 4 5

Consider this

- What did this self-assessment bring up for you?
- How might your responses help you in your career? How might they hold you back?
- What steps can you take in the next one to three weeks to create space for further introspection?
- How are your responses similar to or different from the views of your colleagues?

Add up your score

Tally your score and view your results below.

47–55 Points:

Your answers reflect active thinking and engagement around cultural considerations. Share this assessment with someone who may benefit from talking with you about their results.

38–46 Points:

Your honesty is refreshing! Now try talking and addressing the areas in need of improvement with people who are not like you.

37 Points or Less:

Without meaning harm to others, you may be unconsciously perpetuating culturally biased behaviors. You may find it easier to talk about your results and new insights with someone who is close to you, and whose background is similar to yours. Then, set the intention to create space for introspection.

Source: Derived from Milton J. Bennett, "Towards a Developmental Model of Intercultural Sensitivity," in R. Michael Paige, ed., *Education for the Intercultural Experience,* Yarmouth, ME: Intercultural Press, 1993. Also refer to Janet M. Bennett, "Cultural Marginality: Identity Issues in Intercultural Training," in R. Michael Paige, ed., *Education for the Intercultural Experience.*

Next, check out Tool 2 for a conversation starter worksheet (exhibit G3.3). Using your self-assessment as a conversation starter with your colleagues is a good practice for organizations with a strong learning culture. Tool 2 will equip you with some useful questions and insight on the right environment for holding safe, open, culturally competent conversations.

EXHIBIT G3.3

Tool 2: Staying Open and Confident through Cultural Conversations

I want to give _____ (name) and myself an opportunity to have a conversation about

_____ (aspect or situation involving

culture).

Setting the Stage

I will set the stage for the conversation by

_____

_____

_____

_____

I will create an atmosphere that is inviting by

_____

_____

_____

_____

Observations

Some observations and concrete scenarios that I will share

Intro Messages

Some statements I want to make upfront about _____ (name), this conversation, or what I'm

seeing include

Powerful Questions

Some questions I will ask or ways I will facilitate sharing and learning include the following:

- How do you think we're doing as an organization in reflecting our commitment to acceptance, adaptability, and integration of different cultural views?

- What's the impact (on you)?

- From your vantage point, what might be needed in the future?

- What do you think might be causing this?

- What approaches do you suggest?

- Do you have thoughts on how we might put that into practice?

Ideas and Suggestions

Depending on the direction the conversation goes, I might suggest

EXHIBIT G3.3

Tool 2: Staying Open and Confident through Cultural Conversations, Cont'd

Wrap up and Next Steps

I will make sure _____(name) and I agree on key conversation considerations (e.g., confidentiality, anonymity, expectations, next steps) and will communicate this:

_____

_____

_____

_____

I will follow up on this conversation by: _____ / _____ / _____ (date) and in this way:

_____

_____

_____

_____

After your conversation, consider this

- What did this dialogue bring up for you?
- Where would you say the conversation fell along Bennett's Developmental Model of Intercultural Sensitivity?
- What was the impact of using this tool to guide your thinking before and during the conversation?
- What's noteworthy?
- What's next?

What you do as a manager of a social change organization is so important. I hope you'll come back to this tool regularly. Use it to plan conversations during your one-on-one meetings with staff, or with volunteer leaders seeking to select a diverse slate of new volunteer members to the board or to a committee. Refer to it as you think about building more trusting peer-to-peer relationships and smoothing out miscommunication or misunderstandings. Basically, as you go about your work, look for opportunities to reflect and discuss culture as a lens on interpersonal communication and dynamics.

Sometimes you will come across objections to intercultural competency. Tool 3 helps you prepare strategies to overcome these objections (exhibit G3.4).

At this juncture in the guide, pause to take note of how your self-assessment connects to your work as a leader. As demographic shifts continue on a macro level, imagine how much more the intercultural competence skills you're practicing here will help you in your career down the line.

EXHIBIT G3.4

Tool 3: Developing Strategies to Overcome Objections to Intercultural Competency

As you practice intercultural competence, consider that you will not always work with people who have the same appreciation for these skills and how they contribute to career and organizational success. Instead of getting frustrated, there's a much easier way to overcome objections to intercultural competency: anticipate objections and strategically address them.

Let's practice! Read each objection statement below and construct a brief response that helps enhance intercultural curiosity.

Anticipating Objections

Objection 1: There are too many considerations and terms. I cannot possibly learn about all of them. Besides, I see everyone as the same. I don't see color or difference.

_____

_____

_____

_____

Objection 2: Resources are thin, so I need a concrete, step-by-step, business-oriented way to sell the organization on investing in intercultural competency. Why should business and work become so personal or "touchy feely?" We should stick to the facts and business at hand.

_____

_____

_____

_____

Objection 3: As someone who is in the minority in my organization, I know what it means to be culturally sensitive. I don't need any lecture or literature on how to practice it.

_____

_____

_____

_____

Objection 4: I keep hearing about changing demographics, but the organization and community that we serve here isn't that diverse. I don't see that changing anytime soon, either. There are only a couple of cultures different from our American culture here, so do we really need to do anything differently?

_____

_____

_____

_____

EXHIBIT G3.4
Tool 3: Developing Strategies to Overcome Objections to Intercultural Competency, Cont'd

Did you catch yourself wanting to confront rather than converse as you read the objections? Remember, the name of the game is understanding and relationship building, which can't happen if you're in defensive mode. When that comes up for you, recognize it as a trigger for the ethnocentric stage (that is, denial, defensiveness, and minimization) on the continuum of Bennett's Developmental Model of Intercultural Sensitivity.

Stay with me. The goal is to use objections as opportunities to practice developing your own sense of intercultural curiosity, and help others do the same.

Inspiring Intercultural Curiosity

Here are ten strategies for inspiring intercultural curiosity:

1. Give others the floor without interrupting, either to agree or disagree.
2. Practice listening with tolerance for ambiguity.
3. Suspend assumptions and value judgments.
4. Monitor the use of humor for appropriateness.
5. Facilitate turn-taking, participation, use of silence.
6. Reduce physical barriers to participation (e.g., room setup, accommodations).
7. Acknowledge each person who shares with the group.
8. Express gratitude that this is a safe environment to have these types of conversations.
9. Wear the hat of a cultural ally and thought partner and position your contributions accordingly.
10. Reinforce that this is not the only opportunity to have a conversation about culture, and offer examples of how to keep it going. Invite others to build on your ideas.

Before moving on, consider also what you would want to add to this list. Then, let's look at how to create the possibility for a regular dialogue about culture so that it becomes as relevant to others as it is to you. That may not happen in one conversation, so it's important to lay the foundation for acceptance, adaptation, and integration.

Making Real Connections: Deepening Dialogue about Intercultural Competence

Find an article from a newspaper, blog, or magazine about culture and organizations. After reading the article, share it with colleagues or your staff to generate conversation about building shared understanding about related cultural considerations in *your* organization, department, or team.

EXHIBIT G3.4

Tool 3: Developing Strategies to Overcome Objections to Intercultural Competency, Cont'd

Sample conversation starters

- What stood out to you in the article?

- What might be the impact on you/us/the organization?

- What are we already doing in that area? (Affirm behavior that aligns with your organization and this article!)

- What more can we do?

- What might that bring us?

- How do you see that working here?

- What resources are available to make that happen? What else might we need?

As you have this conversation, identify opportunities for additional development, training, materials, and so on, to broaden and deepen learning. The extent to which you, and your colleagues, can be clear about real connections and earmarks of cultural competence in the news or in your organization, the more likely you will pick up additional skills that could bring career advancement and organizational advancement later on.

Part B: Facilitating Intercultural Competence in Your Organization

By now you've gone through quizzes and worksheets designed to help you gain a new understanding of where you are in your individual intercultural competence cycle, and how to facilitate others' self-awareness and intercultural curiosity. Now it's time to frame where you might have opportunities for impact at the group and organizational level.

Putting It All Together

Let's face it; some colleagues simply have less practice, and thus comfort, talking about aspects of identity in the context of others. And when we don't talk about intercultural competence as a value or skill, it can feel like a shock when we finally do. Resistance is a natural response to change. So when you're starting to introduce skill building of intercultural competence to a group or organization, expect it to feel initially like a tough pill to swallow, or expect a lack of urgency as though it is a topic to focus on when something goes wrong. Organizations can unintentionally reinforce this thinking by engaging in intercultural competence skill building only after an issue arises. As a social change manager, you have the influence to make business personal. And do so with some flavor that only you can bring! Here's my mental map, in case it helps get your creative juices flowing about how you will incorporate the tools in this guide into your unique nonprofit lifestyle.

Step 1: Preparation

When I feel ready to engage colleagues who question the relevance of intercultural competence, I use Tool 2 to help frame my thinking and approach to the conversation. Sometimes I can recall cultural clues from their cubicles or corner offices (e.g., photos, art, quotes, religious symbols, screen savers) and use these indications of identity and value systems as conversation starters. If I know their objections up front, I use Tool 3 to be thoughtful about objections without coming across as defensive. To effectively weave intercultural competence into a work conversation, it helps to set my intention first (e.g., raising awareness, improving a relationship or communication with my colleague or team). That way, everything I say or do flows from that intention. Remember, an open, friendly attitude will build the relationship.

Step 2: One-on-One Conversations

If it's a one-on-one conversation, I go to their cubicle or office. It's highly likely I will see photos on their desk. Wearing our intercultural competency glasses, we know that photos are clues about an aspect of someone's identity or value system. And depending on someone's notion of the word *family,* starting or participating in a conversation about those photos could be easy or difficult for them and others in the organization. For example, the photos could be of an interracial couple on their wedding day, or of a child sitting in a wheelchair.

I'm a sucker for cute kids, so when I see family photos displayed, it's natural for me to ooh and ahh over them and ask the person about his or her kids. Usually that sparks a great story or dialogue. Then I follow with an acknowledgment or observation such as, "I see you light up when you can talk about your kids and your identity as a mom [dad]. Aren't we fortunate to work in an environment where we can surround ourselves with and discuss important moments in life that keep us motivated during the day? I hope everyone feels as comfortable."

And then I pause. Meanwhile, I'm listening and watching body language for clues related to Bennett's continuum: denial, defense, and minimization or acceptance, adaptation, and integration.

If on the one hand my questions or statements are met with denial, defense, or minimization of differences, then Tool 3 becomes relevant. It's a judgment call. Rome wasn't built in a day, right? So depending on the response and my other options, I may re-engage in a different way at a different time or invite a more influential colleague to do so.

On the other hand, if my questions or statement are met with acknowledgment or curiosity, I'll likely follow up immediately: "Given what we do as an organization, how might we encourage more conversation about identity and its influence in shaping richer nonprofit lives? That way, we could also avoid unintentionally sending a message that it's not important or, worse, not allowed here unless something bad happens first. What do you think?"

Then I pause again and listen. If I hear ideas and others raise similar ones, then I acknowledge any themes. Here's what *not* to do next: Avoid the trap of going into planning and action mode. Your job at this point is to appreciate your colleague's willingness to be generous with his time and ideas and not bog him down with yours. Give him space to determine where to take the conversation with you. He may shift gears and not bring it up again unless you do (for example, if you use the "Making Real Connections" exercise in Tool 3). He may come back to you at another time or take action on his own. As a cultural ally, my job is to inspire, model, and challenge, which takes more than one conversation.

Step 3: Group Conversations

Working with a bunch of "peaches" and "coconuts" takes intentionality. Stay with me. Culture gurus Fons Trompenaars and Charles Hampden-Turner (1997) introduced this topic, and Erin Meyer (2014) covered it in a *Harvard Review* blog post noting:

> Peach cultures like the USA or Brazil people tend to be friendly ("soft") with new acquaintances. They smile frequently at strangers, move quickly to first-name usage, share information about themselves, and ask personal questions of those they hardly know. But after a little friendly interaction with a peach, you may suddenly get to the hard shell of the pit where the peach protects his real self and the relationship suddenly stops.
>
> In coconut cultures such Russia and Germany, people are initially more closed off from those they don't have friendships with. They rarely smile at strangers, ask casual acquaintances personal questions, or offer personal information to those they don't know intimately. But over time, as coconuts get to know you, they become gradually warmer and friendlier. And while relationships are built up slowly, they also tend to last longer.

The current combination of peaches and coconuts in a group is one consideration. Another, particularly for social change leaders, is the combination the organization needs in the future in order to achieve its objectives. With this in mind, I initiate meaningful group conversations that foster intercultural competence starting with a self-assessment (Tool 1), or I use Tool 4, which looks at ten behavior statements that relate specifically to the role of social change organization managers (exhibit G3.5). Think carefully about your answers in Tool 4—the more accurate they are, the more insight you'll gain into the organization and into the person you can influence the most: you.

EXHIBIT G3.5

Tool 4: Intercultural Competency Behaviors of an Effective Social Change Manager

Rank in order your responses from 1 (least important behavior) to 10 (most important behavior). Then share the statements with your department or team. Work together to reach a shared view of the order of importance from 1 to 10. Use each choice to complete this sentence: "An effective social change manager ... "

My Ranking		Group Ranking
	A. partners with various identity-based organizations to create ties in the community	
	B. understands the different cultural norms and preferences of coworkers and organizational stakeholders	
	C. proactively offers information to make coworkers feel comfortable	
	D. is flexible and creative in finding alternate ways of informing and communicating with coworkers	
	E. cultivates productive relationships with coworkers	
	F. treats all coworkers and other organizational stakeholders with dignity and respect	
	G. gives necessary information in ways that people of various backgrounds and tenure with the organization can understand	
	H. knows how to work within the system to make changes that benefit people of various backgrounds and tenure with the organization	
	I. takes pride in helping coworkers and organizational stakeholders feel welcome and involved in organizational decision making	
	J. solicits and uses feedback to improve interactions with coworkers and organizational stakeholders	

Source: Developed by The Coordinating Council of Broward Multicultural Board. Adapted in part from their Cultural Competency Tool Kit for Broward County, Florida, May 2007.

It's important to point out that your responses and the group's responses may shift over time. The pace of that shift depends in part on the action steps you take in developing individual and group dialogue and plans centered on intercultural competence.

Making It Your Own

From here, continue to incorporate your own voice and style as you reuse this tool and others to hone and refine individual, team, and organizational developmental opportunities for fostering intercultural competence. Stay in touch along the way so we can grow in this work together!

Oh, before you go, remember:

- **Knowledge does not necessarily lead to competence.** For example, reading up on the Millennial generation does not necessarily equip you to effectively and appropriately engage them.

- **Contact does not necessarily lead to competence.** Just because your neighbor is African-American does not necessarily equip you to effectively and appropriately engage all African-Americans.

- **Interaction may lead to a reduction of stereotypes.** Interacting with gay or lesbian couples who are married can challenge or support your previously held notions of love and family.

The best practice of intercultural competence is pretty simple: to practice! In short, here's what it takes:

- **Curiosity and flexible thinking.** With each interpersonal encounter, consider what's more important—being right or facilitating effective and appropriate interaction across cultures.

- **Facilitating ongoing learning and immersion experiences.** Actively making time to facilitate sharing and learning about different cultures, work style preferences, and interpersonal experiences makes it stick.

- **Reducing anxiety about differences by leveraging them in the work of the organization.** Acknowledge the connection between diversity and mission fulfillment as often as you can.

An organization with staff and volunteers committed to practicing intercultural competence stands to reap the following rewards:

- **Diversity, but not at any cost.** On the one hand, whether deliberate or not, sometimes diversity brings inefficiency and confusion. On the other hand, "sameness" in background and viewpoints will only take an organization so far. Practicing intercultural competence can turn differences into organizational assets.

- **Breakthroughs in productivity with fewer clashes of expectations.** With intercultural competence as a lens for understanding intentions and behaviors, managers save time from running interference between staff or volunteers and instead spend it productively in facilitating opportunities for understanding important differences.

- **Smart approaches for rewarding "invisible" stars in staff and volunteer ranks.** Do you really know who your organizational superstars are, or do you know those who are the most vocal or sponsored? For social change managers who practice intercultural competence, it is almost impossible to take "invisibles" and the value they deliver for granted.

For the past three months, I have been writing this guide while living it. Sometimes using these tools got me looking in a mirror with mascara running down my cheeks and hair like a rat's nest. More often than not, thankfully, transformation occurs at the individual and organizational level. This guide ends in the same place it started: with you, and a relentless support of your talent and growth as a social change organization professional. I hope this guide has shown you how to start harnessing the results you seek to help change the world.

REFERENCES

Introduction

Aguinis, H., & Kraiger, K. (2009). Benefits of training and development for individuals and teams, organizations, and society. *Annual Review of Psychology, 60*(1), 451–474. doi:10.1146/annurev.psych.60.110707.163505

Asghar, R. (2014, January). What millennials want in the workplace (and why you should start giving it to them). *Forbes*. Retrieved from www.forbes.com/sites/robasghar/2014/01/13/what-millennials-want-in-the-workplace-and-why-you-should-start-giving-it-to-them/

B Lab. (2014). Retrieved from www.bcorporation.net

Blumenthal, B. (2003). *Investing in capacity building: Guide to high-impact approaches.* New York: Foundation Center.

Bromberger, A. (n.d.). Social enterprise: A lawyer's perspective. Retrieved from www.alissamickels.com/BrombergerSE.pdf

Bureau of Labor Statistics. (2014). Labor force statistics from the current population survey. www.bls.gov/cps/cpsaat03.htm

Carpenter, H., Clarke A., & Gregg, R. (2013). Nonprofit needs assessment: A profile of Michigan's most urgent professional development needs. Retrieved from http://johnsoncenterforphilanthropy.files.wordpress.com/2013/06/2013-nonprofit-needs-assessment.pdf

Dobin, D. & Tchume, T. (2011). Good in theory, problems in practice: Young professionals' views on popular leadership development strategies. Retrieved from http://ynpn.org/wp-content/uploads/YNPN_National_Report_FOR WEBSITE.pdf

interSector Partners. (2014). LC3 statistics. Retrieved from www.intersectorl3c.com/l3c_tally.html

Komives, S. R., Lucas, N., & McMahon, T. R. (2006). *Exploring leadership: For college students who want to make a difference* (2nd ed.). San Francisco: Jossey-Bass.

National Center for Charitable Statistics. (2014). Quick facts about nonprofits. Retrieved from nccs.urban.org/statistics/quickfacts.cfm

Nonprofit HR Solutions. (2013, March). *2013 nonprofit employment trends survey.* Retrieved from www.nonprofithr.com/wp-content/uploads/2013/03/2013-Employment-Trends-Survey-Report.pdf

Nonprofit Workforce Coalition. (2009, July). Welcome to the Nonprofit Workforce Coalition blog. Retrieved from nonprofitworkforce. blogspot.com/2009/07/welcome-to-nonprofit-workforce.html

Pynes, J. E. (2009). *Human resources management for public and nonprofit organizations: A strategic approach* (3rd ed.). San Francisco: Jossey-Bass.

Riechmann, S. W., & Grasha, A. F. (1974). A rational approach to developing and assessing the construct validity of a student learning style scales instrument. *The Journal of Psychology, 87*(2), 213–223. doi:10.1080/00223980.1974.9915693

Salamon, L., Sokolowski, W. S., & Geller, S. (2012). Holding the fort: Nonprofit employment during a decade of turmoil. *Nonprofit Data Bulletin, 39.* www.ccss.jhu.edu.

Stahl, R. (2013). Talent philanthropy: Investing in nonprofit people to advance nonprofit performance. *The Foundation Review, 5*(3). doi:10.9707/1944–5660.1169

Chapter 1: Why Talent Development?

Bridgespan Group. The 70–20–10 Model. Retrieved from www.bridgespan.org/getattachment/2bfae3b6–2815–4cd5–803a-62147735d603/The-70–20–10-Model.aspx

Colorado Nonprofit Association and Pathfinders Solutions. (2012). Crafting pathways: A Colorado nonprofit talent development report. Retrieved from www.coloradononprofits.org/wp-content/uploads/CraftingPathways.pdf

Genis, M. (2008). So many leadership programs, so little change: Why many leadership development efforts fall short. *Journal for Nonprofit Management. 12*(1), 32–40.

Heldrich, J., Zukin, C., & Szeltner, M. (2012). Talent report: What workers want in 2012. Center for Workforce Development Rutgers, The State University of New Jersey. Retrieved from https://netimpact.org/sites/default/files/documents/what-workers-want-2012.pdf

Krause, J. (2014). Avoiding high turnover begins with making the right hire. Retrieved from www.linkedin.com/today/post/article/20140617141517–13362262-avoiding-high-turnover-begins-with-making-the-right-hire

Light, M., & Light, P. (2006). Which light is right? The impending leadership deficit crisis. *Nonprofit Quarterly*, Fall, 70–72.

Merriam, S. B. (2001). Andragogy and self-directed learning: Pillars of adult learning theory. *New Directions for Adult and Continuing Education. 89.* San Francisco, CA: Jossey-Bass.

Nonprofit HR Solutions. (2013, March). *2013 nonprofit employment trends survey.* Retrieved from www.nonprofithr.com/wp-content/uploads/2013/03/2013-Employment-Trends-Survey-Report.pdf

O'Connell, M., & Kung, M.-C. (2007). The cost of employee turnover. *Industrial Management, 49*(1), 14–19.

O'Neill, M. (2005). Developmental contexts of nonprofit management education. *Nonprofit Management and Leadership, 16*(1), 5–17. doi:10.1002/nml.87

Paton, R., Mordaunt, J., & Cornforth, C. (2007). Beyond nonprofit management education: Leadership development in a time of blurred boundaries and distributed learning. *Nonprofit and Voluntary Sector Quarterly, 36*(4_suppl), 148S–162S. doi:10.1177/0899764007305053

Rabin, R. (2014). Blended learning for leadership: The CCL approach. Retrieved from www.ccl.org/leadership/pdf/research/BlendedLearningLeadership.pdf

Ridder, H.-G., Piening, E. P., & Baluch, A. M. (2012). The third way reconfigured: How and why nonprofit organizations are shifting their human resource management. *VOLUNTAS: International Journal of Voluntary and Nonprofit Organizations, 23*(3), 605–635. doi:10.1007/s11266–011–9219-z

Ronquillo, J. C., Hein, W. E., & Carpenter, H. (2013). Reviewing the literature on leadership in nonprofit organizations. In Ronald J. Burke & Cary L. Cooper (Eds.), *Human resource management in the nonprofit sector: Passion, purpose and professionalism.* Northampton, MA: Edward Elgar.

Stahl, R. (2013). Talent philanthropy: Investing in nonprofit people to advance nonprofit performance. *The Foundation Review, 5*(3). doi:10.9707/1944–5660.1169

Chapter 2: The Organizational Learning Assessment

Bess, K., Perkins, D., & McCown, D. (2011). Testing a measure of organizational learning capacity and readiness for transformational change in human services. *Journal of Prevention & Intervention in the Community, 39*(1), 35–49.

Cullen, K. L., Palus, C. J., & Appaneal, C. (2014). Developing network perspective: Understanding the basics of social networks and their role in leadership. Retrieved from www.ccl.org/leadership/pdf/research/developingNetworkPerspective.pdf

Garvin, D., Edmondson, A., & Gino, F. (2008). Is yours a learning organization? *Harvard Business Review.* Retrieved from hbr.org/2008/03/is-yours-a-learning-organization/ar/1

Lehmen, W., Greener, J., & Simpson, D. (2002). Assessing organizational readiness for change. *Journal of Substance Abuse Treatment*, 22(4), 197–209.

Lerch, J., et al. (2011). Organizational readiness in corrections. *Federal Probation*, 75(1), 5–10.

Marsick, V., & Watkins, K. (2003). Demonstrating the value of an organization's learning culture: The dimensions of the learning organization questionnaire. *Advances in Developing Human Resources*, 5(2), 132–151.

Chapter 3: Social Change Competencies

Boyatzis, R. E., Goleman, D., & Rhee, K. (2000). Clustering competence in emotional intelligence: Insights from the Emotional Competence Inventory (ECI). In R. Bar-On & J. D. A. Parker (Eds.), *Handbook of Emotional Intelligence* (pp. 343–362). San Francisco, CA: Jossey-Bass.

Carpenter, H., Clarke A., & Gregg, R. (2013). Nonprofit needs assessment: A profile of Michigan's most urgent professional development needs. Retrieved from johnsoncenterforphilanthropy.files.wordpress.com/2013/06/2013-nonprofit-needs-assessment.pdf

Emerging Practitioners in Philanthropy. (2013). Measuring a leader. Retrieved from www.epip.org/our-leadership-moments/measuring-a-leader/

Gangani, N., McLean, G. N., & Braden, R. A. (2006). A competency-based human resource development strategy. *Performance Improvement Quarterly*, 19(1), 127–139. doi:10.1111/j.1937–8327.2006.tb00361.x

Goleman, D. (2005). *Emotional intelligence: Why it can matter more than IQ* (10th anniversary edition.). New York: Bantam Books.

Hunter, J. E. (1986). Cognitive ability, cognitive aptitudes, job knowledge, and job performance. *Journal of Vocational Behavior*, 29(3), 340–362. doi:10.1016/0001–8791(86)90013–8

Liker, J., Convis, G. L., & Meskimen, J. (2012). *The Toyota way to lean leadership: Achieving and sustaining excellence through leadership development*. New York: McGraw-Hill.

Lucia, A. D., & Lepsinger, R. (1999). *The art and science of competency models: Pinpointing critical success factors in organizations*. San Francisco, CA: Pfeiffer.

National Institutes of Health. (2014). Competencies proficiency scale. Retrieved from http://hr.od.nih.gov/workingatnih/competencies/proficiencyscale.htm

Otting, L. G. (2007). *Change your career: Transitioning to the nonprofit sector* (Original edition.). New York: Kaplan.

Pynes, J. E. (2009). *Human resources management for public and nonprofit organizations: A strategic approach* (3rd ed.). San Francisco, CA: Jossey-Bass.

Rodriguez, D., Patel, R., Bright, A., Gregory, D., & Gowing, M. K. (2002). Developing competency models to promote integrated human resource practices. *Human Resource Management, 41*(3), 309–324. doi:10.1002/hrm.10043

Rouson, B. (2009). Key terms for cultural competency in P. St. Onge (Ed.), *Embracing cultural competency: A roadmap for nonprofit capacity builders.* Saint Paul, MN: Fieldstone Alliance.

Salovey, P., & Mayer, J. D. (1990). Emotional intelligence. *Imagination, cognition, and personality, 9*, 185–211.

Shippmann, J. S., Ash, R. A., Batjtsta, M., Carr, L., Eyde, L. D., Hesketh, B., . . . Sanchez, J. I. (2000). The practice of competency modeling. *Personnel Psychology, 53*(3), 703–740. doi:10.1111/j.1744–6570.2000.tb00220.x

Tan, C. (2012). *Search inside yourself: The unexpected path to achieving success, happiness (and world peace)* (1st print ed.). New York: HarperOne.

Tupes, E. C., & Christal, R. E. (1961). *Recurrent personality factors based on trait ratings.* (Technical Report ASD-TR-61–97). Lackland Air Force Base, TX: Personnel Laboratory, Air Force Systems Command.

Watson, P. (2009). Four quadrant model of emotional intelligence. Retrieved from http://smartgrowth.com/pdf/four_quadrant_model.pdf

Chapter 4: Creating Job Descriptions

FLSA (Fair Labor Standards Act). (n.d.). Retrieved from www.flsa.com/coverage.html

Nonprofit HR Solutions. (2013, March). *2013 nonprofit employment trends survey.* Retrieved from www.nonprofithr.com/wp-content/uploads/2013/03/2013-Employment-Trends-Survey-Report.pdf

Opportunity Knocks. (2010). *Nonprofit retention and vacancy report.* Atlanta, GA: Opportunity Knocks.

Preston, A. E. (1994). Women in the nonprofit labor market. In Teresa Odendahl and Michael O'Neill (Eds.), *Women and power in the nonprofit sector* (pp. 39–78). San Francisco, CA: Jossey-Bass.

Solomon, J., & Sandahl, Y. (2007). Stepping up or stepping out: A report on the readiness of next generation nonprofit leaders. Retrieved from http://ynpn.org/wp-content/uploads/stepping_up.pdf

Sources for Job Descriptions (Presented in Order of Exhibits 4.8 through 4.22)

Board Chair

Board Chair Job Description. Retrieved from www.bridgespan.org/Nonprofit_Jobs/Position_Details.aspx?jobId=11650

www.bridgespan.org/Publications-and-Tools/Hiring-Nonprofit-Leaders/
Nonprofit-Job-Descriptions/Board-Member-Job-Descriptions/Chairman-of-
the-Board-Job-Description.aspx#.U3Yk6IFdX_M

Board Treasurer

Board Treasurer Job Description. Retrieved May 7, 2014, from www.bridge
span.org/Nonprofit_Jobs/Position_Details.aspx?jobId=10970

www.nonprofitcentral.biz/blog/what-is-the-role-of-a-treasurer/

Executive Director

Executive Director Job Description. Retrieved from https://autodesk.taleo.net/
careersection/adsk_gen/jobdetail.ftl?lang=en&job=14WD14856&src=JB-10120

Chief Operating Officer/Operations Manager

Sustainability accounting standards board—www.sasb.org/engage/work-sasb/
chief-operating-officer/

Chief Operating Officer Job Description. Retrieved from nonprofitprofessionals
.com/searches/WKKF-COO.pdf

crenyc.org/_blog/News_and_Views/post/cre-search—-turning-point—-chief-
operating-officer/

www.jccworks.com/Search.htm?ID=050983A4&utm_source=Indeed&utm_
medium=organic&utm_campaign=Indeed

Human Resources Manager

Human Resources Manager Job Description. Retrieved from www.edjoin.org/
JobDescription.aspx?descriptionID=117255

www.indeed.com/viewjob?cmp=Mosaic-North-Central-Iowa&t=Human+
Resource+Specialist&jk=860054b36cf6c9ab&sjdu=QwrRXKrqZ3CNX5W-
O9jEvVwTvy1_dmtfLQDZksb8zfcc7uyo_YkVwgZydNLzt50xvJZ4drJUCz
mUdsZuXEByPtIeMMg2wkhZDWd5RpxdV4

www.indeed.com/cmp/Tienda-Inc/jobs/Human-Resource-Manager-b94e6e4b39
068af0

Development Director

Development Director Job Description. Retrieved from www.bridgespan.org/
getattachment/8bc7b576-fd29–406d-b88d-87410654a52c/Sample-Director-
Development-Job-Description-Small.aspx

Program Manager

www.technoserve.org/jobs/program-manager-volunteer-consultant-program

Program Manager Job Description. Retrieved from www.indeed.com/viewjob?cmp=Women%27s-Empowerment&t=Program+Manager+Local+Non+Profit&jk=a7af2dd9fe70074b&sjdu=QwrRXKrqZ3CNX5W-O9jEvboqH3KsCi-ZpW0p65RLM2WGoFrgtFIwVMvroRnqPwmpqQOiqk_r-kXaLhiN2cBejXrf9C0YsFiM6ZlW_VCZOEo

Volunteer Coordinator

Volunteer Coordinator Job Description. Retrieved from www4.recruitingcenter.net/Clients/curohs/PublicJobs/controller.cfm?jbaction=JobProfile&Job_Id=10984&esid=az

www.smartrecruiters.com/ChicagoArchitectureFoundation/76939994-volunteer-coordinator-open-house-chicago-

www.indeed.com/viewjob?cmp=The-Urban-League-of-Greater-OKC&t=Public+Relation+Volunteer+Coordinator&jk=3bc8fe05972ff528&sjdu=QwrRXKrqZ3CNX5W-O9jEvQOURiBK2fpQ4vUAeoCKDMVKPRHyFlfg2MPv-Fe-RMznVYQ695yEiIKAQcpvElEuvgKBGI_WbYANQPBKKcOo9-I0Nm_SJd9fWSAsMFSKnXIb

Administrative Assistant

Administrative Assistant Job Description. Retrieved from www.careerbuilder.com/jobseeker/jobs/jobdetails.aspx?sc_cmp1=js_jrp_jobclick&APath=2.21.0.0.0&job_did=JHS6WD6065VSD67J02B&showNewJDP=yes&IPath=JRKV0D

www.indeed.com/viewjob?jk=8503796696ad373a&q=Non+Profit+Administrative+Assistant&tk=18o2n37of1a2272l&from=web

Marketing Coordinator

Marketing Coordinator Job Description. Retrieved from www.appone.com/MainInfoReq.asp?R_ID=749020&B_ID=56&fid=1&Adid=&ssbgcolor=FFFFFF&SearchScreenID=708

www.barefootstudent.com/atlanta/jobs/internship/nonprofit_marketing_event_coordinator_internship_162597?utm_source=Indeed&utm_medium=organic&utm_campaign=Indeed

www.npo.net/job/marketing-development-coordinator/60339?action=search&13=illinois&utm_source=Indeed&utm_medium=organic&utm_campaign=Indeed

Program Officer

Program Officer Job Description. Retrieved from jobs.cof.org/jobseeker/job/ 17195162/Program%20Officer/__company__/?vnet=0&keywords=board& max=25#sthash.EjEBKxQm.dpuf

Program Associate

Program Coordinator/Associate Job Description. Retrieved from www.indeed .com/cmp/Sobrato-Family-Foundation/jobs/Program-Associate-890b3e5539 f5c43e

Program Coordinator Job Description. Retrieved from www.indeed.com/viewjob? jk=3a085ee12b81806b&from=tellafriend&utm_source=jobseeker_emails&utm_ medium=email&cd%20-=tell_a_friend

www.indeed.com/viewjob?jk=94ce36db298db83c&from=tellafriend&utm_source =jobseeker_emails&utm_medium=email&cd%20-=tell_a_friend

Director of Donor Services

Director of Donor Services Job Description. Retrieved from www.americanred cross.apply2jobs.com/ProfExt/index.cfm?fuseaction=mExternal.showJob& RID=43608&CurrentPage=14&sid=106

rwu.interviewexchange.com/jobofferdetails.jsp;jsessionid=F793C5157016B3A143 AEB953107F20E6?JOBID=48979

Evaluator

Evaluator Job Description. Retrieved from www.bridgespan.org/getmedia/9dd9f d57-dedb-4afe-b17c-795dd9f46386/Director-of-Evaluation-and-Innovation_ Horizons-for-Homeless-Children.pdf.aspx

www.bridgespan.org/getmedia/85b4cf7e-91db-4a6c-94a8–6d5802619ad9/ Director-of-Learning-and-Evaluation_Latin-American-Youth-Center.pdf.aspx

Chapter 5: Mapping Competencies and Proficiency Levels to Job Descriptions

Bloom, B. S., Engelhart, M. D., Furst, E. J., Hill, W. H., & Krathwohl, D. R. (1956). *Taxonomy of educational objectives: The classification of educational goals.* Handbook I: Cognitive domain. New York, NY: David McKay.

Dreyfus, H. L., & Dreyfus, S. E. (1986). *Mind over machine: The power of human intuition and expertise in the age of the computer.* Oxford, UK: Basil Blackwell.

Hassad, M. (2005). Importance of a job description. *Entrepreneur*. Retrieved from www.entrepreneur.com/article/78506

Tan, C. (2012). *Search inside yourself: The unexpected path to achieving success, happiness (and world peace)* (1st print ed.). New York, NY: HarperOne.

Tyler, K. (2013, January). Job worth doing: Update descriptions. *HR Magazine 58*(1). Retrieved from www.shrm.org/publications/hrmagazine/editorialcontent/2013/0113/pages/0113-job-descriptions.aspx#sthash.RWqkpuWR.dpuf

Chapter 6: The Individual Professional Development Assessment

Fiske, S. T., & Taylor, S. E. (1991). *Social cognition* (2nd ed.). New York, NY: McGraw-Hill.

Gangani, N., McLean, G. N., & Braden, R. A. (2006). A competency-based human resource development strategy. *Performance Improvement Quarterly, 19*(1), 127–139. doi:10.1111/j.1937–8327.2006.tb00361.x

Pynes, J. E. (2009). *Human resources management for public and nonprofit organizations: A strategic approach* (3rd ed.). San Francisco, CA: Jossey-Bass.

Shippmann, J. S., Ash, R. A., Batjtsta, M., Carr, L., Eyde, L. D., Hesketh, B., . . . Sanchez, J. I. (2000). The practice of competency modeling. *Personnel Psychology, 53*(3), 703–740. doi:10.1111/j.1744–6570.2000.tb00220.x

Chapter 7: The Individual Learning Styles Assessment

Cassidy, S. (2004). Learning styles: An overview of theories, models, and measures. *Educational Psychology: An International Journal of Experimental Educational Psychology, 24*(4), 419–444, doi:10.1080/0144341042000228834

Curry, L. (1987). Integrating concepts of cognitive or learning style: A review with attention to psychometric standards. Ottawa, ON: Canadian College of Health Sciences.

Ferrell, B. G. (1983). A factor analytic comparison of four learning-styles instruments. *Journal of Educational Psychology, 75*(1), 33–39. doi:10.1037/0022–0663.75.1.33

Jonassen, D. H., & Grabowski, B. L. (1993). *Handbook of individual differences learning and instruction*. New York, NY: Routledge.

Riding, R. J., & Rayner, S. (1998). *Cognitive styles and learning strategies: Understanding style differences in learning and behaviour*. London, UK: David Fulton.

Riechmann, S. W., & Grasha, A. F. (1974). A rational approach to developing and assessing the construct validity of a student learning style scales instrument. *The Journal of Psychology, 87*(2), 213–223. doi:10.1080/00223980.1974.9915693

Tough, A. M. (1979). *The adult's learning projects: A fresh approach to theory and practice in adult learning.* Ontario, Canada: Ontario Institute for Studies in Education.

Chapter 8: Developing Organizational Goals and Setting Objectives

Aryee, S., Chay, Y. W., & Chew, J. (1996). The motivation to mentor among managerial employees: An interactionist approach. *Group & Organization Management, 21*(3), 261–277. doi:10.1177/1059601196213002

Aryee, S., Wyatt, T., & Stone, R. (1996). Early career outcomes of graduate employees: The effect of mentoring and ingratiation. *Journal of Management Studies, 33*(1), 95–118. doi:10.1111/j.1467–6486.1996.tb00800.x

Business Model Foundry. (2014). Retrieved from www.businessmodel generation.com/

Bryson, J. M. (2011). *Strategic planning for public and nonprofit organizations: A guide to strengthening and sustaining organizational achievement* (4th ed.). San Francisco, CA: Jossey-Bass.

Chao, G. T., Walz, P., & Gardner, P. D. (1992). Formal and informal mentorships: A comparison on mentoring functions and contrast with nonmentored counterparts. *Personnel Psychology, 45*(3), 619–636. doi:10.1111/j.1744–6570.1992 .tb00863.x

Cherniss, C. (2007). The role of emotional intelligence in the mentoring process. In B. R. Ragins & K. E. Kram (Eds.), *The handbook of mentoring at work: Theory, research, and practice* (pp. 427–446). Los Angeles: Sage.

Doran, G. T. (1981). There's a SMART way to write management's goals and objectives. *Management Review, 70*(11), 35–36.

Goleman, D. (2005). *Emotional intelligence: Why it can matter more than IQ* (10th anniversary ed.). New York: Bantam Books.

Graziano, W. G., & Eisenberg, N. (1997). Agreeableness: A dimension of personality. In R. Hogan, S. Briggs, & J. Johnson, *Handbook of personality psychology*. San Diego, CA: Academic Press.

Rabin, R. (2014). *Blended learning for leadership: The CCL approach.* Retrieved from www.ccl.org/leadership/pdf/research/BlendedLearningLeadership.pdf

Ragins, B. R., & Kram, K. E. (2007). *The handbook of mentoring at work: Theory, research, and practice.* Los Angeles: Sage.

Salovey, P., & Mayer, J. D. (1990). Emotional intelligence. *Imagination, Cognition, and Personality, 9,* 185–211.

Turban D. B., & Lee, F. K. (2007). The role of personality in mentoring relationships. In B. R. Ragins & K. E. Kram (2007), *The handbook of mentoring at work: Theory, research, and practice* (pp. 21–50). Los Angeles: Sage.

Chapter 9: Setting Individual Goals and Objectives

Campbell, D. J., & Lee, C. (1988). Self-appraisal in performance evaluation: Development versus evaluation. *Academy of Management Review, 13*(2), 302–314. doi:10.5465/AMR.1988.4306896

Rabin, R. (2014). Blended learning for leadership: The CCL approach. Retrieved from www.ccl.org/leadership/pdf/research/BlendedLearningLeadership.pdf

Chapter 10: Implementing the Plan

Carpenter, H., Clarke A., & Gregg, R. (2013). Nonprofit needs assessment: A profile of Michigan's most urgent professional development needs. Retrieved from johnsoncenterforphilanthropy.files.wordpress.com/2013/06/2013-nonprofit-needs-assessment.pdf

CompassPoint Nonprofit Services. Peer Group Agenda. Authenticity Circles Peer Learning Groups. Retrieved from www.compasspoint.org/sites/default/files/documents/SVForum/Peer%20Coaching%20Quick%20Reference%20Tool%20and%20Member.pdf

Davidson, C. (2013). Essential tool kit for peer learning and peer teaching. Retrieved from www.hastac.org/blogs/cathy-davidson/2013/06/04/essential-tool-kit-peer-learning-and-peer-teaching

Executive Mentor Program, College of Business Administration, Kansas State University. (n.d.). 7 tips for being a good mentee. Retrieved from https://cba.k-state.edu/current-students/documents/executive-mentor/Tips%20for%20being%20a%20good%20mentee.pdf

Fellner, K., Keleher, T., & Oritz, E. (2008). *Work with me: Intergenerational conversations for nonprofit leadership*. Washington, DC: National Council of Nonprofit Associations.

Kirkpatrick, D. L., & Kirkpatrick, J. D. (2006). *Evaluating training programs: The four levels* (3rd ed.). San Francisco: Berrett-Koehler.

McFarlane, H. (2007). *Board mentoring handbook*. Retrieved from maytree.com/PDF_Files/BoardMentoringHandbook.pdf

MindTools. (n.d.). Kirkpatrick's four-level training and evaluation model. Retrieved from www.mindtools.com/pages/article/kirkpatrick.htm

Molnar, J., & Watts, B. (2002). *Structured on the job training: Effectively training employees with employees*. Morgantown, VA: Center for Entrepreneurial Studies and Development. Retrieved from www.cesd.wvu.edu/Assets/White_Paper_PDFS/SJT_Training_Employees.pdf

Paul, R., & Elder, L. (2014). *The miniature guide to critical thinking concepts and tools* (7th ed.). Tomales, CA: Foundation for Critical Thinking.

Rooke, D. & Torbert, W. R. (2005, April). Seven transformations of leadership. *Harvard Business Review, 83*(4), 66–76.

Scontrino, M. P., & Powell, J. K. (2013). Developmental plan for on-the-job learning. Retrieved from www.scontrino-powell.com/wp-content/uploads/2013/06/Developmental-Plan-Template-for-On-the-Job-Learning.pdf

South Delta Mentor Mentee Form. Retrieved from www.jfs.ohio.gov/owd/WorkforceProf/Docs/South-Delta-Mentor-Mentee-Agreement-Forms.doc

Tan, C. (2012). *Search inside yourself: The unexpected path to achieving success, happiness (and world peace)* (1st print ed.). New York: HarperOne.

Torbert, W. R. (2004). *Action inquiry: The secret of timely and transforming leadership.* San Francisco, CA: Berrett-Koehler.

Tough, A. M. (1979). *The adult's learning projects: A fresh approach to theory and practice in adult learning.* Ontario, Canada: Ontario Institute for Studies in Education.

Chapter 11: Organizational Evaluation and Performance Assessment

Bonner, L., & Obergas, J. (n.d.). Nonprofit leadership development: A model for identifying and growing leaders in the nonprofit sector. Retrieved from www.deweykaye.com/assets/documents/DK_NonprofitLeadershipStudy.pdf

Gangani, N., McLean, G. N., & Braden, R. A. (2006). A competency-based human resource development strategy. *Performance Improvement Quarterly, 19*(1), 127–139. doi:10.1111/j.1937–8327.2006.tb00361.x

Independent Sector. (2014). Independent Sector's value of volunteer time. Retrieved from www.independentsector.org/volunteer_time

McConnell, C. R. (1986). Employee evaluations. *AORN Journal, 44*(6), 996–997. doi:10.1016/S0001 2092(07)65483-0

O'Connell., & Kung, M.-C. (2007). The cost of employee turnover. *Industrial Management, 49*(1), 14–19.

Rabin, R. (2014). Blended learning for leadership: The CCL approach. Retrieved from www.ccl.org/leadership/pdf/research/BlendedLearningLeadership.pdf

Wiese, D. S., & Buckley, M. R. (1998). The evolution of the performance appraisal process. *Journal of Management History (Archive), 4*(3), 233–249. doi:10.1108/13552529810231003

Guide 2: Talent Investing: Raising and Granting Funds to Develop Social Change Leadership

Council on Foundations. (2009). *Career pathways to philanthropic leadership: Baseline report.* Washington, DC.

Durfee Foundation. (2011). *The Durfee Foundation: The first 50 years.* Retrieved from durfee.org/about/publications/

Golensky, N. (2014). Why nonprofit leaders need to focus on protecting themselves as much as they protect others. Retrieved from www.nextlevelnonprofits.com/why-nonprofit-leaders-need-to-focus-on-protecting-themselves-as-much-as-they-protect-others/

Light, P. (2004). *Sustaining nonprofit performance: The case for capacity building and the evidence to support it.* Washington, DC: Brookings Institution.

Linnell, D. & Wolfred, T. (2009). Creative disruption: Sabbaticals for capacity building and leadership development in the nonprofit sector. CompassPoint and Third Sector New England. Retrieved from www.compasspoint.org/creativedisruption

Marino, M. (2011). *Leap of reason: Managing to outcomes in an era of scarcity.* Washington, DC: Venture Philanthropy Partners.

Nonprofit HR Solutions. (2013) *2013 nonprofit employment trends survey.* Retrieved from www.nonprofithr.com/wp-content/uploads/2013/03/2013-Employment-Trends-Survey-Report.pdf

O'Leonard, K. (2014). *The corporate learning factbook: Benchmarks, trends, and analysis of the U.S. training market.* Available to research members at www.bersin.com/library or for purchase at www.bersin.com/factbook.

Pifer, A. (1982). *Speaking out: Reflections on thirty years in foundation work.* Washington, DC: Council on Foundations.

Roadmap, DataCenter, & National Organizers Alliance. (2012). The wages of peace and justice: 2012 national compensation survey of social justice organizations. Retrieved from www.datacenter.org/wp-content/uploads/RoadMap_SalarySurvey_ExecSummary.July_2012.pdf

Ryan, B. (2013). *Five-year evaluation of the flexible leadership awards.* San Francisco: Evelyn and Walter Haas, Jr. Fund. Retrieved from www.haasjr.org/sites/default/files/pdfs/FLA_Evaluation.pdf

Sage HRMS. (2013). *Return on employee investment: Increasing competitiveness through your biggest asset.* Retrieved from na.sage.com/~/media/site/Sage%20HRMS/pdf/SageHRMS_ROEI.pdf

Stahl, R. (2013). Talent philanthropy: Investing in nonprofit people to advance nonprofit performance. *The Foundation Review, 5*(3), 35–49. Retrieved from www.talentphilanthropy.org/research

Tierney, T. (2006). *The nonprofit sector's leadership deficit.* Boston, MA: The Bridgespan Group.

Guide 3: A Practical Guide on Intercultural Competence for Nonprofit Managers

Association of University Centers on Disabilities (AUCD) Multicultural Council. Adapted in part from Promoting Cultural Diversity and Cultural Competency Self-Assessment Checklist for Personnel Providing Services and Support to Children with Special Health Needs and Their Families by Tawara D. Goode, Georgetown University Child Development Center.

Bennett, M. J. (1993). Towards a developmental model of intercultural sensitivity. In R. Michael Paige (Ed.), *Education for the intercultural experience*. Yarmouth, ME: Intercultural Press.

Bennett, J. M. (1993). Cultural marginality: Identity issues in intercultural training. In R. Michael Paige (Ed.), *Education for the intercultural experience*. Yarmouth, ME: Intercultural Press.

Bennett, W. J. (2011). *The index of leading cultural indicators*. Colorado Springs, CO: Doubleday Religious.

Coordinating Council of Broward Multicultural Board. (2007). Cultural competency tool kit for Broward County, Florida.

Hall, E. T. (1989). *Beyond culture*. New York, NY: Random House.

Hofstede, G. (2001). *Culture's consequences: Comparing values, behaviors, institutions, and organizations across nations* (2nd ed.). Thousand Oaks, CA: Sage.

Meyer, Erin. (2014). One reason cross-cultural small talk is so tricky. *Harvard Business Review Blog Network*. Retrieved from http://blogs.hbr.org/2014/05/one-reason-cross-cultural-small-talk-is-so-tricky/

Trompenaars, F., & Hampden-Turner, C. (1997). *Riding the waves of culture*. New York, NY: McGraw-Hill.

Index

Page references followed by *fig* indicate an illustrated figure; followed by *t* indicate a table; followed by *e* indicate an exhibit.

A

Achiever action logic, 333*t*

Action logics (development stages), 333*fig*

Action words: creating proficiency level descriptions using, 134; identify proficiency levels based on, 135*t*, 140; identifying and associating with proficiency level, 141*e*; realigned to proficiency level, 140, 142*e*–152*t*

Administrative assistants: position sub-competencies for, 75; sample responsibilities of, 121*e*–122*e*

Adult learning. *See* Learning

Advanced proficiency level: action words used for, 134–135; description of, 134, 136*t*; IPDA–Evaluation Stage scores for, 372*e*, 373*e*; Position Mapping Form on, 188*e*–191*e*; Proficiency Mapping Worksheet across a Department or an Organization, 192*e*; writing job descriptions and process for mapping the, 137–187*e*

Advocacy and public policy competency: as core social change competency, 67; creating Talent Map for competencies including, 206–231*t*; executive director job responsibilities by, 137*t*–138*t*; executive director proficiency level in, 152*t*; included in multiple job descriptions with other competencies, 98–131*e*; IPDA–Evaluation Stage of the, 370*e*, 371*e*, 372*e*, 373*e*; IPDA for board chair, 300*fig*; IPDA for development coordinator, 305*fig*; IPDA for executive director, 303*fig*; IPDA for program association, 307*fig*; Position Mapping Form on, 188*e*–191*e*; realigned executive director job responsibilities and, 143*t*; revised job description for executive director on, 153*e*; sub-competencies for, 76–77. *See also specific job position*

Advocacy and public policy proficiency mapping: comparisons between developmental director and development director, 168*t*; for grantmaking organization, 175*t*, 176*t*, 184*e*, 290*fig*; for midsized organization, 167*t*, 169*t*, 173*e*, 288*fig*; Proficiency Mapping Worksheet across a Department or an Organization, 192*e*; for small grassroots organization, 165*t*, 267*fig*, 285*fig*; for volunteer-run organization, 158*t*, 159*t*, 162*e*, 282*fig*

Aguinis, H., 16

Alchemist action logic, 333*t*

Aryee, S., 270

Asghar, R., 7

Avoidant learning style: description of, 237*t*; Individual Learning Styles Assessment (ILSA) of, 237*e*–243*e*; learning activities based on, 252*t*; Learning Styles Map for grantmaking organization, 258*fig*, 289*fig*; Learning Styles Map for midsized organization, 256*fig*, 287*fig*; Learning Styles Map for small grassroots organization, 246*fig*, 254*fig*, 266*fig*, 284*fig*; Learning Styles Map for volunteer-run organization, 253*fig*; practice of ILSA in different organizations to identify, 252–259; professional development preferences for, 271*t*; scoring and interpreting ILSA results on, 244–252*t*

B

B corporations: competency for financial management of, 78; number of certified, 6; professional development goal-setting in, 264; social change focus by, 16

B Lab, 6

Baby Boomer workforce, 7

Baluch, A. M., 18

Benefit corporations. *See* B corporations

Bess, K., 36

Bloom, B. S., 134

Bloom's learning taxonomy, 134*e*

Board chairs. *See* President/board chairs